FOODWAYS OF THE ANCIENT ANDES

AMERIND STUDIES IN ANTHROPOLOGY

Series Editor, **Eric J. Kaldahl**

AMERIND STUDIES
IN ANTHROPOLOGY

FOODWAYS OF THE ANCIENT ANDES

TRANSFORMING DIET, CUISINE, AND SOCIETY

EDITED BY

Marta Alfonso-Durruty and Deborah E. Blom

THE UNIVERSITY OF
ARIZONA PRESS
TUCSON

The University of Arizona Press
www.uapress.arizona.edu

We respectfully acknowledge the University of Arizona is on the land and territories of Indigenous peoples. Today, Arizona is home to twenty-two federally recognized tribes, with Tucson being home to the O'odham and the Yaqui. Committed to diversity and inclusion, the University strives to build sustainable relationships with sovereign Native Nations and Indigenous communities through education offerings, partnerships, and community service.

ISBN-13: 978-0-8165-4869-9 (hardcover)
ISBN-13: 978-0-8165-5660-1 (paperback)
ISBN-13: 978-0-8165-4870-5 (ebook)

Cover design by Leigh McDonald
Cover art from rawpixel.com
Typeset by Sara Thaxton in 10.5/14 Adobe Caslon Pro and Trade Gothic LT Std

Library of Congress Cataloging-in-Publication Data
Names: Alfonso-Durruty, Marta P., editor. | Blom, Deborah E., 1967– editor.
Title: Foodways of the ancient Andes : transforming diet, cuisine, and society / edited by Marta Alfonso-Durruty and Deborah E. Blom.
Other titles: Amerind studies in anthropology.
Description: Tucson : University of Arizona Press, 2023. | Series: Amerind studies in anthropology | Includes bibliographical references and index.
Identifiers: LCCN 2022030149 (print) | LCCN 2022030150 (ebook) | ISBN 9780816548699 (hardcover) | ISBN 9780816548705 (ebook)
Subjects: LCSH: Indians of South America—Food—Andes Region. | Food—Social aspects—Andes Region.
Classification: LCC F2230.1.F66 F66 2023 (print) | LCC F2230.1.F66 (ebook) | DDC 613.2089/9808612—dc23/eng/20220823
LC record available at https://lccn.loc.gov/2022030149
LC ebook record available at https://lccn.loc.gov/2022030150

Printed in the United States of America
♾ This paper meets the requirements of ANSI/NISO Z39.48-1992 (Permanence of Paper).

CONTENTS

Part IV. Building the Inka Empire with Sacred and High-Status Foods

Part V. Future Directions and Conclusion

    Some Concluding Thoughts   347
    Susan D. deFrance

    Contributors   *357*
    Index   *365*

ACKNOWLEDGMENTS

We would like to express our gratitude to the Amerind Museum for this transforming opportunity. Our deepest thanks to the Amerind's CEO, Dr. Eric Kaldahl, who welcomed and guided us at all stages of this process. Thanks to all members of the Amerind and the University of Arizona Press; your constant support and careful attention to detail have made completing this project, even amid the Covid-19 pandemic, an enriching and rewarding experience. We are especially thankful for the authors' intellectual contributions, their quick responses, and their open, insightful, and enriching discussions. Most of all, we would like to thank the Andean peoples, past and present, who have given us the great honor to learn by studying the lives of their ancestors and for generously sharing with us their words and wisdom. The Andes' devastating beauty will always stay with us.

FOODWAYS OF THE ANCIENT ANDES

Introduction

Transforming Foods in the Ancient Andes

*Deborah E. Blom, Marta Alfonso-Durruty,
and Susan D. deFrance*

A synergistic process of mutual production and transformation characterizes our relationship with food. We skillfully transform our food—
cooking, mixing, and modifying ingredients—to enhance its nutrient
value and alter its taste (Pollan 2013; Wrangham 2009). Similarly, while
foods meet our nutritional needs, cooking and eating embody social and
symbolic dimensions that transform our bodies into material (bio)culture
(Bourdieu 1984; Douglas 1972; Lèvi-Strauss 1997; Mead 1997; Sofaer
2006). Meals too can be viewed as simultaneously material and discursive phenomena, and the *chaînes opératoires* of human thoughts, actions,
and bodily techniques that go into preparing them are ideal avenues to
view the ways in which humans interact with their physical and cultural
environments (see Briggs 2018; Cadena and Moreano 2012; Goody 1982;
Hastorf 2018; Mauss [1935] 2006; Mintz and Du Bois 2002; Peres and
Deter-Wolf 2018). The Andean region's cultural and environmental diversity provides a unique locale for the study of food (Cuéllar 2013; Klarich 2010; Knudson, Torres-Rouff, and Stojanowski 2015; Turner et al.
2018; Velasco and Tung 2021). Embracing this diversity and the rich ethnohistoric and archaeological record of the region, this volume addresses
key sociopolitical and ontological questions about ancient foodways and
uses a variety of methods to investigate how foods and peoples were
mutually transformed in the ancient Andes.

Archaeologists are left to infer food, diet, and cuisine from material
left behind (e.g., food remains, vessels, and tools) and from the chemical signatures of diets incorporated into human and animal bone. We
can also draw from ethnographic and ethnohistorical accounts of more
recent societies to aid our endeavors to reconstruct behaviors. While we
cannot uncritically impose this information onto the past, we can use
generalized insights from ethnohistory and ethnography to inform our

understandings of ancient Andean social organization and ontologies about the world (e.g., Lozada and Tantaleán 2019; Murra 1975; Swenson and Roddick 2018). To quote Tristan Platt (2016, 199),

> The word 'Andean' . . . does not deny historical change. . . . On the contrary, it can refer to Andean societies which have been conquered by the Incas, invaded by the Spanish, and incorporated into nation-states, combining threads of continuity and change in their actions and reactions to a constantly transforming context.

It is with these threads of continuity and change in mind that the scholarship included in this volume explores diversity in food, diet, and cuisine across time/space[1] over the *longue durée* in the ancient Andes.

Throughout time, Andean peoples rose to the challenges of climatic and sociopolitical changes that affected their access to resources (see also Juengst et al. 2021; Bruno et al. 2021). The resilient pre-Columbian Andean peoples prioritized, scaled, diversified, and embraced new as well as previously developed subsistence strategies and food resources. When all else failed, in the face of environmental degradation and state collapse that severely impacted their needs, they turned to local resources and enacted the power of their extended families.

ANDEAN FOODWAYS: LANDSCAPES, INGENUITY, AND TASTE

Whether communities were living in the western coastal deserts, the stark and frigid highlands, or the lush eastern slopes bordering the Amazon, the landscape heavily shaped Andean foodways (Wilson and McCool, this volume). Cultural palatability and pertinence were also central in determining which available and abundant foodstuffs people chose. Creative and tenacious ecological knowledge was essential to make the most of the diverse Andean ecological zones, as demonstrated by the millennia-long practices of maintaining lands or establishing trade and

---

1. In Andean cosmology, time and space are essentially one, as illustrated in the Quechua word *pacha*, which is translated "tiempo, suelo, lugar," or "time, soil, place" (González Holguín 1608; George Urioste, personal communication, 2002).

exchange networks in multiple, vertically aligned altitudinal zones to access essential or desired nonlocal products (Murra 1972; see also Baitzel et al. and Berryman and Blom, this volume; for a critical analysis of the "verticality" model as an economic system, see Van Buren 1996; Van-Valkenburgh 2019). Other practices focused on using labor and ingenuity to intensify local Andean food production, sometimes turning "marginal zones" into highly productive agricultural fields.

The organization of labor was necessary for many elements of food production in the Andes, such as agricultural innovations that extended growing seasons or the amount of cultivable land. The chapters in this volume document the power of these practices, which included irrigation (see Baitzel et al.; Chiou; and Knudson et al., this volume), raised fields (Berryman and Blom, this volume), the use of fertilizers (Santana-Sagredo et al., this volume), and even composting (Chiou, this volume). As they altered the landscape, Andean peoples also transformed perishable foods into those that could be stored for months, if not years, such as by drying fish, meat (*charki*), and potatoes (*chuño*) (Castro 2010) and fermenting maize (*Zea mays*), manioc (*Manihot esculenta*), and the fruit of *molle* (*Schinus molle*) and *algarrobo* (*Prosopis* sp.; the fruit is typically called *algarroba*) into beer (*chicha*) (Jennings and Bowser 2009; Moore 1989; Murra 2017; Bélisle, Alaica, and Brown; Biwer, Alaica, and Quiñonez Cuzcano; and Weber and Young, this volume). Storage was key, whether preparing for times of shortage or amassing surplus for prestige negotiations. The chapters of this volume present diverse ways that archaeologists can use to track the processing and storage of foods, which range from analyzing vessels used for preparing food, storage vessels, and large-scale food storage infrastructure (*collqas*), to the study of microscopic evidence of food alterations such as grinding, fermentation, and cooking (Alconini; Chiou; Bélisle, Alaica, and Brown; Berryman and Blom; Biwer, Alaica, and Quiñonez Cuzcano; and Weber and Young, this volume).

Andean meals, today and in the past, typically included starchy tubers, quinoa, wild or cultivated plants, meat (e.g., camelids [llama and alpaca] and guinea pig), and fish boiled in soups or stews or roasted when feeding larger groups (for a discussion of comfort and nostalgia regarding food, see Chiou, this volume). Andean dietary flexibility is also documented through the incorporation of new and foreign foods,

even as staples (Baitzel et al. and Belmar et al., this volume; Kennedy and
VanValkenburgh 2016; Paredes and Hopkins 2018). In some instances,
people valued difficult-to-obtain foods over readily available and nutri-
tious local resources (Berryman and Blom; Miller et al., this volume).
Archaeological, ethnohistoric, and ethnographic evidence indicates that
the inclusion of two geographically limited seasonings, salt and capsicum
pepper (*ají*), was "the absolute minimum of comfort which divided acceptable subsistence from deprivation" (Salomon [1986] 2007, 88). Thus,
to provide a "proper" meal in most locales, imported ingredients were
essential. As discussed below, the need to access nonlocal ingredients
(e.g., maize) was even greater for prestige negotiations, and in these cases
the host required quantities larger than those that could be carried by
humans alone. Highland-adapted South American camelids, llamas and
alpacas, were both cherished for their meat and wool, while llamas were
valuable beasts of burden in the Andes. Even in the driest desert of the
world (Santana-Sagredo et al. this volume), Andean communities de-
vised ways to successfully herd their own camelids to transport valued
resources to be shared with others and to move nonlocal food items that
diversified diets and buffered against scarcity.

ANDEAN COMMENSALITY: RECIPROCITY, POLITICS, EXTRAORDINARY FOODS, AND ONTOLOGIES

The human relationship with food in the Andes is simultaneously biological, cultural, and social. Drinking and eating together (commensality) transcends biology as a principal means of creating kinship and
relationships (Weismantel 1995; see also Bray; Scaffidi, Vang, and Tung,
this volume). While eating, borders between bodies can become porous,
and transcorporeality allows one to eat with and for others, even those
separated in time and space, such as geographically distant loved ones or
dead ancestors (Weismantel 1991; Bray, this volume). Among the living,
it is not through genetics, but through feeding, that kinship is formed,
even between parents and children.

   In addition to being essential for establishing solidarity, Andean commensality is significant in exchanges of reciprocal labor on which Andean
social and economic systems are built (Allen 1988; Gose 1994, 9–11; Isbell
1978, 167–77; Mayer 2002; Murra 2017; Rostworowski de Diez Canseco

2013, 259–60). Individuals work their land by exchanging deferred labor (*ayni*) with equals (friends and family) in their social network, and they must provide food and drink when they receive aid[2] or secure promises of future labor.[3] When organizing public work projects, higher-status recipients of labor do not reciprocate in kind (*ayni*) but partially remunerate workers with food, drink, and goods as well as wages (*mink'a*[4]). This labor debt is never fully repaid, and the social asymmetry is publicly reified through commensality. Therefore, cooking and serving, rather than being viewed as marginalized "housework," are imbued with power, power that women can often exercise by controlling the order in which guests are served, the type of serving vessels used, and the quantity and quality of the food and drink provided (Gose 1994, 11; see also Jennings and Bowser 2009; Weismantel 1988).

Gastro-politics are revealed in competitive feasting and other performative aspects of consumption and meaning attributed to food (Appadurai 1981). Ordinary, everyday food can be transformed into extraordinary foods (see discussions in Bélisle, Alaica, and Brown; Biwer, Alaica, and Quiñonez Cuzcano; and Bray, this volume; see also Belmar et al.; Weber and Young, this volume; Weismantel 1991). Important in making food extraordinary are the properties of the food (e.g., psychoactive qualities, color), the location where ingredients are grown (e.g., sanctified fields of the Inka, exotic locales), who prepares the food and drink (e.g., the "chosen women" [*aclla*] of the Inka), the use of special serving wares, the time and location of food consumption (e.g., festival days, graveside, public plaza), unusual quantities, special guests (e.g., the dead or earth spirits), and the sacred properties assigned to them (e.g., substantiation). Extraordinary meals or foods, especially those served at feasts, can be used to generate harmony but can also signify differences in class, gender, and other forms of social hierarchy (e.g., Bray, 2003; Scaffidi, Vang, and Tung, this volume).

One of the more transformative foods throughout history in the Andes is chicha beer (Jennings and Bowser 2009; Moore 1989; Weismantel 1991). Chicha was sometimes part of daily household commensality but

2. Mayer (2002) characterizes this food sharing as an acknowledgment of service rendered.

3. The food sharing, according to Mayer (2002), is a way to "seal the deal."

4. *Mink'a*: highly asymmetrical corvée labor that was used by the Inkas (*mit'a*) and Spaniards (*mita*) to build and extract resources for the empire.

was most important in larger quantities during public feasts. Throughout this volume, we see the myriad social dynamics that involved chicha as well as its importance in Andean statecraft. Chicha created and signified cosmopolitan identities that integrated local groups into larger cultural spheres (Biwer, Alaica, and Quiñonez Cuzcano; Chiou; and Weber and Young, this volume). Chicha was also the dominant beverage served during the feasts and rituals of ancient Andean states and empires, as we see during the emergence and collapse of the Moche (Chiou), Wari (Bélisle, Alaica, and Brown; Biwer, Alaica, and Quiñonez Cuzcano, this volume), Tiwanaku (Baitzel et al. Berryman and Blom; Knudson et al.; Miller et al., this volume), and Inkas (Alconini; Bray, this volume).

Finally, commensality is essential to reciprocal relationships that intertwine humans with the supernatural, the ancestors, and the sentient Andean landscape (Allen 1988, 2019; Bastien 1978; de la Cadena 2015; Tantaleán 2019; Weismantel 1995; Alconini and Bray, this volume). As described above, food can dissolve boundaries of time, space, and bodies, forging relationships and interdependence. Catherine Allen (2019, 10) writes that Sonqueños, a Quechua-speaking community in the highlands of southern Peru,

> describe their local earth beings [*tiraa kuna*] as *uywaqniykukuna* (those who nurture us, who make us grow up). These powerful places instill and maintain *animu* [individuating energy] for everything within the spheres of their authority. In return for their care, the *tirakuna* expect to be fed with libations of alcohol and the aromas of coca leaves and cooked food. Agriculturalists address the nourishing earth as *Pachamama* (Mother Pacha [Mother World, but also Mother Space-Time]) and in gratitude nourish her just as they do the *tirakuna*.

While humans/kin subsist on food, places and other other-than-humans eat smoke and the air blown over coca leaves (Gose 2018). The free flow of life force between humans and the supernatural is essential to human survival (Allen 2019; Graham 1997; Greenway 1998). If reciprocal obligations to feed each other are not met, hungry ancestors and earth spirits can physically or spiritually drain human bodies, and agricultural fields can become infertile. Feeding and eating are thus intertwined in the social fabric of the Andes.

THE IMPACT OF PLACE AND LONG-DISTANCE INTERACTIONS ON FOODWAYS

This volume begins with two chapters that outline broad changes in foodways over time. Kurt Wilson and Weston McCool examine the relative influence that local environments and sociopolitical integration and complexity had in shaping Andean diets from the Early Intermediate Period to the Late Horizon (~2150–418 yBP).[5] Their large-scale analyses show that ~60%–80% of the diet was explained by the environment, although its influence was incomplete and decreased over time. Their analysis suggests that factors other than sociopolitical complexity, such as greater economic intensification or trade and exchange relationships, played a significant role in dietary changes. Similarly, the direct ways in which culture shaped food and cuisine over millennia are effectively illustrated in the Chiloé Island of northern Patagonia (Chile) from the Late Ceramic Period (~6000 yBP) to European contact. Carolina Belmar and her colleagues found that as the inhabitants came into contact with horticulturalists and European influence, Chiloé's cuisine expanded to incorporate some domesticated plants (maize and potatoes) and new technologies (e.g., ceramics). Even with these changes, Chiloé's people maintained a local "surf and turf" culinary tradition and identity that remains to this day. Importantly, their analysis revealed edible medicines were used in the past as they are today; seaweeds and plants with psychoactive qualities nourished, healed, and transformed minds and bodies.

In the Andes significant interregional interactions involving food began during a period of time that archaeologists typically refer to as "Formative." During these times many Andean people began to settle into larger villages, and regional civic-ceremonial centers emerged. Three chapters in this volume highlight Formative Period sites with monumental architecture in the Andean highlands and the contributions of nonlocal cuisine to local agropastoral subsistence strategies in these centers. One of these studies concerns a site that was part of the broad Chavin Interaction Sphere, a network of interrelated sites that shared religious and ritual practices. In their investigation of the site of Atalla

---

5. Authors provided their own dates and temporal periods in this book. Those interested in debates about the limitations of chronologies can look elsewhere (e.g., Swenson and Roddick 2018).

(~1200–400 BCE) in Huancavelica, Peru, Sadie Weber and Michelle Young focus on the social implications of chicha recipes. Their detailed analysis revealed that foreign cultigens and diverse taxa played important roles, especially in ritual contexts, where people created complex recipes combining maize with algarroba, manioc, or both. Exotic plants were imported to prepare ritual beverages, reinforcing Atalla's exchange relationships and its commitment to and reliance on distant communities.

Elsewhere, on the Taraco Peninsula of Lake Titicaca (Bolivia), Melanie Miller and colleagues examine the complex relationship that the inhabitants had with the land and water around them. Beginning in the Formative Period, and for more than two millennia (1400 BCE–1100 CE), the inhabitants of the peninsula dined on wild and domesticated local resources including quinoa, tubers, camelids, and small game. Their isotopic analyses determined that lake fish were less important in the diets of those living on the peninsula, at least during childhood. The abundance of fish remains, however, suggests that fish may have been used as fertilizer or reserved for adult consumption or for special dishes, perhaps those that fed sentient earth beings. Isotopic evidence of maize in the diets of Formative settlers on the peninsula is echoed at other Late Formative centers with monumental complexes in the southern Lake Titicaca Basin, such as the city of Tiwanaku ~15 km away and in the Desaguadero Valley just to the south (Berryman and Blom, this volume).

FOOD, POWER, AND STATUS IN EARLY STATES AND EMPIRES

Several chapters in this volume provide insights into the nature of expansive empires and the variety of experiences of those living within communities transformed through their interaction with two Middle Horizon (ca. 600–1000 CE) polities, the Tiwanaku and Wari. The rise and fall of Tiwanaku (ca. 550–1100 CE) had a transformative effect on food, diet, and cuisine for many individuals living in urban neighborhoods and rural hamlets in the Tiwanaku altiplano heartland in the southern Lake Titicaca Basin. Carrie Anne Berryman and Deborah Blom found that some individuals in the heartland consumed only local food resources while others accessed large quantities of meat and maize chicha associated with state-sponsored feasts. Some of these highland individuals consumed as much maize as contemporaneous maize agriculturalists living in diasporic Tiwanaku settlements in the distant western lowlands. In their isotopic examination of the diets of individuals buried in Tiwanaku-affiliated sites in the Moquegua Valley (Peru), Kelly Knudson and colleagues found that dietary variation, in general and across individuals' life cycles, was not structured by sex or age but by occupational or community-based identities. Their study reveals that in addition to disparate amounts of maize, inhabitants likely consumed a relatively high proportion of legumes, a foodstuff not previously considered important in this region.

Focused on territory controlled or influenced by the Wari Empire (600–1000 CE) in the South-Central Andes, two chapters contrast the meals shared in private with the extraordinary foods of commensality consumed in public spaces. Véronique Bélisle, Aleksa Alaica, and Matthew Brown assessed how the inhabitants of Ak'awillay, a local center in Cusco (~3,300 masl), promoted unity through the household preparation of mundane local food resources served in plain, small vessels for public consumption. In contrast to the simple public meals, those consumed in the privacy of homes included exotic ingredients brought from afar. Matthew Biwer, Aleksa Alaica, and Patricia Quiñonez Cuzcano studied foodways in Quilcapampa La Antigua, a roadside outpost of the Wari Empire in the middle Sihuas Valley (Arequipa, Peru, ~1,600 masl). While food was mostly processed in the outlying areas of the site, those eating in the core enjoyed meatier cuts of llama and alpaca and conducted intense brewing activities that focused on chicha made from molle and maize. Quilcapampa's cuisine included ají, quinoa, local and wild game as well as *wilka* (a hallucinogenic plant that could be added to chicha), legumes, fruit, and shellfish brought to the outpost from the coast. In contrast to Ak'awillay, public commensality at Quilcapampa included a more diverse range of food items, which may indicate that patron-client feasts were important for integrating local leaders into the Wari Empire.

FOOD DURING TIMES OF TROUBLE: CONFLICT, INSTABILITY, AND COLLAPSE

So we might fully understand social complexity in the Andes, four chapters encourage us to appreciate the myriad of ways in which societies responded during times of warfare, climate change, and political collapse.

Beth Scaffidi, Natasha Vang, and Tiffiny Tung bring the reality of warfare and violence to light in their study of human remains from Uraca, a
cemetery in the Lower Majes Valley of Arequipa, Peru, during a time of
increased violence in the late Early Intermediate Period–early Middle
Horizon (ca. 200–750 CE). Their study of "isobiographies" showed that
individuals whose crania were removed and made into "trophy heads"
were fed more maize through early childhood and adolescence than individuals whose bodies were buried intact. This suggests a unique social
upbringing that made these individuals into high-status combatants who
would suffer later-life trauma and whose bodies would be transformed
into trophies after death.

Several chapters in the volume discuss the Late Intermediate Period
(LIP), a time characterized by the loss of the political integration of the
Middle Horizon. Wilson and McCool show that in general, diets in the
LIP were not markedly different from earlier periods, but Berryman and
Blom report that after the collapse of the Tiwanaku state (ca. 1100 CE),
diets in the altiplano heartland became less diverse and more local than
at any time in the previous 2,500 years. The contraction of dietary diversity in the Lake Titicaca Basin is in stark contrast to the experience in
the Tiwanaku-descendant, diasporic Cabuza community of Los Batanes
studied by Sarah Baitzel and colleagues in the Sama Valley of southern
Peru. After the collapse of the Tiwanaku state, agropastoralists living in
this coastal-highland ecotone were no longer constrained by state political
integration. The result was relatively expansive foodways, which included
seafood and a wide range of wild and domesticated plants and animals
from various altitudinal zones. In another example of LIP ingenuity, Francisca Santana-Sagredo and her coauthors apply stable isotope analyses to
camelid fibers from animals and textiles interred in the Pica 8 cemetery
in the Atacama Desert, northern Chile. By applying standard methods to
a new substrate, they discovered that even in the driest land in the world,
Andean peoples' creativity and knowledge allowed them to herd camelids
by possibly feeding these animals highly fertilized crops. Having their
own llama caravans allowed them to import goods from distant lands.

In contrast to the relative prosperity of the LIP in the Southern Andes, Katherine Chiou's study provides a view of life amid the instability
of prolonged and severe flooding and droughts. During the Late Moche
Period (600–800 CE), inhabitants of Cerro Chepén, in the Jequetepeque

Valley, responded to food scarcity and conflict by hastily constructing household compounds on hillside terraces below an elite hilltop fortress. Chiou presents a detailed GIS (Geographic Information System) visualization of the food remains from a six-room multileveled household compound. The relatively small range of ingredients identified were prepared, cooked, and consumed in particular "taskscapes," which included a compost bin that further illustrates the inhabitants' frugality and self-reliance. While these households grappled with food insecurity, the elite living above conspicuously consumed diverse food items (e.g., marine resources, fruits, and maize chicha), possibly with psychoactive substances added. In describing abandonment offerings, Chiou asks us to consider that memories of the locales we live in and the foods we eat during times of trouble may be those that bring us the most comfort and nostalgia in later years.

BUILDING THE INKA EMPIRE WITH SACRED AND HIGH-STATUS FOODS

During the expansion of the Inka Empire (ca.1400–1540), food was used in prestigious feasts and festivals and in offerings to royalty, ancestors, and other-than-human beings. At the height of the empire, the extraction of nonlocal products (e.g., metals, coca, and maize) involved increasingly complex interactions with distant communities. In two of these Inka provinces, the Kallawaya (Bolivia) and the Diaguita (Chile) peoples used very different strategies to establish reciprocal, sociopolitical, economic, and ritual relationships that signaled, through food, both state incorporation and the special relationship that some communities and individuals had with the empire. Inka interactions with the sacred are also visible on Mount Kaata (Bolivia), a sacred mountain divinity (*apu*). Information from archaeology, ethnography, and ethnohistory aid in understanding the Andean ontological relationships with food.

Marta Alfonso-Durruty, Nicole Misarti, and Andrés Troncoso examine the dietary impact of the Inka Empire on the Diaguita populations from the Semi-Arid Region of Northern Chile (SARNC). Nonviolent Inka-Diaguita relations likely facilitated the Diaguita's access to camelids of diverse origins. At the same time, Diaguita's consumption of maize declined and was likely restricted to a few individuals whose eating or drinking maize signaled their closeness to the Inka state. Most maize produced in the SARNC was consumed by other peoples who also participated in the Inka State's redistributing network. Sonia Alconini's exquisite analysis of evidence from Kaata Pata (Bolivia) shows the power that cuisine, place, and other-than-human beings had on the status negotiations between local elites (Kallawaya) and the Inka. Kaata Pata united vast exchange networks and occupied the heart of Mount Kaata. Periodic lavish commensal celebrations reinforced communal cohesion and the group-divinity relation, and simultaneously these feasts publicized emerging social differences. The complex interaction of reciprocal relations between groups and divinities allowed the Inka to gain access to the eastern tropic networks, while the local Kallawayas became important Inka representatives.

Tamara Bray explores food and Andean ontologies through ethnographic and ethnohistoric documents. Her study demonstrates that food is not just an inert substance that symbolizes something (e.g., identity, belonging, and ethnicity) but a transformative material culture that bonded porous, transcorporeal, human bodies to various Andean other-than-human beings. In this manner, Andean commensality created and maintained social worlds while it also transcended and dissolved ontological boundaries, reinforcing the interdependent and relational qualities of the Andean cosmospace. While our Western world views often overemphasize the symbolic and nutritional roles of foods and cuisines, Bray eloquently refocuses our attention on the deeper social meaning of culinary behavior, particularly in a setting where all matter has power that requires and demands human participation.

FUTURE DIRECTIONS AND CONCLUSION

In the concluding chapter, Susan deFrance draws out various theoretical and methodological challenges for archaeologists and ethnohistorians studying foodways and provides suggestions for future directions. In doing so, she highlights themes introduced in this volume, which are intertwined with uniquely Andean cultural and geographical characteristics. She asks us to consider problems of equifinality, methodological limitations, and the information gained from overlapping and sometimes contradictory data sets. DeFrance asks us to examine the definitions and implications of terms commonly used by archaeologists to describe the remains of food and food-related behaviors and encourages us to think about how biases inherent in some of these terms might inadvertently shape our interpretations and obscure the nature of the relationship between past people and food.

As a whole, the anthropological, archaeological, and bioarchaeological research presented in this volume offers a diverse set of theoretical perspectives and methodological approaches. The contributing authors, who have studied or worked in more than ten different countries, present a variety of worldviews. By including areas that were previously seen as marginal or extreme and peoples not fully incorporated into the empires and states of their times, the volume presents a more inclusive picture of the human experience. Contextual interpretations and the integration of Andean concepts illustrate the richness and ingenuity of Andean peoples and showcase how foods and people mutually transformed one another in the Andean past.

REFERENCES

Allen, Catherine J. 1988. *The Hold Life Has: Coca and Cultural Identity in an Andean Community*. Washington, DC: Smithsonian Institution Press.

Allen, Catherine J. 2019. "Righting Imbalance: Striving for Well-Being in the Andes." *Science, Religion and Culture* 6 (1): 6–14. https://doi.org/10.17582/journal.src/2019.6.1.6.14.

Appadurai, Arjun. 1981. "Gastro-Politics in Hindu South Asia." *American Ethnologist* 8 (3): 494–511. https://doi.org/10.1525/ae.1981.8.3.02a00050.

Bastien, Joseph W. 1978. *Mountain of the Condor: Metaphor and Ritual in an Andean Ayllu*. Prospect Heights, Ill.: Waveland Press.

Bourdieu, Pierre. 1984. *Distinction: A Social Critique of the Judgement of Taste*. Translated by Richard Nice. Cambridge, Mass.: Harvard University Press.

Bray, Tamara L. 2003. "To Dine Splendidly: Imperial Pottery, Commensal Politics and the Inca State." In *The Archaeology and Politics of Food and Feasting in Early State and Empires*, edited by Tamara L. Bray, 93–142. New York: Kluwer Academic; Plenum.

Briggs, Rachel V. 2018. "Detangling Histories of Hominy: A Historical Anthropological Approach." In *Baking, Bourbon, and Black Drink: Foodways Archaeology in the American Southeast*, edited by Tanya M. Peres and Aaron Deter-Wolf, 160–73. Tuscaloosa: University of Alabama Press.

Bruno, Maria C., José M. Capriles, Christine A. Hastorf, Sherilyn C. Fritz, D. Marie Weide, Alejandra I. Domic, and Paul A. Baker. 2021. "The Rise and

Fall of Wiñaymarka: Rethinking Cultural and Environmental Interactions in the Southern Basin of Lake Titicaca." *Human Ecology* 49 (2): 131–45. https://doi.org/10.1007/s10745-021-00222-3.

Cadena, Bibiana, and Carolina Moreano. 2012. "La Alimentación en Tiempos Pretéritos: Una Reflexión acerca de la Trascendencia de la Comida en la Cultura y en el Entorno Biológico de las Poblaciones Humanas." In *Las Manos en la Masa: Arqueologías, Antropologías e Historias de la Alimentación en Suramérica*, edited by María del Pilar Babot, María Marschoff, and Francisco Pazzarelli, 339–60. Córdova: Universidad Nacional de Córdova.

Castro, Victoria. 2010. "Sabores Ancestrales: Caza, Recolección y Producción de Alimentos en el Norte Prehispano." In *Historia y Cultura de la Alimentación en Chile: Miradas y Saberes Sobre Nuestra Culinaria*, edited by Carolina Sciolla, 27–62. Santiago, Chile: Catalonia.

Cuéllar, Andrea M. 2013. "The Archaeology of Food and Social Inequality in the Andes." *Journal of Archaeological Research* 21 (2): 123–74. http://www.jstor.org/stable/42635578.

de la Cadena, Marisol. 2015. *Earth Beings*. Durham, N.C.: Duke University Press.

Douglas, Mary. 1972. "Deciphering a Meal." *Daedalus* 101 (1): 61–81. http://www.jstor.org/stable/20024058.

González Holguín, Diego. 1608. *Vocabulario de la Lengua General de Todo el Perú Llamada Lengua Qquichua o del Inca*. Lima: Francisco del Canto. http://www.bibliotecanacionaldigital.gob.cl/visor/BND:9530.

Goody, Jack. 1982. *Cooking, Cuisine and Class: A Study in Comparative Sociology*. Cambridge: Cambridge University Press.

Gose, Peter. 1994. *Deathly Waters and Hungry Mountains: Agrarian Ritual and Class Formation in an Andean Town*. Toronto: University of Toronto Press.

Gose, Peter. 2018. "The Semi-Social Mountain: Metapersonhood and Political Ontology in the Andes." *HAU: Journal of Ethnographic Theory* 8 (3): 488–505.

Graham, Margaret A. 1997. "Food Allocation in Rural Peruvian Households: Concepts and Behavior Regarding Children." *Social Science and Medicine* 44 (11): 1697–709. https://doi.org/10.1016/s0277-9536(96)00372-3.

Greenway, Christine. 1998. "Hungry Earth and Vengeful Stars: Soul Loss and Identity in the Peruvian Andes." *Social Science & Medicine* 47 (8): 993–1004. https://doi.org/https://doi.org/10.1016/S0277-9536(98)00163-4.

Hastorf, Christine A. 2018. *The Social Archaeology of Food: Thinking about Eating from Prehistory to the Present*. New York: Cambridge University Press.

Isbell, Billie Jean. 1978. *To Defend Ourselves: Ecology and Ritual in an Andean Village*. Prospect Heights, Ill.: Waveland Press.

Jennings, Justin, and Brenda J. Bowser. 2009. "Drink, Power, and Society in the Andes: An Introduction." In *Drink, Power, and Society in the Andes*, edited by Justin Jennings and Brenda J. Bowser, 1–27. Gainesville: University Press of Florida.

Juengst, Sara L., Dale L. Hutchinson, Karen Mohr Chávez, Sergio J. Chávez, Stanislava R. Chávez, John Krigbaum, Theresa Schober, and Lynette Norr. 2021. "The Resiliency of Diet on the Copacabana Peninsula, Bolivia." *Journal of Anthropological Archaeology* 61:101260. https://doi.org/10.1016/j.jaa.2020.101260.

Kennedy, Sarah A., and Parker VanValkenburgh. 2016. "Zooarchaeology and Changing Food Practices at Carrizales, Peru Following the Spanish Invasion." *International Journal of Historical Archaeology* 20 (1): 73–104. http://www.jstor.org/stable/26174192.

Klarich, Elizabeth, ed. 2010. *Inside Ancient Kitchens: New Directions in the Study of Daily Meals and Feasts.* Boulder: University Press of Colorado.

Knudson, Kelly J., Christina Torres-Rouff, and Christopher M. Stojanowski. 2015. "Investigating Human Responses to Political and Environmental Change Through Paleodiet and Paleomobility." *American Journal of Physical Anthropology* 157 (2): 179–201. https://doi.org/10.1002/ajpa.22694.

Lèvi-Strauss, Claude. 1997. "The Culinary Triangle." In *Food and Culture: A Reader*, edited by Carole Counihan and Penny Van Esterik, 28–35. New York: Routledge.

Lozada, María Cecelia, and Henry Tantaleán. 2019. *Andean Ontologies: New Archaeological Perspectives.* Gainesville: University Press of Florida.

Mauss, Marcel. (1935) 2006. "Techniques of the Body." In *Techniques, Technology and Civilization*, edited by Nathan Schlanger, 77–96. New York: Berghahn Books.

Mayer, Enrique. 2002. "The Rules of the Game in Andean Reciprocity." In *The Articulated Peasant: Household Economies in the Andes*, 105–42. Cambridge, Mass.: Westfield.

Mead, Margaret. 1997. "The Changing Significance of Food." In *Food and Culture: A Reader*, edited by Carole Counihan and Penny Van Esterik, 11–19. New York: Routledge.

Mintz, Sidney W., and Christine M. Du Bois. 2002. "The Anthropology of Food and Eating." *Annual Review of Anthropology* 31:99–119. http://www.jstor.org/stable/4132873.

Moore, Jerry D. 1989. "Pre-Hispanic Beer in Coastal Peru: Technology and Social Context of Prehistoric Production." *American Anthropologist* 91 (3): 682–95. https://doi.org/10.1525/aa.1989.91.3.02a00090.

Murra, John V. 1972. "El 'Control Vertical' de un Máximo de Pisos Ecológicos en la Economía de las Sociedades Andinas." In *Visita de la Provincia de León de Huánuco en 1562: Iñigo Ortiz de Zúñiga, Visitador.* Vol. 2, *Visita de los Yacha y Mitmaqkuna Cuzqueños Encomendados en Juan Sanchez Falcon*, edited by John V. Murra, 429–76. Huánuco: Universidad Nacional Hermilio Valdizán.

Murra, John V. 1975. *Formaciones Económicas y Políticas del Mundo Andino.* Lima: Instituto de Estudios Peruanos.

Murra, John V. 2017. "Reciprocity, the Anthropological Alternative to Exotic Explanations." In *Reciprocity and Redistribution in Andean Civilizations: Transcript of the Lewis Henry Morgan Lectures at the University of Rochester, April 8th–17th, 1969*, prepared by Freda Yancy Wolf and Heather Lechtman, 19–34, Chicago: Hau Books.

Paredes, Rossana, and Allison L. Hopkins. 2018. "Dynamism in Traditional Ecological Knowledge: Persistence and Change in the Use of Totora (*Schoenoplectus californicus*) for Subsistence in Huanchaco, Peru." *Ethnobiology Letters* 9 (2): 169–79. http://www.jstor.org/stable/26607685.

Peres, Tanya M., and Aaron Deter-Wolf. 2018. "Introduction: Foodways Archaeology in the South East." In *Baking, Bourbon, and Black Drink*, edited by Tanya M. Peres and Aaron Deter-Wolf, 1–10. Tuscaloosa: University of Alabama Press.

Platt, Tristan. 2016. "Avoiding 'Community Studies': The Historical Turn in Bolivian and South Andean Anthropology." In *A Return to the Village: Community Ethnographies and the Study of Andean Culture in Retrospective*, edited by Francisco Ferreira and Billie Jean Isbell, 199–231. London: Institute of Latin American Studies, School of Advanced Study, University of London.

Pollan, Michael. 2013. *Cooked: A Natural History of Transformation*. New York: Penguin Press.

Rostworowski de Diez Canseco, María. 2013. *Historia del Tahuantinsuyu*. Lima: Instituto de Estudios Peruanos.

Salomon, Frank. (1986) 2007. *Native Lords of Quito in the Age of the Incas: The Political Economy of North Andean Chiefdoms*. New York: Cambridge University Press. https://epdf.pub/native-lords-of-quito-in-the-age-of-the-incas-the-political-economy-of-north-andbbf4ac07ff58a13dbf3f66fd4826281a63817.html.

Sofaer, Joanna R. 2006. *The Body as Material Culture: A Theoretical Osteoarchaeology*. Cambridge: Cambridge University Press.

Swenson, Edward, and Andy P. Roddick. 2018. "Rethinking Temporality and Historicity from the Perspective of Andean Archaeology." In *Constructions of Time and History in the Ancient Andes*, edited by Edward Swenson and Andrew P. Roddick, 3–44. Boulder: University Press of Colorado.

Tantaleán, Henry. 2019. "Andean Ontologies." In *Andean Ontologies: New Archaeological Perspectives*, edited by María Cecilia Lozada and Henry Tantaleán, 1–48. Gainesville: University Press of Florida.

Turner, Bethany L., Véronique Bélisle, Allison R. Davis, Maeve Skidmore, Sara L. Juengst, Benjamin J. Schaefer, R. Alan Covey, and Brian S. Bauer. 2018. "Diet and Foodways Across Five Millennia in the Cusco Region of Peru." *Journal of Archaeological Science* 98:137–48. https://doi.org/10.1016/j.jas.2018.07.013.

Van Buren, Mary. 1996. "Rethinking the Vertical Archipelago: Ethnicity, Exchange, and History in the South Central Andes." *American Anthropologist* 98 (2): 338–51.

Van Valkenburgh, Parker. 2019. "The Past, Present, and Future of Transconquest Archaeologies in the Andes." *International Journal of Historical Archaeology* 23 (4): 1063–80. https://doi.org/10.1007/s10761-018-0484-z.

Velasco, Matthew C., and Tiffiny A. Tung. 2021. "Shaping Dietary Histories: Exploring the Relationship Between Cranial Modification and Childhood Feeding in a High-Altitude Andean Population (1100–1450 CE)." *Journal of Anthropological Archaeology* 62:101298. https://doi.org/10.1016/j.jaa.2021.101298.

Weismantel, Mary J. 1988. *Food, Gender, and Poverty in the Ecuadorian Andes.* Philadelphia: University of Pennsylvania Press.

Weismantel, Mary J. 1991. "Maize Beer and Andean Social Transformations: Drunken Indians, Bread Babies, and Chosen Women." *MLN* 106 (4): 861–79. https://doi.org/10.2307/2904628.

Weismantel, Mary. 1995. "Making Kin: Kinship Theory and Zumbagua Adoptions." *American Ethnologist* 22 (4): 685–704. http://www.jstor.org/stable/646380.

Wrangham, Richard. 2009. *Catching Fire: How Cooking Made Us Human.* New York: Basic Books.

PART I

THE IMPACT OF PLACE AND LONG-DISTANCE INTERACTIONS ON FOODWAYS

1

The Environmental Null

Documenting the Changing Influence of Physical and
Social Environments on Prehistoric Andean Diets

Kurt M. Wilson and Weston C. McCool

Andean studies of the impact of social and political processes on diet
have a long history (Hastorf and Johannessen 1993; Pozorski 1979;
Turner and Klaus 2020; Tykot, Burger, and van der Merwe 2006) and
have provided invaluable information on issues such as imperial impacts
(Bray 2003; Toyne et al. 2017; Williams and Murphy 2013), cooperation
(Stanish, Tantaleán, and Knudson 2018), fertilization of crops (Finucane
2007), socioeconomic specialization (Marsteller, Zolotova, and Knudson
2017), and social inequality and complex societies (Cuéllar 2013; Quilter
and Stocker 1983) in pre-Hispanic Andean life. However, quantifying
sociopolitical factors is difficult, and thus, studies have rarely attempted
to estimate the relative degree of influence social factors may have had on
Andean diets. Here we quantify the influence of the local environment
on diet across four time periods to begin to assess the changing influence
of social factors on Andean diets.

BACKGROUND

Isotopic studies on prehistoric peoples have shown sex (Coltrain and
Janetski 2013) and status (Ambrose, Buikstra, and Krueger 2003; Kellner and Schoeninger 2012), among other factors, can directly influence
diet. Lower-status individuals may be prevented from consuming certain
goods because of elite manipulation of food items for status, wealth, signaling, or labor control (see deFrance 2009 for an overview). Additionally, inequality may significantly constrain the options individuals have
for movement or decision making (Wilson and Codding 2020), which
could alter their consumption practices. Sex-based dietary differences can
reflect divergent strategies. For example, women, particularly mothers,

may be more likely to make risk-averse subsistence decisions for daily provisioning of children (Codding, Bird, and Bird 2011; Hawkes, O'Connell, and Blurton Jones 1995). These and other aspects of social life that contribute to the transformative nature of food may therefore influence diet either through limiting individuals' access to high-ranking foods or by facilitating expanded access to such resources. Further, the food consumed may signify identity and build mundane-transcending bonds that enabled individuals to construct inter- and intragroup identities and sacred meaning (Bray, this volume).

However, the physical environment in which individuals live also exerts a strong influence on diet (Wilson et al. 2022). Andean settlement and mobility patterns were often designed to access resources in multiple ecozones (see Contreras 2010 overview). Further, numerous studies show that ecological patterning strongly affects resource acquisition decisions, transitions, and diets (Browman 1997; Greaves and Kramer 2014; Hawkes and O'Connell 1992; Piperno and Pearsall 1998). In the Andes, dietary reconstructions using stable isotope biogeochemistry have a long history (Burger and van der Merwe 1990; Kellner and Schoeninger 2008; Knudson, Peters, and Cagigao 2015; Knudson, Torres-Rouff, and Stojanowski 2015; McCool, Anderson, and Kennett 2021; Turner et al. 2018; Toyne et al. 2017). Comparison of stable carbon and nitrogen values has allowed Andean researchers to identify maize in diets (Finucane 2009; Tung et al. 2020), the level of reliance on marine resources (King et al. 2018), weaning ages (Greenwald et al. 2019), and more. To evaluate the effects of the environment on diet, Wilson et al. (2022) documented that across a sample of ~1,700 Andean individuals spanning the Preceramic to the Late Horizon, climatic and demographic factors explain ~80% of the variation in bone collagen $\delta^{15}N$ and ~66% of $\delta^{13}C$ values, with changing climates accounting for the majority of the effect. This suggests that local ecology was a strong constraint on the resources individuals consumed, although social factors were also likely at play, particularly during the Late Horizon.

In this study, our goal is to evaluate the changing importance of physical versus social environments on Andean diets by assessing the variation in $\delta^{15}N$ and $\delta^{13}C$ in the Central Andes (map 1.1) across four time periods: the Early Intermediate Period (EIP) (~2,150–1,350 yBP), Middle Horizon (MH) (~1,350–950 yBP), Late Intermediate Period

(LIP) (~950–480 yBP), and Late Horizon (LH) (~480–418 yBP).[1] Generally, the EIP is assumed to be the least complex of these four periods because of the absence of major state formations, and it is followed by the LIP, when state formations broke down (Covey 2008; Parsons, Hastings, and Matos 1997). While empires in the MH (Wari and Tiwanaku) and LH (Inka) share some characteristics, the scope of the empire building by the Inka makes the LH the most complex of the four periods. These general temporal patterns (Moseley 2001; Rivera 1991; Silverman and Isbell 2008) varied in space (Dulanto 2008; Moore and Mackey 2008) but are used here as proxies for variation in social effects and political complexity.

PREDICTIONS

Based on foraging theory (Smith and Winterhalder 1992; Stephens and Krebs 1986), the physiographic structure of the Andes, and prior work (Wilson et al. 2022), we expect climatically structured resource abundance to heavily influence diet. However, other influences—such as imperial pressures, decisions, or control over resource distribution (D'Altroy and Hastorf 2001) and changing social dimensions of dietary items (Hastorf and Johannessen 1993; Staller 2006)—should also vary in their power to explain diets. Empires may impose dietary constraints (e.g., limit access to status-signaling foods; Hastorf and Johannessen 1993) but can also expand access to nonlocal foods through trade and redistribution (Patterson 2012) while social dimensions may incentivize consumption for identity or signaling. These processes are expected to decrease the amount of diet explained by the local environment. Thus, if social or sociopolitical effects caused dietary changes, we expect the environment's influence on the diet to vary by period and be greatest during the EIP, followed by the LIP, MH, and LH, when it would have had the smallest impact. While oversimplified, and complicated by intraperiod spatial variation in sociopolitical complexity, these predictions are used to assess the changing impact of social processes on diet in the Andes.

---

1. While chronological boundaries vary by region, we rely on the general Andean chronology established by Moseley (2001, 22–23), as the data set spans the entirety of Peru and Northern Chile.

METHODS

The analysis of stable isotope $\delta^{13}C$ and $\delta^{15}N$ values from bone collagen in ~1,600 individuals (Wilson et al. 2022) considers six environmental variables: distance to coast (m), elevation above sea level (masl), mean temperature (°C), mean precipitation (mm/day), temperature seasonality (sd in °C × 100), and precipitation seasonality (sd in mm/day × 100). Results are analyzed with generalized additive models (GAMs; Wood 2017), a form of multivariate nonlinear statistical models conducted in the R statistical environment (R Core Team 2021).

DATA

Individuals from archaeological contexts in Peru, northern Chile, and the Titicaca Basin with stable isotope values for $\delta^{13}C‰$ and $\delta^{15}N‰$ from purified bone collagen were categorized by age and time period based on the reporting author's estimates. Individuals below the age of 5 years were excluded to control for nursing effects. Only individuals that belonged to the EIP ($\delta^{15}N$, $n = 318$; $\delta^{13}C$, $n = 318$), MH ($\delta^{15}N$, $n = 385$; $\delta^{13}C$, $n = 396$), LIP ($\delta^{15}N$, $n = 612$, $\delta^{13}C$, $n = 625$), and LH ($\delta^{15}N$, $n = 255$; $\delta^{13}C$, $n = 257$) (map 1.1; fig. 1.1) are included in the analyses. Stable isotope values represent the weighted average of an individual's long-term diet, although in subadults the time span is shorter because carbon turns over more rapidly (Hedges et al. 2007; Seifert and Watkins 1997). As a necessary simplification, we assumed individuals' burial locations are roughly representative of the type of environment in which they lived. All individual and site data are available in Wilson et al. (2022) or upon request from Kurt M. Wilson.[2]

Prehistoric climatic variables were generated using the PaleoView Paleoenvironmental Reconstruction Tool (Fordham et al. 2017) based on TRaCE-21ka experiments (Liu et al. 2009). Through this tool, estimated means for temperature, precipitation, and temperature and precipitation seasonality are calculated at 20-year intervals from 11,000 yBP to 140 yBP in 2.5 × 2.5 degree latitude-longitude grids. Using the site coordinates for each individual, the climatic variable values at every 20-year

---

2. R code to replicate analyses is hosted at https://github.com/wilsonkurt /env_null_andeaniso.

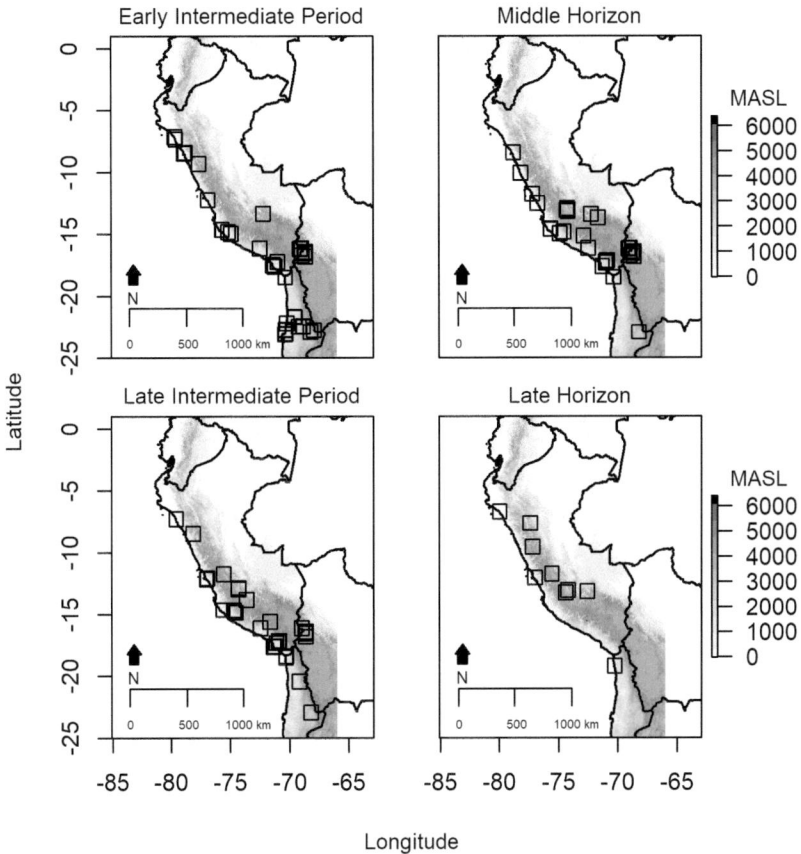

Map 1.1 Maps of sites (*black squares*) from which individuals' isotope records were obtained by time period. Grayscale shows the elevation in meters above sea level (masl) for each site. Figures created by Kurt M. Wilson and Weston C. McCool.

interval within the individual's time window are extracted and averaged using the rgdal package in R (Bivand et al. 2019). For individuals who have been radiocarbon dated, the calibrated radiocarbon date range BP at two standard deviations (δ) is used to establish their time window. This process provides each individual with estimated climatic values relative to their location in space and time.

Site elevation was extracted from a digital elevation model (DEM) for the study area generated through the USGS EarthExplorer tool and

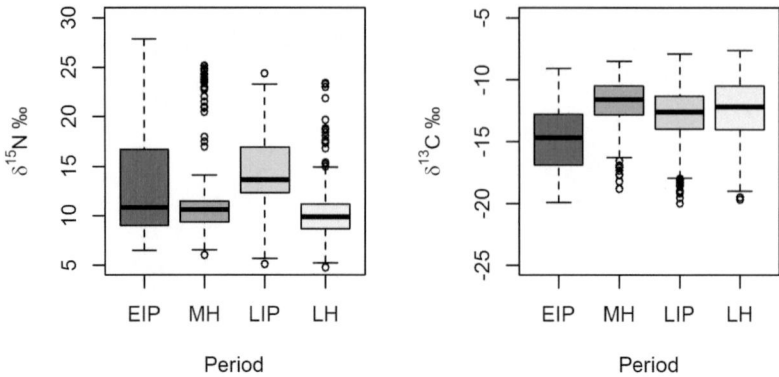

Figure 1.1 Boxplots showing the distribution of isotope data (δ^{15}N and δ^{13}C) by time period. Figures created by Kurt M. Wilson and Weston C. McCool.

the site coordinates.[3] Elevation is included because it can correlate with climatic variables and strongly influence Andean flora and fauna (Pulgar Vidal 1981; Seltzer and Hastorf 1990; Trawick 2003). For distance to coast, world vector shorelines data from the NOAA Global Self-consistent, Hierarchical, High-resolution Geography Database (Wessel and Smith 1996) is used to calculate the Euclidean distance (m) between the nearest coastal point and the site coordinates.

STATISTICAL ANALYSES

Individuals from the same site and period are expected to have more similar diets than others. Thus, site-based autocorrelation in the response variables (δ^{13}C and δ^{15}N) is evaluated by comparing expected versus observed Moran's I values on an inverse distance matrix using the ape package in R (Paradis and Schliep 2019). When the Moran's I test indicates individuals from the same site are more similar than expected by chance, we account for this autocorrelation in the statistical model. We also confirm that the duration of the temporal window for the individual does not influence their dietary value.

Correlation test diagnostics determine whether predictor variables exhibited collinearity. Collinearity is deemed present when the strength

3. "EarthExplorer," United States Geological Survey, https://earthexplorer.usgs.gov/.

of correlation between pairwise comparisons of variables is >0.70 (Dormann et al. 2013). The only uniformly collinear variables are distance to coast (m) and elevation (masl), indicating they are functionally the same. Thus, distance to the coast is dropped from the analysis, as elevation more directly aligns with natural regions (Pulgar Vidal 1981).

The relationship between environment and diet is analyzed with two series of four GAMs. Two final GAMs comprising all individuals incorporated in the analysis ($\delta^{15}N$, $n = 1,570$; $\delta^{13}C$, $n = 1,596$) are constructed for comparative purposes as well. The GAMs estimate linear and nonlinear (smooth) fits between response and predictor variables. Smoothing parameters are estimated using generalized cross validation and constrained to the lowest number of knots possible in order to maximize parsimony and avoid overfitting. With a continuous response variable, our models specify a Gaussian distribution with an identity link. Each explanatory model is constructed to evaluate how well dietary $\delta^{13}C$ and $\delta^{15}N$ are explained as a function of climate and elevation while controlling for the effects of site autocorrelation by including site .id as a random effect. All climate variables are included as parametric terms (linear relationship) while elevation is included as a smoothed term (nonlinear). For each model, we report the proportion of deviance explained and r^2 values for the whole model and the estimate (slope) and p value (p) for each parametric predictor. For smoothed terms, we report the p value (p). Model diagnostics evaluate the distribution of model residuals, check whether smoothed model terms are adequately smoothed, and check for overdispersion. Outputs are visualized as bar plots showing the percent deviance explained for $\delta^{13}C$ and $\delta^{15}N$ by environmental variables in each period.

RESULTS

Both $\delta^{15}N$ ($I_{obs} = 0.55$, $I_{exp} < -0.01$, $p < .0001$) and $\delta^{13}C$ ($I_{obs} = 0.53$, $I_{exp} < -0.01$, $p < .0001$) contain significant positive autocorrelation by site, indicating that individuals at the same site are more likely to share dietary isotope values than would be expected by random chance. Thus, site.id is included in explanatory models as a control.

Results reveal that the explanatory power of environment on dietary $\delta^{15}N$ and $\delta^{13}C$ varies over time (table 1.1; fig. 1.2). During the EIP no variables exhibit collinearity, and thus all are included in the statistical model.

Table 1.1 Summary of generalized additive model results reporting the estimate (slope) indicating the direction of the relationship for each parametric term, p-value for each term, plus the adjusted r^2 value, percent deviance explained, and number of individuals included for each time period whole-model GAM

Variable	EIP		MH		LIP		LH		All Individuals	
	slope	p	slope	p	slope	p	slope	p	slope	p
δ^{15}N‰										
Mean temperature	−0.93	.0016**	0.26	.1520	−0.41	–	0.29	.1300	−0.28	.0253*
Mean precipitation	−3.65	.0045**	0.02	.8390	−2.56	.0221*	−0.45	.2110	−2.37	.0000***
Temperature seasonality	0.04	.1357	0.02	.1100	–	–	0.10	.0000***	0.02	.0136*
Precipitation seasonality	−19.72	.0000***	–	–	–	.9949	–	–	−12.28	.0000***
Elevation	–	.0005**	–	.4430	–	.6530	–	.0147*	–	.0000***
site.id	–	.0000***	–	.0000***	–	.0000***	–	.0060**	–	.0000***
Adjusted r^2	0.91		0.70		0.64		0.89		0.83	
Deviance explained	92.3%		72.3%		65.8%		89.7%		84.4%	
n (number of sites)	318 (41)		385 (36)		612 (34)		255 (10)		1570 (121)	
Mean ‰	13.35		10.30		14.66		11.71		12.85	
Median ‰	10.85		9.90		13.66		10.60		11.58	
sd ‰	5.82		2.75		3.64		4.43		4.49	

δ¹³C‰

Mean temperature	-0.29	.0110*	0.12	.7988	-0.06	–	-0.32	.0039**	-0.21	.0554*
Mean precipitation	-0.54	.0731	0.17	.9604	0.98	.0526	-0.09	.5366	-0.06	.5239
Temperature seasonality	-0.01	.10019	-0.00	.3655	–	–	0.47	.3944	-0.01	.0016**
Precipitation seasonality	-5.70	.0000***	–	–	–	.0506	–	–	-0.82	.8017
Elevation	–	.0000***	–	.0000***	–	.0000***	–	.0022**	–	.0000***
site.id	–	.0000***	–	.0000***	–	.0000***	–	.0000***	–	.0000***
Adjusted r²	0.88		0.55		0.53		0.44		0.66	
Deviance explained	88.9%		58.0%		55.0%		45.9%		68.1%	
n (number of sites)	318 (41)		396 (37)		625 (37)		257 (10)		1596 (125)	
Mean ‰	-14.94		-12.55		-12.87		-12.03		-13.07	
Median ‰	-14.70		-12.20		-12.61		-11.60		-12.63	
sd ‰	2.56		2.68		2.26		1.98		2.58	

Note: Also included are the mean and sd values of δ¹⁵N‰ and δ¹³C‰ per time period.

* $p < .05$; ** $p < .01$; *** $p < .001$

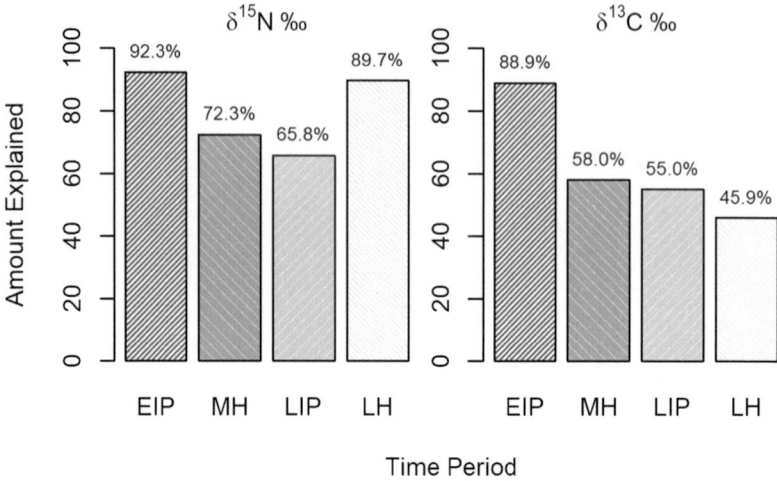

Figure 1.2 Percent of the variation (deviance) in δ¹⁵N and δ¹³C explained by each model during each time period. See table 1.1 for variables contributing to the deviance explained by time period and isotope. Figures created by Kurt M. Wilson and Weston C. McCool.

Mean temperature, mean precipitation, seasonality of precipitation, elevation, and site.id are significant predictors and together explain 92.3% of the deviance in δ¹⁵N. Mean temperature, seasonality of precipitation, elevation, and site.id explain 88.9% of the variance in δ¹³C.

During the MH, mean and seasonality of precipitation exhibit strong collinearity (>0.70). Therefore, seasonality was removed from the model. Only site.id is a significant predictor of δ¹⁵N during this period, explaining 72.3% of the deviance. Elevation and site.id are significant predictors of δ¹³C, explaining 58.0% of the variance.

Throughout the LIP, mean precipitation is collinear with both temperature and precipitation seasonality (>0.70). Temperature and precipitation seasonality were removed in favor of keeping mean precipitation. For δ¹⁵N, mean precipitation and site.id are significant and explain 65.8% of the deviance. Elevation and site.id are significant predictors of δ¹³C and explain 55.0% of the deviance.

In the LH, temperature and precipitation seasonality are strongly collinear (>0.70), Thus, precipitation seasonality was removed from the statistical model. Together, temperature seasonality, elevation, and site.id

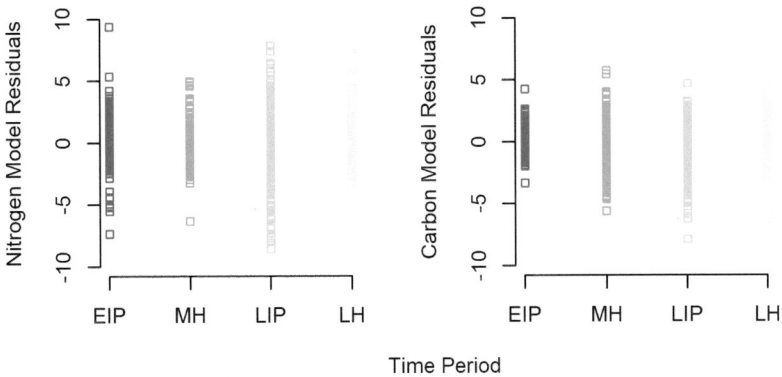

Figure 1.3 Distribution of model residuals (deviance left unexplained by the models) for each time period. EIP $\delta^{13}C$ and LH $\delta^{15}N$ residuals are more tightly condensed than others. LIP $\delta^{15}N$ residuals are more dispersed. Figures created by Kurt M. Wilson and Weston C. McCool.

explain 89.7% of the deviance in $\delta^{15}N$. For $\delta^{13}C$, mean temperature, elevation, and site.id predict 45.9% of the deviance.

Across all individuals included, the variables combine to explain 84.4% of the deviance in $\delta^{15}N$ and 68.1% in $\delta^{13}C$ (table 1.1). Model diagnostics for each GAM show that residuals are normally distributed around zero and that elevation is generally adequately smoothed, indicating the models perform well to predict variation in dietary isotopes.

Figure 1.3 shows the distribution of the residual variation left unexplained by our models for each time period. In general, the distribution in the residuals is comparable across periods, however, EIP carbon and LIP nitrogen show diverging patterns. The distribution of residuals is tighter for EIP carbon than the other periods, while LIP nitrogen possesses a wider dispersion.

DISCUSSION

Across the four time periods, the explanatory power of environment on dietary isotope signatures varies drastically, ranging from explaining as much as 92% of the variance to as little as 46%. This suggests the importance of the environment in constraining diet fluctuated significantly over the past 2,000 years in the Andes. These results also suggest that sociocultural influences on diet varied considerably by period in the past, generally becoming more important later in time. However, the observed variation does not follow our predictions regarding the influence of sociopolitical complexity.

EVALUATION OF SOCIOPOLITICAL PREDICTIONS

The results suggest that something, apart from the local environment, influenced diet more heavily later in time, but they do not support the predictions about sociopolitical complexity. As predicted, the EIP isotope values are almost completely explained by the local environments (>92% of the variance in $\delta^{15}N$ and >88% for $\delta^{13}C$). During the MH and LH periods, states influenced settlement (Bongers et al. 2020; Covey et al. 2013), trade (Stanish et al. 2010; Vinton et al. 2009), levels of violence (Andrushko and Torres 2011; D'Altroy 2015), and the importance of maize and chicha for social signaling (Hastorf and Johannessen 1993; Kellner and Schoeninger 2008), but their effect on diet is unclear. The pattern of decreased $\delta^{13}C$ variance explained in these periods would fit the expectation of state-level influence but does not address the variance explained in LIP $\delta^{13}C$ nor the suite of $\delta^{15}N$ patterns (fig. 1.2). The discrepancy in variance explained during the LIP may relate to the spatial variability in complexity, with sociopolitical complexity rising on the coasts but falling in the highlands. This possibility warrants further study.

The fact that no environmental variable significantly predicts $\delta^{15}N$ during the MH is surprising given that environment should influence resources (Pulgar Vidal 1981; Smith and Winterhalder 1992), and prior work has shown climatic environmental factors have significant effects (Wilson et al. 2022). The lack of statistical significance may result from unmeasured aspects of the local environment being more important than those captured by TRaCE-21ka here. Alternatively, it is possible that during the MH, social aspects overrode local conditions driving protein intake. Some studies suggest that Wari's influence in diets during the MH differed from others (Turner et al. 2018) by increasing dietary diversity (Buzon et al. 2012), though others have reported diets were not driven by direct Wari influence (Tung and Knudson 2018).

Finally, if greater complexity had a uniform effect, not evidenced in the percent deviance explained, we would anticipate the pattern in the distribution of MH and LH residuals to be similar to each other and different from those in the EIP and LIP. But the patterns found (fig. 1.3) do not suggest sociopolitical complexity is directly mediating diets in consistent manners.

INTENSIFICATION

Whereas sociopolitical complexity influence is not directly supported by our results, economic intensification may be suggested. Economic intensification resulting from population increases creating crises (Malthus 1798) or incentivizing innovation (Boserup 1965) can generate technological or production shifts in resource economies, particularly subsistence. Such shifts include subsistence strategy changes (Weitzel and Codding 2016), innovation in techniques (Dillehay and Kolata 2004), or increased reliance on lower-ranked resources with higher sustainable yields (Winterhalder and Goland 1993). However, population change is not the only potential cause of intensification; environmental shifts (Dillehay and Kolata 2004) and changing social values of foods (Thomas and Andrus 2008; Thomas 2014) may also result in intensifying production of subsistence resources.

After the EIP, $\delta^{13}C$ values increased (fig. 1.1, right panel) most likely due to the influence of maize agriculture. Concurrent with this dietary shift, the intensity of terrace use increased, with expansion beginning in the MH (Pearsall 2008) and culminating during the LH (Murra 1960). Over this same period, population sizes (Wilson et al. 2022, fig. 2) and the social importance of maize (Hastorf and Johannessen 1993) likely rose. If intensification in the Andean subsistence economy were occurring not because of local climatic change but as the result of changing populations, the social importance of maize, or trade demands, intensification would result in decreasing influence of environmental factors on dietary intake over time, the exact pattern shown in our $\delta^{13}C$ results (fig. 1.2). This would also fit with the reality that the LIP may not be, overall, less complex than the MH. Additionally, vertical migration (Fehren-Schmitz et al. 2014) and horizontal exchange between specialized groups (Marsteller, Zolotova, and Knudson 2017) continued to occur in the LIP despite the collapse of interregional highland states while coastal states emerged (Moore and Mackey 2008). These aspects of interconnectivity may be outcomes of intensification in strategies. Further, the heightened levels of violence and warfare during the LIP may have prompted maize intensification (McCool 2020), which could also decrease the predictive strength of local environments. Such intensification would explain the decreasing predictive power over time.

Our $\delta^{15}N$ results generally follow a pattern expected from intensification as well, though with implications for mediating effects by sociopolitical structures. As expected, the predictive power of the environment on $\delta^{15}N$ decreases over time (fig. 1.2). Figure 1.1 (left panel) also suggests the dispersion in diet decreases over time, though mediated by period. The MH and LH $\delta^{15}N$ is narrowly spread relative to EIP and LIP. The LIP pattern, in particular, may suggest that although intensification continued, as evidenced by decreased predictive power of the environment, diminished imperial structures resulted in more localized responses, hence the wide variation in values. This may also be suggested by the residuals (fig. 1.3), which show LIP $\delta^{15}N$ residuals are significantly wider than any other period. During the MH and LH, proximate effects of intensification may be organized by broader political structures, resulting in the narrowed range of dietary $\delta^{15}N$ (fig. 1.1) and model residuals (fig. 1.3).

The 89.7% of $\delta^{15}N$ deviance explained in the LH is unexpected and does not fit an intensification prediction. This value may be a factor of sampling bias, as most LH individuals are from coastal or highland locations, where we may expect $\delta^{15}N$ to be more environmentally driven through the use of marine resources or camelids. If mid-elevation individuals' $\delta^{15}N$ were less influenced by environment, it may not be captured in our data. It is also possible that during this period, dietary inputs diverged, with those contributing more heavily to $\delta^{15}N$ driven by local environments and those contributing to $\delta^{13}C$ driven by social pressures. Despite this anomalous outcome, the possibility for socioculturally driven intensification as a dominant factor in Andean diets is intriguing. This would also be supported by the reduced number of environmental variables being significant over time while site.id remains consistent, suggesting that while environmental influences decreased, an unobserved process influenced all individuals who were buried at a site.

While we cannot test whether the cause of intensification may be variation in the social importance of certain subsistence products, changing markets, labor demands, shifting ontologies around the meaning of food, or something else, the patterns in our results are suggestive of resource intensification driven by social factors causing decreased environmental predictive power on diets over time. Future research employing different techniques or splits in the data may enable the teasing out of the causative potential of various social and environmental factors. Adding data for each individual on primary and secondary subsistence methods, distances from religious or imperial centers, the relative level of inequality within the community, or factoring in dimensions such as sex and age may begin to unveil the key social factors influencing Andean diets and their transformative effects. Subsequent chapters in this volume explore several of these possibilities, documenting how the sacred and symbolic may influence consumption.

CONCLUSION

Here we employed an environmental null approach, documenting how much influence environment had on diets to estimate how the relative influence of environmental and social factors changed over time. We find that environment exerts a strong influence on diet (60%–80%), with that influence waning over time. Sociopolitical complexity did not have a consistent influence on overall diet, but social aspects of life may be responsible for, on average, 20% to 40% of what is consumed. It is possible that over time, individuals in the Andes were driven to intensify their subsistence economies because of social pressures such as population growth, changing social significances of food, interpersonal violence, or trade demands. While the results of this environmental null model suggest both physical and social environments influenced Andean diets over time, future work improving the quantification of social factors and identifying more fine-grain environmental data will be important to more thoroughly evaluate the complex relationships of environment, individual interaction, and social influences.

REFERENCES

Ambrose, Stanley H., Jane Buikstra, and Harold W. Krueger. 2003. "Status and Gender Differences in Diet at Mound 72, Cahokia, Revealed by Isotopic Analysis of Bone." *Journal of Anthropological Archaeology* 22 (3): 217–26. https://doi.org/10.1016/S0278-4165(03)00036-9.

Andrushko, Valerie A., and Elva C. Torres. 2011. "Skeletal Evidence for Inca Warfare from the Cuzco Region of Peru." *American Journal of Physical Anthropology* 146 (3): 361–72. https://doi.org/10.1002/ajpa.21574.

Bivand, Roger, Timothy H. Keitt, Edzer Pebesma, and Barry Rowlingson. 2019. "Rgdal: Bindings for the Geospatial Data Abstraction Library." The R Project for Statistical Computing. https://cran.r-project.org/web/packages/rgdal/index.html.

Bongers, Jacob L., Nathan Nakatsuka, Colleen O'Shea, Thomas K. Harper, Henry Tantaleán, Charles Stanish, and Lars Fehren-Schmitz. 2020. "Integration of Ancient DNA with Transdisciplinary Dataset Finds Strong Support for Inca Resettlement in the South Peruvian Coast." *Proceedings of the National Academy of Sciences* 117 (31): 18359–68. https://doi.org/10.1073/pnas.2005965117.

Boserup, Esther. 1965. *The Conditions of Agricultural Growth: The Economics of Agrarian Change Under Population Pressure*. Chicago: Aldine.

Bray, Tamara. 2003. "Inka Pottery as Culinary Equipment: Food, Feasting, and Gender in Imperial State Design." *Latin American Antiquity* 14 (1): 3–28.

Browman, David L. 1997. "Pastoral Risk Perception and Risk Definition for Altiplano Herders." *Nomadic Peoples New Series* 1 (1): 22–36.

Burger, Richard L., and Nikolaas J. van der Merwe. 1990. "Maize and the Origin of Highland Chavin Civilization: An Isotopic Perspective." *American Anthropologist* 92 (1): 85–95.

Buzon, Michele R., Christina A. Conlee, Antonio Simonetti, and Gabriel J. Bowen. 2012. "The Consequences of Wari Contact in the Nasca Region During the Middle Horizon: Archaeological, Skeletal, and Isotopic Evidence." *Journal of Archaeological Science* 39 (8): 2627–36. https://doi.org/10.1016/j.jas.2012.04.003.

Codding, Brian F., Rebecca Bliege Bird, and Douglas W. Bird. 2011. "Provisioning Offspring and Others: Risk-Energy Trade-Offs and Gender Differences in Hunter-Gatherer Foraging Strategies." *Proceedings of the Royal Society B: Biological Sciences* 278 (1717): 2502–9. https://doi.org/10.1098/rspb.2010.2403.

Coltrain, Joan Brenner, and Joel C. Janetski. 2013. "The Stable and Radio-Isotope Chemistry of Southeastern Utah Basketmaker II Burials: Dietary Analysis Using the Linear Mixing Model SISUS, Age and Sex Patterning, Geolocation and Temporal Patterning." *Journal of Archaeological Science* 40 (12): 4711–30. https://doi.org/10.1016/j.jas.2013.07.012.

Contreras, Daniel A. 2010. "Landscape and Environment: Insights from the Prehispanic Central Andes." *Journal of Archaeological Research* 18 (3): 241–88. https://doi.org/10.1007/s10814-010-9038-6.

Covey, R. Alan. 2008. "Multiregional Perspectives on the Archaeology of the Andes During the Late Intermediate Period (c. AD 1000–1400)." *Journal of Archaeological Research* 16 (3): 287–338. https://doi.org/10.1007/S10814-008-9021-7.

Covey, R. Alan, Brian S. Bauer, Véronique Bélisle, and Lia Tsesmeli. 2013. "Regional Perspectives on Wari State Influence in Cusco, Peru (c. AD 600–1000)." *Journal of Anthropological Archaeology* 32 (4): 538–52. https://doi.org/10.1016/j.jaa.2013.09.001.

Cuéllar, Andrea M. 2013. "The Archaeology of Food and Social Inequality in the Andes." *Journal of Archaeological Research* 21: 123–74. https://doi.org/10.1007/s10814-012-9061-x.

D'Altroy, Terence N. 2015. *The Incas*. 2nd ed. West Sussex: Wiley Blackwell.

D'Altroy, Terence N., and Christine A. Hastorf. 2001. *Empire and Domestic Economy*. New York: Kluwer Academic.

deFrance, Susan D. 2009. "Zooarchaeology in Complex Societies: Political Economy, Status, and Ideology." *Journal of Archaeological Research* 17 (2): 105–68. https://doi.org/10.1007/s10814-008-9027-1.

Dillehay, Tom D., and Alan L. Kolata. 2004. "Long-Term Human Response to Uncertain Environmental Conditions in the Andes." *Proceedings of the National Academy of Sciences* 101(12): 4325–30. https://www.pnas.org/doi/10.1073/pnas.0400538101.

Dormann, Carsten F., Jane Elith, Sven Bacher, Carsten Buchmann, Gudrun Carl, Gabriel Carré, Jaime R. García Marquéz, et al. 2013. "Collinearity: A Review of Methods to Deal with it and a Simulation Study Evaluating Their Performance." *Ecography* 36 (1): 27–46. https://doi.org/10.1111/j.1600-0587.2012.07348.x.

Dulanto, Jalh. 2008. "Between Horizons: Diverse Configurations of Society and Power in the Late Pre-Hispanic Central Andes." In *The Handbook of South American Archaeology*, edited by Helaine Silverman and William H. Isbell, 761–82. New York: Springer.

Fehren-Schmitz, Lars, Wolfgang Haak, Bertil Mächtle, Florian Masch, Bastien Llamas, Elsa Tomasto Cagigao, Volker Sossna, et al., 2014. "Climate Change Underlies Global Demographic, Genetic, and Cultural Transitions in Pre-Columbian Southern Peru." *Proceedings of the National Academy of Sciences* 111 (26): 9443–48. https://doi.org/10.1073/pnas.1403466111.

Finucane, Brian Clifton. 2007. "Mummies, Maize, and Manure: Multi-tissue Stable Isotope Analysis of Late Prehistoric Human Remains from the Ayacucho Valley, Peru." *Journal of Archaeological Science* 34 (12): 2115–24. https://doi.org/10.1016/j.jas.2007.02.006.

Finucane, Brian Clifton. 2009. "Maize and Sociopolitical Complexity in the Ayacucho Valley, Peru." *Current Anthropology* 50 (4): 535–45. https://doi.org/10.1086/599860.

Fordham, Damien A., Frédérik Saltré, Sean Haythorne, Tom M. L. Wigley, Bette L. Otto-Bliesner, Ka Ching Chan, and Barry W. Brook. 2017. "PaleoView: A Tool for Generating Continuous Climate Projections Spanning the Last 21,000 Years at Regional and Global Scales." *Ecography* 40 (11): 1348–58. https://doi.org/10.1111/ecog.03031.

Greaves, Russell D., and Karen L. Kramer. 2014. "Hunter-Gatherer Use of Wild Plants and Domesticates: Archaeological Implications for Mixed Economies Before Agricultural Intensification." *Journal of Archaeological Science* 41:263–71.

Greenwald, Alexandra M., Deborah Blom, Natalya Zolotova, and Kelly Knudson. 2019. "Stable Isotope Measures of Weaning Age and Early Childhood Diet in the Ancient Andes: Variation in Early Life Experiences and Health Outcomes Across Status and Sex in Tiwanaku-Affiliated Sites in Peru and Bolivia." *American Journal of Physical Anthropology* 168:91.

Hastorf, Christine A., and Sissel Johannessen. 1993. "Pre-Hispanic Political Change and the Role of Maize in the Central Andes of Peru." *American Anthropologist* 95 (1): 115–38.

Hawkes, Kristen, and James F. O'Connell. 1992. "On Optimal Foraging Models and Subsistence Transitions." *Current Anthropology* 33 (1): 63–66.

Hawkes, Kristen, James F. O'Connell, and N. G. Blurton Jones. 1995. "Hadza Children's Foraging: Juvenile Dependency, Social Arrangements and Mobility Among Hunter-Gatherers." *Current Anthropology* 36: 688–700.

Hedges, Robert E. M., John G. Clement, C. David L. Thomas, and Tamsin C. O'Connell. 2007. "Collagen Turnover in the Adult Femoral Mid-Shaft: Modeled from Anthropogenic Radiocarbon Tracer Measurements." *American Journal of Physical Anthropology* 133 (2): 808–16. https://doi.org/10.1002/ajpa.20598.

Kellner, Corina M., and Margaret J. Schoeninger. 2008. "Wari's Imperial Influence on Local Nasca Diet: The Stable Isotope Evidence." *Journal of Anthropological Archaeology* 27 (2): 226–43. https://doi.org/10.1016/j.jaa.2007.12.003.

Kellner, Corina M., and Margaret J. Schoeninger. 2012. "Dietary Correlates to the Development of Nasca Social Complexity (AD 1–750)." *Latin American Antiquity* 23 (4): 490–508. https://doi.org/10.7183/1045-6635.23.4.490.

King, Charlotte L., Andrew R. Millard, Darren R. Gröcke, Vivien G. Standen, Bernardo T. Arriaza, and Siân E. Halcrow. 2018. "Marine Resource Reliance in the Human Populations of the Atacama Desert, Northern Chile: A View from Prehistory." *Quaternary Science Reviews* 182:163–74. https://doi.org/10.1016/j.quascirev.2017.12.009.

Knudson, Kelly J., Ann H. Peters, and Elsa Tomasto Cagigao. 2015. "Paleodiet in the Paracas Necropolis of Wari Kayan: Carbon and Nitrogen Isotope Analysis of Keratin Samples from the South Coast of Peru." *Journal of Archaeological Science* 55:231–43. https://doi.org/10.1016/j.jas.2015.01.011.

Knudson, Kelly J., Christina Torres-Rouff, and Christopher M. Stojanowski. 2015. "Investigating Human Responses to Political and Environmental Change Through Paleodiet and Paleomobility." *American Journal of Physical Anthropology* 157 (2): 179–201. https://doi.org/10.1002/ajpa.22694.

Liu, Zhengyu, B. L. Otto-Bliesner, Feng He, E. C. Brady, Robert Tomas, P. U. Clark, A. E. Carlson, et al. 2009. "Transient Simulation of Last Deglaciation with a New Mechanism for Bølling-Allerød Warming." *Science* 325 (5938): 310–14. https://doi.org/10.1126/science.1171041.

Malthus, Thomas R. 1798. *An Essay on the Principle of Population, as it Affects the Future Improvement of Society, with Remarks on the Speculations of Mr. Godwin, M. Condorcet, and Other Writers*. London: Lawbook Exchange.

Marsteller, Sara J., Natalya Zolotova, and Kelly J. Knudson. 2017. "Investigating Economic Specialization on the Central Peruvian Coast: A Reconstruction of Late Intermediate Period Ychsma Diet Using Stable Isotopes." *American Journal of Physical Anthropology* 162 (2): 300–17. https://doi.org/10.1002/ajpa.23117.

McCool, Weston C. 2020. "The Human Ecology of Conflict: A Case Study From the Prehispanic Nasca Highlands of Peru." PhD diss., University of California, Santa Barbara.

McCool, Weston C., Amy S. Anderson, and Douglas J. Kennett. 2021. "Using a Multimethod Life History Approach to Navigate the Osteological Paradox: A Case Study from the Nasca Highland." *American Journal of Physical Anthropology* 175 (4): 816–33. https://doi.org/10.1002/ajpa.24279.

Moore, Jerry D., and Carol J. Mackey. 2008. "The Chimú Empire." In *The Handbook of South American Archaeology*, edited by Helaine Silverman and William H. Isbell, 783–807. New York: Springer.

Moseley, Michael E. 2001. *The Incas and Their Ancestors: The Archaeology of Peru*. Rev. ed. London: Thames and Hudson.

Murra, John V. 1960. "Rite and Crop in the Inca State." In *Culture in History: Essays in Honor of Paul Raudin*, edited by Stanley Diamond, 393–407. New York: Columbia University Press.

Paradis, Emmanuel, and Klaus Schliep. 2019. "Ape 5.0: An Environment for Modern Phylogenetics and Evolutionary Analyses in R." *Bioinformatics* 35 (3): 526–28. https://doi.org/10.1093/bioinformatics/bty633.

Parsons, Jeffrey R., Charles M. Hastings, and Ramiro Matos. 1997. "Rebuilding the State in Highland Peru: Herder-Cultivator Interaction During the Late Intermediate Period in the Tarama-Chinchaycocha Region." *Latin American Antiquity* 8 (4): 317–41. https://doi.org/10.2307/972106.

Patterson, Thomas C. 2012. "Distribution and Redistribution." In *A Handbook of Economic Anthropology*, 2nd ed., edited by James G Carrier, 194–209. Cheltenham: Edward Elgar.

Pearsall, Deborah M. 2008. "Plant Domestication and the Shift to Agriculture in the Andes." In *The Handbook of South American Archaeology*, edited by Helaine Silverman and William H. Isbell, 105–20. New York: Springer.

Piperno, Dolores R., and Deborah M. Pearsall. 1998. *The Origins of Agriculture in the Lowland Neotropics*. San Diego, Calif.: Academic Press.

Pozorski, Shelia G. 1979. "Prehistoric Diet and Subsistence of the Moche Valley, Peru." *World Archaeology* 11 (2): 163–84.

Pulgar Vidal, Javier. 1981. *Geografía del Perú: Las Ocho Regiones Naturales del Perú*. 8th ed. Lima: Editorial Universo.

Quilter, Jeffrey, and Terry Stocker. 1983. "Subsistence Economies and the Origins of Andean Complex Societies." *American Anthropologist* 85 (3): 545–62.

R Core Team. 2021. R: A Language and Environment for Statistical Computing. The R Project for Statistical Computing, Vienna. https://www.R-project.org/.

Rivera, Mario A. 1991. "The Prehistory of Northern Chile: A Synthesis." *Journal of World Prehistory* 5 (1): 1–47. https://doi.org/10.1007/BF00974731.

Seifert, Mark F., and Bruce A. Watkins. 1997. "Role of Dietary Lipid and Antioxidants in Bone Metabolism." *Nutrition Research* 17 (7): 1209–28. https://doi.org/10.1016/S0271-5317(97)00090-0.

Seltzer, Geoffrey O., and Christine A. Hastorf. 1990. "Climatic Change and Its Effect on Prehispanic Agriculture in the Central Peruvian Andes." *Journal of Field Archaeology* 17 (4): 397–414.

Silverman, Helaine, and William Isbell. 2008. *Handbook of South American Archaeology.* New York: Springer Science and Business Media.

Smith, Eric Alden, and Bruce Winterhalder. 1992. *Evolutionary Ecology and Human Behavior.* New Brunswick, N.J.: Transaction.

Staller, John E. 2006. "The Social, Symbolic, and Economic Significance of *Zea Mays* L. in the Late Horizon Period." In *Histories of Maize: Multidisciplinary Approaches to the Prehistory, Linguistics, Biogeography, Domestication, and Evolution of Maize*, edited by John E. Staller, Robert H. Tykot, and Bruce F. Benz, 449–67. New York: Routledge.

Stanish, Charles, Edmundo de la Vega, Michael Moseley, Patrick Ryan Williams, Cecilia Chávez J., Benjamin Vining, and Karl LaFavre. 2010. "Tiwanaku Trade Patterns in Southern Peru." *Journal of Anthropological Archaeology* 29 (4): 524–32. https://doi.org/10.1016/j.jaa.2010.09.002.

Stanish, Charles, Henry Tantaleán, and Kelly Knudson. 2018. "Feasting and the Evolution of Cooperative Social Organizations Circa 2300 BP in Paracas Culture, Southern Peru." *Proceedings of the National Academy of Sciences* 115 (29): E6716–E6721. https://doi.org/10.1073/pnas.1806632115.

Stephens, David W., and John R. Krebs. 1986. *Foraging Theory.* Princeton, N.J.: Princeton University Press.

Thomas, David H. 2014. "The Shellfishers of St. Catherine's Island: Hardscrabble Foragers or Farming Beachcombers?" *Journal of Island and Coastal Archaeology* 9 (2): 169–82. https://doi.org/10.1080/15564894.2013.840874.

Thomas, David H., and C. Fred T. Andrus. 2008. "Native American Landscapes of St. Catherine's Island, Georgia." In *Anthropological Papers of the American Museum of Natural History*, no. 88. New York: American Museum of Natural History.

Toyne, J. Marla, Warren B. Church, Jose Luis Coronado Tello, and Ricardo Morales Gamarra. 2017. "Exploring Imperial Expansion Using an Isotopic Analysis of Paleodietary and Paleomobility Indicators in Chachapoyas, Peru." *American Journal of Physical Anthropology* 162 (1): 51–72. https://doi.org/10.1002/ajpa.23085.

Trawick, Paul B. 2003. *The Struggle for Water in Peru: Comedy and Tragedy in the Andean Commons*. Stanford, Calif: Stanford University Press.

Tung, Tiffiny A., Tom D. Dillehay, Robert S. Feranec, and Larisa R. G. DeSantis. 2020. "Early Specialized Maritime and Maize Economies on the North Coast of Peru." *Proceedings of the National Academy of Sciences* 117 (51): 32308–19. https://doi.org/10.1073/pnas.2009121117.

Tung, Tiffiny A., and Kelly J. Knudson. 2018. "Stable Isotope Analysis of a Pre-Hispanic Andean Community: Reconstructing Pre-Wari and Wari Era Diets in the Hinterland of the Wari Empire, Peru." *American Journal of Physical Anthropology* 165 (1): 149–72. https://doi.org/10.1002/ajpa.23339.

Turner, Bethany L., Véronique Bélisle, Allison R. Davis, Maeve Skidmore, Sara L. Juengst, Benjamin J. Schaefer, R. Alan Covey, and Brian S. Bauer. 2018. "Diet and Foodways Across Five Millennia in the Cusco Region of Peru." *Journal of Archaeological Science* 98:137–48. https://doi.org/10.1016/j.jas.2018.07.013.

Turner, Bethany L., and Haagen D. Klaus. 2020. "Theorizing Food and Power in the Ancient Andes." In *Diet, Nutrition, and Foodways on the North Coast of Peru*, edited by Bethany L. Turner and Haagen D. Klaus, 11–28. Cham: Springer.

Tykot, Robert H., Richard L. Burger, and Nikolaas J. van der Merwe. 2006. "The Importance of Maize in Initial Period and Early Horizon Peru." In *Histories of Maize: Multidisciplinary Approaches to the Prehistory, Linguistics, Biogeography, Domestication, and Evolution of Maize*, edited by John E. Staller, Robert H. Tykot, and Bruce F. Benz, 187–97. New York: Routledge.

Vinton, Sheila Dorsey, Linda Perry, Karl J. Reinhard, Calogero M. Santoro, and Isabel Teixeira-Santos. 2009. "Impact of Empire Expansion on Household Diet: The Inka in Northern Chile's Atacama Desert." *PLoS One* 4 (11): e8069. https://doi.org/10.1371/journal.pone.0008069.

Weitzel, Elic M., and Brian F. Codding. 2016. "Population Growth as a Driver of Initial Domestication in Eastern North America." *Royal Society Open Science* 3 (8): 160319. http://dx.doi.org/10.1098/rsos.160319.

Wessel, Pål, and Walter H. F. Smith. 1996. "A Global, Self-Consistent, Hierarchical, High-Resolution Shoreline Database." *Journal of Geophysical Research: Solid Earth* 101 (B4):8741–43. https://agupubs.onlinelibrary.wiley.com/doi/abs/10.1029/96JB00104.

Williams, Jocelyn S., and Melissa S. Murphy. 2013. "Living and Dying as Subjects of the Inca Empire: Adult Diet and Health at Puruchuco-Huaquerones, Peru." *Journal of Anthropological Archaeology* 32 (2): 165–79.

Wilson, Kurt M., and Brian F. Codding. 2020. "The Marginal Utility of Inequality: A Global Examination Across Ethnographic Societies." *Human Nature* 31:361–86. https://doi.org/10.1007/s12110-020-09383-4.

Wilson, Kurt M., Weston C. McCool, Simon C. Brewer, Nicole Zamora-Wilson, Percy J. Schryver, Roxanne Lois F. Lamson, Ashlyn M. Huggard,

Joan Brenner Coltrain, Daniel A. Contreras, and Brian F. Codding. 2022. "Climate and Demography Drive 7000 Years of Dietary Change in the Central Andes." *Scientific Reports* 12 (2026). https://doi.org/10.1038/s41598-022 -05774-y.

Winterhalder, Bruce, and Carol Goland. 1993. "On Population, Foraging Efficiency, and Plant Domestication." *Current Anthropology* 34 (5): 710–15.

Wood, Simon N. 2017. *Generalized Additive Models: An Introduction with R.* Boca Raton, Fla.: Chapman and Hall/CRC.

2

What is Cooking in the Pots of the Chiloé Archipelago?

Plant Use Trajectories Through Ceramic Residue Analysis

Carolina Belmar, Omar Reyes, Augusto Tessone, Manuel San Román, and Flavia Morello

The Chiloé Archipelago (41°–43° S, map 2.1) was a place of contact and interaction between different sociocultural systems (Álvarez et al. 2019) located north (horticulturalists) and south (marine hunter-gatherers and fisherman) of the Gulf of Corcovado (43°S; Cooper 1917, 1946; Reyes et al. 2019a, 2019b; Urbina, Reyes, and Belmar 2020; map 2.1). Contact with horticultural groups toward the Late Holocene (~1000 BP, pre-Hispanic Late Ceramic Period; Aldunate 1996; Cooper 1917, 1946; Menghin 1962) and the arrival of the first Europeans (sixteenth century) introduced new elements (pottery and domesticated plants and animals) and exposed Chiloé's peoples to culinary traditions that may have altered their consumption of plants (Belmar et al. 2021; Reyes et al. 2019b; Urbina 2016). To assess the impact of these social interactions on plant consumption, we study the microfossils contained in the use residues of ceramic sherds recovered from seven sites on Chiloé Island.

THE HISTORY OF CHILOÉ

Chiloé Island, located in the Chiloé Archipelago of northern Patagonia (~41°30´–47°S), is particularly rich in marine resources (mollusks, fish, birds, and marine mammals) and presents vegetation composed mostly of evergreen forests and a terrestrial fauna limited mainly to small Mammalia (Luebert and Pliscoff 2006; Muñoz and Yáñez 2009; Navarro and Pequeño 1979; Osorio and Reid 2004; Vuilleumier 1985). The first evidence of human occupation in the Chiloé Archipelago dates to the Middle Holocene (~6000 cal. yBP) and corresponds to marine hunter-gatherer and fishing groups who had high levels of social interaction and

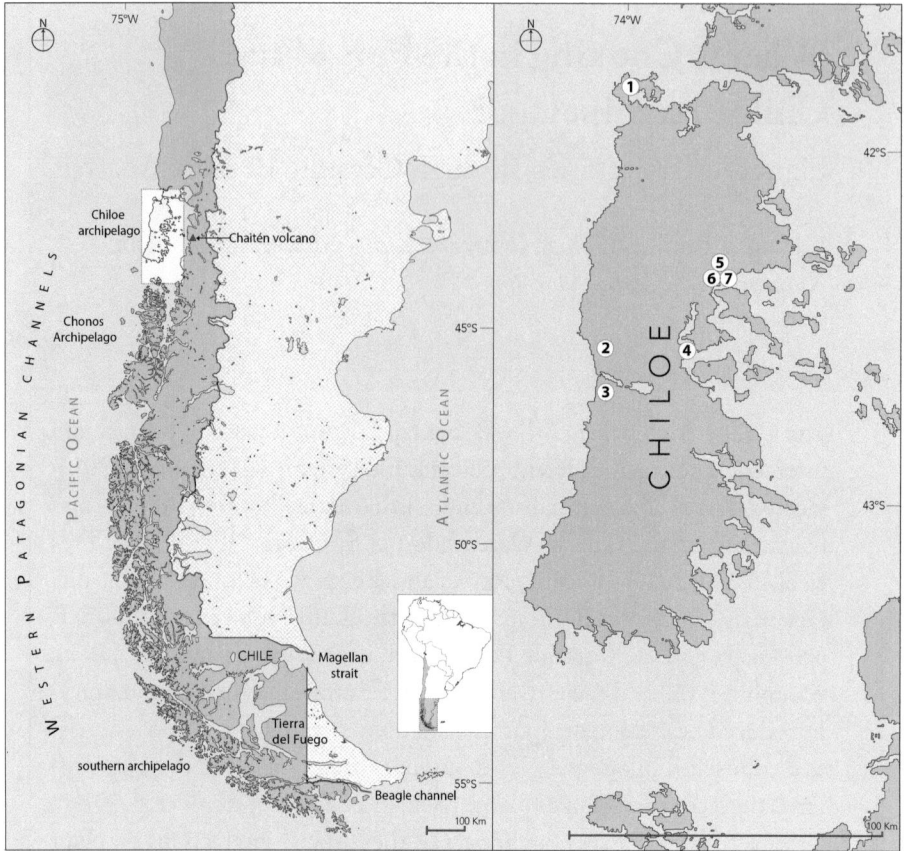

Map 2.1 Location of the study area and archaeological sites, *1*, Puente Quilo. *2*, Cucao Norte 1. *3*, Tricolor. *4*, Tauco 1. *5*, Lomas de San Juan. *6*, Álamos de San Juan. *7*, San Juan 1. Image by Carolina Belmar and Omar Reyes.

cultural integration at a wider regional scale (Álvarez et al. 2008; Flores, Broitman, and Rivas 2010; Legoupil 2005; Munita 2007; Ocampo and Rivas 2004; Reyes et al. 2020; Reyes, Méndez, and San Román 2019a; Rivas and Ocampo 2010; Rivas, Ocampo, and Aspillaga 1999; Sierralta et al. 2019; Stern 2018). Zooarchaeological and isotopic studies reveal that during the Middle and Late Holocene the diet was mostly composed of marine resources that were gathered (mollusks), hunted (sea lions, dolphins, and birds), and fished. Small-to-medium-size inland mammals (e.g., *Pudu pudu* and *Myocastor coypus*) along with the consumption of wild plants (e.g., strawberry, *Fragaria chiloensis*; chaura, *Gaultheria mucronata*; nalca, *Gunnera tinctoria*), seaweed, and edible grasses, complemented the diet (Belmar et al. 2021; González 2019).

Toward the Late Holocene, contact with northern horticultural groups (~1000 BP; Aldunate 1996; Cooper 1917, 1946; Menghin 1962), resulted in the presence of pottery, the production of lithic tools related to horticultural activities, and changes in the zooarchaeological assemblages (Álvarez et al. 2008; Rivas and Ocampo 2010). These new technologies (pottery) and foods (domesticated plants and animals) may have been an initial trigger for the decrease in the consumption of marine resources and an increased emphasis on terrestrial C_3 plants, including some with medicinal and psychoactive properties (e.g., *Desfontainia spinosa* and *Latua* pubiflora; Belmar et al. 2021).

The first European records (sixteenth century) described the presence of crops such as maize, potato, and quinoa and possibly domesticated animals (*Lama* sp. and dogs; de Bibar [1558] 1979; de Ercilla [1569] 2009; de Goicueta 1558). European contact led to profound cultural transformations, interrupted the long subsistence tradition of Chiloé, and resulted in the increased consumption of terrestrial proteins (Rivas and Ocampo 2010; Reyes et al. 2019b; Reyes 2020; Reyes et al. 2022; Urbina, Reyes, and Belmar 2020).

FOOD AS IDENTITY

The study of food preparation can inform us about cultural continuities and changes. In the Chiloé Archipelago, the contact with groups that brought new technologies resulted in novel social interactions and changes in cultural practices including plant use in both food and medicinal recipes. While ethnographic studies among the Kawésqar (Emperaire 1963) describe how plants were eaten fresh as they were picked, the presence of archaeological pit holes, or *curantos*, document the existence of cooking techniques that preceded the introduction of pottery in Chiloé (Catrumán site dated to 1830 yBP; Munita, Mera, and Álvarez 2016). Once pottery was incorporated, it likely affected food preparation because of properties, such as thermal conductivity, that affect the transformation of foodstuffs (Atalay and Hastorf 2006; Lévi-Strauss [1964] 1968).

Following Goody (1995) we consider that the phases of food production are interwoven with different social practices (acquisition and production, distribution, preparation, consumption, and disposal) and that different preparations are related to ideological, political, and economic dimensions. Thus, food production, preparation, and consumption can be powerful expressions of identity intrinsically intertwined with social life, as they are commonly done following guidelines that are remembered and repeated within the group (Atalay and Hastorf 2006; Hastorf 2017; Twiss 2007, 2019).

Recipes are *chaînes opératoires* of daily preparations that involve ingredients, settings, actors, postures, and senses (Hastorf 2017). The corpus of preparations of a group, the collection and use of ingredients and their proportions, and the technology used in all these phases are equally important for the correct use of their properties (Etkin and Ross 1991), including those of medicinal or sacred plants that constitute "edible medicine," where nutrition and religion become entangled (Etkin and Ross 1991; Etkin 2006). Sacred plants are "in the indigenous conception, . . . distinguished from exclusively medicinal plants because they not only contain curative properties but are able to bring the consumer to a state of heightened consciousness comparable to an ecstatic trance, modifying his perception and bringing him into contact with supernatural planes" (Llamazares, Martínez, and Funes 2004, 263). The psychoactive effects of these plants are curative, and thus they are prepared and consumed under observance.

To evaluate changes in the consumption and preparation of foods in Chiloé, we must first consider pottery as a technology that directly affects the preparation (cooking) of food. Additionally, we must assess the introduction of ingredients that required new forms of acquisition, production behaviors, and preparations. The goal of this chapter is to evaluate these changes through the analysis of microfossil assemblages contained in the residues adhered to ceramic sherds.

MATERIALS AND METHODS

We analyzed residues from 110 ceramic sherds found at seven coastal archaeological sites in the Chiloé Archipelago (table 2.1, map 2.1). The chronological sequence of these sites was established with radiocarbon

Table 2.1 Archaeological sites in Chiloé where analyzed ceramic sherds were recovered

Site	Altitude of base deposit (masl)	Distance from shoreline (m)	Approximate size (m²)	Maximum thickness (cm)	Cultural component	Pottery period	Chronology BP ^{14}C cal, TL, or estimated	Principal characteristics of the site
Puente Quilo 1[a]	3	10	800	130	Middle and Late Holocene marine hunter-gatherer	Late Ceramic	~6000 (^{14}C) Type of ceramic	Dense shell midden with multiple occupations since the Middle Holocene
San Juan 1[b]	6	30	17,000	230	Middle to Late Holocene marine hunter-gatherer	Late Ceramic	~6000 (^{14}C) 475 (TL)	Dense shell midden with multiple occupations since the Middle Holocene
Lomas de San Juan[c]	110	600	170	40	Late occupations	Late ceramic Historic European tradition	Undated Type of materials	Shell discard area
Álamos de San Juan[c]	150	900	160	30	Late occupations	Late Ceramic Historic	Undated Type of materials	Discrete shell midden
Tauco 1[b]	2	0–10	400	230	Late Holocene marine hunter-gatherer	Late Ceramic	~3200 (^{14}C) Type of ceramic	Dense shell midden with multiple occupations since the Late Holocene
Cucao Norte 1[c]	13	150	44	20	Late Holocene marine hunter-gatherer	Late Ceramic	230 (TL)	Discrete shell midden
Tricolor[c]	96	800	35,000	60	Late Holocene marine hunter-gatherers	Late Ceramic	715 (TL)	Extensive dispersal of lithic and ceramic material in dunes

[a] Rivas, Ocampo, and Aspillaga (1999), Rivas and Ocampo (2010), Ocampo and Rivas (2004).
[b] Reyes et al. (2020).
[c] This volume.

and thermoluminescence (ceramic) dates. Cultural components and site occupations were defined using archaeofaunal, lithic, ceramic, and bio-anthropological data (Rivas and Ocampo 2010; Reyes et al. 2020). Some of these settlements were formed by successive Middle and Late Holocene marine hunter-gatherer occupations. Others only date back to the last 200 years. All sites contained ceramic components in their upper levels, with ceramic sherds assigned to (1) the Late Ceramic Period (pre-Hispanic), which has similar characteristics to the Late Ceramic Period in neighboring areas in southern Chile (Adán et al. 2016); (2) the Historic ceramic, which may correspond to postcontact Indigenous groups that acquired European elements: and (3) traditional European pottery (Palma and Alfaro 2019; Reyes et al. 2020; table 2.2, fig. 2.1). Indeterminate ceramics correspond to those that lack diagnostic elements to assign them to a specific ceramic type but have sufficient traits to group them in larger categories, such as Prehispanic or Historic (Palma and Alfaro 2019).

Microfossil study of the sherds (Coil et al. 2003) included the recovery of all categories of microremains with the least damaging recovery methods—in this case, dry and/or wet scraping (Babot 2007) of the internal surface of the sherds. Sediment samples from the archaeological sites were obtained to control for residue contamination. Sampling and handling protocols were followed to reduce sample degradation and contamination (Belmar et al. 2015).

Samples were examined under a BM2100POL petrographic microscope at magnification 200× and 400×. Twiss, Seuss, and Smith (1969), ICPN (Madella, Alexandre, and Ball 2005), and ICSN[1] nomenclatures guided the description of phytoliths and starch grains. Our own and published microfossil reference collections were consulted to establish taxonomic affinity (Albornoz 2015; Belmar 2019; Gonzalez 2019; Korstanje and Babot 2007; Pearsall 2010). The ubiquity score of the identified taxa was calculated to estimate the recurrence of certain plants among the samples (Popper 1988).

Damage detected in the microfossils was registered to identify processing methods in food preparation (e.g., gelatinization, which indicates the exposure to water and heat, thermal alteration due to exposure to

---

1. International Code for Starch Nomenclature, http://www.fossilfarm.org /ICSN/Code.html.

Table 2.2 Origin and cultural assignment of the ceramic sherds and percentage of the sample subjected to microfossil analysis of the use residues

Site	Pre-Hispanic						Historic						Indeter-minate		Total Indeter-minate		Overall total		Sample taken for microfossil analysis	
	Late Period		Indeter-minate		Total Pre-Hispanic		European Tradition		Indeter-minate		Total Historic									
	n	%	n	%	n	%	n	%	n	%	n	%	n	%	n	%	n	%	n	%
Puente Quilo	90	100.0	0	0.0	90	100.0	0	0.0	0	0.0	0	0.00	0	0.0	0	0.0	90	100.0	53	58.9
Lomas de San Juan	34	75.6	1	2.2	35	77.8	3	6.7	3	6.7	6	13.30	4	8.9	4	8.9	45	100.0	17	37.8
Álamos de San Juan	1	6.3	7	43.8	8	50.0	0	0.0	8	50.0	8	50.0	0	0.0	0	0.0	16	100.0	9	56.3
San Juan 1	10	52.6	8	42.1	18	94.7	0	0.0	0	0.0	0	0.0	1	5.3	1	5.3	19	100.0	6	31.6
Cucao Norte 1	4	100.0	0	0.0	4	100.0	0	0.0	0	0.0	0	0.0	0	0.0	0	0.0	4	100.0	4	100.0
Tricolor	37	43.5	46	54.1	83	97.6	0	0.0	0	0.0	0	0.0	2	2.4	2	2.4	85	100.0	17	20.0
Tauco 1	4	80.0	0	0.0	4	80.0	0	0.0	0	0.0	0	0.0	1	20.0	1	20.0	5	100.0	4	80.0

Source: Palma and Alfaro (2019).

Figure 2.1 Ceramic sherds. *A*, *B*, Prehispanic pottery, tricolor. *C*, European tradition pottery, Lomas de San Juan. Image by Carolina Belmar and Omar Reyes.

heat, damage caused by crushing or grinding; Babot 2007). To unveil the uses of the plants identified and their preparations, we revised ethnohistorical documents and ethnobotanical descriptions available for the area.

RESULTS

One type of seaweed and a variety of wild and domesticated plants were identified (table 2.3). Taxa with high ubiquity scores (table 2.3) included a species of seaweed known as *cochayuyo* (*Durvillaea antarctica*) on sherds from Cucao Norte 1, Tauco 1, and Álamos de San Juan. Among wild plants, high ubiquity scores were recorded for grasses (Poaceae and Panicoide) in Tricolor, Cucao Norte 1, Lomas de San Juan, and Álamos de San Juan. Nalca (*Gunnera tinctoria*) had high ubiquity scores in San Juan 1. Among domesticated plants, the highest ubiquity of maize (*Zea mays*) was found in Álamos de San Juan.

The sherds from the Late Ceramic Period are associated with edible plants, including domesticates (maize, beans, and potatoes), seaweeds, and plants with medicinal and psychoactive properties such as *miyaye* (*Datura* sp.) and *latué* (*Latua pubiflora*; fig. 2.2, table 2.4). The historic sherds from Lomas de San Juan and Álamos de San Juan are linked with the processing of edible seaweed, edible wild and domesticated plants (potato and maize), as well as *miyaye* (table 2.4). The European pottery of Lomas de San Juan 1 is associated with grass, *nalca*, and *cochayuyo*.

We found clear differences in the variety of damages per type of pottery (figs 2.3, 2.4). The Late Ceramic Period pottery is associated with the highest diversity of damages (eight types), in comparison to Historic (five types) and European ceramics (two types)[2] (Babot 2007). The more frequent alteration found in all ceramic types is the brown coloring of phytoliths associated with thermo-alteration (fig. 2.4*A*). The detection of damaged hilum in starch grains can also be related to thermo-alterations used at different moments (e.g., toasting grains before grinding). The presence of fissures, darkened hilum or loss of birefringence of starch grains, and fracture of phytoliths (fig. 2.4*B*) are related to milling or grinding (figs 2.4*C*, 2.4*D*), which facilitate cooking. Thus, we recognize plants and seaweed in these ceramic sherds as well as different types of

---

2. The sample size of each ceramic type may influence these differences.

Table 2.3 Ubiquity score (US) and identification of plants and seaweed taxa

Site/sample	Wild			Domesticated			Seaweed		
	Scientific name	Common name	US (%)	Scientific name	Common name	US (%)	Scientific name	Common name	US (%)
Puente Quilo (n = 53)	Datura sp.[a]	Miyaye[g]/Jimson weed	1.9	Zea mays[e]	Maize	5.7			
	Oxalis sp.[b]	Oxalis genus	3.8						
	Amomyrtus luma[c]	Cauchao[g]	3.8						
	Latua pubiflora[a]	Latué	7.5						
	Panioidea[d]	Grass	1.9						
San Juan 1 (n = 6)	Poaceae[d]	Grass	62.5	Zea mays[e]	Maize	12.5			
	cf. Gaultheria mucronata[b]	Chaura	12.5						
	Gunnera tinctoria[b]	Nalca[g]/Chilean rhubarb	50.0						
Lomas de San Juan (n = 17)	cf. Chenopodium[e]	Paico and quinoa genus	5.6	Solanum sp. tuberosum[e]	Potato	11.1	D. antarctica[f]	Cochayuyo	44.4
	cf. Gaultheria mucronata[b]	Chaura[g]	11.1	Phaseolus vulgaris[e]	Bean	5.6			
	cf. Gunnera tinctoria[b]	Nalca[g]/Chilean rhubarb	5.6						
	cf. Ribes magellanicum[b]	Zarzaparilla[g]/currant	5.6						
	Panicoidea[d]	Grass	5.6						
	Poaceae[d]	Grass	88.9						

Site	Taxon	Common name	%	Cultigen		%	Algae		%
	Poaceae[d]	Grass	90.0	*Solanum* sp. *tuberosum*[e]	Potato	10.0	*D. antarctica*[f]	Cochayuyo	90.0
Álamos de San Juan (*n* = 9)	cf. *Berberis darwinii*[b]	Michay[g]/barberry	10.0	*Zea mays*[e]	Maize	40.0			
	cf. *Datura stramonium*[a]	Miyaye[g]/Jimson weed	20.0						
	cf. *Gunnera tinctoria*[b]	Nalca[g]/Chilean rhubarb	20.0						
Tauco 1 (*n* = 4)	*Berberis microphylla*[b]	Michay[g]/barberry	25.0				*D. antarctica*[f]	Cochayuyo	50.0
	Latua pubiflora[a]	Latué[g]	25.0						
Cucao Norte 1 (*n* = 4)	cf. *Gaultheria mucronata*[b]	Chaura[g]	20.0				*D. antarctica*[f]	Cochayuyo	80.0
	Poaceae[d]	Grass	100						
Tricolor (*n* = 17)	Poaceae[d]	Grass	100	*Zea mays*[e]	Maize	5.6	*D. antarctica*[f]	Cochayuyo	5.6

[a] Albornoz (2015).
[b] Belmar (2019).
[c] González (2019).
[d] Twiss, Suess, and Smith (1969), Pearsall (2010).
[e] Korstanje and Babot (2007).
[f] Boraso et al. (2004), Collantes et al. (2002).
[g] Native name.

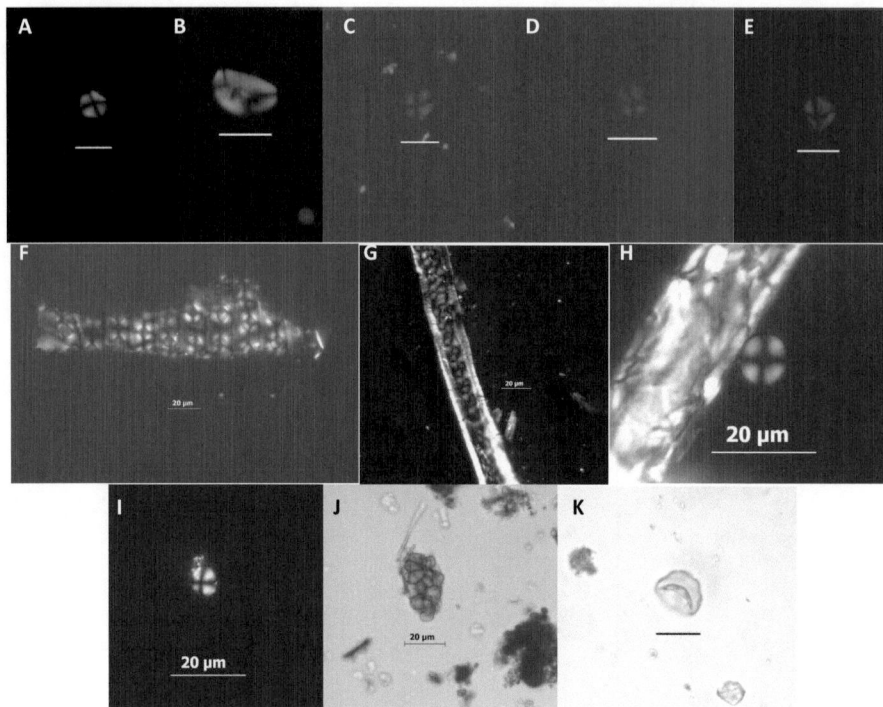

Figure 2.2 *A, Gunnera tinctoria* starch grain, San Juan 1. *B, Phaseolus vulgaris* starch grain, Lomas de San Juan. *C, Solanum* sp. *tuberosum* starch grain, Lomas de San Juan. *D, Solanum* sp. *tuberosum*, Lomas de San Juan. *E, Zea mays* starch grain, Álamos de San Juan. *F, Latua pubiflora* starch grain, Puente Quilo. *G, Latua pubiflora* starch grain, Puente Quilo. *H, Zea mays* starch grain, Puente Quilo. *I, Amomyrtus luma* starch grain, Puente Quilo. *J, Durvillaea antarctica* ooginia, Tauco 1. *K, Datura* sp. cystolith, Álamos de San Juan 1. Scale 20μ. Image by Carolina Belmar and Omar Reyes.

processing. The gelatinized state of starch grains of undetermined plants shows exposure to heat and water and is related to fermentation. Grass-like plants, Chilean rhubarb, chaura, cauchao, as well as maize and potato were ground and then cooked.

DISCUSSION

Several dimensions of foods, ingredients, preparation, and the impact of pottery introduction were assessed in this study. A wide range of wild

Table 2.4 Plant and seaweed microfossils identified in use residue from Late Ceramic, Historical, and European pottery

Taxa	Late Ceramic pottery							Historical pottery		European pottery
	Puente Quilo 1	San Juan 1	Lomas de San Juan	Álamos de San Juan	Tauco 1	Cucao Norte 1	Tricolor	Lomas de San Juan	Álamos de San Juan	Lomas de San Juan
Wild										
Amomyrtus luma	X									
Berberis microphylla					X					
cf. *Berberis darwinii*									X	
cf. *Chenopodium* sp.								X	X	
Datura sp.	X			X				X	X	
Gaultheria mucronata						X				
Gunnera tinctoria									X	X
Latua pubiflora					X					
Oxalis sp.	X									
Panicoide	X									
Poaceae		X	X	X		X	X	X	X	X
Ribes magallenicum		X	X							
Domesticated										
Zea mays	X	X					X		X	
Solanum sp. *tuberosum*			X					X	X	
Phaseolus vulgaris			X							
Seaweed										
Durvillaea antarctica		X	X	X	X	X	X	X	X	X

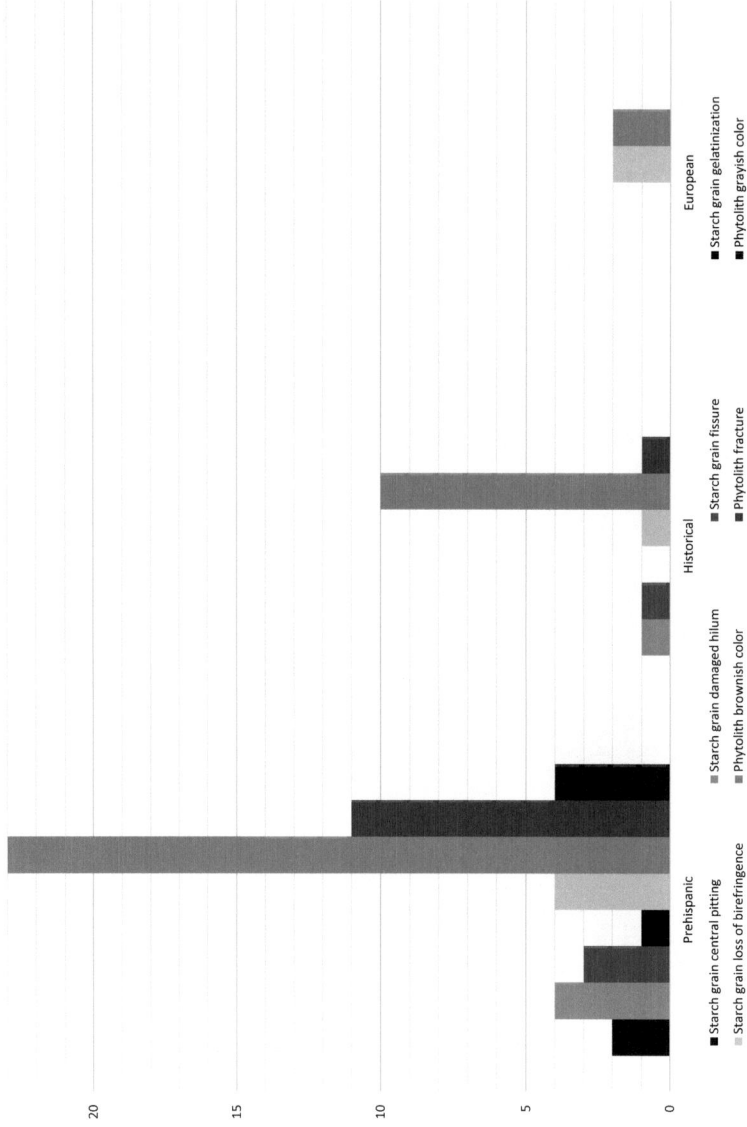

Figure 2.3 Types of microfossil damage by ceramic type. Image by Carolina Belmar and Omar Reyes.

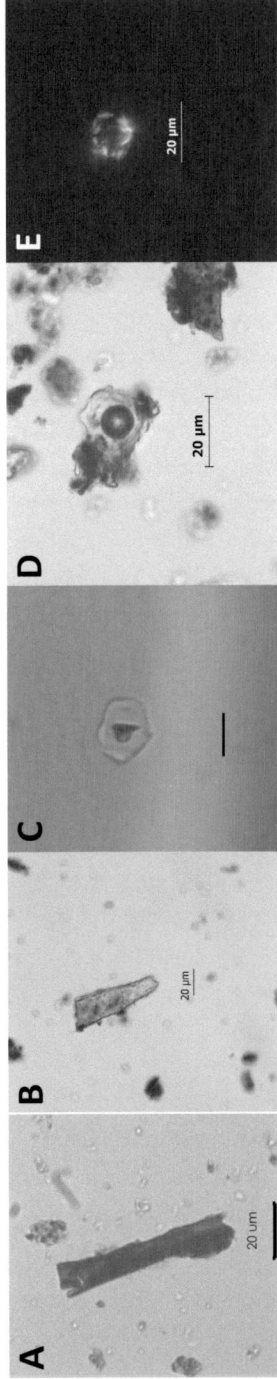

Figure 2.4 Microfossil damages. *A*, Phytolith that was exposed to heat, San Juan site. *B*, Fractured phytolith, Tauco 1. *C*, Starch grain with darkened hilum, Puente Quilo. *D*, Starch grain with darkened hilum, Tauco 1. *E*, Gelatinized starch grain, Puente Quilo. Scale 20μ. Image by Carolina Belmar and Omar Reyes.

and domesticated plants as well as seaweeds (*cochayuyo*) was used for food and medicinal preparations in Chiloé. The continuity of some wild plants and *cochayuyo* consumed by marine hunter-gatherers since the Middle Holocene (Belmar et al. 2021) signals the existence of traditional ingredients that have a long local trajectory. These ingredients form part of current typical recipes and are crucial components of Chiloé's identity (Montecino 2004; Twiss 2007). Domesticated plants mark the addition of new ingredients to these preparations more than the replacement of previous ones. It is possible that new ingredients led to the creation of new recipes. But since residues sum the history of use of an artifact, we can only identify ingredients but not their combinations.

The types of preparations are an important part of food's *chaîne opératoire*. The damages identified in microfossils reveal that some plants were milled (such as grasslike plants, Chilean rhubarb, chaura, cauchao, maize, and potato), while others were toasted or cooked with water. Given ethnohistorical and ethnobotanical information, we must consider the preparation of fermented and unfermented drinks made of fruits and grains (e.g., maize) that were ground and cooked (de Mösbach [1955] 1999) as well as that of infusions based on medicinal and psychoactive plants (de Mösbach [1955] 1999; Jerez 2013; Plath 1981).[3] Every type of preparation includes a series of steps and guidelines that lead to a final product. This is particularly true when making fermented fruit drinks or preparations with sacred plants that aim to retrieve their medicinal and psychoactive properties with the goal of eliciting specific effects in the individual (Etkin and Ross 1991; Hastorf 2017). Even though cooking occurred in *curantos* before the arrival of pottery to the island, the introduction of pottery is related to the transformations of the ingredient's physical and chemical characteristics (Etkin and Ross 1991; Hastorf 2017) from raw to cooked and from unfermented to fermented, and these transformations, through consumption, altered the state of Chiloé's people, especially through the consumption of sacred plants.

One seaweed taxon and ten of the thirteen identified plant taxa have known medicinal and curative properties. Two of them, *miyaye* (*Datura*

---

3. Documents show that the plants identified in this analysis were consumed as infusions, not ointments or cataplasms, which would also require some cooking-like preparation.

sp.) and *latué* (*Latua pubiflora*), are important sacred plants in southern Chile that contain highly toxic alkaloids. Both plants have been traditionally used in Mapuche-Huilliche communities (de Mösbach [1955] 1999; Jerez 2013), by the *machi* (healers, diviners, and priests) for healing and communication with the other world (Lenz 1905–1910, 785; Jerez 2013; de Mösbach [1955] 1999; Munizaga 1960; Plath 1981; Plowman, Gyllenhaal, and Lindgren 1971; Serrano 1934). These plants and seaweed fall into the fused categories of edible medicines, or transformative foods that can cure diseases and illnesses (de Mösbach [1955] 1999; Etkin and Ross 1991; Jerez 2013).

In synthesis, the history of the human occupation of the Chiloé Archipelago can be described through the history of food where more than 6,000 years of marine-based diet complemented with the consumption of wild plants and seaweed were followed (ca. 1000 yBP) by the addition of domesticated plants and preparations in ceramic vessels. The greatest change resulted from European contact, which increased the importance of terrestrial foods configuring a sea and land (*mar y tierra*) diet that is characteristic of current Chiloé's culinary traditions.

CONCLUSIONS

The incorporation of new technologies in Chiloé (pottery and domesticated plants) was accompanied by changes in lithic and zooarchaeological assemblages and required new forms of acquisition (harvesting) that probably transformed the structure and understanding of this marine landscape. However, the constant presence of *cochayuyo* and wild plants were part of a long tradition in which plants and seaweeds were used as foods and, in some instances, constituted the basis for edible medicines.

ACKNOWLEDGMENTS

Funded by a ANID-FONDECYT 1170726, 1210045 grant. Our thanks to National Geographic EC-52996R-19 and Simon Sierralta for allowing access to the Puente Quilo collection and to Doris Barría, Armando Bahamonde, Carolina and Consuelo Bahamonde (San Juan), Francisco Aude (Tauco); Felipe Montiel, Director of the Municipal Museum of

Castro; and the archaeology team of Ximena Albornoz, Francisco Cayla, Pablo González, Javier Cárcamo, Karol González, Silvia Alfaro, and Gabriela Palma.

REFERENCES

Adán, Leonor, Rodrigo Mera, Ximena Navarro, Roberto Campbell, Daniel Quiroz, and Marco Sánchez. 2016. "Historia Prehispánica en la Región Centro-Sur de Chile: Cazadores-Recolectores Holocénicos y Comunidades Alfareras (ca. 10.000 años a ca. 1550 años d.C.)." In *Prehistoria en Chile: Desde sus Primeros Habitantes Hasta los Incas*, edited by Fernanda Falabella, Carlos Aldunate, Mauricio Uribe, and Lorena Sanhueza, 401–41. Santiago: Editorial Universitaria.

Albornoz, Ximena. 2015. "Colección de Referencia de Microrrestos vegetales: Especies Psicoactivas y Aromáticas de los Andes Centro-Sur." In *Avances y Desafíos Metodológicos en Arqueobotánica: Miradas Consensuadas y Diálogos Compartidos desde Sudamérica*, edited by Carolina Belmar and Verónica Lema, 497–516. Santiago: Impresos New Grafic.

Aldunate, Carlos. 1996. "Mapuche: Gente de la Tierra." In *Nueva Historia de Chile desde los Orígenes Hasta Nuestros Días*, edited by Nicolás Cruz, Pablo Whipple, and Carlos Aldunate, 111–34. Santiago: Zig-Zag.

Álvarez, Ricardo, Doina Munita, Jaime Fredes, and Rodrigo Mera. 2008. *Corrales de Pesca en Chiloé*. Valdivia, Chile: Imprenta América.

Álvarez, Ricardo, Doina Munita, Rodrigo Mera, Italo Borlando, Francisco Ther-Ríos, David Núñez, Carlos Hidalgo, and Philip Hayward. 2019. "Rebounding from Extractivism: The History and Re-assertion of Traditional Weir-Fishing Practices in the Interior Sea of Chiloé." *Shima* 13 (2): 155–73.

Atalay, Sonya, and Christine Hastorf. 2006. "Food, Meals, and Daily Activities: Food *Habitus* at Neolithic Çatalhöyük." *American Antiquity* 71 (2): 283–319. https://doi.org/10.2307/40035906.

Babot, María Pilar. 2007. "Granos de Almidón en Contextos Arqueológicos: Posibilidades y Perspectivas a partir de Casos del Noroeste Argentino." In *Paleoetnobotánica del Cono Sur: Estudios de Casos y Propuestas Metodológicas*, edited by Bernarda Marconetto, Nurit Oliszewski, and María P. Babot, 95–125. Córdoba: Universidad Nacional de Córdoba.

Belmar, Carolina. 2019. *Los Cazadores-Recolectores y las Plantas en Patagonia: Perspectivas desde el Sitio Cueva Baño Nuevo 1, Aisén*. Santiago: Social Ediciones.

Belmar, Carolina, Luciana Quiroz, Hermann Niemeyer, María Planella, Ximena Albornoz, Fernanda Meneses, Silvia Alfaro, Carolina Carrasco, Kathy Collao-Alvarado, and Javier Echeverría. 2015. "Condiciones Previas para el Uso de Marcadores Arqueobotánicos y Químicos en Estudios Arqueológicos Sobre Complejos Fumatorios: Una Propuesta de Protocolo para Manipulación del Objeto y Toma de Muestras." *Intersecciones en Antropología* 15:497–501.

Belmar, Carolina, Omar Reyes, Ximena Albornoz, Augusto Tessone, Manuel San Román, Flavia Morello, and Ximena Urbina. 2021. "Evaluando el Consumo y Uso de Plantas entre Cazadores-Recolectores Pescadores Marinos a través del Estudio del Tártaro Dental Humano en los Canales Septentrionales de Patagonia (41°30′–47°S)." *Chungará Revista Chilena de Antropología* 53 (3): 400–418. http://dx.doi.org/10.4067/S0717-73562021005001701.

Boraso, Alicia, Alicia Rico, Susana Perales, Laura Pérez, and Hilda Zalazar. 2004. *Algas Marinas de la Patagonia: Una Guía Ilustrada*. Buenos Aires: Fundación de Historia Natural Félix de Azara.

Coil, James, Alejandra Korstanje, Steven Archer, and Christine Hastorf. 2003. "Laboratory Goals and Considerations for Multiple Microfossil Extraction in Archaeology." *Journal of Archaeological Science* 30 (8): 991–1008. https://doi.org/10.1016/S0305-4403(02)00285-6.

Collantes, Gloria, Ana Merino, and Verónica Lagos. 2002. "Fenología de la Gametogénesis, Madurez de Conceptáculos, Fertilidad y Embriogénesis en *Durvillaea antarctica* (Chamisso) Hariot (Phaeophyta, Durvillaeales)." *Revista de Biología Marina y Oceanografía* 37 (1): 83–112. http://dx.doi.org/10.4067/S0718-19572002000100009.

Cooper, John. 1917. *Analytical and Critical Bibliography of the Tribes of Tierra del Fuego and Adjacent Territory*. Washington, D.C.: Smithsonian Institution. https://repository.si.edu/handle/10088/15530?show=full.

Cooper, John. 1946. "The Chono." In *Handbook of South American Indians*. Vol. 1, *The Marginal Tribes*, edited by James Steward, 47–54. Washington, D.C.: Smithsonian Institution. https://repository.si.edu/handle/10088/34955.

de Bibar, Geronimo. (1558) 1979. *Crónica y Relación Copiosa y Verdadera de los Reinos de Chile*. Berlín: Edición de L. Sáez-Godoy, Bibliotheca Ibero-Americana, Colloquium Verlag.

de Ercilla, Alonso. (1569) 2009. *La Araucana*. Madrid: Edición de Isaías Lerner, Cátedra.

de Goicueta, Miguel. 1558. *Derrotero y Viaje de Juan Ladrillero*. Sevilla: Archivo General de Indias.

de Mösbach, Ernesto W. (1955) 1999. *Botánica Indígena de Chile*. 2nd ed. Santiago: Editorial Andrés Bello.

Emperaire, Joseph. 1963. *Los Nómades del Mar*. Santiago: Ediciones de la Universidad de Chile.

Etkin, Nina. 2006. *Edible Medicines: An Ethnopharmacology of Food*. Tucson: University of Arizona Press.

Etkin, Nina, and Paul Ross. 1991. "Should We Set a Place for Diet in Ethnopharmacology?" *Journal of Ethnopharmacology* 32 (1): 25–36. https://doi.org/10.1016/0378-8741(91)90100-R.

Flores, Carola, Bernardo Broitman, and Pilar Rivas. 2010. "Changes in the Subsistence Strategy of Prehistoric Intertidal Gathering: The Pre-Ceramic and Ceramic Coastal Hunter-Gatherers of Reloncaví Sound, Chile." In

Comparative Perspectives on the Archaeology of Coastal South America, edited by Robyn Cutright, Enrique López-Hurtado, and Alexander Martí, 64–76. Pittsburgh: Center for Comparative Archaeology, University of Pittsburgh, Pontificia Universidad Católica del Perú, Ministerio de Cultura del Ecuador.

González, Karol. 2019. *Uso de Recursos Vegetales por Grupos Cazadores-Recolectores Marítimos en el Sitio San Juan 1, Chiloé (6.000–2.000 años cal. AP)*. Santiago: Memoria Para Optar al Título Profesional de Arqueólogo(a), Escuela de Arqueología, Universidad Alberto Hurtado.

Goody, Jack. 1995. *Cocina, Cuisine y Clase: Estudio de Sociología Comparada*. Barcelona: Gedisa Editorial.

Hastorf, Christine. 2017. *The Social Archaeology of Food: Thinking About Eating from the Prehistory to the Present*. Cambridge: Cambridge University Press. https://doi.org/10.1017/9781316597590.

Jerez, Jimena. 2013. *Plantas Mágicas: Guía Etnobotánica de la Región de los Ríos*. Valdivia: Ediciones Kultrún.

Korstanje, Alejandra, and María P. Babot. 2007. "A Microfossil Characterization from South Andean Economic Plants." In *Plants, People and Places: Recent Studies in Phytholithic Analysis*, edited by Marco Madella and Debora Zurro, 41–72. Cambridge: Oxbow Books.

Legoupil, Dominique. 2005. "Recolectores de Moluscos Tempranos en el Sureste de la Isla de Chiloé: Una Primera Mirada." *Magallania* 33 (1): 51–61. http://dx.doi.org/10.4067/S0718-22442005000100004.

Lenz, Rodolfo. 1905–1910. *Diccionario Etimológico*. Santiago: Universidad de Chile.

Lévi-Strauss, Claude. (1964) 1968. *Mitológicas I: Lo Crudo y lo Cocido*. Mexico City: FCE.

Llamazares, Ana, Carlos Martínez, and Florencia Funes. 2004. "Principales Plantas Sagradas de Sudamérica." In *El Lenguaje de los Dioses. Arte, Chamanismo y Cosmovisión Indígena en Sudamérica*, edited by Ana Llamazares and Carlos Martínez, 259–85. Buenos Aires: Editorial Biblios.

Luebert, Federico, and Patricio Pliscoff. 2006. *Sinopsis Bioclimática y Vegetacional de Chile*. Santiago: Editorial Universitaria. https://www.uchile.cl/publi caciones/141285/sinopsis-bioclimatica-y-vegetacional-de-chile.

Madella, Marco, Anne Alexandre, and Terry Ball. 2005. "International Code for Phytolith Nomenclature. 1.0." *Annals of Botany* 96:253–60. https://doi.org /10.1093/aob/mci172.

Menghin, Osvaldo. 1962. *Estudios de Prehistoria Araucana: Studia Praehistorica 2*. Buenos Aires: Centro Argentino de Estudios Prehistóricos.

Montecino, Sonia. 2004. *Cocinas Mestiza de Chile: La Olla Deleitosa*. Santiago: Moran.

Munita, Doina. 2007. "Materias Primas Líticas en Sitios Costeros del Extremo Sur Septentrional de Chile Dispersión y Aprovisionamiento." In *Arqueología de Fuego-Patagonia: Levantando Piedras, Desenterrando Huesos . . . y Develando Arcanos*, edited by Flavia Morello, Mateo Martinic, Alfredo Prieto, and Gabriel Bahamonde, 189–203. Punta Arenas, Chile: CEQUA.

Munita, Doina, Rodrigo Mera, and Ricardo Álvarez. 2016. "Una Historia de Mil años." In *Chiloé*, edited by Benjamín Lira, Hernán Rodríguez, and Lucia Santa Cruz, 58–185. Santiago, Chile: Museo de Arte Precolombino.

Munizaga, Carlos. 1960. "Uso Actual de Miaya (*Datura stramonium*) por los Araucanos de Chile." *Revista Universitaria* 23:43–45.

Muñoz, Andrés, and José Yáñez. 2009. *Mamíferos de Chile*. Santiago: CEA Ediciones.

Navarro, Jorge, and Germán Pequeño. 1979. "Peces Litorales de los Archipiélagos de Chiloé y los Chonos, Chile." *Revista Biología Marina* 16: 205–309. https://rbmo.uv.cl/articulos/peces-litorales-de-los-archipielagos-de-chiloe-y-los-chonos-chile/.

Ocampo, Carlos, and Pilar Rivas. 2004. "Poblamiento Temprano de los Extremos Geográficos de los Canales Patagónicos: Chiloé e Isla Navarino 1." *Chungará Revista Chilena de Antropología* 36 (1): 317–31. http://dx.doi.org/10.4067/S0717-73562004000300034.

Osorio, Cecilia, and David Reid. 2004. "Moluscos Marinos Intermareales y Submareales entre la Boca del Guafo y el Estero Elefantes, sur de Chile." *Investigaciones Marinas* 32 (2): 71–89. http://dx.doi.org/10.4067/S0717-71782004000200006.

Palma, Gabriela, and Silvia Alfaro. 2019. *Informe de Análisis Cerámico de Sitios Arqueológicos de la Provincia de Chiloé, Región de Los Lagos*. Informe Proyecto FONDECYT N°1170726. Santiago: Fondo de Ciencia y Tecnología de Chile.

Pearsall, Deborah. 2010. *Paleoethnobotany: A Handbook of Procedures*. Walnut Creek, Calif.: Left Coast Press.

Plath, Oreste. 1981. *Folklore Médico Chileno*. Santiago: Editorial Nacimiento.

Plowman, Timothy, Lars Gyllenhaal, and Jan Lindgren. 1971. "*Latua pubiflora*— Magic Plant from Southern Chile." *Botanical Museum Leaflets* 23 (2): 61–92.

Popper, Virginia. 1988. "Selecting Quantitative Measurements in Paleoethnobotany." In *Current Paleoethnobotany: Analytical Methods and Cultural Interpretations of Archaeological Plant Remains*, edited by Christine Hastorf and Virginia Popper, 53–71. Chicago: University of Chicago Press.

Reyes, Omar. 2020. *The Settlement of the Chonos Archipelago, Western Patagonia, Chile*. New York: Springer.

Reyes, Omar, Carolina Belmar, Manuel San Román, Flavia Morello, and Ximena Urbina. 2020. "Avances en la Secuencia Cronológica del Mar Interior de Chiloé, Patagonia Occidental: Sitios Arqueológicos San Juan 1, Tauco 1 y 2." *Magallania* 48 (1): 173–84. http://dx.doi.org/10.4067/S0718-22442020000 0100173.

Reyes, Omar, César Méndez, and Manuel San Román. 2019a. "Cronología de la Ocupación Humana en los Canales Septentrionales de Patagonia Occidental,

Chile." *Intersecciones en Antropología* 20 (2): 153–65. https://doi.org/10.37176/iea.20.2.2019.449.

Reyes, Omar, Augusto Tessone, Carolina Belmar, Manuel San Román, Flavia Morello, Mauricio Moraga, and Ximena Urbina. 2022. "Cambios y Continuidades en la Subsistencia e Interacción entre Sociedades Cazadoras-Recolectoras Marinas y Agro-Alfareras durante el Holoceno Tardío en el Archipiélago Septentrional, Patagonia, Chile." *Latin American Antiquity* 33. https://doi.org/10.1017/laq.2022.38.

Reyes, Omar, Augusto Tessone, Manuel San Román, and César Méndez. 2019b. "Dieta e Isótopos Estables de Cazadores Recolectores Marinos en los canales Occidentales de Patagonia, Chile." *Latin American Antiquity* 30 (3): 550–68. https://doi.org/10.1017/laq.2019.40.

Rivas, Pilar, and Carlos Ocampo. 2010. "La Adaptación Humana al Bosque en la Isla de Chiloé: Estrategias Adaptativas en el Litoral Septentrional de los Canales Patagónicos." In *Actas del XVII Congreso Nacional de Arqueología Chilena*, 2:1449–60. Valdivia: Ediciones Kultrún.

Rivas, Pilar, Carlos Ocampo, and Eugenio Aspillaga. 1999. "Poblamiento Temprano de los Canales Patagónicos: El Núcleo Ecotonal Septentrional." *Anales del Instituto de la Patagonia* 27:221–30. http://bibliotecadigital.umag.cl/handle/20.500.11893/1349.

Serrano, Anotonio. 1934. "El Uso del Tabaco y Vegetales Narcotizantes entre los Indígenas de América." *Revista Geográfica Americana* 2 (15): 415–25. https://issuu.com/quantulumcumque/docs/serrano.

Sierralta, Simón, Ayelén Delgado, Patricia Kelly, and Sandra Rebolledo. 2019. "Cronología Absoluta en los Canales Septentrionales, el Mar Interior y la Costa Pacífica Austral." In *Arqueología de la Patagonia: El Pasado en las Arenas*, 167–79. Argentina: Altuna.

Stern, Charles R. 2018. "Obsidian Sources and Distribution in Patagonia, Southernmost South America." *Quaternary International* 468: 190–205. https://doi.org/10.1016/j.quaint.2017.07.030.

Twiss, Katheryn. 2007. "We Are What We Eat." In *The Archaeology of Food and Identity*, edited by Katheryn Twiss, 1–15. Carbondale: Southern Illinois University.

Twiss, Katheryn. 2019. *The Archaeology of Food: Identity, Politics and Ideology in the Prehistoric and Historic Past*. Cambridge: Cambridge University Press.

Twiss, Page, Erwin Suess, and R. Smith. 1969. "Morphological Classification of Grass Phytoliths." *Soil Science Society of America Journal* 33 (1): 109–15. https://doi.org/10.2136/sssaj1969.03615995003300010030x.

Urbina, Ximena. 2016. "Traslados de Indígenas de la Patagonia Occidental Insular a Chiloé en los Siglos XVI, XVII y XVIII." In *América en Diásporas: Esclavitudes y Migraciones Forzadas (Siglos XVI–XIX)*, edited by Jaime Valenzuela, 381–411. Santiago: Instituto de Historia, Pontificia Universidad Católica de Chile; RiL editores.

Urbina, Ximena, Omar Reyes, and Carolina Belmar. 2020. "Canoeros en Chiloé: De Facilitadores de las Navegaciones Españolas en los Archipiélagos de Los Chonos y de Guayaneco, a Productores y Comerciantes, 1567–792." *Chungará: Revista Chilena de Antropología* 52 (2): 335–46. http://dx.doi.org/10.4067/S0717-73562020005000702.

Vuilleumier, François. 1985. "Forest Birds of Patagonia: Ecological Geography, Speciation, Endemism, and Faunal History." *Ornithological Monographs* 36:255–304. https://www.jstor.org/stable/40168287.

3

Eating Local, Drinking Imported

Chicha Recipes, Emulative Desire, and Identity Formation at Atalla, Huancavelica, Peru

Sadie L. Weber and Michelle E. Young

People's relationships with food are perhaps best encapsulated by Jean Brillat-Savarin's (1999) words: "Tell me what you eat, and I will tell you who you are" (8). Taste and food preferences are socially constructed, and as such, cuisines encode and communicate complex social information about both individual and group identity. Through food, people establish, perform, and reinforce their group and personal identities, which may be defined along multiple axes, including gender, status, ethnicity, religion, and place of origin (e.g., Bray 2003; Hastorf 2017). The "semiotic virtuosity" of food lies in its capacity to construct social relations, either transmitting messages of solidarity or, conversely, reinforcing hierarchies of segmentation and difference (Appadurai 1981). In this chapter we explore the social implications of an almost three-thousand-year-old *chicha*[1] recipe that we identified through the analysis of starch granules on materials excavated from Atalla, an archaeological site located in the south-central highlands of Peru.

The consumption of maize chicha is a communal activity that marks celebrations, commemorates the completion of shared tasks, and crystalizes social relationships and identities within and among contemporary groups in the Andes (Allen 1988, 2009; Weismantel 1991). The act of drinking and the qualities of chicha itself carry significant symbolic power within these interactions (Goldstein, Goldstein, and Williams 2009). Chicha also served as a cornerstone of ritual commensality dating back into the precontact era (e.g., Jennings 2005; Goldstein and Coleman 2004), and consequently, this fermented beverage played a significant role in structuring relations of sociality (Bray 2012). Although we cannot assume that chicha played the same role or carried the same

---

1. A lightly fermented beverage of indigenous American origin.

associations in the precontact past as it does today, archaeological evidence suggests that the ritual consumption of maize chicha has been practiced by Andean societies since at least the Formative Period (e.g., Burger 1992).

The Formative Period (1200–400 BCE) is broadly considered a time of increased social cohesion and long-distance interaction during which some groups in the Central Andes intensified their agricultural regimes with incipient sedentarism while others continued to practice more mobile lifeways specialized in the husbandry of domesticated camelids. As sedentary communities increased in size and number, this period witnessed the emergence of regional civic-ceremonial centers (fig. 3.1), many of which functioned as pilgrimage destinations that participated in the Chavín Interaction Sphere (Brown 2017; Burger 2008; Nesbitt, Matsumoto, and Cavero Palomino 2019; Young, forthcoming), a term that refers to trade networks associated with shared material cultural and ritual practices.

Maize chicha was consumed as a ritual beverage at several of these Formative Period ceremonial centers, including the preeminent cult site of Chavín de Huántar itself (Burger 1992, 138; Mesía 2014). Isotopic signatures of human bone from Chavín de Huántar demonstrate infrequent consumption of maize, suggesting that it was reserved for special occasions or ritual purposes (Burger and van der Merwe 1990). Ritual consumption of maize also occurred at contemporaneous centers such as Cerro Blanco in the Nepeña Valley (Ikehara, Paipay, and Shibata 2013) and Campanayuq Rumi in the Ayacucho highlands (Matsumoto, Cavero Palomino, and Gutierrez Silva 2013). Based on the evidence for maize chicha consumption at these ceremonial sites, we suggest that the ritual consumption of maize chicha was a practice popularized through the Chavín Interaction Sphere.

Atalla, an ancient village with a monumental temple complex located at 3,550 masl in the highlands of Huancavelica, Peru, functioned as one such civic-ceremonial center that participated in the Chavín Interaction Sphere (map 3.1) (Young 2020). Between 1000 and 800 BCE, Atalla grew into the largest village in the region, serving as a node of exchange and ritual practice. Our analysis of microbotanical remains from Atalla confirms that a wide variety of plants was used at Atalla, including cultigens that cannot grow within the site's immediate area because of its high

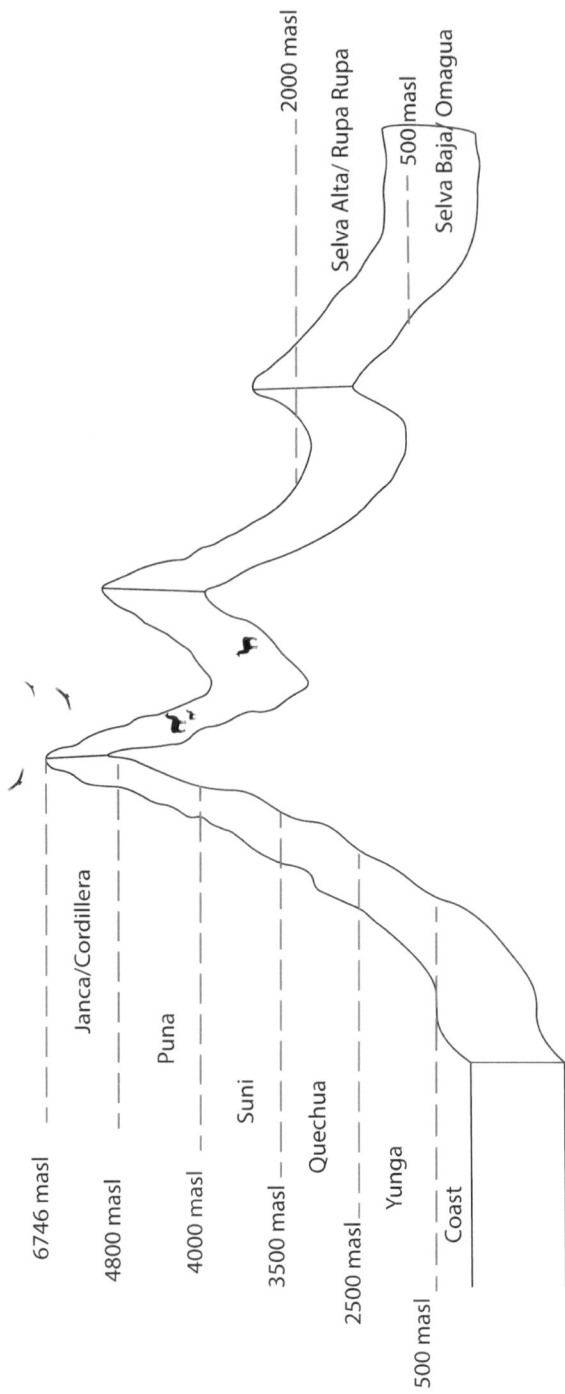

Figure 3.1 Schematic of the vertically stratified ecozones as classified by Javier Pulgar-Vidal in the Central Andean region. Image by S. L. Weber.

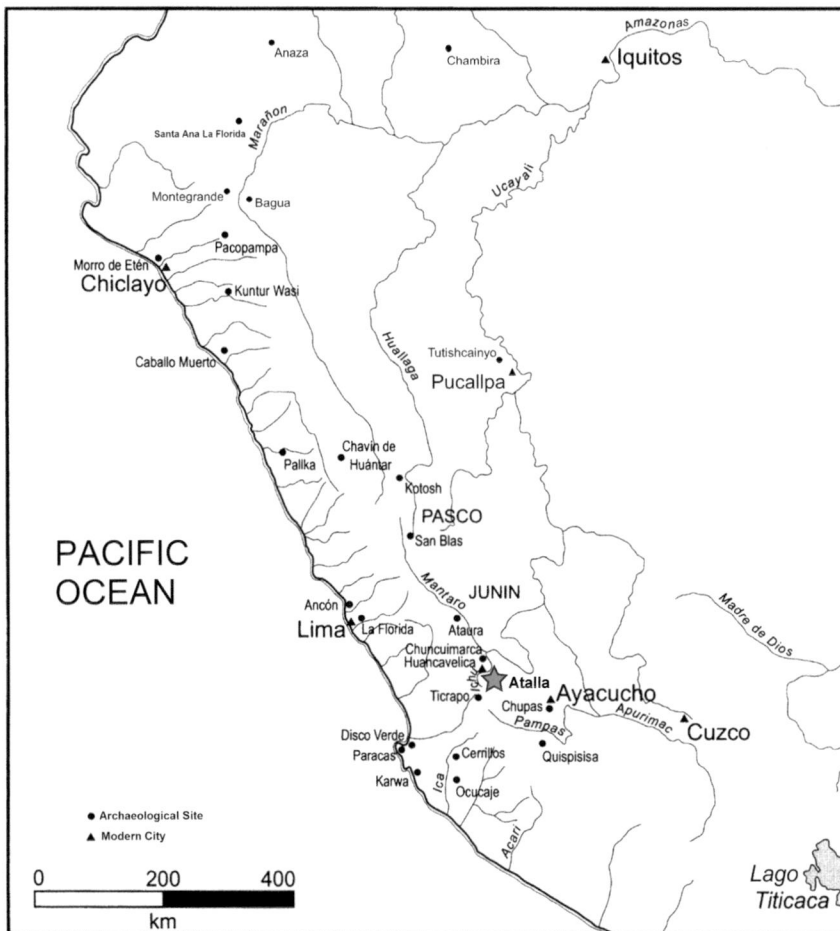

Map 3.1 Formative Period sites in the Central Andean region. The gray star indicates the location of Atalla. Redrawn from Burger (1992). Image by S. L. Weber.

altitude. Our findings include ground, boiled, and probably fermented starches that point to the consumption of a specialized chicha recipe involving a combination of maize, manioc, and algarroba, a blend that has yet to be identified elsewhere in the precontact Andes. The lowland plants identified at Atalla offer material evidence for close ties between groups in Huancavelica and communities on the south coast of Peru. We argue that the culinary knowledge required to prepare such nonlocal foodstuffs at Atalla demonstrates more intimate connections between these groups than just down-the-line trade.

METHODS

Tubers and other underground storage organs (USOs) form key components of Andean cuisine and diet, making up ~40% of highland diets in recent times (Leonard and Thomas 1988, 251).[2] Despite their near ubiquity, USOs are difficult to identify in highland Andean macrobotanical assemblages because of their poor archaeological preservation resulting from year-round changes in moisture, lack of hard seed coats, and the ways they are traditionally prepared and consumed (e.g., grated or boiled, and finally, eaten completely). Thus in areas where macrobotanical preservation is poor, microbotanical analyses provide a useful tool for identifying the presence of comestibles. Microbotanical analysis of microremains extracted from artifacts also provides a degree of certainty in the intentionality involved in the ancient preparation and consumption of these products as opposed to macroremains, which may be found unassociated with artifacts within the soil matrix of an excavation.

To better understand subsistence and interaction at Atalla, we analyzed starch granules, which vary morphologically by taxon, making them particularly useful for studies of diet and cuisine (Henry 2014). The ceramic fragments (n = 133) and stone tools (n = 24) sampled for this study were selected from a variety of contexts at the site. Before microbotanical sampling, the ceramic fragments and stone tools had been processed in the field lab through washing, storage in plastic bags, and labeling by provenience. The specimens were then washed again separately to diminish the chances of cross contamination within the laboratory bags or contamination by modern foods. Since contamination of modern starches is common in even the cleanest of laboratory settings (Crowther et al. 2014), control samples were taken from the water and containers used for this process as well as from the working surfaces (both in the field in Peru and in the laboratory in the United States) to ensure

---

2. These data were collected in 1988 from Nuñoa, Peru, when agrarian reform and increased access to nonlocal foods had already decreased tuber consumption from ~70% of the diet to 40%.

that cross contamination had not occurred. Each sampled ceramic fragment and stone tool was placed into a disposable plastic container into which 10 mL of distilled water was added. The artifacts were physically agitated with an electric sonicating toothbrush to release any microremains trapped in superficial imperfections. The samples extracted from the artifacts were allowed to dry completely, after which ~25 µL of a 1:1 solution of distilled water and glycerol was added. The dried sample and solution were then homogenized by agitation and added to a microscope slide. The sample was then covered with a glass coverslip and sealed with clear nail polish. The microremains were analyzed under brightfield and cross-polarized light for rapid identification of starch granules based on morphology and established nomenclature.[3] All archaeological microremains were compared to images of modern reference samples (e.g., Babot 2003; Giovannetti et al. 2008; Pagán-Jiménez 2015). The starch granules were also assessed for damage in the form of fissures, pitting, swelling, loss of birefringence, or diminished distinction in the extinction cross, which can be indicative of various forms of processing such as cooking and fermentation (Babot 2003; Dozier and Jennings 2021). However, as starches are cooked for longer periods of time, they gradually lose essential diagnostic characteristics, which can impair their identification (Henry, Hudson, and Piperno 2009). Nonetheless, we successfully identified many granules to the genus level, and we inferred the preparation method from the type of damage observed.

RESULTS

A consideration of the ancient cultivation range of different plant species is essential to define what constitutes a "local" or imported crop. Although the marked changes in altitude across the Andes create distinct ecological zones, modern interpretations of paleoclimate data suggest that the vertical ecozones defined by Pulgar-Vidal (1941; fig. 3.1) are not necessarily representative of ancient climatic conditions. Oxygen isotope data from the Huascarán ice core demonstrate that the Formative Period climate was colder and drier than that of today, representing an average

---

3. International Code for Starch Nomenclature, http://fossilfarm.org/ICSN /Code.html.

upshift of 150 meters in limits of the ecozones (Thompson et al. 1995). We have taken these colder precontact climatic conditions between 1000 and 500 BCE into account when inferring "local" versus "nonlocal" cultigens. Thus, while maize currently grows near Atalla, the Formative Period climate would have required residents to control maize fields at lower elevations or import their maize from lowland groups.

Microbotanical analysis confirms the use of common highland Andean plant taxa as well as various nonlocal plant taxa at Atalla. Twelve different categories of starches were identified, seven of which we consider to be nonlocal plants that could not have grown at Atalla's elevation. These include achira (*Canna indica*), maize (*Zea mays*), manioc (*Manihot esculenta*), sacha papa (*Dioscorea* sp.), sweet potato (*Ipomoea batatas*), chili pepper (*Capsicum* sp.), and algarroba (*Prosopis* sp.).[4] Local plants identified include potato (*Solanum tuberosum)*, olluco (*Ullucus tuberosus*), and grasses (Poaceae) as well as starches that are likely chenopods (fig. 3.2). The highest overall diversity in starches and frequency of nonlocal taxa occurred in samples taken from ceremonial contexts, and although there were nonlocal taxa used in the residential sector, their presence in domestic areas was far less common (table 3.1). This suggests that more variety, particularly dishes that incorporated lowland plants, were prepared and served in ritual contexts compared to the more limited range of plants consumed in domestic settings.

Our data suggest that maize, manioc, and algarroba were prepared together in a fermented beverage that was consumed at Atalla during the Formative Period. The appearance of more than one plant species in any given sample was observed in 38% of the samples that yielded starches (*n* = 20). Maize was nearly ubiquitous, appearing in 10 of 13 contexts, while manioc and algarroba were less common, each appearing in only 3 of 13 contexts surveyed. Many, if not all, of the ceramic vessels sampled were probably used more than once, complicating our ability to infer specific dishes; however, the production of chicha typically requires the consistent use of specific, consistently used vessels. These vessels are called *cántaros borrachos*, or drunk jars, and are used only to inoculate the brew with native yeasts to ensure a successful fermentation (de Florio

---

4. In Spanish-speaking countries, *algarrobo* largely refers to trees in the genus *Prosopis*, while the fruit of these trees is referred to as *algarroba*.

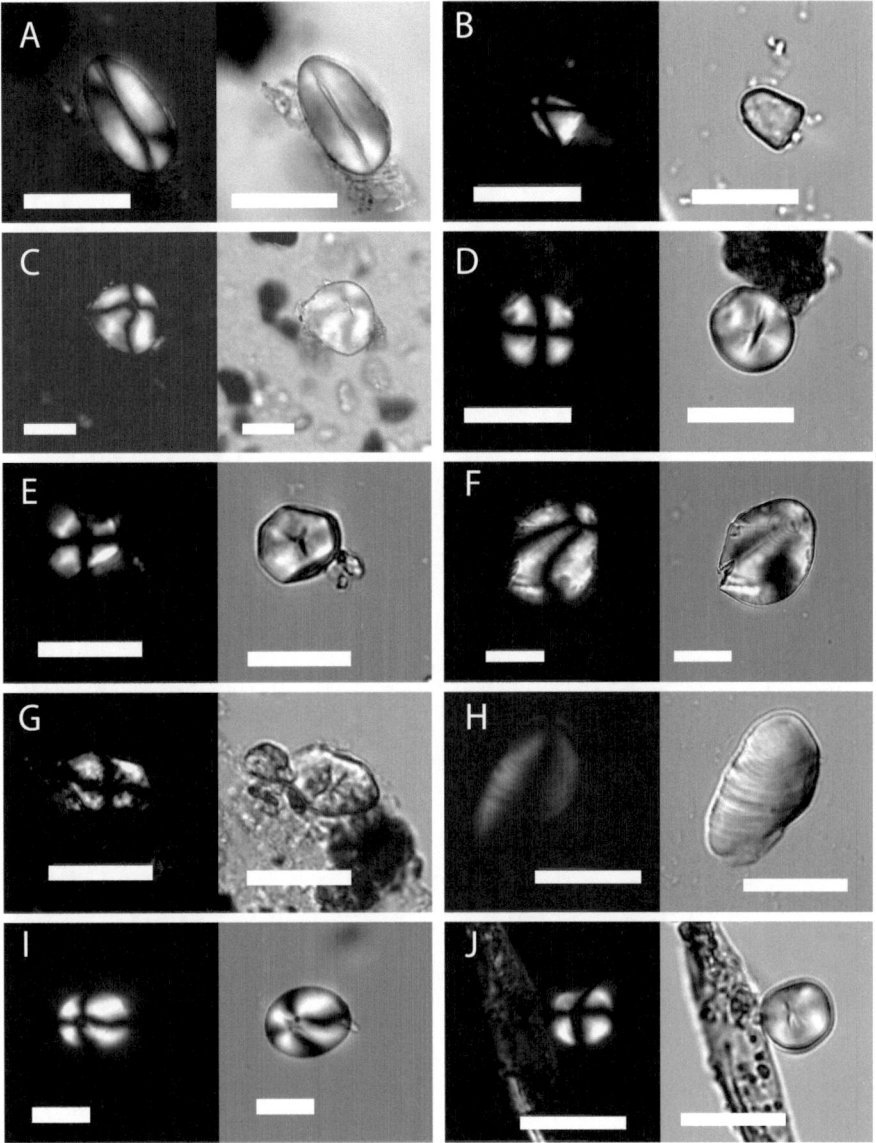

Figure 3.2 Exemplary starch granules. The darker images on the left of each subfigure are fully crossed-polarized, while the lighter images are brightfield images. *A*, *Capsicum* sp. *B*, *Dioscorea* sp. *C*, *Ipomoea* sp. *D*, *Manihot* sp. *E*, *Zea mays*. *F*, *Solanum tuberosum*. *G*, *Prosopis* sp. *H*, Canna sp. *I*, *Ullucus tuberosus*. *J*, *Chenopodium* sp. The scale bar in each image is 20 μm. The starches in *F* and *H*, while most exemplary of their respective taxa, are damaged. Image by S. L. Weber.

Table 3.1 Summary of the locations of plant taxa identified at Atalla

	Civic-ceremonial contexts: Orjon Cancha						Residential contexts: Sumaq Wasi and Achka Wasikuna							
	OC-1	OC-2	OC-A	OC-B	OC-C	SW-3	SW-4	SW-F	SW-N	AW-5	AW-G	AW-H	AW-I	AW-K
Amaranthaceae (Pseudocereals)	—	—	—	X	—	—	—	—	—	—	—	—	—	—
Canna sp.* (achira)	—	X	—	X	—	X	—	—	—	X	—	—	—	—
Capsicum sp.* (chili pepper)	—	—	—	—	—	—	—	—	—	—	—	—	—	—
Dioscorea sp.* (yam/sacha papa)	X	—	—	X	—	—	—	—	—	—	—	—	—	—
Ipomoea sp.* (sweet potato)	—	—	X	X	—	—	—	—	—	—	—	—	—	—
Manihot sp.* (manioc)	X	—	—	X	—	—	—	—	—	—	X	—	—	—
Prosopis sp.* (algarroba)	—	—	—	X	—	—	—	X	—	—	X	—	—	—
Phaseolus sp. (bean)	X	—	—	—	—	—	—	X	—	—	—	—	—	—
Poaceae (grasses)	X	X	—	X	—	X	—	X	X	X	—	X	X	X
Solanum sp. (potato)	X	X	—	—	X	X	—	X	—	X	X	X	—	X
Ullucus sp. (olluco)	—	—	—	X	—	—	—	X	—	—	X	X	—	—
Zea sp.* (maize)	X	X	X	X	—	X	—	X	X	—	X	X	X	X

Note: Taxa in bold print are a particular focus of this chapter. Asterisks indicate nonlocal taxa. Dashes indicate absence, and X's indicate presence.

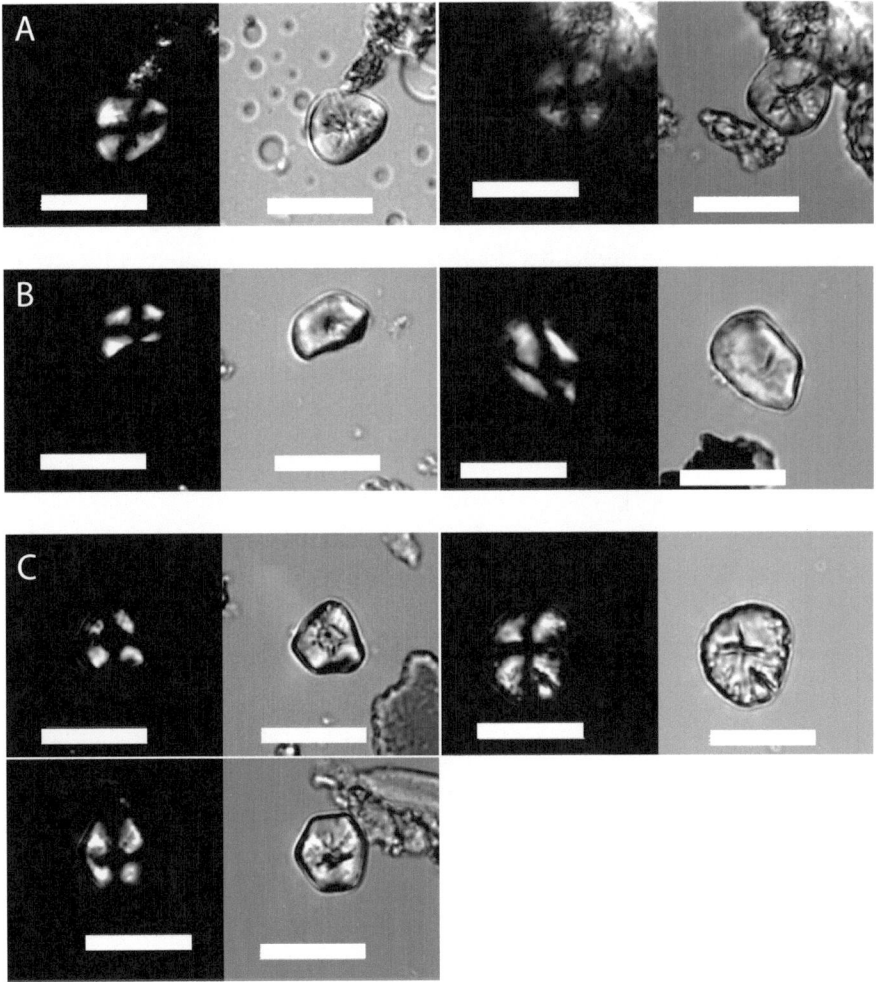

Figure 3.3 Starch granules with diagnostic damage. *A*, Manioc starch granules with evidence for fermentation (intensive fissuring). *B*, Algarroba starches with evidence for grinding (pitting) and boiling (indistinct crosses). *C*, Maize starches exhibiting evidence of grinding (pitting) and fermentation (fissuring). Image by S. L. Weber.

Ramírez 1995, 93). Evidence for fermented maize and manioc along with algarroba is the most common combination of any co-occurring cultigens, and their presence within the same vessels strongly suggests a distinctive chicha recipe using these three ingredients rather than the product of repeated use with different dishes. This combination of ingredients was identified in an undecorated neckless *olla* (MB29), a necked jar (MB69), and a small burnished bowl (MB75), suggesting that these vessel forms represent chicha preparation and serving vessels at Atalla. The recurrence of these three nonlocal ingredients to produce a distinctive chicha also highlights the importance of foreign cultigens for the Atalla community and suggests intensive contact with lowland peoples. These finds suggest that Atalla's increasing engagement in interregional exchange with the Peruvian south coast may have been motivated by the social and religious exigencies of producing increasingly larger quantities of maize- and manioc-based, algarroba-flavored chicha.

DISCUSSION

EATING LOCAL: EXPLOITATION OF LOCAL FLORA AND FAUNA

While the variety of nonlocal plants at Atalla indicates that residents had regular interactions with peoples from other regions, daily cuisine shared at Atalla was primarily highland in origin. Potatoes, olluco, and pseudocereals identified at the site are typical of dietary habits in the Peruvian highlands during the Formative Period as attested by macrobotanical, microbotanical, and stable isotope data from contemporaneous highland ceremonial sites like Chavín de Huántar (Sayre 2010), Campanayuc Rumi (Matsumoto 2010), and Chavín de Huántar (Burger and van der Merwe 1990). The microbotanical evidence for the exploitation of local products at Atalla is complemented by both the zooarchaeological data and stable oxygen ($\delta^{18}O$) isotope analysis of the faunal assemblage. Zooarchaeological analyses revealed that meat sources consumed at the site were entirely of local, highland origin and that residents butchered locally raised camelids on-site in addition to exploiting them for fleece and transport (Weber 2019). Camelids made up the majority (82%–85%) of the taxonomically identifiable specimens, with minor contributions from deer, small mammals, and birds (Weber 2019, 79). Stable oxygen isotope ($\delta^{18}O$) analysis conducted on camelid teeth from Atalla provides supporting evidence that camelids were used to transport resources between the highlands and lowlands (Weber 2019, 79). Thus, while Atalla residents' diets consisted primarily of highland tubers, pseudocereals, and meat, they imported nonlocal plants to produce specialized foods and beverages for ritual purposes.

DRINKING IMPORTED: MAIZE, MANIOC, AND ALGARROBA CHICHA

Despite the highland origin of the faunal assemblage and much of the botanical assemblage, Atalla residents also had access to nonlocal plant foods. The use of these "foreign" resources would have required specific preparation knowledge, as incorporating exotic plants can have dangerous effects. For example, bitter manioc must be processed through a series of time-intensive tasks (fermentation, soaking, and drying) to remove harmful cyanogenic compounds before the plant is safe for consumption (Cardoso et al. 2005). Migrants, pilgrims, or traders may have brought agricultural products or prepared foodstuffs to exchange at ceremonial centers, and they may have taught Atalla's residents to prepare these foods.

Furthermore, the presence of fermented manioc starch granules suggests that chicha containing manioc was produced on-site from whole, fresh tubers. Unprocessed, nonlocal foodstuffs would have risked spoiling if not prepared and consumed soon after harvesting. Manioc in particular spoils within three days after it is harvested if no preservation methods are used (Kay 1987; Piperno and Pearsall 1998). Furthermore, fermented beverages made from manioc are generally made using fresh tubers and are meant to be consumed soon after they're prepared (Sztutman 2008). Thus, the timely production of fermented chicha would have required direct contact through the expedient sourcing of perishable products, and perhaps labor, from communities at lower altitudes. Atalla residents' demand for a specific type of nonlocal beverage would have necessitated sustained, intimate connections with distant communities or trading partners who provided both access to nonlocal foods and knowledge of their preparation.

DRINK IN THE ANDEAN CONTEXT

Although algarroba and manioc are not what typically come to mind when we speak of chicha in the Andes, there are several ethnographic, historical, and archaeological precedents in South America for the use of these ingredients in fermented beverages. While today the word *chicha* is most commonly associated with maize-based drafts, Spanish chroniclers used it as a catchall term to describe any indigenous drink—fermented or not—regardless of the region in which it was identified (Cutler and Cardenas 1947; Goldstein, Coleman Goldstein, and Williams 2009). For instance, ancient peoples fermented other foodstuffs such as *molle* (*Schinus molle*), a berry produced by an evergreen tree native to the Andes, to create a chicha associated with Wari cultural identity (Goldstein and Coleman 2004; Goldstein, Coleman Goldstein, and Williams 2009; Sayre et al. 2012; Valdez 2012). Recent ethnohistoric and archaeological studies have also highlighted the importance of regionally specific beverages as markers of local cuisine and symbols of group identity (Bray 2003; Lema, Capparelli, and Martínez 2012; Orgaz 2012; Weismantel 2009). We briefly review some ethnographic and archaeological examples of manioc- and algarroba-based beverages that hint at the wide variety of regional drink recipes that incorporated these ingredients and that may have existed in the precontact Andes.

For peoples living in the adjacent tropical lowlands, manioc beers, in addition to maize-based beverages, are central to ritual and domestic life and are considered food as well as intoxicants (Apolinário 2019; Noelli and Brochado 1998). Manioc (*Manihot escultenta* var. Crantz), which is also known as cassava or yuca, is a perennial shrub that has been domesticated and cultivated primarily as a root crop. Manioc roots, both of the bitter and sweet varieties, are rich in starch, making this plant a desirable staple that can be turned into flour, fermented, or eaten whole (Piperno and Pearsall 1998). However, the bitter variety must be processed to be safe to eat (Cardoso et al. 2005). While more commonly associated with the eastern tropical lowlands, manioc was consumed on the Peruvian coast by the Late Preceramic (ca. 4200–1800 BCE; Ugent, Pozorski, and Pozorski 1982).[5]

---

5. However, given the morphology of the manioc starches from Atalla, it appears that *both* Amazonian and coastal manioc were imported to Atalla (Weber 2019, 132).

Although drinks made from algarroba are not as extensively documented in the Central Andes as those made from maize, the diverse uses of algarroba, the fruit from the algarrobo,[6] in foods and beverages point to its regional importance, particularly in northwest Argentina, northern Chile, and parts of coastal Peru. Algarrobo (*Prosopis* sp.) is a leguminous tree native to dry regions of South America that produces sweet, edible seed pods. *Añapa* and *ulpo* are two nonfermented algarroba beverages from the southern Andes, the latter being produced by mixing maize and algarroba flours to make a drink or porridge. Ulpo, in particular, is traditionally consumed by shepherds and underweight or ill children because of its high caloric content and relative ease of preparation (Capparelli and Lema 2011). *Aloja* is a fermented algarroba beverage from northwestern Argentina and northern Chile, which served as a distinctive cultural marker during the Inka conquest (Orgaz 2012). Today, on Peru's north coast, algarroba is frequently used in the production of *algarrobina*,[7] a sweet syrup used to flavor drinks and other foods, and less commonly in *yupisín*, a drink made by boiling the pods (Grados and Cruz 1996). We suggest that the specific chicha recipe of maize, manioc, and algarroba identified at Atalla may represent an antecedent to these contemporary, ethnographically documented beverages from other parts of the Andes.

Plants and foodstuffs used to prepare chichas are deeply intertwined with notions of social organization and regional and ethnic identity. In particular we point to the significance of the algarrobo tree in the study area in question. Today on Peru's south coast, Silverman (1993) reported that *chicha de huarango*, an algarroba chicha, is produced in the summer when the fruits are in season. She suggests that algarrobo represents the physical embodiment of south coast *ayllus*,[8] which were organized into groups of households known as *huarangas* (Silverman 1993). Furthermore, the myths and oral histories of the Ica Valley refer to places where huarangos grow as good places to settle, and the trees themselves are honored for their ability to provide for humans (Beresford-Jones 2004). The fermented beverage incorporating maize, manioc, and algarroba that we have identified from the highland site of Atalla would have been

---

6. Also referred to as *huarango*.

7. Also known as *arrope de algarroba*.

8. A fictive or biological kin group.

inalienable from its cultural associations with the lowland places and people from whence these plants were sourced.

ETHNOBOTANICAL IDENTITIES

When archaeologists move beyond the identification of plant species to the reconstruction of recipes, new interpretive possibilities emerge offering insights into ancient social relationships and identities. One's knowledge and use of a range of plants for food, drink, medicine, decoration, or industrial uses creates a kind of "ethnobotanical identity" that reinforces a person's cultural affiliation and place in society. This is particularly true in the ancient Central Andes, a region with such a stark range of environmental zones and microclimates where one's knowledge of and access to plant resources would have been limited by geographical region. Nonetheless, well-connected highland settlements, such as Atalla, were afforded access to nonlocal foodstuffs from lower-elevation areas during the Formative Period. This meeting of culinary cultures between the groups from these different regions may have prompted the development of consumption restrictions aimed at establishing and maintaining group identity or status (Gaoue et al. 2017; Hastorf 2017, 127–28; Vinton et al. 2009). Thus the use of foodstuffs with inalienable ties to peoples on the south coast by Atalla residents demonstrates an explicit desire to physically and symbolically link these two groups of people. The pervasiveness of nonlocal plant resources across both the domestic and public sectors of the site suggests that "exotic" foodstuffs were not restricted to a subset of Atalla's residents. However, the greatest diversity of different plant species was recorded in the temple, which suggests that consumption of nonlocal foods was a part of the ceremonies taking place there (see table 3.1). It seems likely that coastal peoples may have been invited to partake in these festivities during certain times of the year.

Even limited or inconsistent access to and use of foreign foodstuffs expresses desire, often because of a product's indexical relationship with that foreign culture or association with worldliness and prestige. Globally, alcoholic beverages (particularly wine) have typically served as elite commodities with important roles in ritual (Dietler 2006). For example, Celtic leaders imported Etruscan wines and associated drinking paraphernalia as a means of elevating their local political status by flaunting their wealth and connection to a global economy (Dietler 1990). Studies on other comestible commodities, such as black pepper and sugar (Mintz 1985; Sheridan 1994), have demonstrated how the demand for certain flavors can play a significant role in driving long-distance exchange. Such exotic flavoring agents are often value laden, and motivation for their acquisition lies in an emulative desire for the status such goods can confer (Hastorf 2017, 149). Through this lens, algarroba-flavored beverages at Atalla may have been sought after for their indexical relationship with an emergent cosmopolitan identity that was developing across Chavín centers during the Formative Period (e.g., Young, forthcoming).

CONCLUSION

If commensality is "aimed at the construction of social bonds and networks" (Bray 2012, 205), then what kinds of bonds and networks were forged at Atalla with a chicha crafted from maize, manioc, and algarroba? Within the context of the ritual practices emerging during the Andean Formative Period, a maize-based chicha may have projected a prestigious, cosmopolitan identity associated with the Chavín Interaction Sphere, while the specific variation of adding manioc and algarroba reflects an intimate relationship with peoples from the Peruvian south coast. Consumption of this "exotic" chicha can be interpreted as a ritual strategy that reinforced exchange relationships, just as annual festivals bring together contemporary herders and agriculturalists—who depend on exchange with one another—into ritual activities and exogamous marriage alliances that renew their mutual commitment and reliance (e.g., Paerregaard 1992). Isbell's (1977, 84–88) observation of *Yarqa Aspiy*,[9] carried out in chapels located at the transition between ecological zones, further underscores the mediating role of rituals in symbolically unifying individuals residing in different ecozones. This recipe—so far only identified at Atalla—may have been a regional innovation that projected the worldly status of Atalla residents and invited coastal communities to participate in the social world of the Huancavelica highlands. Further investigation of chicha recipes from contemporaneous communities will be necessary to confirm or challenge this hypothesis.

---

9. The ritualized communal cleaning of irrigation canals (Isbell 1977).

This study demonstrates how the importation of nonlocal foods acts as both driver and mediator of intercultural interaction in the south-central Andes. Based on our microbotanical results, we propose that Atalla residents prepared and consumed a special chicha produced with nonlocal knowledge from nonlocal plants. This evidence suggests that the Chavín Interaction Sphere was characterized by direct contact between groups living in the highlands and adjacent lowland zones and that these interaction networks were at least partially motivated by a desire to acquire nonlocal foodstuffs. Furthermore, these "exotic" food preferences may have been part of a wider social realignment of the Atalla community toward a supraregional cosmopolitan identity that was emerging throughout the Chavín Interaction Sphere at this time (e.g., Young 2020, forthcoming). By moving beyond a simple examination of the constituent elements of food and diet, this study demonstrates the analytical potential of identifying specific recipes in the archaeological record. Furthermore, we contribute a deeper understanding of the origins of chicha and the diversity of ancient Andean culinary practices using the lens of commensality to approach these culinary innovations as desired products and strategies of social involvement that structured the ancient Andean world.

REFERENCES

Allen, Catherine J. 1988. *The Hold Life Has: Coca and Cultural Identity in an Andean Community*. Washington, D.C.: Smithsonian Institution Press.

Allen, Catherine J. 2009. "'Let's Drink Together, My Dear!' Persistent Ceremonies in a Changing Community." In *Drink, Power, and Society in the Andes*, edited by Justin Jennings and Brenda J. Bowser, 28–48. Gainesville: University Press of Florida.

Apolinário, Juciene R. 2019. "Sabores, Saberes e o 'Pão Dos Trópicos': Contatos Interétnicos entre Indígenas e Colonizadores a Partir da Circulação e Uso da Mandioca." *Patrimônio e Memória* 15 (1): 28–46.

Appadurai, Arjun. 1981. "Gastro-Politics in Hindu South Asia." *American Ethnologist* 8 (3): 494–511. https://doi.org/10.1525/ae.1981.8.3.02a00050.

Babot, María Del Pilar. 2003. "Starch Grain Damage as an Indicator of Food Processing." In *Phytolith and Starch Research in the Australian-Pacific-Asian Regions: The State of the Art*, edited by Diane M. Hart and Lynley A. Wallis, 69–81. Canberra: Pandanus Books.

Beresford-Jones, David G. 2004. "Pre-Hispanic Prosopis-Human Relationships on the South Coast of Peru: Riparian Forests in the Context of Environmental and Cultural Trajectories of the Lower Ica Valley." PhD diss., University of Cambridge.

Bray, Tamara L. 2003. "Inka Pottery as Culinary Equipment: Food, Feasting, and Gender in Imperial State Design." *Latin American Antiquity* 14 (1): 3–28. https://doi.org//10.2307/972232.

Bray, Tamara L. 2012. "Ritual Commensality Between Human and Non-Human Persons: Investigating Native Ontologies in the Late Pre-Columbian Andean World." *Journal for Ancient Studies* 2:197–212.

Brillat-Savarin, Jean Anthelme. 1999. *The Physiology of Taste, or, Meditations on Transcendental Gastronomy.* Translated by M. F. K. Fisher. Washington, D.C.: Counterpoint Press.

Brown, Nicholas E. 2017. "Chawin and Chavín: Evidence of Interregional Interaction Involving the Peruvian Central Highlands During the Late Initial Period." *Ñawpa Pacha* 37 (2): 87–109. https://doi.org/10.1080/00776297.2017 .1390354.

Burger, Richard L. 1992. *Chavin and the Origins of Andean Civilization.* London: Thames and Hudson.

Burger, Richard L. 2008. "Chavin de Huantar and Its Sphere of Influence." In *The Handbook of South American Archaeology,* edited by Helaine Silverman and William H. Isbell, 681–706. New York: Springer.

Burger, Richard L., and Nikolaas J. van der Merwe. 1990. "Maize and the Origin of Highland Chavin Civilization: An Isotopic Perspective." *American Anthropologist* 92 (1): 85–95.

Capparelli, Aylen, and Verónica Lema. 2011. "Recognition of Post-Harvest Processing of Algarrobo (*Prosopis* spp.) as Food from Two Sites of Northwestern Argentina: An Ethnobotanical and Experimental Approach for Desiccated Macroremains." *Archaeological and Anthropological Sciences* 3 (1): 71–92. https://doi.org/10.1007/s12520-011-0052-5.

Cardoso, A. Paula, Estevao Mirione, Mario Ernesto, Fernando Massaza, Julie Cliff, M. Rezaul Haque, and J. Howard Bradbury. 2005. "Processing of Cassava Roots to Remove Cyanogens." *Journal of Food Composition and Analysis* 18 (5): 451–60. https://doi.org/10.1016/j.jfca.2004.04.002.

Crowther, Alison, Michael Haslam, Nikki Oakden, Dale Walde, and Julio Mercader. 2014. "Documenting Contamination in Ancient Starch Laboratories." *Journal of Archaeological Science* 49 (1): 90–104. https://doi.org/10.1016/j.jas .2014.04.023.

Cutler, Hugh C., and Martin Cardenas. 1947. "Chicha, a Native South American Beer." *Botanical Museum Leaflets* 13 (3): 51–5.

de Florio Ramírez, Enrique. 1995. "Elaboración Tradicional de Chicha de Jora." *Ciencia y Desarrollo* 1:92–96.

Dietler, Michael. 1990. "Driven by Drink: The Role of Drinking in the Political Economy and the Case of Early Iron Age France." *Journal of Anthropological Archaeology* 9 (4): 352–406. https://doi.org/10.1016/0278-4165(90)90011-2.

Dietler, Michael. 2006. "Alcohol: Anthropological/Archaeological Perspectives." *Annual Review of Anthropology* 35 (1): 229–49. https://doi.org/10.1146/annu rev.anthro.35.081705.123120.

Dozier, Crystal A., and Justin Jennings. 2021. "Identification of Chicha de Maiz in the Pre-Columbian Andes Through Starch Analysis: New Experimental Evidence." In *Andean Foodways: Pre-Columbian, Colonial, and Contemporary Food and Culture*, edited by John E. Staller: 187–204. Cham: Springer International.

Gaoue, Orou G., Michael A. Coe, Matthew Bond, Georgia Hart, Barnabas C. Seyler, and Heather McMillen. 2017. "Theories and Major Hypotheses in Ethnobotany." *Economic Botany* 71 (3): 269–87. https://doi.org/10.1007/s12 231-017-9389-8.

Giovannetti, Marco A., Verónica S. Lema, Carlos G. Bartoli, and Aylen Capparelli. 2008. "Starch Grain Characterization of *Prosopis chilensis* (Mol.) Stuntz and *P. Flexuosa* DC, and the Analysis of Their Archaeological Remains in Andean South America." *Journal of Archaeological Science* 35 (11): 2973–85. https://doi.org/10.1016/j.jas.2008.06.009.

Goldstein, David J., and Robin C. Coleman. 2004. "*Schinus molle* L. (Anacardiaceae) *Chicha* Production in the Central Andes." *Economic Botany* 58 (4): 523–9.

Goldstein, David J., Robin C. Coleman Goldstein, and Patrick R. Williams. 2009. "You Are What You Drink: A Sociocultural Reconstruction of PreHispanic Fermented Beverage Use at Cerro Baúl, Moquegua, Peru." In *Drink, Power, and Society in the Andes*, edited by Justin Jennings and Brenda J. Bowser, 133–65. Gainesville: University Press of Florida.

Grados, Nora, and Gaston Cruz. 1996. "New Approaches to Industrialization of Algarrobo (*Prosopis pallida*) Pods in Peru." In *Prosopis: Semiarid Fuelwood and Forage Tree Building Consensus for the Disenfranchised*, edited by Peter Felker and James Moss, 25–42. Washington D.C.: Center for Semi-Arid Forest Resources.

Hastorf, Christine A. 2017. *The Social Archaeology of Food*. New York: Cambridge University Press.

Henry, Amanda G. 2014. "Formation and Taphonomic Processes Affecting Starch Granules." In *Method and Theory in Paleoethnobotany*, edited by John M. Marston, Jade d'Alpoim Guedes, and Christina Warinner, 35–50. Boulder: University Press of Colorado.

Henry, Amanda G., Holly F. Hudson, and Dolores R. Piperno. 2009. "Changes in Starch Grain Morphologies from Cooking." *Journal of Archaeological Science* 36 (3): 915–22. https://doi.org/10.1016/j.jas.2008.11.008.

Ikehara, Hugo C., J. Fiorella Paipay, and Koichiro Shibata. 2013. "Feasting with Zea Mays in the Middle and Late Formative North Coast of Peru." *Latin American Antiquity* 24 (2): 217–31. https://doi.org/10.7183/1045-6635.24.2.217.

Isbell, Billie Jean. 1977. *To Defend Ourselves: Ecology and Ritual in an Andean Village*. Prospect Heights, Ill.: Waveland Press.

Jennings, Justin. 2005. "La Chichera y El Patrón: Chicha and the Energetics of Feasting in the Prehistoric Andes." *Archeological Papers of the American Anthropological Association* 14 (1): 241–59. https://doi.org/10.1525/ap3a.2004.14.241.

Kay, Daisy. 1987. *Tropical Root Crops*. 2nd ed. London: Tropical Development and Research Institute.

Lema, Verónica S., Aylen Capparelli, and Analia Martínez. 2012. "Las Vías del Algarrobo: Antiguas Preparaciones Culinarias en el Noroeste Argentino." In *Las Manos en la Masa: Arqueologías, Antropologías e Historias de la Alimentación en Suramérica*, edited by María Del Pilar Babot, María Marschoff, and Francisco Pazzarelli, 639–66. Córdoba: Universidad Nacional de Córdoba.

Leonard, William R., and R. Brooke Thomas. 1988. "Changing Dietary Patterns in the Peruvian Andes." *Ecology of Food and Nutrition* 21 (4): 37–41. https://doi.org/10.1080/03670244.1988.9991039.

Matsumoto, Yuichi. 2010. "The Prehistoric Ceremonial Center of Campanayuq Rumi: Interregional Interactions in the South-Central Highlands of Peru." PhD diss., Yale University.

Matsumoto, Yuichi, Yuri Cavero Palomino, and Roy Gutierrez Silva. 2013. "The Domestic Occupation of Campanayuq Rumi: Implications for Understanding the Initial Period and Early Horizon of the South-Central Andes of Peru." *Andean Past* 1:169–213.

Mesía, Christian. 2014. "Festines y Poder en Chavín de Huántar Durante el Formativo Tardío en los Andes Centrales." *Chungará Revista Chilena de Antropología* 46 (3): 313–44. http://dx.doi.org/10.4067/S0717-73562014000300002.

Mintz, Sidney W. 1985. *Sweetness and Power: The Place of Sugar in Modern History*. New York: Penguin Books.

Nesbitt, Jason, Yuichi Matsumoto, and Yuri Cavero Palomino. 2019. "Campanayuq Rumi and Arpiri: Two Civic-Ceremonial Centers on the Southern Periphery of the Chavín Interaction Sphere." *Ñawpa Pacha* 39 (1): 57–75. https://doi.org/10.1080/00776297.2019.1580834.

Noelli, Francisco Silva, and José Proenza Brochado. 1998. "O Cauim e as Beberagens dos Guarani e Tupinambá: Equipamentos, Técnicas de Preparacção e Consumo." *Revista do Museu de Arqueologia e Etnologia* 8: 117–28. https://doi.org/10.11606/issn.2448-1750.revmae.1998.109531.

Orgaz, Martín. 2012. "Chicha y Aloja: Inkas y Autoridades Locales en el Sector Meridional del Valle de Yocavil—Catamarca—Argentina." *Surandino Monográfico* 2 (2): 1–38.

Paerregaard, Karsten. 1992. "Complementarity and Duality: Oppositions Between Agriculturists and Herders in an Andean Village." *Ethnology* 31 (1): 15–26. https://doi.org/10.2307/3773439.

Pagán-Jiménez, Jaime R. 2015. *Almidones: Guía de Material Comparativo Modernos del Ecuador para los Estudios Paleoetnobotánicos en el Neotrópico*. Buenos Aires: Aspah Ediciones.

Piperno, Dolores R., and Deborah M. Pearsall. 1998. *The Origins of Agriculture in the Lowland Neotropics*. New York: Academic Press.

Pulgar-Vidal, Javier. 1941. "Las Ocho Regiones Naturales del Perú." *Terra Brasilis*, no. 3, 1–20. https://doi.org/10.4000/terrabrasilis.1027.

Sayre, Matthew P. 2010. "Life Across the River: Agricultural, Ritual, and Production Practices at Chavín de Huántar, Perú." PhD diss., University of California, Berkeley.

Sayre, Matthew, David Goldstein, William Whitehead, and Patrick Williams. 2012. "A Marked Preference." *Ñawpa Pacha* 32 (2): 231–58. https://doi.org/10 .1179/naw.2012.32.2.231.

Sheridan, Richard B. 1994. *Sugar and Slavery: An Economic History of the British West Indies, 1623–1775*. Kingston, Jamaica: Canoe Press, University of West Indies Press.

Silverman, Helaine. 1993. *Cahuachi in the Ancient Nasca World*. Iowa City: University of Iowa Press.

Sztutman, Renato. 2008. "Cauim, Substância e Efeito: Sobre o Consumo de Bebidas Fermentadas entre os Ameríndios." In *Drogas e Cultura: Novas Perspectivas*, edited by Beatriz Caiuby Labate, Sandra Lucia Goulart, Mauricio Fiore, Edward MacRae, and Henrique Carneiro, 219–50. Salvador: Edufba.

Thompson, L. G., E. Mosley-Thompson, M. E. Davis, P.-N. Lin, K. A. Henderson, J. Cole-Dai, J. F. Bolzan, and K-b Liu. 1995. "Late Glacial Stage and Holocene Tropical Ice Core Records from Huascaran, Peru." *Science* 269 (5220): 46–50. https://doi.org/10.1126/science.269.5220.46.

Ugent, Donald, Shelia Pozorski, and Thomas Pozorski. 1982. "Archaeological Potato Tuber Remains from the Casma Valley of Peru." *Economic Botany* 36 (2): 182–92. https://doi.org/10.1007/BF02858715.

Valdez, Lidio M. 2012. "Molle Beer Production in a Peruvian Central Highland Valley." *Journal of Anthropological Research* 68 (1): 71–93. https://doi.org/10 .3998/jar.0521004.0068.103.

Vinton, Sheila Dorsey, Linda Perry, Karl J. Reinhard, Calogero M. Santoro, and Isabel Teixeira-Santos. 2009. "Impact of Empire Expansion on Household Diet: The Inka in Northern Chile's Atacama Desert." *PLoS One* 4 (11): e8069. https://doi.org/10.1371/journal.pone.0008069.

Weber, Sadie L. 2019. "Pulling Abundance out of Thin Air: The Role of Camelid Pastoralism at 3000 B.P." PhD diss., Harvard University.

Weismantel, Mary. 1991. "Maize Beer and Andean Social Transformations: Drunken Indians, Bread Babies, and Chosen Women." *MLN* 106 (4): 861–79. https://doi.org/10.2307/2904628.

Weismantel, Mary. 2009. "Have a Drink: Chicha, Performance, and Politics." In *Drink, Power, and Society in the Andes*, edited by Justin Jennings and Brenda J. Bowser, 257–77. Gainesville: University Press of Florida.

Young, Michelle E. 2020. "The Chavín Phenomenon in Huancavelica, Peru: Interregional Interaction, Ritual Practice, and Social Transformations at Atalla." PhD diss., Yale University.

Young, Michelle E. Forthcoming. "Horizon, Interaction Sphere, Cult? A View of the 'Chavín Phenomenon' from Huancavelica." In *Reconsidering the Chavín Phenomenon in the 21st Century*, edited by R. Burger and J. Nesbitt. Washington, D.C.: Dumbarton Oaks.

4

Eating from the Earth on the Shores of Lake Titicaca

A Multimethod Approach to Understanding
the Diets of Taraco Peninsula Inhabitants

*Melanie J. Miller, Maria C. Bruno, José M. Capriles, Iain
Kendall, Richard P. Evershed, and Christine A. Hastorf*

Archaeologists study foodways because eating reveals people's relationships with their environment, economics, politics, and values (Hastorf 2017b). Exciting recent developments in Andean archaeological scholarship, noted throughout this volume, are helping to unravel the dynamic ways residents adapted their diets to diverse locales across time, and incorporating Indigenous ontologies broadens our interpretations and engages with data in a more culturally meaningful manner. By using the frame of Indigenous American animistic concepts of sentience and interaction in our inquiries into the long-term resilience of Andean residents, we are able to envision and understand past food activities in a more nuanced way. The Andean "cosmospace" (Bray, this volume) and the earth beings (*achachillas*) that reside throughout the landscape (Alconini, this volume) inform us about the required interactions of successful living through gifting, often called feeding (Allen 2016; de la Cadena 2015). Thus, the gifting of food is not just a necessity for organic things but also the basis of human society that nurtures all beings, from the landscape to the ancestors. What animates all of this is the life force (*sami*) that moves between beings through nurturing (*uywaña*). This interactive nurturing is the basis for the resilient success that the altiplano residents have had over the millennia of their existence throughout the Lake Titicaca Basin. It is the history of this resilience of feeding that we attempt to uncover here.

Decades of archaeological research on the Taraco Peninsula in the southern Lake Titicaca Basin have focused on gathering evidence of the subsistence practices of its early inhabitants (map 4.1). The Taraco

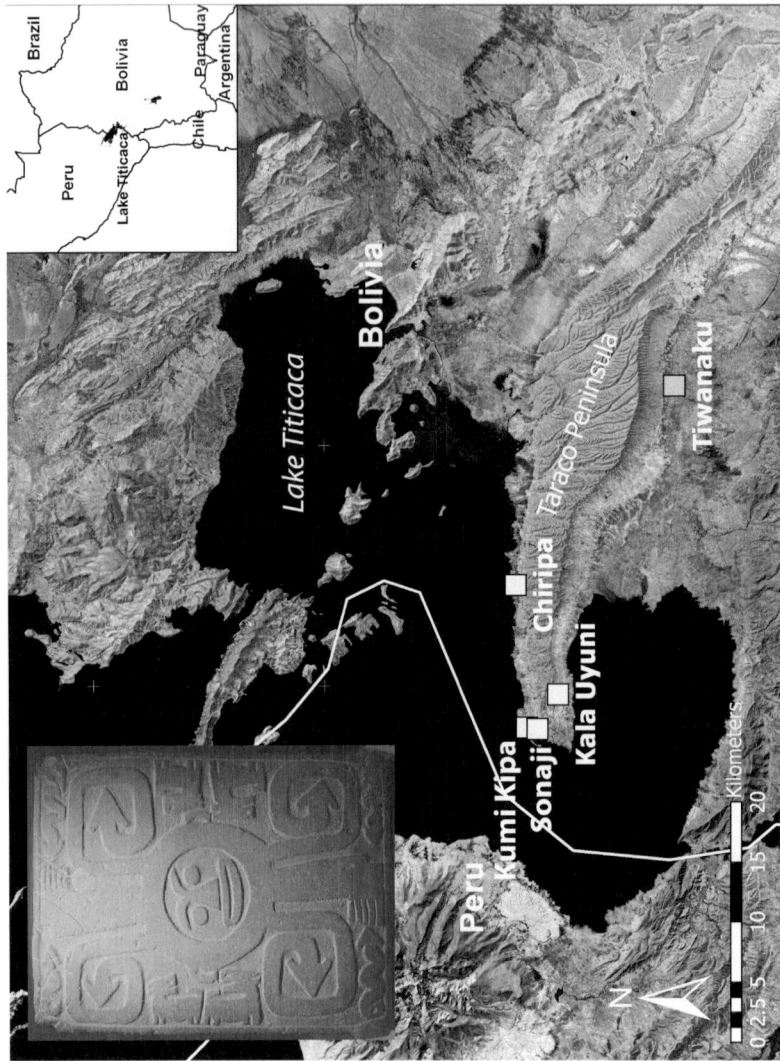

Map 4.1 Taraco Peninsula and the southern Lake Titicaca Basin, Bolivia. *White squares* = excavated sites discussed in the text. *Gray square* = Middle Horizon center of Tiwanaku. *Upper-left*, a picture of the Sami stone. J. M. Capriles, C. A. Hastorf.

Archaeological Project (TAP) has targeted the archaeological record of food practices (botanicals, fauna, lithics, ceramics, human remains) as a window into the daily lives and experiences of the people who lived there. The significance of our work is the large amount of high-quality archaeological data we have accumulated, which provides a deep multimethod view of human diets over time.

Archaeological studies of human foodways rely on material evidence of the plants, animals, and fungi that humans consumed. Most forms of evidence, such as faunal and archaeobotanical analyses from recovered excavated materials, are indirect in that they are traces of foods that were discarded. These fragments cannot tell us specifically who was consuming those foods, when, in what proportions, or what the meanings of a meal were. One of the most commonly employed direct methods of measuring diet is stable isotope analysis of human bone collagen, which uses skeletal chemistry to reconstruct individual dietary patterns (Ambrose and Krigbaum 2003). In combination with other data sources, stable isotopes can help to clarify what people ate in the past and how their food habits reflected biocultural and ecological aspects of their life experiences. This is particularly important in a region like Lake Titicaca, where multiple lines of evidence reveal that local inhabitants farmed quinoa and tubers, herded camelids, hunted small game, gathered plants across their landscape, and fished in the lake. Out of this mix of resources, we encountered challenges in unpacking lake versus terrestrial foods, particularly fish and maize. This chapter highlights how combining data sets from macroremains (animal bones, wood, and seeds) and microremains (starches, phytoliths, isotopes, genetics, and proteomics) can solve old problems and bring new questions about eating to light.

EARLY FOODWAYS ON THE TARACO PENINSULA

Since 1992, TAP has studied the first settled communities in the Lake Titicaca Basin through the influence of the region's first large polity, Tiwanaku (Hastorf 1999). The fertile altiplano landscape, situated above 3800 masl, provides zones to gather, hunt, fish, cultivate, and herd. While people foraged in this part of the Andean highlands for millennia, the earliest settling began around 1400 BCE with what archaeologists call the Formative Period, which is divided into three phases (Early, Middle, and Late) with transitions determined by cultural and material changes (Bruno et al. 2021). On the peninsula these transitions date to ~800 BCE (Early to Middle) and ~200 BCE (Middle to Late). The first community structures, sunken courts with plastered and painted stone walls, were built during the Early Formative at a few settlements around the basin, including Chiripa. The houses were more ephemeral, made of sod and adobe. The Middle Formative sees larger communal structures at more settlements that include stepped platforms topped with small chambers. The main cultural change occurs during the Late Formative, when earlier communal structures are abandoned and new elaborate platforms are built. Throughout the Formative, the materialization of community noted in the architecture as well as the imagery that was cut in stone and painted on ceramics illustrates these animating ontologies of nurturing, feeding, and life force (Hastorf 2007, 2017a; map 4.1). The Formative communities eventually coalesced to form Tiwanaku, a major, long-lived ceremonial center. The Taraco Peninsula defines the northeastern edge of the Tiwanaku Valley, where the Tiwanaku capital developed during the first millennium CE (Janusek 2006; Kolata 2003). Despite its proximity to Tiwanaku (~15 km), there is little evidence for Tiwanaku's influence on the Taraco Peninsula up until around CE 600. Over time, the people who settled on the Taraco Peninsula developed deep relationships with plants, animals, water, and land, which we examine here.

THE ARCHAEOBOTANICAL EVIDENCE

Systematic collection of over 800 flotation samples from four sites (Chiripa, Kala Uyuni, Kumi Kipa, and Sonaji) provide a robust database of carbonized macrobotanical remains organized by phase, context, and site. They have been quantified by ubiquity and density (Bruno 2014; Whitehead 2007; Langlie 2008). These remains include wood charcoal and fragments of storage tissue (parenchyma) from tubers but are dominated by seeds from both domesticated and wild plants. The abundance of seeds is probably due to the burning of camelid dung for fuel in this mostly treeless region (Bruno and Hastorf 2016; Hastorf and Wright 1998). Phytoliths and starch grains have been analyzed from soils, lithic and ceramic artifacts, and human teeth from Chiripa and Kala Uyuni. These microanalyses have been particularly important in detecting the rare presence of maize (*Zea mays*) in the sequence (Logan, Hastorf, and Pearsall 2012; Reilly 2017).

Archaeobotanical analyses identify local staple food crops as well as specialized, exotic foods (fig. 4.1*A*). Across both the Formative and Tiwanaku times, farmers focused on two major crop types: tubers—the most archaeologically visible being potatoes (*Solanum tuberosum* spp.) and oca (*Oxalis tuberosa*)—and seeds—quinoa (*Chenopodium quinoa*) and kañawa (*Chenopodium pallidicaule*). Over time, quinoa remains steady while tubers appear to increase (Bruno 2014). Scant maize macrobotanical fragments appear in the Late Formative, increasing only in the Tiwanaku Period. Maize starch grains are present in vessels from the Middle Formative through Tiwanaku times. The earliest maize was probably introduced from other regions as a specialty food, but farmers eventually selected for a variety that could be grown in temperate areas along the shoreline.

THE ZOOARCHAEOLOGICAL EVIDENCE

Faunal material was systematically collected from all excavated sediments using ¼ inch screens and heavy fractions (0.5 mm) of the flotation samples (Capriles et al. 2014; Moore et al. 2010). The Number of Identified Specimens (NISP), Minimum Number of Individuals (MNI), and weight were recorded from selected contexts. Most flotation heavy fractions were sorted into class-level taxonomic categories to estimate densities and ubiquity (fig. 4.1*B*).

Camelid bone dominates the TAP faunal assemblage (97% of all screened bone), indicating that llamas (*Lama glama*) and alpacas (*Viguna pacos*) were used for transportation, wool, meat, dung fertilizer, and fuel. Camelid species, age determinations, and body size estimates are derived from comparative osteological analyses as well as consideration of archaeological contextual information. The bone frequencies suggest that camelids slowly increased in importance over time, probably because of increasing human population and trade rather than environmental changes (Bruno et al. 2021).

Birds and fish are the resources most directly associated with Lake Titicaca (fig. 4.1*B*). A variety of birds and their eggs were brought to the settlements at a low but fairly steady rate. Approximately two dozen

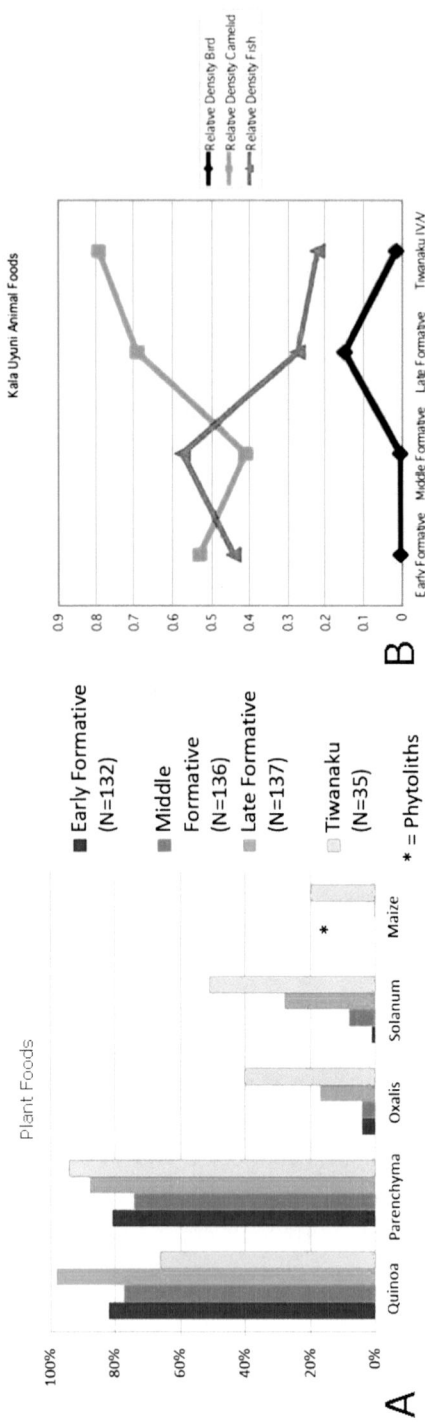

Figure 4.1 Food data through time. *A*, ubiquity (percent presence) of macrobotanical remains of the major plant food categories by time period: quinoa seeds, fragments of parenchyma interpreted to be remnants of tubers, and seeds of *Oxalis* spp. and *Solanum* spp. While these seeds could also come from wild species, we interpret their increased presence as indicative of tuber cultivation (Bruno 2014). The presence of maize in the Middle Formative is indicated by microbotanicals and shown here by an asterisk. Macrobotanical maize kernel and cob fragments are subsequently represented by the bars (note that the Late Formative is only 1%). *B*, relative density data for different faunal bone categories (birds, camelids, fish) over time at the site of Kala Uyuni (data courtesy of Katherine Moore). M. C. Bruno, J. M. Capriles, C. A. Hastorf.

different species of fish belonging to two genera have been described for Lake Titicaca, and many have been exploited and consumed by humans. Most species are killifish of the genus *Orestias*, a small fish ranging from a few to less than 20 cm (Parenti 1984). The catfish genus *Trichomycterus* includes at least two benthic species distributed in the lake and its tributaries.

Lake Wiñaymarka has a dynamic history owing to it being quite shallow and changing area and depth with weather and climatic events (fig. 4.2). The relationship between Lake Titicaca fish evidence and the changing levels of the lake over time has been investigated using the heavy fraction fish remains ($n = 367$; Capriles et al. 2014). It has been hypothesized that people used more lake resources when lake levels were higher, as people did not have to travel as far to reach the shore. However, recent data do not support this pattern (Weide et al. 2017; Bruno et al. 2021). The highest density of fish bone (from flotation samples) is found in the Early and Middle Formative Periods, when lake levels were low, while fish bone densities decline in the Late Formative and Tiwanaku phases as lake levels began to rise (fig. 4.2; Abbott et al. 1997; Weide et al. 2017). The lake dynamically fluctuated throughout the period of study, yet fishing persisted as a low but steady activity (fig. 4.2; Bruno et al. 2021).

STABLE ISOTOPIC EVIDENCE FOR FOODWAYS

STABLE ISOTOPE BACKGROUND: CARBON (Δ^{13}C) AND NITROGEN (Δ^{15}N)

The chemistry of human skeletal remains informs us about what a person ate during life (Lee-Thorp 2008). While human teeth record information about a persons' diet during childhood (when most teeth develop; Wright and Schwarcz 1998), human bone chemistry documents the average diet from at least the final decade before death (Fahy et al. 2017). We included tooth samples for dietary reconstruction because previous isotopic testing showed inconsistent chemical preservation of bone for individuals buried on the Taraco Peninsula. Using carbon (δ^{13}C) and nitrogen (δ^{15}N) data from dentin collagen, we focused on childhood diets, which may be the same or different from the diets of adults (Miller, Agarwal, and Langebaek 2018; Miller et al. 2020).

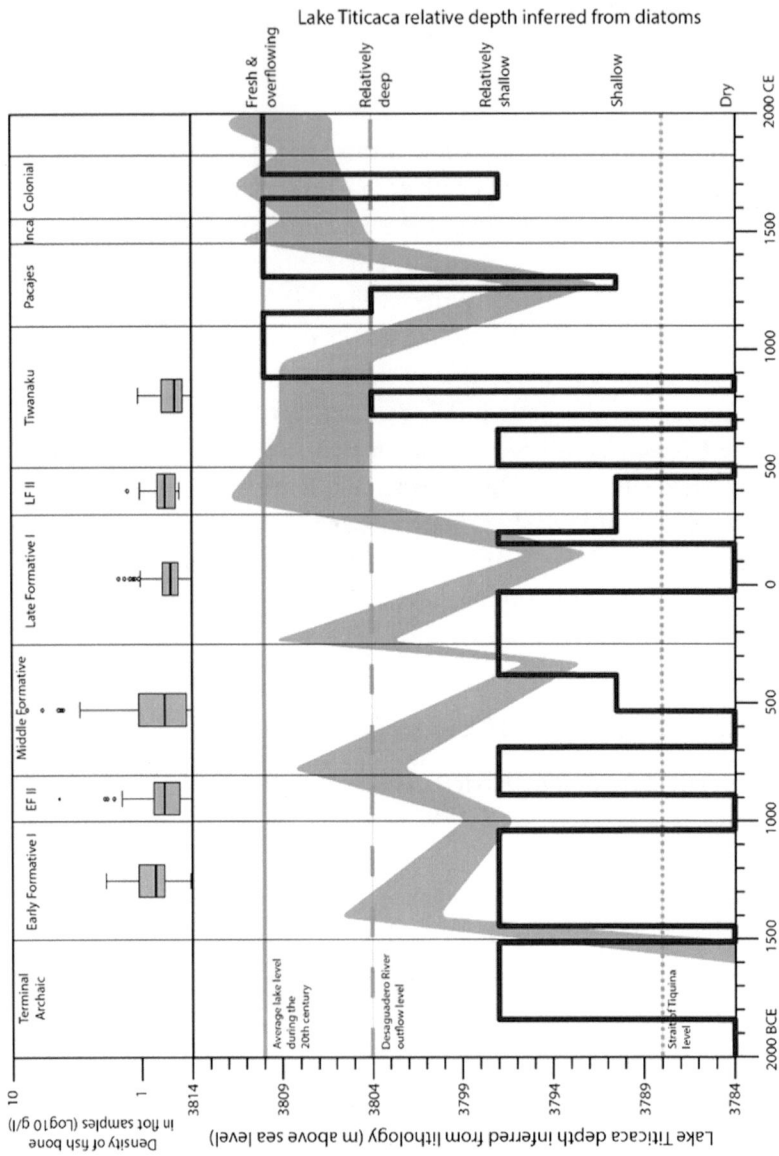

Figure 4.2 *Upper plot,* changing fish bone densities (g/l) in flotation samples over time. *Lower plot,* lake level changes over time as documented by Abbott et al. (1997; *light gray band*), in comparison to lake levels inferred from recent diatom research by Weide et al. (2017; *dark gray line*). M. C. Bruno, J. M. Capriles, C. A. Hastorf.

Like most archaeological isotopic dietary reconstruction studies, we rely on bulk collagen analysis, which studies complete and intact collagen molecules (Ambrose and Krigbaum 2003). Collagen, a structural protein, can be broken down into its individual amino acids, the "building blocks" of proteins, containing carbon, nitrogen, hydrogen, and oxygen. Individual amino acids have the potential to be studied using the stable isotope chemistry of each of those elements. Further, since collagen preferentially routes some amino acids directly from dietary sources into its own structure, we can study those specific amino acids derived from skeletal collagen as an indicator of their original dietary source (McMahon et al. 2010; Fogel and Tuross 2003). Amino acids can be (i) essential, meaning they must be derived from the diet and cannot be synthesized de novo by the body, (ii) conditionally essential, meaning the body can synthesize this form from other amino acids but usually demand outstrips production so dietary sourcing is required, or (iii) nonessential, meaning they can be created by the body (Wang et al. 2013; Reeds 2000). Evershed and coworkers have been studying the relationships between amino acids extracted from collagen, and a few amino acids have been identified as being useful for archaeological studies of human diets (Corr et al. 2009; Styring et al. 2015; Webb et al. 2018). The research presented here focuses on the compound-specific amino acid isotopic analysis of glycine (Gly, conditionally essential) and phenylalanine (Phe, essential), which can be useful for disentangling terrestrial and aquatic resource use in human diets and which are an opportunity to further understand human foodways in the dynamic environment of the ancient Taraco Peninsula peoples (Webb et al. 2018).

BULK STABLE ISOTOPE DATA

A large number of modern plants collected in the southern Lake Titicaca region were analyzed (Miller 2005; Miller et al. 2021). Initial results confirmed most of the terrestrial cultivated plants investigated showed typical C_3 plant values ($\delta^{13}C$ range from −25‰ to −20‰), while only the maize showed typical C_4 plant values ($\delta^{13}C$ around −12‰ to −10‰; fig. 4.3A). A number of plants from Lake Wiñaymarka were analyzed. These plants showed a very wide range of $\delta^{13}C$ values, from −28‰ to −3‰ (Miller, Capriles, and Hastorf 2010). This finding suggests there

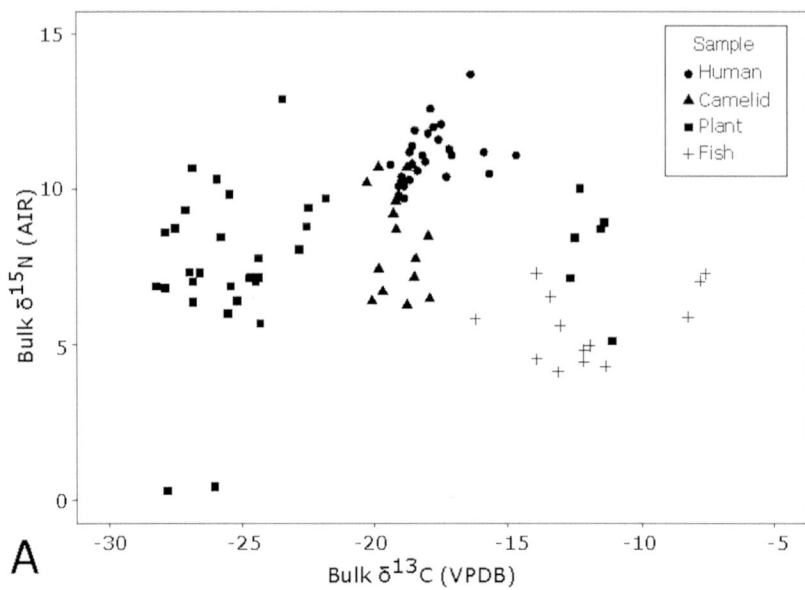

A

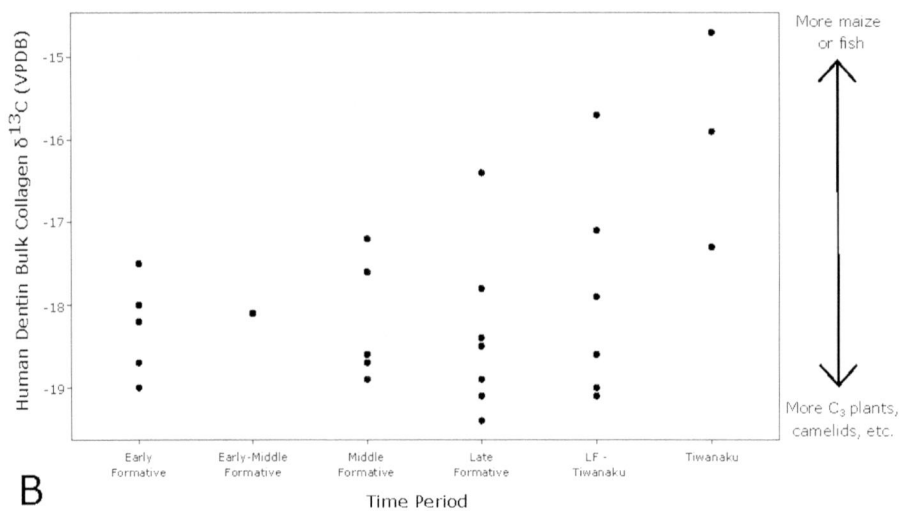

B

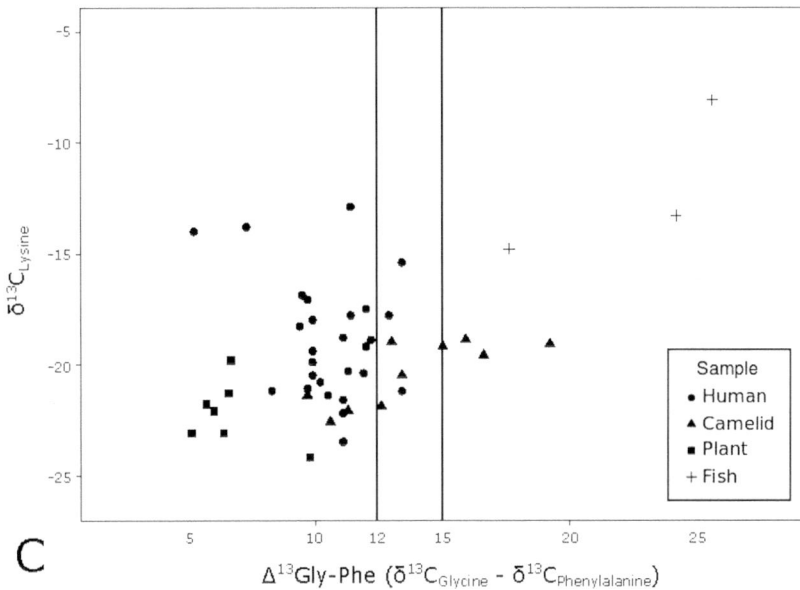

C

δ¹³C_Lysine

Δ¹³Gly-Phe (δ¹³C_Glycine − δ¹³C_Phenylalanine)

Sample
• Human
▲ Camelid
■ Plant
+ Fish

Figure 4.3 *A*, stable carbon and nitrogen isotope values for bulk samples (human tooth dentin collagen, camelid bone collagen, fish collagen, and cultivated plant tissues). Note that plant samples have not been Suess corrected, and therefore ancient plants were approximately +1.5‰ more positive than the values observed here. *B*, δ¹³C values of bulk dentin collagen from Taraco Peninsula humans plotted by time period. Note that in the Late Formative and Tiwanaku Periods, there are a handful of individuals with higher δ¹³C values, suggesting the consumption of some lake fish, maize, or both. *C*, Compound-specific amino acid stable isotope values for ancient Taraco Peninsula humans (*circle*), camelids (*triangle*), fish (*cross*), and modern plants (*square*). Δ¹³C_Gly-Phe values greater than 15‰ indicate aquatic ecosystem resource consumption, while Δ¹³C_Gly-Phe values less than 12‰ suggest terrestrial-based diets. Note all fish have Δ¹³C_Gly-Phe above 15‰, all humans have Δ¹³C_Gly-Phe values below 15‰, while the camelids show a wide range of Δ¹³C_Gly-Phe values including a few greater than 15‰, suggesting they were feeding on the lake shores. M. J. Miller, M. C. Bruno, J. M. Capriles, I. Kendall, R. P. Evershed, and C. A. Hastorf.

may be a downstream effect on the animals, including humans, that consumed lake plants (Miller, Capriles, and Hastorf 2010).

Fish from the lake had higher than expected carbon isotopes (δ^{13}C averaging around −12‰), with many having δ^{13}C values that overlap the range of typical terrestrial C_4 plants (Miller et al. 2010). Additionally, the nitrogen isotope ranges for maize and fish overlapped (fig. 4.3*A*). We realized we had a conundrum on our hands; as anthropologists who are interested in understanding the role of various foods over time, we have two important potential food sources, fish and maize, which cannot be resolved using traditional bulk δ^{13}C and δ^{15}N isotope methods. This became particularly problematic when we turned to the human stable isotope data.

We analyzed a permanent tooth from 28 individuals buried on the Taraco Peninsula spanning from the Early Formative to Tiwanaku time periods (fig. 4.3*A*, *B*). Dentin collagen samples were extracted from the cemento-enamel junction or tooth root in order to avoid the earliest forming part of the tooth structure (crown), which can record breastfeeding and weaning in early-developing teeth (such as first molars, incisors, canines). The Taraco individuals had dentin collagen δ^{13}C values ranging from −19.4‰ to −14.7‰ (n = 28; average = −17.9‰, sd = 1.2‰), and δ^{15}N$_{coll}$ values ranged from +9.7‰ to +13.7‰ (n = 28; average = +11.1‰, sd = 0.9‰; see Miller et al. 2021 for details). Given a δ^{13}C diet-collagen offset of approximately +5‰, the corresponding diets would have averaged around −25‰ to −20‰. Therefore, the human carbon and nitrogen isotope values indicate that people's diets were dominated by C_3 plants, such as tubers and quinoa, and animals (such as camelids) consuming C_3 plants.

We expected to find isotopic evidence of some people consuming a more mixed diet given the proximity of settlements to the lake and the appearance of fish remains within the archaeological contexts. Thus, we were especially surprised to see no significant isotopic evidence of fish consumption in the human dentin chemistry for individuals living in the Early and Middle Formative Periods when we find relatively denser concentrations of fish presence (figs 4.2, 4.3*B*). We had hypothesized that individuals living during those times would have mixed diets, relying on resources from both the land and the lake for their meals, fluctuating as the lake did, assuming the residents engaged with the lake as they do today. Instead, we see very little isotopic evidence of fish in the bulk isotope data from the Early and Middle Formative Taraco Peninsula inhabitants. A few individuals living in the Late Formative and Tiwanaku time periods did show higher bulk dentin collagen $\delta^{13}C$ values, around −16‰ to −15‰, indicating that they consumed some fish and/or maize (fig. 4.3B). We suspected that maize was the likely ingredient driving this dietary shift because it was gaining value around this time (fig. 4.1A). However, we could not rule out the possibility that fish were being eaten.

We found ourselves with complicated, interrelated food data sets: botanical samples indicating the importance of terrestrial protein-rich cultigens, such as quinoa, and faunal data sets that suggested fish and camelids were utilized in varying amounts over time. The local iconography suggests both land and water animate beings were important to the residents (map 4.1, Sami stone image). The isotope data left us with two lingering issues. First, were fish or maize being consumed regularly? And second, would it be possible to sort out whether maize or fish increased the $\delta^{13}C$ bulk dentin values in those Late Formative and Tiwanaku individuals?

COMPOUND-SPECIFIC AMINO
ACID STABLE ISOTOPE DATA

In 2018 we were able to disentangle the roles of terrestrial and aquatic foods in the peninsular diets. Glycine (Gly) and phenylalanine (Phe) have proven particularly useful for distinguishing between terrestrial and aquatic resource consumption (Webb et al. 2018). One of the critical identifying measures is the $\Delta^{13}C_{Gly-Phe}$ value, which is simply the subtraction of $\delta^{13}C_{Phe}$ from $\delta^{13}C_{Gly}$. Species whose $\Delta^{13}C_{Gly-Phe}$ values are >15‰ have been shown to be aquatic species and their consumers, while those with $\Delta^{13}C_{Gly-Phe}$ values of ≤12‰ are terrestrial species (Webb et al. 2018). We analyzed seven modern plant samples (six *Chenopodium quinoa* samples and a *chuño* freeze-dried *Solanum* potato), ten archaeological camelid bone samples, and three Lake Titicaca archaeological fish bone samples to get baseline compound-specific amino acid (CSAA) data for these major food groups that inhabited terrestrial and aquatic ecosystems, respectively (fig. 4.3C). The fish from Lake Titicaca had unique $\delta^{13}C$ values for a number of amino acids when compared to the camelids and plants, suggesting that multiple amino acids may have utility as freshwater resource markers for this environment (Miller et al. 2021). Specifically, the $\Delta^{13}C_{Gly-Phe}$ values of the modern plant samples ranged from 5.1‰ to 9.8‰ (within the expected terrestrial range), while the fish had $\Delta^{13}C_{Gly-Phe}$ values ranging from 17.6‰ to 25.6‰ (within the expected aquatic range; $\Delta^{13}C_{Gly-Phe}$ >15‰; Webb et al. 2018). Interestingly the camelids had a wide range of $\Delta^{13}C_{Gly-Phe}$ values, from 9.7‰ to 19.2‰, four of whom had $\Delta^{13}C_{Gly-Phe}$ >15‰, suggesting significant aquatic resource consumption for those camelids, probably by grazing on lakeshore resources (Miller et al. 2021).

We also analyzed 27 of the same human teeth that we sampled for bulk dentin collagen using a CSAA approach (Miller et al. 2021). The Taraco Peninsula peoples had $\Delta^{13}C_{Gly-Phe}$ values ranging from 5.2‰ to 13.4‰ (average = 10.6‰; sd = 1.8‰); all the individuals studied had $\Delta^{13}C_{Gly-Phe}$ values <15‰, with only a few individuals having values greater than 12‰ (fig. 4.3C). Therefore, no individuals appear to have relied on fish as a major dietary protein component; instead, their $\Delta^{13}C_{Gly-Phe}$ values confirm the centrality of terrestrial plants and animals in their diets.

Three individuals had $\Delta^{13}C_{Gly-Phe}$ values around 13‰; two were from the Middle Formative (L8536 and L8625), and one was from the Late Formative (L9105). These three individuals are not the same individuals who have higher bulk $\delta^{13}C$ dentin collagen values. Therefore, we suggest that these three individuals with $\Delta^{13}C_{Gly-Phe}$ values around 13‰ were probably consuming more fish from the lake than their peers (either more frequently or in greater quantity on periodic occasions), but they still were not relying on the lake as a primary resource for food, particularly for protein. Further, the handful of individuals from the Late Formative and Tiwanaku Periods with higher bulk $\delta^{13}C$ values in the range of −16‰ to −15‰ (L7119, L7692, L5268) probably consumed maize, which lead to their higher carbon isotope values, rather than fish, because their corresponding $\Delta^{13}C_{Gly-Phe}$ values are in the terrestrial range (note L5264 did not have amino acid isotope data, so we cannot say whether their bulk $\delta^{13}C$ was influenced by fish or by maize). The hint of maize captured in the teeth of only a few peninsular people and scarce presence of maize botanical evidence further supports the relative rarity of this food in local diets despite proximity to the Tiwanaku center, where maize may have been consumed more widely (Berryman and Blom, this volume). Further, these individuals were children when they consumed maize, leaving us to wonder about the social conditions that brought them to imbibe or eat this highly valued but certainly uncommon and probably nonlocally grown food. If maize was valued as a special food that marked group belonging or identity, then the consumption of maize (as a food or a drink), particularly by a young person, might be significant as part of socializing children into particular roles or community membership.

CONCLUSIONS

The archaeobotanical data tell us of the continuing prominence of the key staple crops—quinoa, and tubers. The faunal remains emphasize a shifting importance of fish and camelids over time. The isotopic data indicate that terrestrial plants and animals were central and that lake resources were a smaller than expected part of Taraco Peninsula inhabitant's diets (Miller et al. 2021). Despite the presence of fish remains in archaeologically excavated contexts, fish did not appear to be a dietary staple during childhood. So, what do we make of the presence of fish bones in the archaeological record but the lack of evidence for these fish in the human tooth isotope chemistry, and what might that inform us about the resident's relationship with the land and the lake?

Recent studies of modern Lake Titicaca fish (Monroy et al. 2014) have documented a larger range of carbon and nitrogen bulk isotope values for endemic species than our previous study (Miller et al. 2010), so it is possible that human bulk dentin isotope values may have some influence from fish. However, the dentin collagen amino acid data do not currently support the hypothesis that fish were a prominent protein source. It is critical to remember that we sampled permanent teeth for this study, and teeth record the diet from discrete periods of childhood/ adolescence. During these periods of early life, children may have been eating foods that could have differed from those consumed by adults (Miller, Agarwal, and Langebaek 2018). Future research will reexamine the possibility of studying Taraco Peninsula people's bone collagen to characterize diet during adulthood; perhaps fish were preferred by adults rather than children, and we are missing it because we are not examining the correct life stage when it was a dietary component.

Furthermore, because fish are relatively small and provide much less meat than camelids, it is possible their consumption was complementary to other agricultural resources and was reserved for special occasions. In fact, there are "fish pits" where very dense whole fish evidence was uncovered in several locations and times, particularly clustered in Formative contexts (Moore et al. 2010). These features held few other organic species in them, suggesting they might have been fermenting locales (Hastorf 1999) or the trash remains from special feasting occasions. It is also possible that fish were used for other purposes on the peninsula, such as fertilizer for agricultural fields (Santana-Sagredo et al. 2021; Szpak 2014). Taken together, we believe that it is most likely that fish were consumed but in very small quantities or relatively rarely such that the fish chemical signal is masked by the sheer volume of terrestrial protein foods to which residents had access (quinoa is a protein-rich grain after all). These results also support the increasingly important, but as yet relatively imperceptible, maize input in the diet of the Late Formative and Tiwanaku phase residents.

Importantly, this work demonstrates the value of utilizing multiple lines of evidence to tease apart and clarify a more nuanced understanding of ancient foodways. Here, different dietary data sets both complement and complicate one another, and we are left with both a better understanding of past food decisions and more questions. We believe these findings challenge us to confront our own biases about foods and thinking about protein sources in particular. Many of us modern archaeologists working in the Lake Titicaca Basin see the lake and assume it would have been a critical subsistence resource for local peoples over time, particularly for dietary protein through the consumption of lake fish. Our own perspectives and biases color our view of the landscapes around us and the people we study; we see particular resources as having more or less importance relative to our own cultural values. However, dietary protein can come in many forms, and animal flesh is but one, with plants offering their own forms of protein to human diets.

Our long-term investigation of the diets of the Taraco Peninsula residents reflects both the steadiness in their diet and the complexity of its study. Each method that we have applied to this topic provides critical information, which while clarifying some aspects of past diets further complicates our vision of them as the data work independently and synergistically. The inhabitants of the Taraco Peninsula were versatile in their cuisine ingredients and most certainly used products from both the land and the lake in their diets and in other aspects of their daily lives. This evidence illustrates people's strong bond to the land and water—as seen in their images—and that they had a different engagement with the lake than they did with the land, which fed them. Perhaps the lake was more powerful and less easy to nurture and thus to receive food from. It could be that the residents used the lake resources to feed the land beings, as seen in the fish-dense pits of the Formative times, and the isotopic values that suggest some camelids foraged on or were fed aquatic resources. With these results we can begin to see that the residents had different relationships with the earth beings than the lake beings, while domains would have required feeding and care.

REFERENCES

Abbott, Mark B., Michael W. Binford, Mark Brenner, and Kerry R. Kelts. 1997. "A 3500¹⁴C Yr High-Resolution Record of Water-Level Changes in Lake Titicaca, Bolivia/Peru." *Quaternary Research* 47 (2): 169–80. https://doi.org/10.1006/qres.1997.1881.

Allen, Catherine J. 2016. "The Living Ones: Miniatures and Animation in the Andes." *Journal of Anthropological Research* 72 (4): 416–41.

Ambrose, Stanley H., and John Krigbaum. 2003. "Bone Chemistry and Bioarchaeology." *Journal of Anthropological Archaeology* 22 (3): 193–99. https://doi.org/10.1016/S0278-4165(03)00033-3.

Bruno, Maria C. 2014. "Beyond Raised Fields: Exploring Farming Practices and Processes of Agricultural Change in the Ancient Lake Titicaca Basin of the Andes." *American Anthropologist* 116 (1): 1–16. https://doi.org/10.1111/aman.12066.

Bruno, Maria C., José M. Capriles, Christine A. Hastorf, Sherilyn C. Fritz, D. Marie Weide, Alejandra I. Domic, and Paul A. Baker. 2021. "The Rise and Fall of Wiñaymarka: Rethinking Cultural and Environmental Interactions in the Southern Basin of Lake Titicaca." *Human Ecology* 49 (2): 131–45. https://doi.org/10.1007/s10745-021-00222-3.

Bruno, Maria C., and Christine A. Hastorf. 2016. "Gifts from the Camelids: Archaeobotanical Insights into Camelid Pastoralism Through the Study of Dung." In *The Archaeology of Andean Pastoralism*, edited by José M. Capriles and Nicholas Tripcevich, 55–65. Albuquerque: University of New Mexico Press.

Capriles, José M., Katherine M. Moore, Alejandra I. Domic, and Christine A. Hastorf. 2014. "Fishing and Environmental Change During the Emergence of Social Complexity in the Lake Titicaca Basin." *Journal of Anthropological Archaeology* 34:66–77. https://doi.org/10.1016/j.jaa.2014.02.001.

Corr, Lorna T., Michael P. Richards, Colin Grier, Alexander Mackie, Owen Beattie, and Richard P. Evershed. 2009. "Probing Dietary Change of the Kwäday Dän Ts'ìnchị Individual, an Ancient Glacier Body from British Columbia. II. Deconvoluting Whole Skin and Bone Collagen $\delta^{13}C$ Values via Carbon Isotope Analysis of Individual Amino Acids." *Journal of Archaeological Science* 36 (1): 12–18. https://doi.org/10.1016/j.jas.2008.06.027.

de la Cadena, Marisol. 2015. *Earth Beings.* Durham, N.C.: Duke University Press.

Fahy, G. E., C. Deter, R. Pitfield, J. J. Miszkiewicz, and P. Mahoney. 2017. "Bone Deep: Variation in Stable Isotope Ratios and Histomorphometric Measurements of Bone Remodelling within Adult Humans." *Journal of Archaeological Science* 87:10–6. https://doi.org/10.1016/j.jas.2017.09.009.

Fogel, Marilyn L., and Noreen Tuross. 2003. "Extending the Limits of Paleodietary Studies of Humans with Compound Specific Carbon Isotope Analysis of Amino Acids." *Journal of Archaeological Science* 30 (5): 535–45. https://doi.org/10.1016/S0305-4403(02)00199-1.

Hastorf, Christine A. 1999. "Recent Research in Paleoethnobotany." *Journal of Archaeological Research* 7 (1): 55–103. https://doi.org/10.1007/BF02446085.

Hastorf, Christine A. 2007. "Archaeological Andean Rituals: Performance, Liturgy, and Meaning." In *The Archaeology of Ritual*, edited by Evangelos Kyriakidis, 77–107. Los Angeles: Cotsen Institute of Archaeology, University of California.

Hastorf, Christine A. 2017a. "The Actions and Meanings of Visible and Hidden Spaces at Formative Chiripa." *Ñawpa Pacha* 37:1–22. https://doi.org/10.1080/00776297.2017.1390925.

Hastorf, Christine A. 2017b. *The Social Archaeology of Food: Thinking About Eating from Prehistory to the Present.* Cambridge: Cambridge University Press.

Hastorf, Christine A., and Melanie F. Wright. 1998. "Interpreting Wild Seeds from Archaeological Sites: A Dung Charring Experiment from the Andes." *Journal of Ethnobiology* 18 (2): 211–27.

Janusek, John Wayne. 2006. "The Changing 'Nature' of Tiwanaku Religion and the Rise of an Andean State." *World Archaeology* 38 (3): 469–92. https://doi.org/10.1080/00438240600813541.

Kolata, Alan L. 2003. "The Social Production of Tiwanaku: Political Economy and Authority in a Native Andean State." In *Tiwanaku and Its Hinterland: Archaeology and Paleoecology of an Andean Civilization.* Vol. 2, *Urban and Rural Archaeology*, edited by Alan L. Kolata, 449–72. Washington, D.C.: Smithsonian Institution Press.

Langlie, BrieAnna S. 2008. "Paleoethnobotanical Analysis of Formative Chiripa, Bolivia." Senior honors thesis, University of California, Berkeley.

Lee-Thorp, J. A. 2008. "On Isotopes and Old Bones." *Archaeometry* 50 (6): 925–50. https://doi.org/10.1111/j.1475-4754.2008.00441.x.

Logan, Amanda L., Christine A. Hastorf, and Deborah M. Pearsall. 2012. "'Let's Drink Together': Early Ceremonial Use of Maize in the Titicaca Basin." *Latin American Antiquity* 23 (3): 235–58. https://doi.org/10.7183/1045-6635.23.3.235.

McMahon, Kelton W., Marilyn L. Fogel, Travis S. Elsdon, and Simon R. Thorrold. 2010. "Carbon Isotope Fractionation of Amino Acids in Fish Muscle Reflects Biosynthesis and Isotopic Routing from Dietary Protein." *Journal of Animal Ecology* 79 (5): 1132–41. https://doi.org/10.1111/j.1365-2656.2010.01722.x.

Miller, Melanie J. 2005. "What's in That Pot? Using Stable Isotope Analysis to Understand Cuisines of the Taraco Peninsula, Bolivia, 1500 BC–AD 1000." Senior honors thesis, University of California, Berkeley.

Miller, Melanie J., Sabrina C. Agarwal, and Carl H. Langebaek. 2018. "Dietary Histories: Tracing Food Consumption Practices from Childhood Through Adulthood Using Stable Isotope Analysis." In *Children and Childhood in Bioarchaeology*, edited by Patrick Beauchesne and Sabrina C. Agarwal, 262–93. Gainesville: University Press of Florida.

Miller, Melanie J., José M. Capriles, and Christine A. Hastorf. 2010. "The Fish of Lake Titicaca: Implications for Archaeology and Changing Ecology Through Stable Isotope Analysis." *Journal of Archaeological Science* 37 (2): 317–27. https://doi.org/10.1016/j.jas.2009.09.043.

Miller, Melanie J., Yu Dong, Kate Pechenkina, Wenquan Fan, and Siân E. Halcrow. 2020. "Raising Girls and Boys in Early China: Stable Isotope Data Reveal Sex Differences in Weaning and Childhood Diets During the Eastern Zhou Era." *American Journal of Physical Anthropology* 172 (4): 567–85. https://doi.org/10.1002/ajpa.24033.

Miller, Melanie J., Iain Kendall, José M. Capriles, Maria C. Bruno, Richard P. Evershed, and Christine A. Hastorf. 2021. "Quinoa, Potatoes, and Llamas Fueled Emergent Social Complexity in the Lake Titicaca Basin of the Andes." *Proceedings of the National Academy of Sciences* 118 (49): e2113395118. https://doi.org/10.1073/pnas.2113395118.

Monroy, M., A. Maceda-Veiga, N. Caiola, and A. De Sostoa. 2014. "Trophic Interactions Between Native and Introduced Fish Species in a Littoral Fish Community." *Journal of Fish Biology* 85:1693–706. https://doi.org/10.1111/jfb.12529.

Moore, Katherine, Maria Bruno, José M. Capriles, and Christine Hastorf. 2010. "Integrated Contextual Approaches to Understanding Past Activities Using Plant and Animal Remains from Kala Uyuni, Lake Titicaca, Bolivia." In *Integrating Zooarchaeology and Paleoethnobotany: A Consideration of Issues, Methods, and Cases*, edited by Amber M. VanDerwarker and Tanya M. Peres, 173–203. New York: Springer.

Parenti, Lynne R. 1984. "A Taxonomic Revision of the Andean Killifish Genus *Orestias* (Cyprinodontiformes, Cyprinodontidae)." *Bulletin of the American Museum of Natural History* 178 (2): 197–214. http://hdl.handle.net/2246/575.

Reeds, Peter J. 2000. "Dispensable and Indispensable Amino Acids for Humans." *Journal of Nutrition* 130 (7): 1835S–40S. https://doi.org/10.1093/jn/130.7.1835S.

Reilly, Sophie E. 2017. *Meals in Motion: Ceramic and Botanical Investigations of Foodways in the Late Formative and Tiwanaku IV/V, Lake Titicaca Basin, Bolivia.* Master's thesis, McMaster University.

Santana-Sagredo, Francisca, Rick J. Schulting, Pablo Méndez-Quiros, Ale Vidal-Elgueta, Mauricio Uribe, Rodrigo Loyola, Anahí Maturana-Fernández, et al. 2021. "'White Gold' Guano Fertilizer Drove Agricultural Intensification in the Atacama Desert from AD 1000." *Nature Plants* 7 (2): 152–8. https://doi.org/10.1038/s41477-020-00835-4.

Styring, Amy K., Rebecca A. Fraser, Rose-Marie Arbogast, Paul Halstead, Valasia Isaakidou, Jessica A. Pearson, Marguerita Schäfer, et al. 2015. "Refining Human Palaeodietary Reconstruction Using Amino Acid $\delta^{15}N$ Values of Plants, Animals and Humans." *Journal of Archaeological Science* 53:504–15. https://doi.org/10.1016/j.jas.2014.11.009.

Szpak, Paul. 2014. "Complexities of Nitrogen Isotope Biogeochemistry in Plant-Soil Systems: Implications for the Study of Ancient Agricultural and Animal Management Practices." *Frontiers in Plant Science* 5:1–19. https://doi.org/10.3389/fpls.2014.00288.

Wang, Weiwei, Zhenlong Wu, Zhaolai Dai, Ying Yang, Junjun Wang, and Guoyao Wu. 2013. "Glycine Metabolism in Animals and Humans: Implications for Nutrition and Health." *Amino Acids* 45:463–77. https://doi.org/10.1007/s00726-013-1493-1.

Webb, Emily C., Noah V. Honch, Philip J. H. Dunn, Anna Linderholm, Gunilla Eriksson, Kerstin Lidén, and Richard P. Evershed. 2018. "Compound-Specific Amino Acid Isotopic Proxies for Distinguishing Between Terrestrial and Aquatic Resource Consumption." *Archaeological and Anthropological Sciences* 10 (1): 1–18. https://doi.org/10.1007/s12520-015-0309-5.

Weide, D. Marie, Sherilyn C. Fritz, Christine A. Hastorf, Maria C. Bruno, Paul A. Baker, Stephane Guedron, and Wout Salenbien. 2017. "A ~6000 Yr Diatom Record of Mid- to Late Holocene Fluctuations in the Level of Lago Wiñaymarca, Lake Titicaca (Peru/Bolivia)." *Quaternary Research* 88 (2): 179–92. https://doi.org/10.1017/qua.2017.49.

Whitehead, William T. 2007. "Exploring the Wild and Domestic: Paleoethnobotany at Chiripa, a Formative Site in Bolivia." PhD diss., University of California, Berkeley.

Wright, L. E., and H. P. Schwarcz. 1998. "Stable Carbon and Oxygen Isotopes in Human Tooth Enamel: Identifying Breastfeeding and Weaning in Prehistory." *American Journal of Physical Anthropology* 106:1–18. https://doi.org/10.1002/(SICI)1096-8644(199805)106:1<1::AID-AJPA1>3.0.CO;2-W.

PART II

FOOD, POWER, AND STATUS IN EARLY
STATES AND EMPIRES

5

Transforming Food in the Tiwanaku Heartland

Maize and the Rise and Fall of Sociopolitical Complexity in the Southern Lake Titicaca Basin

Carrie Anne Berryman and Deborah E. Blom

As early as 1400 BCE, the inhabitants of the southern Lake Titicaca Basin (Bolivia) had a variety of resources available to them as agropastoralists living near one of the largest lakes in South America (Miller et al., this volume). They dined on the meat of fish, wild animals, and domesticated camelids, and they consumed a variety of highland-adapted wild and domesticated plants such as quinoa and tubers. Between 500 and 1100 CE, the ceremonial center of Tiwanaku became the seat of power for one of the first state-level societies in the Americas (Albarracín-Jordán 1996; Janusek 2004b, 2008; Kolata 1993, 1996, 2003a; Ponce [1972] 1981; Vranich and Stanish 2013). At 3,800 masl, the seemingly barren environment in which Tiwanaku developed appears an unlikely setting for the growth of a major urban center. Yet at its height around 800 CE, the city supported an estimated 15,000–20,000 inhabitants, completed the construction of the massive Akapana pyramid, and probably managed more than 70 km^2 of raised-field agriculture in the surrounding *pampas*. During this time, Tiwanaku built strategic trade alliances and, in some cases, established colonial enclaves to obtain lowland resources such as tropical fruits, chili peppers, psychotropic plants, coca, and maize. Many of these agricultural imports were significant not as dietary supplements but for their sociopolitical value. Most notably, in the form of beer, or *chicha*, maize was transformed to serve as a key element of rituals and feasts in the Andes (Hastorf and Johannessen 1993; Jennings et al. 2005; see also the chapters in this volume by Alconini; Scaffidi, Vang, and Tung; and Weber and Young).

Both authors contributed equally to this chapter.

By turning ordinary food into the extraordinary, many ancient states of the Andes and elsewhere used feasting as significant elements in the creation and maintenance of political authority and social differentiation (see Alconini; Bélisle, Alaica, and Brown; and Biwer, Alaica, and Quiñonez Cuzcano, this volume; Bray 2003; Dietler and Hayden [2001] 2010; Hastorf 2016; Hayden and Villeneuve 2011; Goldstein 2003; Klarich 2010; Nash 2010). Evidence suggests that public feasts have been an important arena for commensal politics in the southern Lake Titicaca Basin region since at least the Middle Formative (Hastorf 2003). At the height of Tiwanaku's expansion, the scale of public feasts increased on an unprecedented scale. Communal feasts with the consumption of maize chicha and camelid meat were significant forums for the negotiation of status and prestige within Tiwanaku society, and it is this strong connection between food and politics that inspired this study.

Critical to understanding Tiwanaku sociopolitical organization is determining who took part in commensal events and the distribution and consumption of food resources acquired through local versus nonlocal production. Archaeological data provide insight into production as well as indirect evidence of consumption in general; however, overlapping, but distinct, isotopic and dental data can provide direct evidence of consumption at the level of the individual. Revealing how consumption patterns varied among subpopulations of Tiwanaku society allows a more nuanced understanding of the degree to which certain factions contributed to and were affected by the Tiwanaku state and the role of feasting in Tiwanaku political authority and social differentiation.

THE SOUTHERN LAKE TITICACA BASIN (WIÑAYMARKA)

The chapter by Miller and colleagues sets the stage for our work with a discussion of the Early and Middle Formative on the Taraco Peninsula (see Bruno et al. 2021 for a thorough discussion of the temporal changes in the southern Lake Titicaca Basin, or "Wiñaymarka"). During the Late Formative (200 BCE–500 CE), several larger politico-religious centers developed, each with a network of multiple surrounding rural communities (Janusek 2008, 2018; Stanish 2003; Smith 2016). In addition to Kala Uyuni on the Taraco Peninsula (Miller et al., this volume), major centers in the southern Lake Titicaca Basin included the site of Lukurmata in the Katari Valley (Bermann 1994); the Tiwanaku Valley site of Tiwanaku, which was relatively small at this time; and the more prominent sites of Khonkho Wankane and Iruhito in the Desaguadero Valley (Janusek 2005; Marsh 2012; Pérez Arias 2014; map 5.1). Probably these sacred, sunken court complexes and their associated rituals of consumption—such as feasting, ancestor veneration, and renewal—were used by elites as a means of consolidating power and/or generating and maintaining tradition and social memory (Couture 2002; Logan, Hastorf and Pearsall 2012; Roddick and Hastorf 2010; Pérez Arias 2014; Smith 2016; Stanish 2003).

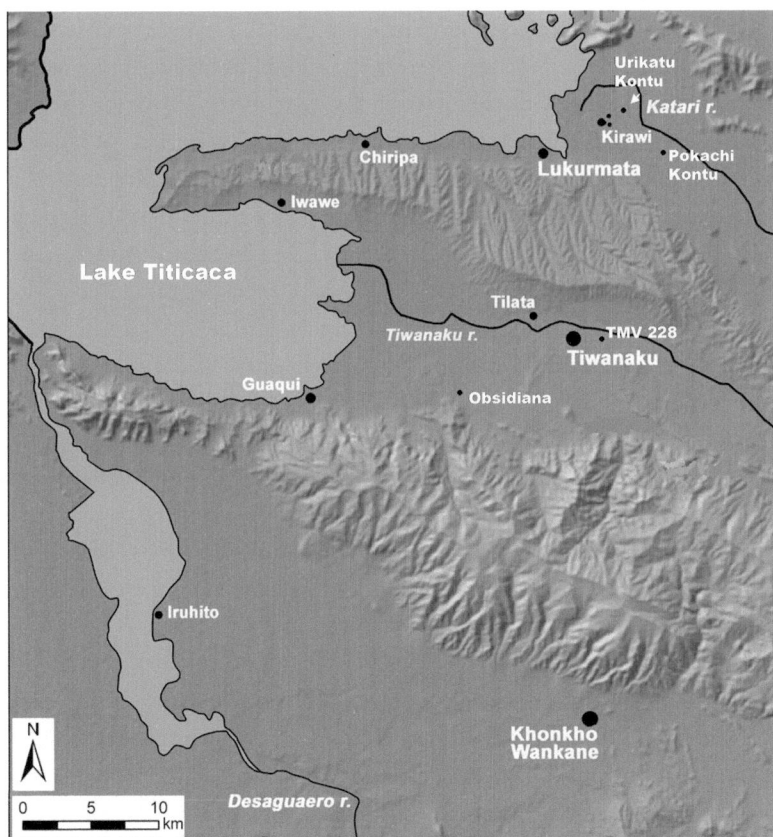

Map 5.1 Southern Titicaca Basin sites mentioned in this text. Illustration by Berryman and Blom.

During the Middle Horizon Tiwanaku Period (500–1100 CE, Tiwa-naku IV/V) evidence for increasing sociopolitical complexity through centralization, control, and expansion is evident as Tiwanaku emerged as a major polity in the southern basin (Albarracín-Jordán 1996; Janusek 2004b, 2008; Kolata 1993, 1996, 2003a; Ponce [1972] 1981; Vranich and Stanish 2013). The now ~6.5 km² city of Tiwanaku rose to become the preeminent ceremonial center in the area. Increased social differentiation within residential barrios established around the ceremonial core was reflected in class, identity, occupational specialization, and residential mobility (Becker 2017; Janusek 2005; Knudson and Blom 2009). In the Katari Valley, Lukurmata became the second most important center in the basin, probably serving as an administrative center for Tiwanaku and overseeing agricultural production within the expansive raised-field systems of the Koani Pampa (Bermann 1994). Tiwanaku's influence also spread beyond the Titicaca Basin to the east and west, where they ob-tained lowland resources such as tropical fruits, chili peppers, psychotro-pic plants, coca, and maize by building strategic trade alliances and, in some cases, establishing colonies such as the coastal valley "hinterland" sites in Moquegua, Peru, and northern Chile described in the chapter in this volume by Knudson and colleagues (see also Baitzel 2018; Blom 2005; and Goldstein 2005).

Much evidence indicates that feasting intensified during the apogee of Tiwanaku. Excavations within Tiwanaku's ceremonial core revealed dense middens indicating large-scale feasts, with the remains of butch-ered llamas, communal serving wares, hallucinogenic snuff tubes, as well as vessels dedicated to the storage, fermentation, and consumption of chicha, including *kerus*, *ollas*, and *tinajas*, styles which appear throughout the South Central Andes as a hallmark of Tiwanaku influence (Alconini 1995; Couture and Sampeck 2003; Goldstein 2003; Kolata 2003b; Man-zanilla 1992; Janusek 2004b). Akapana East, a compound neighboring the Akapana monument at the center of the site, appears to have served as a preparation area for large feasting events, with paleobotanical evi-dence indicating that maize was being imported off the cob, suggest-ing large-scale provisioning, in contrast to the way it was entering some other households (Janusek 2003; Wright, Hastorf, and Lennstrom 2003). While paleobotanical analyses indicate that on average maize was second to quinoa as the most important crop in the region (Bruno 2014), the importance of maize at this time is clear, as is the fact that the presence and quantity of maize throughout the cities and surrounding settlements was not uniform (Wright, Hastorf, and Lennstrom 2003).

Coinciding with patterns seen elsewhere during the Late Intermediate Period, the Post-Tiwanaku, or Pacajes, Period (1100–1400 CE) followed the disintegration of the Tiwanaku polity in the altiplano (Janusek 2004a). While the exact nature of Tiwanaku disintegration is debated, the exploitative, hierarchical nature of Tiwanaku politics probably created a volatile political environment (Langlie and Arkush 2016) exacerbated by long-term drought (Arnold et al. 2021; Kolata et al. 2000). State-associated cultural practices were abandoned, including artistic styles, the generation of surplus, and vertical exchange. Populations dispersed from the lowland colonies (see Baitzel et al., this volume), as well as the Tiwanaku center, where some monuments were defaced and elite residences burned. Hierarchical distinctions blurred, and many settled into small, fortified hilltop settlements, indicating that this was a period of political turmoil in the region.

MATERIALS AND METHODS

In order to gain insight into the impact of the Tiwanaku state on diet in the southern Lake Titicaca Basin, we focused on several sites in the Tiwanaku, Katari, and Desaguadero valleys. Detailed information on these sites can be found in numerous chapters from two edited manuscripts (Kolata 1996, 2003a) and our previous work (Berryman 2010; Blom 2005). The Tiwanaku Valley sample comes from the urban center of Tiwanaku as well as small rural settlements throughout the valley (Albarracín-Jordán and Mathews 1990). Katari Valley sites include the urban center of Lukurmata and several rural sites (Janusek and Kolata 2003). Desaguadero Valley sites include the major settlements of Khonkho Wankane and Iruhito. Our comparative lowland sample derives from the Tiwanaku-affiliated complex of Chen Chen in the coastal Moquegua Valley of Southern Peru described in the chapter in this volume by Knudson and colleagues. Using various publications, dissertations, excavation notes, and reports, we (Berryman 2010; Blom 1999) previously assigned individuals to broad temporal categories and compiled detailed descriptions of the various sites and samples presented here.

This research uses several overlapping but distinct isotopic and dental data sets collected by Berryman in the Titicaca Basin and Blom in the Moquegua Valley as well as architectural, ceramic, and faunal data from published sources.

DENTAL INDICATORS OF DIET: CARIES AND WEAR

Dental analyses provide a nondestructive and relatively low cost, if somewhat indirect, measure of overall diet and nutrition (Hillson 1979, 1996; Larsen, Shavit, and Griffin 1991; Powell 1985). Data on dental caries and attrition were collected using the standards recommended by Buikstra and Ubelaker (1994) on 133 individuals from the Moquegua Valley and 121 individuals from the Lake Titicaca Basin: 72 from the Tiwanaku Valley, 40 from the Katari Valley, and 9 from the Desaguadero Valley. Since most dental pathologies are age progressive (Hillson 1996), we considered age distributions when comparing populations. Only adults (defined as greater than 18 years of age) were included, and results here are restricted to the Tiwanaku and Post-Tiwanaku contexts, which have sufficient sample sizes for comparison.

STABLE ISOTOPIC INDICATORS OF DIET

Insights into Andean foodways are increasingly being gained through the use of stable isotopic analyses (see Wilson and McCool, this volume, as well as several chapters that employ these data; see Juengst et al. 2021 for a general overview). Human bone samples for the analysis of stable carbon and nitrogen isotopes were collected from all adults with sufficiently preserved remains. This resulted in 15 samples from the Late Formative, 58 from the Tiwanaku Period, and 15 Post-Tiwanaku/Pacajes Period remains. Here we report on the highlights from a more extensive analysis by Berryman (2010). Details on isotopic sample preparation assessment of sample integrity are outlined in Berryman (2010; see also Tykot 2006), which also includes all of our isotopic and demographic data as well as additional isotopic data from Tomczak (2001) that was performed on the same collections we analyzed.

Information gained from zooarchaeological and paleobotanical studies combined with extensive isotopic data for a wide range of southern

Titicaca Basin fauna and flora (Berryman 2010; Miller et al., this volume) provides us with some important observations to consider when using isotopic data to interpret ancient altiplano diets. In contrast to other Andean areas (e.g., Santana-Sagredo et al., this volume; Cadwallader et al. 2012), altiplano fauna, specifically camelids, were consuming C_3 plants, and maize is the only plant of dietary significance in our contexts that uses a C_4 pathway. Highland staples, such as tubers and quinoa, use the C_3 pathway and have lower carbon isotope ratios ($^{13}C/^{12}C$, or $\delta^{13}C$; between −20‰ and −35‰) while C_4 plants result in higher $\delta^{13}C$ ratios (between −9‰ and −14‰). These benefits are offset by complications.

As described by Miller et al. (this volume), unexpectedly high $\delta^{13}C$ in Lake Titicaca fish makes it difficult to distinguish the consumption of fish from the consumption of maize, especially since the low mean nitrogen isotope ratio ($^{15}N/^{14}N$, or $\delta^{15}N$) for most lake fish is not significantly different from the $\delta^{15}N$ values of available carbohydrate resources. Therefore, variations in $\delta^{15}N$ values primarily reflect differential consumption of terrestrial fauna (and perhaps carnivorous fish), and we need a means of differentiating between consumption of fish, which is predominantly a protein source, and maize, which contains very little protein. Because carbon in bone collagen is primarily (although not completely) derived from dietary protein while carbon in bone apatite carbonate reflects the whole diet, we used the apatite-collagen spacing value ($\Delta^{13}C_{ap-col}$) to determine whether the source of high $\delta^{13}C$ in southern Lake Titicaca Basin humans was fish or maize. Our additional interpretations also draw on valuable models developed from experimental feeding studies (e.g., Froehle, Kellner, and Schoeninger 2010, 2012; Kellner and Schoenigher 2007).

SOUTHERN LAKE TITICACA BASIN DIETS

Our apatite-collagen spacing ($\Delta^{13}C_{ap-col}$) data clearly indicate that a substantial source of high $\delta^{13}C$ in the southern Lake Titicaca Basin humans was most certainly maize (fig. 5.1). Generally, a $\Delta^{13}C_{coll-ap}$ value greater than 4.4‰ indicates that the $\delta^{13}C$ value of dietary protein is more negative than the whole diet (i.e., the primary source of high $\delta^{13}C$ values is a protein-depleted resource such as a C_4 plant, e.g., maize; Ambrose et al. 1997, 351). A $\Delta^{13}C_{ap-col}$ value of approximately 4.4‰ or less indicates that

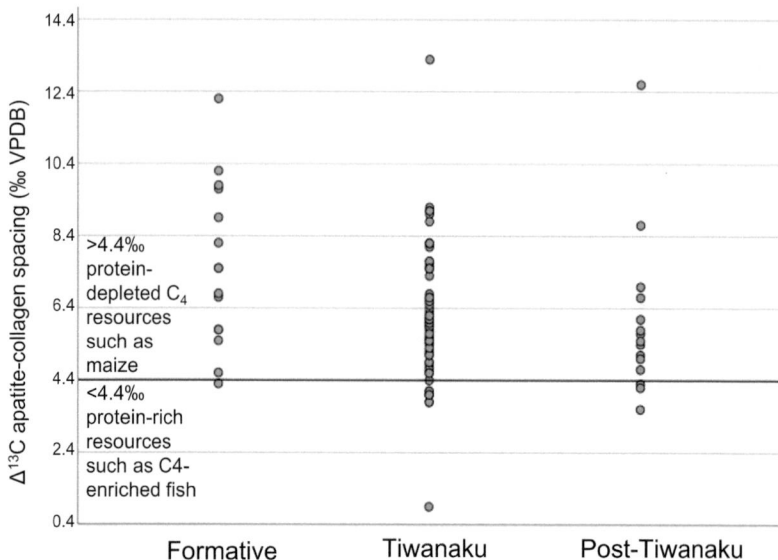

Figure 5.1 $\Delta^{13}C$ apatite-collagen spacing (‰ VPDB) by time. Illustration by Berryman and Blom.

the $\delta^{13}C$ value of dietary protein is more positive than the whole diet (i.e., the primary source of high $\delta^{13}C$ values is a protein-rich resource, such as C_4-enriched fish). Our results using this approach are supported by Miller and colleagues' (this volume) new and more direct method of using compound-specific amino acid analysis for glycine and phenylalanine to discern between fish and maize consumption.

Because we are interested in the impact that the Tiwanaku state had on southern Lake Titicaca Basin diets, we employ various means of comparing differences between Tiwanaku Period diets and those of the earlier Late Formative and later Post-Tiwanaku/Pacajes Periods (table 5.1; figs. 5.2–5.4).

LATE FORMATIVE DIETS

Isotopic data from the Late Formative (LF) are consistent with the majority of individuals relying on C_3 highland-adapted plants, such as quinoa and tubers for their carbohydrate sources, while proteins were derived from C_3-feeding terrestrial herbivores, presumably camelids based on faunal remains (Gladwell 2007; Webster and Janusek 2003). This is

Table 5.1 Descriptive statistics for southern Lake Titicaca Basin isotopic results by time

Time period		$\delta^{13}C_{collagen}$ (‰ VPDB)	$\delta^{13}C_{apatite}$ (‰ VPDB)	$\delta^{15}N$ (‰ AIR)
Late Formative ($n = 15$)	Mean	−18.1	−10.5	10.8
	sd	1.2	2.5	0.9
Tiwanaku ($n = 65$)	Mean	−14.9	−8.7	11.0
	sd	3.0	2.9	1.3
Post-Tiwanaku ($n = 15$)	Mean	−17.7	−11.7	13.2
	sd	1.2	2.1	1.4

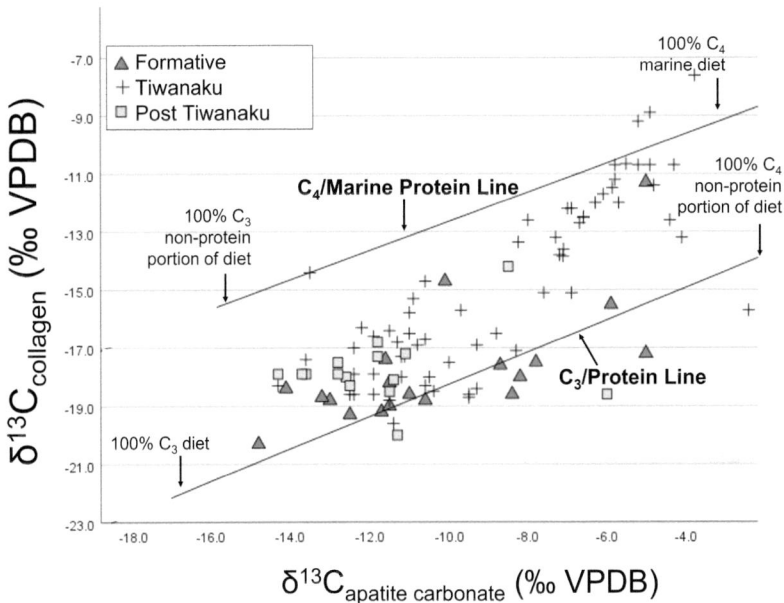

Figure 5.2 Plot by time (Late Formative, Tiwanaku, and Post-Tiwanaku samples) of $\delta^{13}C_{collagen}$ by $\delta^{13}C_{apatite\ carbonate}$, with dietary regression lines from Froehle et al. (2010, 2669; see also Kellner and Schoeninger 2007). Illustration by Berryman and Blom.

not particularly surprising given that zooarchaeological and paleobotanical evidence (see Miller et al., this volume), and dental caries reported elsewhere (Berryman 2010) indicate that populations of the Late Formative were primarily dependent on agropastoral subsistence strategies with less reliance on fishing and hunting.

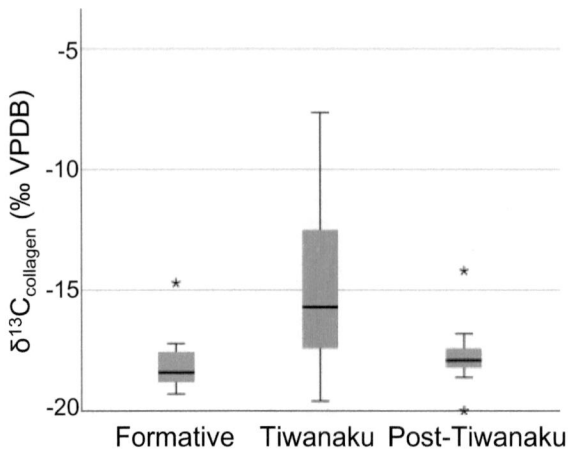

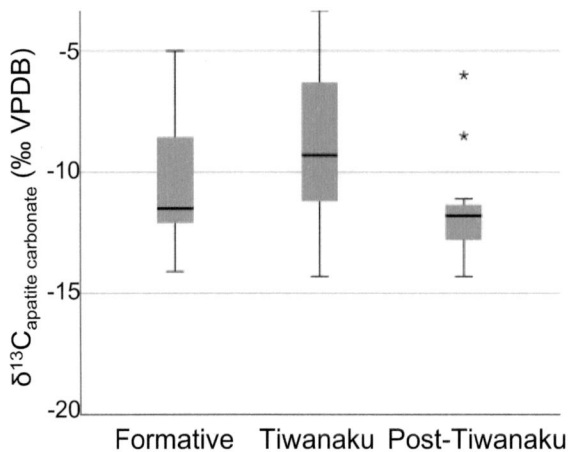

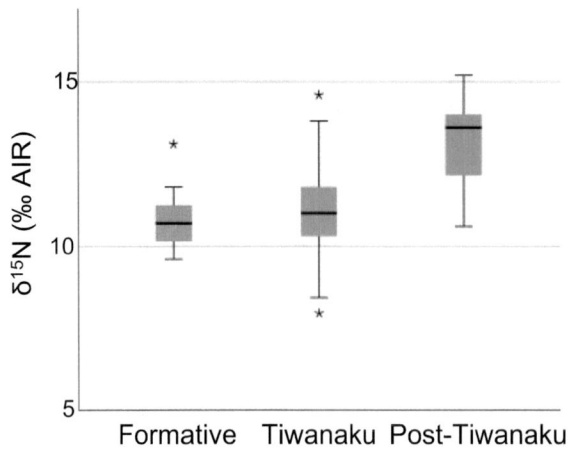

Figure 5.3 Boxplot by time (Late Formative, Tiwanaku, and Post-Tiwanaku samples) for $\delta^{13}C_{collagen}$, $\delta^{13}C_{apatite\ carbonate}$, and $\delta^{15}N$. Illustration by Berryman and Blom.

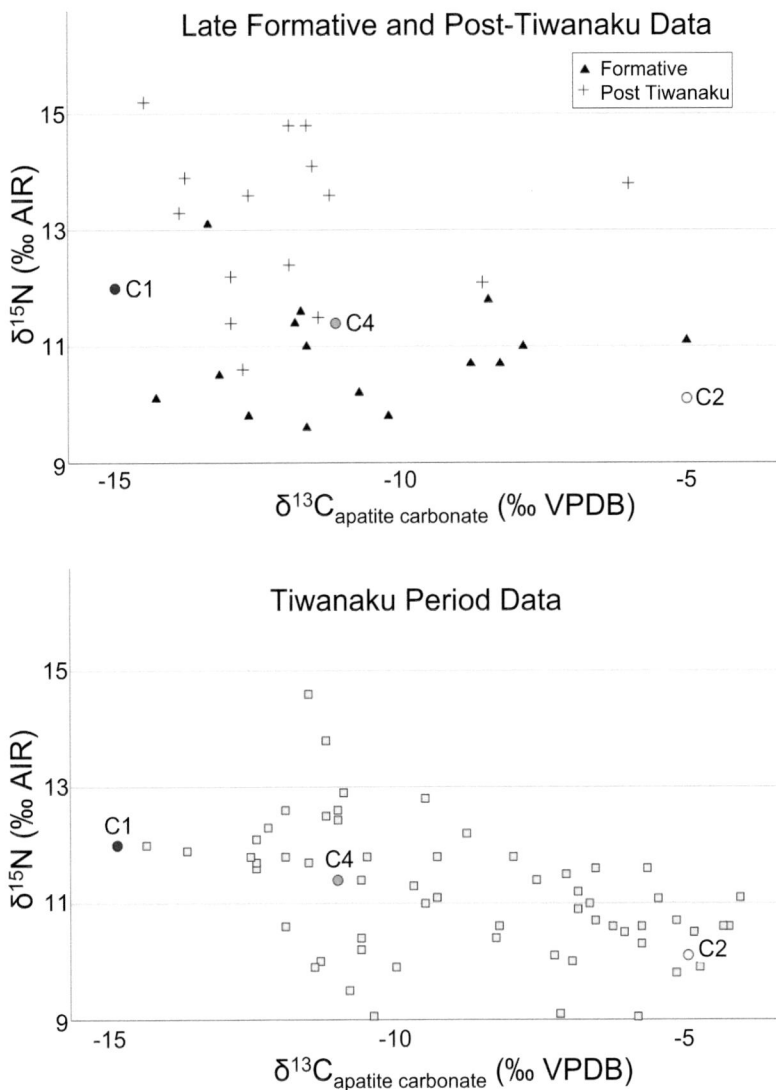

Figure 5.4 Bivariate plot of δ1³C$_{\text{apatite carbonate}}$ by δ¹⁵N (Late Formative and Post-Tiwanaku samples above, Tiwanaku Period sample below) including K-means cluster analysis centroids for dietary estimates by Froehle, Kellner, and Schoeninger (2012) that are located in these ranges. Clusters (C1, C2, and C4) indicate C$_3$:C$_4$ ratio in diet and C$_3$ versus C$_4$ protein source as follows: C1 = 100:0 C$_3$:C$_4$ and C$_3$ protein. C2 = 30:70 C$_3$:C$_4$ and >50% C$_4$ protein. C4 = 70:30 C$_3$:C$_4$ and ≥65% C$_4$ protein. Illustration by Berryman and Blom.

Nevertheless, the diets of some LF individuals had significant quantities of C_4-enriched resources primarily in the form of maize (fig. 5.4). Berryman (2010) has reported that the evidence of maize in the diet was highest in individuals interred in LF centers, such as the city of Tiwanaku and, most notably Khonkho Wankane and Iruhito from the Desaguadero Valley. This contrasts with LF contexts at the Katari Valley center of Lukurmata, where what little C_4 enrichment most individuals had was primarily coming from fish. While this might be unsurprising given Lukurmata's relative proximity to the lake, the lack of significant amounts of fish in the diets of the inhabitants of the Taraco Peninsula (Miller et al., in this volume) would suggest it has more to do with social processes. Unlike Tiwanaku and Khonkho Wankane, no monumental construction had yet begun at Lukurmata during the LF. Although we see some indication of lowland products in the site in the form of sodalite and paraphernalia associated with lowland hallucinogenic plants (Bermann 1994; Janusek 2004b), it appears Lukurmata's inhabitants (at least those we sampled) did not have (or want) opportunities to consume maize like those in the other prominent settlements of the LF.

POST-TIWANAKU DIETS

Our broad temporal comparisons in isotopic data indicate that diets in the Post-Tiwanaku/Late Intermediate Period (PT) were even more homogenous than in the LF. Diets were tightly centered on local altiplano foods. Indications of maize consumption in the individuals we sampled were overall lower than those from the LF, with most of the C_4-enriched resources being fish. In contrast, $\delta^{15}N$ data indicate a substantial increase in PT meat consumption, suggesting greater dependence on pastoralism than ever before. These data are mirrored in the dental data, with caries frequencies similar to those seen in hunter-gatherers. The lack of cariogenic staples in the diet is consistent with the sharp reduction in raised-field agriculture and the number of agricultural implements found in archaeological assemblages during this period. Although vessels associated with chicha consumption continue to be produced, the large *tinajas* and *ollas* necessary for large-scale feasting are absent. It is clear when we examine the Tiwanaku Period data that the dietary variability associated with the presence of the Tiwanaku state was lost during the Post-Tiwanaku Period.

TIWANAKU PERIOD DIETS

The Tiwanaku Period in the southern Lake Titicaca Basin can be characterized as one of dietary expansion and variability unseen before or after Tiwanaku state influence in the altiplano (figs. 5.2–5.5). Certainly, some individuals' isotopic profiles fall within those seen in the LF and PT, but the range of dietary differences is remarkable, especially when we consider the amount of maize consumed. By comparing the Tiwanaku Period altiplano sample as a whole to data from Moquegua Valley Tiwanaku-affiliated settlements, we find that data on tooth wear, dental caries, and the means of the isotopic values indicate an agropastoral lifestyle (Berryman 2010; Indriati 1998). Dental caries rates are similar to those from the LF altiplano contexts as well (see Berryman 2010). Therefore, despite the major intensification of raised-field agriculture during the Tiwanaku Period and the influx of imported maize, the southern Lake Titicaca Basin population as a whole never became pure agriculturalists. Nevertheless, isotopic comparison establishes that some individuals in the altiplano were eating more maize than maize agriculturalists living in Moquegua Valley (see Tomczak 2001). While massive amounts of maize were being imported, stored, fermented, and consumed in the form of chicha, access to this nonlocal prestige good was not uniform across and within Tiwanaku Period sites of Wiñaymarka (fig. 5.4).

Considerable variation is seen in the consumption of maize both between cities and within the large urban center of Tiwanaku (fig. 5.5). Results reveal a statistically significant increase specifically in the consumption of maize at regional centers with monumental architecture, including Tiwanaku, Khonkho Wankane, Iruhito, and Lukurmata. At Lukurmata some individuals had access to more maize, and an overall increase in camelid consumption (and much less fish) is visible corresponding to the construction of monumental architecture at the site and its emergence as the second-largest regional center. However, these changes were not felt by all in these centers, and those living at rural sites (e.g., CK 65 and CK 70) had much less C_4 enrichment in their diets, and most of that was from fish.

The large sample from Tiwanaku Period contexts at the site of Tiwanaku allows for detailed study of intrasite variation (figs. 5.4, 5.5). We present some of the highlights here to illustrate variable access to maize for

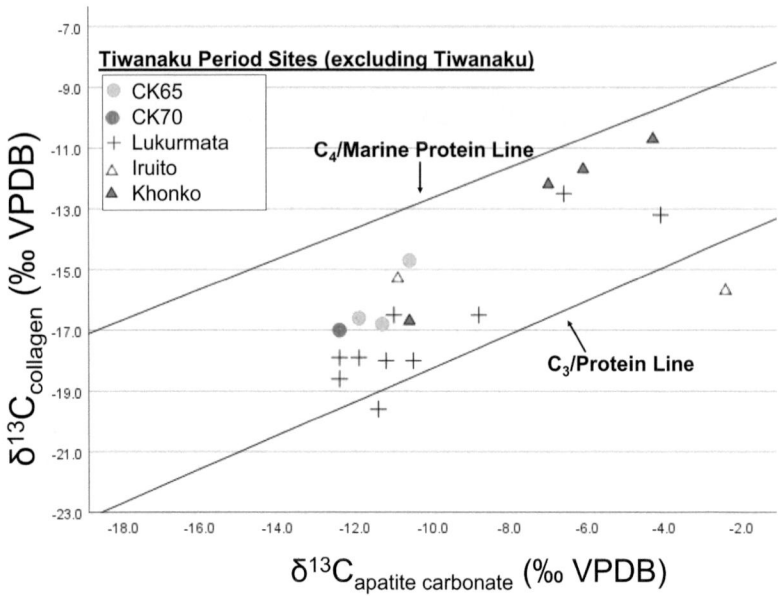

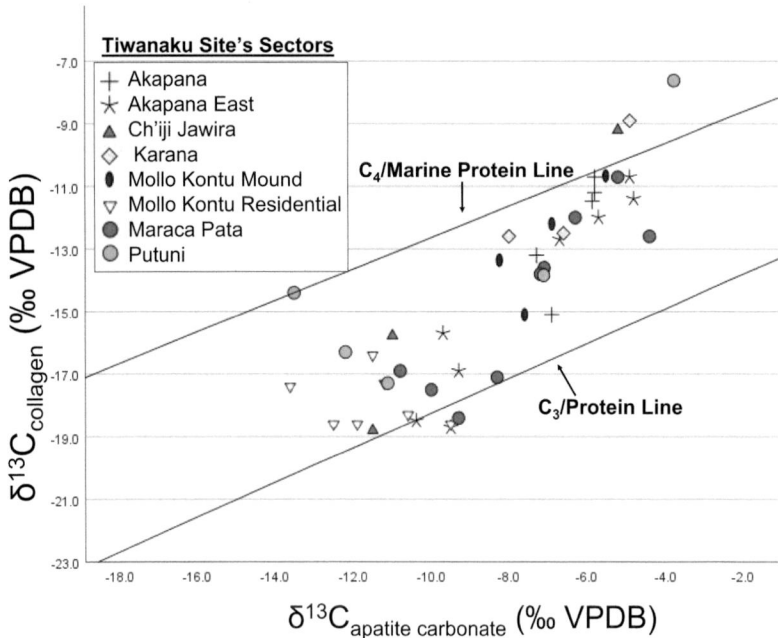

Figure 5.5 Plot of Tiwanaku Period burial locations (site of Tiwanaku by sector below; all other sites above) of $\delta^{13}C_{collagen}$ by $\delta^{13}C_{apatite\ carbonate}$, with dietary regression lines from Froehle, Kellner, and Schoeninger (2010, 2669; see also Kellner and Schoeninger 2007). Illustration by Berryman and Blom.

individuals interred within the site (see Berryman 2010 for more details). Notably, some individuals from Akapana East, the residential compound with the apparent chicha preparation areas discussed above, had $\delta^{13}C$ values that were high even when compared to the maize agriculturalists living in the Moquegua Valley, as did some other individuals interred at the site. Isotopic data also reveal that those in residential compounds on the outskirts of the city had significantly less maize in their diets and more meat, such as those from the Mollo Kontu residential sector. These individuals were more heavily dependent on local crops and were consuming significantly more meat, primarily derived from camelids, an import element of the economy of Mollo Kontu and Tiwanaku in general (Vallières 2016).

In contrast, individuals interred in the Mollo Kontu mound later in the Tiwanaku Period had isotopic signatures and caries rates that indicated significant maize consumption. At other areas of the site, such as Ch'iji Jawira, fish consumption was more prevalent. We also see indications of different diets in the nonlocal outliers from the Putuni palace previously revealed through Sr isotope analyses (Knudson 2008), although most dietary distinctions do not vary with the Sr data and are certainly due to local consumption of resources (see Gagnon and Juengst 2018). Interestingly, no significant differences in diet were observed between males and females, indicating gender was not marked by dietary differences. Overall, the southern Titicaca Basin diet in the Tiwanaku Period can be characterized by its variability both between and within sites and a dramatic increase in access to maize by certain segments of the population.

THE RISE AND FALL OF TIWANAKU SOCIOPOLITICAL COMPLEXITY

Increases in the consumption of imported maize that accompanied the rise of the Tiwanaku state in the Middle Horizon were probably the culmination of escalating competition among regional ceremonial centers that hosted ritual feasts during the LF period. Transforming maize into chicha was a central element of commensal politics and other aspects of altiplano ritual life at these centers, and with the establishment of a colony in Moquegua and other lowland trading partners, Tiwanaku's leaders succeeded in obtaining a large, steady supply of this socially valued extraordinary crop, which they transformed into a distinctive and status-enhancing beverage. This advantage, along with large-scale production of maize chicha by groups of specialists (e.g., Akapana East); the introduction of new ceramic forms for the production, transportation, storage, and consumption of maize chicha; its redistribution at large feasting events; and its virtual disappearance following state disintegration indicate that it was a key element in Tiwanaku's political success. Thus, Tiwanaku's leaders created a social and political climate in which maize chicha, which they could produce on a grand scale, was vital to the construction and maintenance of political authority.

Certain communities and individuals within major centers certainly benefited more than others from their ties to the Tiwanaku state, while many small rural communities in the heartland remained virtually unchanged. Diacritical modes of consumption, including the consumption of large amounts of maize chicha, became an important means of creating and maintaining social differentiation in Tiwanaku society. The homogeneity of Post-Tiwanaku Period diets focused on local crops and a flexible agropastoral lifeway (see Baitzel et al., this volume) indicates that dietary distinctions and the intense social hierarchy of the Tiwanaku Period were effectively leveled with the disintegrations of the Tiwanaku state.

ACKNOWLEDGMENTS

We would like to thank the Amerind Foundation and Eric Kaldahl for allowing space for the intellectual contemplation and reflection that is so precious during these times, and Marta Alfonso-Durruty for being such a wonderful and supportive colleague and friend throughout this pandemic and before and after. We are very grateful for the financial support over the years from the National Science Foundation (BCS-0202329 and SBR-9708001), the Wenner Gren Foundation for Anthropological Research, and Sigma Xi. Several Bolivian colleagues, friends, and institutions, including the Centro de Investigaciones Arqueológicas Antropológicas y Administración de Tiwanaku (CIAAAT), Unidad de Arqueología y Museos (UDAM; and its equivalent over the years such as UNAR and DINAAR), and the Ministerio de Culturas, were essential in providing support, permits, and expertise. Members and directors of Proyecto Jach'a Machaca (John Janusek), Proyecto Jach'a Marka (Nicole

Couture and Maria Bruno), and Proyecto Wila Jawira (Alan Kolata) provided access to collections, important contextual information, and support. We would also like to thank several scholars for their collaboration in providing analyses and data, including Robert Tykot, Amanda Logan, Christine Hastorf, Melanie Miller, and Paula Tomczak. Tiffiny Tung, Tom Dillehay, and Steve Wernke provided countless hours of support and encouragement as members of Carrie Anne's dissertation committee. John Janusek, our collaborator, mentor, and beloved friend; we are forever grateful and miss you dearly.

REFERENCES

Albarracín-Jordán, Juan V. 1996. *Tiwanaku: Arqueología Regional y Dinámica Segmentaria*. La Paz, Bolivia: Plural Editores.

Albarracín-Jordán, Juan V., and James E. Mathews. 1990. *Asentamientos Prehispánicos del Valle de Tiwanaku*. Vol. 1. La Paz, Bolivia: Producciones CIMA.

Alconini Mújica, Sonia. 1995. *Rito, Símbolo e Historia en la Pirámide de Akapana, Tiwanaku: Un Análisis de Cerámica Ceremonial Prehispánica*. La Paz, Bolivia: Editorial Acción.

Ambrose, Stanley H., Brian M. Butler, Douglas B. Hanson, Rosalind L. Hunter-Anderson, and Harold W. Krueger. 1997. "Stable Isotopic Analysis of Human Diet in the Marianas Archipelago, Western Pacific." *American Journal of Physical Anthropology* 104:343–61. https://doi.org/10.1002/(SICI)1096-8644 (199711)104:3<343::AID-AJPA5>3.0.CO;2-W.

Arnold, T. Elliott, Aubrey L. Hillman, Mark B. Abbott, Josef P. Werne, Steven J. McGrath, and Elizabeth N. Arkush. 2021. "Drought and the Collapse of the Tiwanaku Civilization: New Evidence from Lake Orurillo, Peru." *Quaternary Science Reviews* 251: 106693. https://doi.org/10.1016/j.quascirev .2020.106693.

Baitzel, Sarah I. 2018. "Cultural Encounter in the Mortuary Landscape of a Tiwanaku Colony, Moquegua, Peru (AD 650–1100)." *Latin American Antiquity* 29 (3): 421–38. https://doi.org/10.1017/laq.2018.25.

Becker, Sara K. 2017. "Community Labor and Laboring Communities within the Tiwanaku State (C.E. 500–1100)." *Archeological Papers of the American Anthropological Association* 28 (1): 38–53. https://doi.org/10.1111/apaa.12087.

Bermann, Marc. 1994. *Lukurmata: Household Archaeology in Prehispanic Bolivia*. Princeton, N.J.: Princeton University Press.

Berryman, Carrie Anne. 2010. "Food, Feasts, and the Construction of Identity and Power in Ancient Tiwanaku: A Bioarchaeological Perspective." PhD diss., Vanderbilt University.

Blom, Deborah E. 1999. "Tiwanaku Regional Interaction and Social Identity: A Bioarchaeological Approach." PhD diss., University of Chicago.

Blom, Deborah E. 2005. "Embodying Borders: Human Body Modification and Diversity in Tiwanaku Society." *Journal of Anthropological Archaeology* 24 (1): 1–24. https://doi.org/10.1016/j.jaa.2004.10.001.

Bray, Tamara L., ed. 2003. *The Archaeology and Politics of Food and Feasting in Early States and Empires.* New York: Kluwer Academic; Plenum.

Bruno, Maria. 2014. "Beyond Raised Fields: Exploring Farming Practices and Processes of Agricultural Change in the Ancient Lake Titicaca Basin of the Andes." *American Anthropologist* 116 (1): 1–16. https://doi.org/10.1111/aman.12066.

Bruno, Maria C., José M. Capriles, Christine A. Hastorf, Sherilyn C. Fritz, D. Marie Weide, Alejandra I. Domic, and Paul A. Baker. 2021. "The Rise and Fall of Wiñaymarka: Rethinking Cultural and Environmental Interactions in the Southern Basin of Lake Titicaca." *Human Ecology* 49 (2): 131–45. https://doi.org/10.1007/s10745-021-00222-3.

Buikstra, Jane E., and Douglas H. Ubelaker, eds. 1994. *Standards for Data Collection from Human Skeletal Remains: Proceedings of a Seminar at the Field Museum of Natural History.* Arkansas Archaeological Survey Research Series No. 44. Fayetteville: Arkansas Archeological Survey.

Cadwallader, Lauren, David G. Beresford-Jones, Oliver Q. Whaley, and Tamsin C. O'Connell. 2012. "The Signs of Maize? A Reconsideration of What $\delta^{13}C$ Values Say About Palaeodiet in the Andean Region." *Human Ecology* 40 (4): 487–509. https://doi.org/10.1007/s10745-012-9509-0.

Couture, Nicole C. 2002. "The Construction of Power: Monumental Space and Elite Residence at Tiwanaku." PhD diss., University of Chicago.

Couture, Nicole C., and Kathryn E. Sampeck. 2003. "Putuni: A History of Palace Architecture in Tiwanaku." In *Tiwanaku and Its Hinterland: Archaeology and Paleoecology of an Andean Civilization.* Vol. 2, *Urban and Rural Archaeology*, edited by Alan L. Kolata, 226–63. Washington, D.C.: Smithsonian Institution Press.

Dietler, Michael, and Brian Hayden. (2001) 2010. *Feasts: Archaeological and Ethnographic Perspectives on Food, Politics, and Power.* Tuscaloosa: University of Alabama Press.

Froehle, A. W., C. M. Kellner, and M. J. Schoeninger. 2010. "FOCUS: Effect of Diet and Protein Source on Carbon Stable Isotope Ratios in Collagen: Follow up to Warinner and Tuross (2009)." *Journal of Archaeological Science* 37 (10): 2662–70. https://doi.org/10.1016/j.jas.2010.06.003.

Froehle, A. W., C. M. Kellner, and M. J. Schoeninger. 2012. "Multivariate Carbon and Nitrogen Stable Isotope Model for the Reconstruction of Prehistoric Human Diet." *American Journal of Physical Anthropology* 147 (3): 352–69. https://doi.org/10.1002/ajpa.21651.

Gagnon, Celeste Marie, and Sara L. Juengst. 2018. "The Drink Embodied: Theorizing an Integrated Bioarchaeological Approach to the Investigation of

Chicha de Maiz Consumption." *Bioarchaeology International* 2 (3): 206–16. https://doi.org/10.5744/bi.2018.1024.

Gladwell, Randi R. 2007. "El Rango de Machaca (Quimsachata) como Zona de Producción Pastoral: Implicaciones Históricas para Comprender Paisajes del Pasado (investigaciones en 2006)." In *Khonkho e Iruhito: Tercer Informe Preliminar del Proyecto Jach'a Machaca*, edited by John Wayne Janusek and Victor Plaza Martinez, 22–35. Report submitted to the Unidad Nacional de Arqueología, La Paz, Bolivia.

Goldstein, Paul S. 2003. "From Stew-Eaters to Maize-Drinkers: The Chicha Economy and the Tiwanaku Expansion." In *The Archaeology and Politics of Food and Feasting in Early States and Empires*, edited by Tamara L. Bray, 143–72. New York: Kluwer Academic; Plenum.

Goldstein, Paul S. 2005. *Andean Diaspora: The Tiwanaku Colonies and the Origins of South America Empire*. Gainesville: University Press of Florida.

Hastorf, Christine A. 2003. "Andean Luxury Foods: Special Food for the Ancestors, Deities and the Élite." *Antiquity* 77 (297): 545–54. https://doi.org/10.1017/s0003598x00092607.

Hastorf, Christine A. 2016. *The Social Archaeology of Food: Thinking About Eating from Prehistory to the Present*. Cambridge: Cambridge University Press.

Hastorf, Christine A., and Sissel Johannessen. 1993. "Pre-Hispanic Political Change and the Role of Maize in the Central Andes of Peru." *American Anthropologist* 95 (1): 115–38. https://doi.org/10.1525/aa.1993.95.1.02a00060.

Hayden, Brian, and Suzanne Villeneuve. 2011. "A Century of Feasting Studies." *Annual Review of Anthropology* 40 (1): 433–49. https://doi.org/10.1146/annurev-anthro-081309-145740.

Hillson, Simon W. 1979. "Diet and Dental Disease." *World Archaeology* 11 (2): 147–62. https://doi.org/10.1080/00438243.1979.9979758.

Hillson, Simon W. 1996. *Dental Anthropology*. Cambridge: Cambridge University Press.

Indriati, Etty. 1998. "A Dental Anthropological Approach to Coca-Leaf Chewing in the Andes." PhD diss., University of Chicago.

Janusek, John Wayne. 2003. "The Changing Face of Tiwanaku Residential Life: State and Local Identity in an Andean City." In *Tiwanaku and Its Hinterland: Archaeology and Paleoecology of an Andean Civilization*. Vol. 2, *Urban and Rural Archaeology*, edited by Alan L. Kolata, 264–95. Washington D.C.: Smithsonian Institution Press.

Janusek, John Wayne. 2004a. "Collapse as Cultural Revolution: Power and Identity in the Tiwanaku to Pacajes Transition." *Archeological Papers of the American Anthropological Association* 14 (1): 175–209. https://doi.org/10.1525/ap3a.2004.14.175.

Janusek, John Wayne. 2004b. *Identity and Power in the Ancient Andes: Tiwanaku Cities Through Time*. London: Routledge.

Janusek, John Wayne. 2005. "Residential Diversity and the Rise of Complexity in the South-Central Andes." In *Advances in Titicaca Basin Archaeology 1*, edited by Charles Stanish, Amanda B. Cohen, and Mark S. Aldenderfer, 143–73. Los Angeles, Calif.: Cotsen Institute of Archaeology Press.

Janusek, John Wayne. 2008. *Ancient Tiwanaku*. Cambridge: Cambridge University Press.

Janusek, John Wayne, ed. 2018. *Khonkho Wankane: Archaeological Investigations in Jesus de Machaca, Bolivia*. Berkeley: University of California, Berkeley, Archaeological Research Facility.

Janusek, John Wayne, and Alan L. Kolata. 2003. "Prehispanic Rural History in the Rio Katari Valley." In *Tiwanaku and Its Hinterland: Archaeology and Paleoecology of an Andean Civilization*. Vol. 2, *Urban and Rural Archaeology*, edited by Alan L. Kolata, 129–71. Washington D.C.: Smithsonian Institution Press.

Jennings, Justin, Kathleen L. Antrobus, Sam J. Atencio, Erin Glavich, Rebecca Johnson, German Loffler, and Christine Luu. 2005. "Drinking Beer in a Blissful Mood: Alcohol Production, Operational Chains, and Feasting in the Ancient World." *Current Anthropology* 46 (2): 275–303. https://doi.org/10.1086/427119.

Juengst, Sara L., Dale L. Hutchinson, Karen Mohr Chávez, Sergio J. Chávez, Stanislava R. Chávez, John Krigbaum, Theresa Schober, and Lynette Norr. 2021. "The Resiliency of Diet on the Copacabana Peninsula, Bolivia." *Journal of Anthropological Archaeology* 61:101260. https://doi.org/10.1016/j.jaa.2020 .101260.

Kellner, Corina M., and Margaret J. Schoeninger. 2007. "A Simple Carbon Isotope Model for Reconstructing Prehistoric Human Diet." *American Journal of Physical Anthropology* 133 (4): 1112–27. https://doi.org/10.1002/ajpa.20618.

Klarich, Elizabeth, ed. 2010. *Inside Ancient Kitchens: New Directions in the Study of Daily Meals and Feasts*. Boulder: University Press of Colorado.

Knudson, Kelly J. 2008. "Tiwanaku Influence in the South Central Andes: Strontium Isotope Analysis and Middle Horizon Migration." *Latin American Antiquity* 19 (1): 3–23. https://doi.org/10.1017/S104566350000763X.

Knudson, Kelly J., and Deborah E. Blom. 2009. "The Complex Relationship Between Tiwanaku Mortuary Identity and Geographic Origin in the South Central Andes." In *Bioarchaeology and Identity in the Americas*, edited by Kelly J. Knudson and Christopher M. Stojanowski, 194–211. Gainesville: University Press of Florida.

Kolata, Alan L. 1993. *Tiwanaku: Portrait of an Andean Civilization*. Cambridge: Blackwell.

Kolata, Alan L., ed. 1996. *Tiwanaku and Its Hinterland: Archaeology and Paleoecology of an Andean Civilization*. Vol. 1, *Agroecology*. Washington, D.C.: Smithsonian Institution Press.

Kolata, Alan L., ed. 2003a. *Tiwanaku and Its Hinterland: Archaeology and Paleoecology of an Andean Civilization*. Vol. 2, *Urban and Rural Archaeology*. Washington, D.C.: Smithsonian Institution Press.

Kolata, Alan L. 2003b. "Tiwanaku Ceremonial Architecture and Urban Organization." In *Tiwanaku and Its Hinterland: Archaeology and Paleoecology of an Andean Civilization*. Vol. 2, *Urban and Rural Archaeology*, edited by Alan L. Kolata, 175–201. Washington D.C.: Smithsonian Institution Press.

Kolata, Alan L., Michael W. Binford, Mark Brenner, John Wayne Janusek, and Charles Ortloff. 2000. "Environmental Thresholds and the Empirical Reality of State Collapse: A Response to Erickson (1999)." *Antiquity* 74 (284): 424–26. https://doi.org/10.1017/s0003598x00059512.

Langlie, BrieAnna S., and Elizabeth N. Arkush. 2016. "Managing Mayhem: Conflict, Environment, and Subsistence in the Andean Late Intermediate Period, Puno, Peru." In *The Archaeology of Food and Warfare*, edited by Amber M. VanDerwarker and Gregory D. Wilson, 259–89. New York: Springer.

Larsen, Clark Spencer, R. Shavit, and M. C. Griffin. 1991. "Dental Caries Evidence for Dietary Change: An Archaeological Context." In *Advances in Dental Anthropology*, edited by M.A. Kelley and Clark Spencer Larsen, 179–202. New York: Wiley-Liss.

Logan, Amanda L., Christine A. Hastorf, and Deborah M. Pearsall. 2012. "'Let's Drink Together': Early Ceremonial Use of Maize in the Titicaca Basin." *Latin American Antiquity* 23 (3): 235–58. https://doi.org/10.7183/1045-6635.23.3.235.

Manzanilla, Linda. 1992. *Akapana: Una Pirámide en el Centro del Mundo*. Mexico City: Universidad Nacional Autónoma de México, Instituto de Investigaciones Antropológicas.

Marsh, Erik J. 2012. "The Emergence of Tiwanaku: Domestic Practices and Regional Traditions at Khonkho Wankane and Kk'araña." PhD diss., University of California, Santa Barbara.

Nash, Donna J. 2010. "Fine Dining and Fabulous Atmosphere: Feasting Facilities and Political Interaction in the Wari Realm." In *Inside Ancient Kitchens: New Directions in the Study of Daily Meals and Feast*, edited by Elizabeth A. Klarich, 83–110. Boulder: University Press of Colorado.

Pérez Arias, Maribel. 2014. "Feasting and Rank in the Development of Khonkho Wankane." Master's thesis, University of Pittsburgh.

Ponce Sanginés, Carlos. (1972) 1981. *Tiwanaku: Espacio, Tiempo, Cultura; Ensayo de Síntesis Arqueológica*. La Paz, Bolivia: Los Amigos del Libro.

Powell, Mary Lucas. 1985. "The Analysis of Dental Wear and Caries for Dietary Reconstruction." In *The Analysis of Prehistoric Diets*, edited by Robert I. Gilbert Jr. and James H. Mielke, 307–38. London: Academic Press.

Roddick, Andrew P., and Christine A. Hastorf. 2010. "Tradition Brought to the Surface: Continuity, Innovation and Change in the Late Formative Period, Taraco Peninsula, Bolivia." *Cambridge Archaeological Journal* 20 (2): 157–78. https://doi.org/10.1017/s0959774310000211.

Smith, Scott C. 2016. *Landscape and Politics in the Ancient Andes: Biographies of Place at Khonkho Wankane*. Albuquerque: University of New Mexico Press.

Stanish, Charles. 2003. *Ancient Titicaca: The Evolution of Social Complexity in Southern Peru and Northern Bolivia.* Los Angeles: University of California Press.

Tomczak, Paula. 2001. "Prehistoric Socio-Economic Relations and Population Organization in the Lower Osmore Valley of Southern Peru." PhD diss., University of Chicago.

Tykot, Robert H. 2006. "Isotope Analyses and the Histories of Maize." In *Histories of Maize: Multidisciplinary Approaches to the Prehistory, Linguistics, Biogeography, Domestication, and Evolution of Maize*, edited by John E. Staller, Robert H. Tykot, and Bruce F. Benz, 131–42. New York: Routledge.

Vallières, Claudine. 2016. "Camelid Pastoralism at Ancient Tiwanaku: Urban Provisioning in the Highlands of Bolivia." In *The Archaeology of Andean Pastoralism*, edited by José M. Capriles and Nicholas Tripcevich, 67–86. Albuquerque: University of New Mexico Press.

Vranich, Alexei, and Charles Stanish, eds. 2013. *Visions of Tiwanaku.* Los Angeles: Cotsen Institute of Archaeology Press.

Webster, Ann DeMuth, and John Wayne Janusek. 2003. "Tiwanaku Camelids: Subsistence, Sacrifice, and Social Reproduction." In *Tiwanaku and Its Hinterland: Archaeology and Paleoecology of an Andean Civilization.* Vol. 2, *Urban and Rural Archaeology*, edited by Alan L. Kolata, 343–62. Washington, D.C.: Smithsonian Institution Press.

Wright, Melanie F., Christine A. Hastorf, and Heidi A. Lennstrom. 2003. "Pre-Hispanic Agriculture and Plant Use at Tiwanaku: Social and Political Implications." In *Tiwanaku and Its Hinterland: Archaeology and Paleoecology of an Andean Civilization.* Vol. 2, *Urban and Rural Archaeology*, edited by Alan L. Kolata, 384–403. Washington, D.C.: Smithsonian Institution Press.

6

Paleodiet Outside of the Tiwanaku Heartland

Isotopic Analysis of Individuals Buried at Tiwanaku-Affiliated Sites in the Moquegua Valley, Peru

Kelly J. Knudson, Marcos de la Rosa-Martinez, Alexandra Greenwald, and Deborah E. Blom

Between approximately AD 500 and AD 1100, the Tiwanaku polity was an unavoidable presence in the South Central Andes. Tiwanaku affected the daily lives of people in its heartland, the Lake Titicaca Basin, as well as in the widely distributed Tiwanaku-affiliated sites outside of the heartland, such as in the Moquegua Valley of southern Peru. A growing body of research has shown that Tiwanaku impacts were highly variable, both within and between sites (Janusek 2004, 2008; Kolata 1993, 1996–2003; Goldstein 2005; Torres-Rouff 2008, 2011; Torres-Rouff and Knudson 2017). Here we use paleodietary reconstructions, based on carbon and nitrogen isotopic values, to infer food choices and better understand daily life in the site of Chen Chen and other Tiwanaku-affiliated sites in the Moquegua Valley.

The expansion of Tiwanaku-style material culture throughout the South Central Andes reveals that Tiwanaku extended its sociopolitical influence into nearby agriculturally productive areas, particularly in the Moquegua Valley of southern Peru (Janusek 2004, 2008; Kolata 1993, 1996–2003; Goldstein 2005). Although the Lake Titicaca Basin, where Tiwanaku and Tiwanaku-affiliated regional centers are located, was agriculturally productive, the high-altitude zone is not ideal for maize (*Zea mays*) production. However, maize consumption at Tiwanaku and regional centers in the Lake Titicaca Basin increased dramatically after AD 500, and maize was probably a key part of feasting events that involved *chicha*, or maize beer (Berryman and Blom, this volume). Agricultural colonies in the low-altitude Moquegua Valley of southern Peru and the Cochabamba Valley in Bolivia were established to provide this important crop, as well as other low-altitude crops such as chili peppers (*Capsicum* sp.), to people living in the Lake Titicaca Basin (e.g., Goldstein 2005).

In the Moquegua Valley there are three large site complexes (Chen Chen, Omo, and Rio Muerto) with clear material culture ties to Tiwanaku as well as the smaller site complex of Cerro Echenique (Goldstein 2005). At the Moquegua Valley site complexes, residential excavations have shown a commitment to agricultural production and storage of surplus, including agricultural hoes, grinding stones, and storage cists as well as extensive irrigation networks (Goldstein 2005). Salvage excavations at the large cemetery of Chen Chen, which covered more than 10 hectares, demonstrate that there was a large population at the site (Vargas V. 1994; Owen 1997). Direct colonization by the Tiwanaku polity is inferred at Chen Chen through genetic analysis (both biodistance and aDNA) that shows close genetic relationships between Chen Chen and Tiwanaku (Lewis, Buikstra, and Stone 2007; Blom et al. 1998). In addition, strontium isotope analysis has demonstrated the presence of first-generation migrants from the Lake Titicaca Basin (Knudson 2008, 2004; Knudson et al. 2014). While artifact analyses of the mortuary objects included in graves at Chen Chen are ongoing, their homogeneity and generally low quantities do not point to significant status differences in people buried at Chen Chen.

The Tiwanaku-affiliated site complexes of Omo and Rio Muerto also have evidence for extensive agricultural production. In addition, the Omo M10 site also included a monumental temple complex—the only Tiwanaku-style temple in Moquegua—and was probably an important ritual or pilgrimage center in addition to a residential site (Goldstein 1992). Finally, and importantly, the Tiwanaku-affiliated sites in Moquegua were not homogenous, instead consisting of at least two different community or occupational identities based on artifact assemblages and residential architecture. The Chen Chen–style group is associated with maize agriculture and was buried at the sites of Chen Chen, Omo, and Rio Muerto M43, while the Omo-style group is associated with camelid pastoralism and was buried in cemeteries at Rio Muerto M70 (Goldstein 2005).

Given the large numbers of people living in Tiwanaku-affiliated sites in the Moquegua Valley, what dietary choices were they making? How did producing agricultural products for people living in the Lake Titicaca Basin affect their lived experiences? And how did different social identities, such as gender, age, or community identities, influence their diets and food choices?

Theoretically, we address these questions using the framework of social identities, which we define as who individuals thought they were, how they communicated those identities to others, and how others perceived those identities (Knudson and Stojanowski 2009, 5). We recognize that "social identities" is a broad category that encompasses identities that are expected to change throughout the life course, such as age identities, and others that are often, though not always, more stable over the life course, such as gender or ethnic identities (see overviews in Buikstra and Scott 2009; Díaz-Andreu et al. 2005). Social identities can also refer to groups of people who share the same community, occupation, and religion, among others. Dietary choice can be an important aspect of creating, maintaining, and communicating different social identities. In the Andean Middle Horizon, for example, researchers have identified dietary changes related to age identities (e.g., Velasco and Tung 2021), the impact of gender identities on dietary patterns (e.g., Somerville et al. 2015), and how food and drink were used to create and maintain larger community identities (e.g., Berryman 2010; Janusek 2004; Williams and Nash 2021).

Methodologically, we address our questions about the interplay between dietary choices and social identities through isotopic analyses of archaeological human remains. Given the location of Chen Chen and other Moquegua Valley sites in a midaltitude zone well suited for maize agriculture and their role as maize-producing colonies for the Tiwanaku heartland, one might expect that the diet of the people who lived and died in the Moquegua Valley was maize based. However, as Wilson and McCool point out (this volume), dietary choices are not simply determined by the environment. Here we use isotopic indicators of diet to understand the dietary choices of specific individuals buried at Tiwanaku-affiliated Moquegua Valley sites, complementing work on dietary choices at Tiwanaku-affiliated sites in the Lake Titicaca Basin (Berryman and Blom, and Miller et al., this volume). This isotopic approach to Andean paleodiet has been successful in a number of regions (see recent examples in Turner et al. 2019; Tung et al. 2019; Velasco and Tung 2021), and we refer readers to other papers in this volume for more detailed information on carbon and nitrogen isotope analyses in the Andes and the isotopic background (Berryman and Blom, and Miller et al., this volume).

SAMPLING STRATEGY AND METHODS USED

In this study we infer paleodiet from carbon and nitrogen values obtained from bulk collagen from archaeological bone samples from 101 individuals buried at the sites of Chen Chen in the Moquegua Valley (table 6.1). We also reconstruct dietary variability over the life course by collecting sequential serial samples of first and third molar dentinal collagen from six individuals buried at Chen Chen in southern Peru (table 6.2).

Bulk collagen samples from bone represent diet in the last years of life. In contrast, dentinal collagen samples correspond to the diet consumed in the first years of life while the teeth formed. Thus, stable isotope values in dentin mostly reflect particular periods of ontogenetic synthesis. Dentin accumulation in permanent first molars begins at birth at the Dentine Enamel Junction (DEJ), reaching the cemento-enamel junction (CEJ) at ~2.8 years (Hillson 1986, 1996). Dentine deposition continues distally until the completion of the apical root tip (ART) at ~9.5 years of age (Hillson 1986, 1996). In permanent third molars, dentin accumulation begins at the DEJ at ~9–10 years of age, reaching the CEJ at ~14 years, and ART completion is reached by ~21–22 years of age (Hillson 1986, 1996).

Samples were prepared in the Archaeological Chemistry Laboratory at Arizona State University (ASU). To preserve as much information as possible before destructive analysis, all samples were photographed, 3D scanned, and then cast in the ASU Hard Tissue Biology Laboratory. For sequential samples, after cross-sectioning the tooth in the ASU Hard Tissue Laboratory, enamel and cementum were mechanically removed. Bone and dentine samples were demineralized in 0.5M HCl. Thereafter, the tooth was cut into serial microsamples from the root tip to the dentin enamel junction. Serial sections are usually 1–2 mm thick, and samples typically represent 6–12 months of an individual's life. Bone and dentinal collagen samples were rinsed and treated with 0.125M NaOH to remove humic contaminants, solubilized with HCl, and then freeze-dried. Samples were analyzed using a Thermo MAT 253 isotope ratio mass spectrometer with a Costech Elemental Analyzer in the ASU Metals, Environmental, and Terrestrial Analytical Laboratory (METAL). Accuracy and precision were determined through internal and external standards and were 0.2‰. All samples exhibited C:N values consistent

Table 6.1 Carbon and nitrogen isotope data from bone samples from Tiwanaku-affiliated sites M1 (Chen Chen), M10 (Omo), and M43 and M70 (Rio Muerto) in the Moquegua Valley

Site	Specimen or tomb number	Laboratory number	$\delta^{13}C$ collagen (VPDB) (‰)	$\delta^{15}N$ collagen (AIR) (‰)	Reference
M1	681	NA	−11.4	6.2	Tomczak 2001
M1	1573	NA	−12.2	8.0	Tomczak 2001
M1	1600	NA	−13.5	5.9	Tomczak 2001
M1	1847	NA	−13.8	7.7	Tomczak 2001
M1	1968	NA	−14.9	5.6	Tomczak 2001
M1	2188	NA	−14.6	5.3	Tomczak 2001
M1	3660	NA	−13.2	5.4	Tomczak 2001
M1	3715	NA	−11.2	8.1	Tomczak 2001
M1	3718	NA	−14.9	4.8	Tomczak 2001
M1	3835	NA	−14.3	5.6	Tomczak 2001
M1	2798-1	NA	−14.0	5.6	Tomczak 2001
M1	3-Bl	NA	−17.3	10.3 l	Tomczak 2001
M1	ll9	NA	−11.8	7.6	Tomczak 2001
M1	M1-0016	ACL-5349	−14.7	5.8	
M1	M1-0086	ACL-5249	−14.3	4.9	
M1	M1-0086	F1991	−14.3	5.4	
M1	M1-02-026_04	ACL-6923	−11.6	8.0	
M1	M1-02-027_03	ACL-6926	−11.4	6.7	
M1	M1-02-082_04	ACL-6931	−13.2	7.3	
M1	M1-02-106_03	ACL-6934	−14.7	4.7	
M1	M1-02-136_04	ACL-6938	−14.9	5.4	
M1	M1-02-197_04	ACL-6943	−12.9	7.0	
M1	M1-02-250_04	ACL-6947	−13.4	7.0	
M1	M1-02-261_04	ACL-6951	−13.0	6.8	
M1	M1-02-302_01	ACL-6954	−11.9	10.0	
M1	M1-02-385_02	ACL-6956	−14.7	4.4	
M1	M1-02-398_04	ACL-6960	−12.7	5.7	
M1	M1-02-509_03	ACL-6970	−13.8	5.5	
M1	M1-02-513_04	ACL-6974	−13.7	5.1	
M1	M1-02-517_04	ACL-6978	−14.0	5.8	
M1	M1-02-564_03	ACL-6985	−13.2	5.9	
M1	M1-02-588_01	ACL-6988	−11.3	8.0	
M1	M1-02-593_04	ACL-6992	−12.8	7.2	
M1	M1-02-660_01	ACL-6993	−13.6	7.2	
M1	M1-02-705_02	ACL-6995	−14.0	5.7	
M1	M1-02-706_02	ACL-6997	−13.2	6.7	
M1	M1-02-712_04	ACL-7001	−14.3	5.3	
M1	M1-02-823_01	ACL-7002	−14.5	6.4	

(*continued*)

Table 6.1 (*continued*)

Site	Specimen or tomb number	Laboratory number	δ¹³C collagen (VPDB) (‰)	δ¹⁵N collagen (AIR) (‰)	Reference
M1	M1-02-826_02	ACL-7004	−14.2	6.4	
M1	M1-02-826_03	ACL-7005	−14.1	6.4	
M1	M1-02-864_03	ACL-7008	−15.4	4.4	
M1	M1-02-880-02	ACL-7013	−13.9	4.4	
M1	M1-05-070_02	ACL-7015	−14.2	20.6	
M1	M1-05-149_04	ACL-7019	−12.6	7.1	
M1	M1-05-149_05	ACL-7020	−12.4	7.3	
M1	M1-05-152_02	ACL-7023	−13.9	4.8	
M1	M1-05-156_04	ACL-7028	−11.7	7.3	
M1	M1-05-156_05	ACL-7029	−13.3	7.3	
M1	M1-05-174_03	ACL-7032	−12.5	17.6	
M1	M1-05-200_02	ACL-7038	−13.5	6.7	
M1	M1-05-204A_01	ACL-7039	−13.4	5.1	
M1	M1-05-211_03	ACL-7042	−18.9	18.9	
M1	M1-05-240_03	ACL-7046	−13.6	6.3	
M1	M1-05-242_04	ACL-7050	−13.6	5.1	
M1	M1-05-279_02	ACL-7052	−13.9	5.7	
M1	M1-05-311_02	ACL-7056	−13.5	8.1	
M1	M1-05-317_02	ACL-7058	−15.1	6.7	
M1	M1-05-328_04	ACL-7062	−11.0	9.1	
M1	M1-05-329_01	ACL-7063	−13.1	6.7	
M1	M1-05-360_04	ACL-7067	−11.5	7.8	
M1	M1-05-389_03	ACL-7070	−14.0	5.3	
M1	M1-05-395-02	ACL-7072	−13.2	19.5	
M1	M1-05-399_04	ACL-7076	−15.1	4.8	
M1	M1-05-405_02	ACL-7078	−15.1	6.3	
M1	M1-0572	ACL-5301	−14.9	5.1	
M1	M1-0572	F1999	−14.9	5.1	
M1	M1-1091	ACL-5348	−14.6	7.2	
M1	M1-1370	ACL-5226	−13.3	6.4	
M1	M1-88-0046_01	ACL-6735	−13.3	7.1	
M1	M1-88-0113_04	ACL-6739	−14.4	6.1	
M1	M1-88-0122_04	ACL-6743	−13.4	5.7	
M1	M1-88-0148_02	ACL-6745	−13.7	4.6	
M1	M1-88-0164_02	ACL-6747	−14.4	4.9	
M1	M1-88-0169_04	ACL-6751	−13.8	5.3	
M1	M1-88-0177_01	ACL-6752	−12.8	12.8	
M1	M1-88-0210-1_03	ACL-6757	−13.1	5.1	
M1	M1-88-0235_04	ACL-6761	−16.5	9.9	
M1	M1-88-0243_04	ACL-6765	−11.2	9.2	

(*continued*)

Table 6.1 (*continued*)

Site	Specimen or tomb number	Laboratory number	$\delta^{13}C$ collagen (VPDB) (‰)	$\delta^{15}N$ collagen (AIR) (‰)	Reference
M1	M1-88-0256_01	ACL-6766	−15.6	7.4	
M1	M1-88-0262-1_03	ACL-6769	−12.0	5.2	
M1	M1-88-0318_02	ACL-6771	−12.3	6.9	
M1	M1-88-0321_01	ACL-6772	−10.2	12.0	
M1	M1-88-0515_01	ACL-6777	−10.6	8.6	
M1	M1-88-0517_03	ACL-6780	−14.5	5.2	
M1	M1-88-0524_02	ACL-6782	−13.2	4.7	
M1	M1-88-0646_02	ACL-6784	−13.5	5.4	
M1	M1-88-0852_02	ACL-6789	−14.3	5.6	
M1	M1-88-1084_02	ACL-6791	−12.5	6.5	
M1	M1-88-1252_03	ACL-6794	−15.5	5.2	
M1	M1-88-1658-04	ACL-6806	−12.4	9.3	
M1	M1-88-2391_01	ACL-6810	−13.9	9.4	
M1	M1-88-2442_02	ACL-6812	−13.1	4.9	
M1	M1-88-2583_03	ACL-6815	−14.2	6.1	
M1	M1-88-2938_03	ACL-6826	−15.4	5.9	
M1	M1-88-2989_04	ACL-6830	−13.0	9.6	
M1	M1-88-3013_04	ACL-6834	−11.2	9.4	
M1	M1-88-3083_04	ACL-6838	−13.2	5.6	
M1	M1-88-3150_04	ACL-6842	−13.9	5.6	
M1	M1-88-3454_02	ACL-6855	−14.5	4.9	
M1	M1-88-3732_02	ACL-6866	−13.4	8.5	
M1	M1-88-3787_04	ACL-6870	−14.3	5.3	
M1	M1-88-655-03	ACL-6787	−13.8	8.7	
M1	M1-95-271024_01	ACL-6873	−12.5	5.8	
M1	M1-95-271032_04	ACL-6878	−14.1	4.7	
M1	M1-95-302009_04	ACL-6885	−13.0	5.3	
M1	M1-95-302032_03	ACL-6888	−13.3	4.8	
M1	M1-95-302035_02	ACL-6890	−13.3	6.2	
M1	M1-95-302039A_02	ACL-6892	−13.3	4.7	
M1	M1-95-303022_04	ACL-6896	−13.5	6.4	
M1	M1-95-307018_03	ACL-6900	−11.3	14.7	
M1	M1-95-307026_04	ACL-6904	−11.1	15.1	
M1	M1-95-309010_04	ACL-6910	−14.6	5.4	
M1	M1-95-341024_02	ACL-6915	−13.6	5.6	
M1	M1-95-342031_02	ACL-6917	−13.8	5.6	
M1	S/NK.380	NA	−11.6	8.9	Tomczak 2001
M10	B13-2006	s-57	−14.7	5.7	Sandness 1992
M10	M1-7	s-132	−13.0	10.2	Sandness 1992
M10	M2-3	s-133	−13.9	6.8	Sandness 1992

(*continued*)

Table 6.1 (*continued*)

Site	Specimen or tomb number	Laboratory number	δ¹³C collagen (VPDB) (‰)	δ¹⁵N collagen (AIR) (‰)	Reference
M10	M4-5	s-52	−13.9	6.7	Sandness 1992
M10	M5-3	s-53	−12.8	8.0	Sandness 1992
M10	M7-3	s-54	−11.2	8.8	Sandness 1992
M10	S2-2	s-56	−12.0	6.8	Sandness 1992
M10	S6-1	s-130	−9.6	9.7	Sandness 1992
M10	S7-7	s-131	−11.9	8.9	Sandness 1992
M10	S8-2	s-55	−14.5	10.5	Sandness 1992
M43	M43-3018	AS-0052	−13.5	5.9	Somerville et al. 2015
M43	M43-3054	AS-0053	−12.6	6.3	Somerville et al. 2015
M43	M43-3185	AS-0054	−13.0	6.2	Somerville et al. 2015
M43	M43-3233	AS-0055	−10.9	10.7	Somerville et al. 2015
M43	M43-3402	AS-0056	−13.8	5.7	Somerville et al. 2015
M43	M43-3414	AS-0057	−13.5	7.7	Somerville et al. 2015
M43	M43-3435	AS-0058	−12.6	8.6	Somerville et al. 2015
M43	M43-4141	AS-0059	−11.8	9.2	Somerville et al. 2015
M43	M43-4237	AS-0060	−12.2	6.4	Somerville et al. 2015
M43	M43-4345	AS-0061	−10.3	9.7	Somerville et al. 2015
M43	M43-4835	AS-0062	−11.0	8.5	Somerville et al. 2015
M43	M43-4870	AS-0063	−13.0	6.2	Somerville et al. 2015
M43	M43-4878	AS-0064	−11.5	10.6	Somerville et al. 2015
M70	M70-2236	AS-0033	−16.0	9.7	Somerville et al. 2015
M70	M70-2248	AS-0034	−13.3	5.9	Somerville et al., 2015
M70	M70-2276	AS-0035	−11.9	8.0	Somerville et al. 2015
M70	M70-2370	AS-0024	−9.7	8.6	Somerville et al. 2015
M70	M70-2380	AS-0036	−10.4	10.2	Somerville et al. 2015
M70	M70-2456	AS-0037	−10.9	9.8	Somerville et al. 2015
M70	M70-2478	AS-0038	−13.4	5.9	Somerville et al. 2015
M70	M70-2495	AS-0025	−11.6	6.1	Somerville et al. 2015
M70	M70-2621	AS-0026	−14.9	8.4	Somerville et al. 2015
M70	M70-2642	AS-0027	−12.3	9.0	Somerville et al. 2015
M70	M70-2787	AS-0028	−12.5	7.8	Somerville et al. 2015
M70	M70-2840	AS-0039	−11.8	10.2	Somerville et al. 2015
M70	M70-2877	AS-0029	−9.7	9.4	Somerville et al. 2015
M70	M70-2896	AS-0030	−13.2	10.6	Somerville et al. 2015
M70	M70-2956	AS-0031	−11.3	10.4	Somerville et al. 2015
M70	M70-2985	AS-0032	−13.2	9.8	Somerville et al. 2015
M70	M70-2999	AS-0040	−11.6	8.6	Somerville et al., 2015
M70	M70-4429	AS-0065	−10.3	9.7	Somerville et al., 2015
M70	M70-4443	AS-0066	−10.3	9.6	Somerville et al., 2015
M70	M70-4468	AS-0067	−13.4	9.2	Somerville et al., 2015

Note: NA = not available.

Table 6.2 Carbon and nitrogen isotope data from sequential dentinal collagen samples from the Tiwanaku-affiliated site of Chen Chen, Moquegua Valley, Peru

Laboratory number	Specimen or tomb number	Sample type	$\delta^{13}C$ collagen (VPDB) (‰)	$\delta^{15}N$ collagen (AIR) (‰)	Serial Section age (y)
ACL-6758a	M1-88-0235_01	LLM1	NA	NA	9.0
ACL-6758b	M1-88-0235_01	LLM1	NA	NA	8.3
ACL-6758c	M1-88-0235_01	LLM1	−18.9	10.9	7.5
ACL-6758d	M1-88-0235_01	LLM1	−18.4	10.8	6.8
ACL-6758e	M1-88-0235_01	LLM1	−18.7	10.5	6.0
ACL-6758f	M1-88-0235_01	LLM1	−18.2	10.6	5.3
ACL-6758g	M1-88-0235_01	LLM1	−18.1	10.3	4.5
ACL-6758h	M1-88-0235_01	LLM1	−17.9	10.1	3.8
ACL-6758i	M1-88-0235_01	LLM1	−17.6	9.8	3.0
ACL-6758j	M1-88-0235_01	LLM1	−16.9	9.8	2.6
ACL-6758k	M1-88-0235_01	LLM1	NA	NA	2.2
ACL-6758l	M1-88-0235_01	LLM1	−17.6	10.6	1.8
ACL-6758m	M1-88-0235_01	LLM1	−18.6	10.7	1.4
ACL-6758n	M1-88-0235_01	LLM1	−19.1	11.9	1.0
ACL-6760a	M1-88-0235_01	LLM1	−18.0	11.5	21.0
ACL-6760b	M1-88-0235_01	LLM1	−17.6	11.2	20.3
ACL-6760c	M1-88-0235_01	LLM1	−17.7	10.9	19.6
ACL-6760d	M1-88-0235_01	LLM1	−15.6	10.5	18.9
ACL-6760e	M1-88-0235_01	LLM1	−13.9	10.3	18.2
ACL-6760f	M1-88-0235_01	LLM1	−15.9	10.6	17.5
ACL-6760g	M1-88-0235_01	LLM1	−17.3	10.9	16.8
ACL-6760h	M1-88-0235_01	LLM1	−15.4	10.7	16.1
ACL-6760i	M1-88-0235_01	LLM1	−14.4	10.4	15.4
ACL-6760j	M1-88-0235_01	LLM1	NA	NA	14.7
ACL-6760k	M1-88-0235_01	LLM1	−16.7	11.1	14.0
ACL-6760l	M1-88-0235_01	LLM1	−18.5	11.1	12.2
ACL-6760m	M1-88-0235_01	LLM1	−18.2	10.9	10.3
ACL-6760n	M1-88-0235_01	LLM1	−18.7	11.3	8.5
ACL-6795a	M1-88-1400_01	ULM1	−14.2	6.2	9.0
ACL-6795b	M1-88-1400_01	ULM1	−13.6	6.1	8.0
ACL-6795c	M1-88-1400_01	ULM1	−14.3	5.9	7.5
ACL-6795d	M1-88-1400_01	ULM1	−12.3	6.3	7.0
ACL-6795e	M1-88-1400_01	ULM1	−11.9	6.5	6.5
ACL-6795f	M1-88-1400_01	ULM1	−12.9	6.5	6.0
ACL-6795g	M1-88-1400_01	ULM1	−13.4	5.9	5.0
ACL-6795h	M1-88-1400_01	ULM1	−14.4	5.5	4.5
ACL-6795i	M1-88-1400_01	ULM1	−12.8	5.4	4.0

(continued)

Table 6.2 (*continued*)

Laboratory number	Specimen or tomb number	Sample type	$\delta^{13}C$ collagen (VPDB) (‰)	$\delta^{15}N$ collagen (AIR) (‰)	Serial Section age (y)
ACL-6795j	M1-88-1400_01	ULM1	−12.9	5.4	3.5
ACL-6795k	M1-88-1400_01	ULM1	−12.9	5.6	3.0
ACL-6795l	M1-88-1400_01	ULM1	−12.4	6.0	2.5
ACL-6795m	M1-88-1400_01	ULM1	−12.0	7.8	2.0
ACL-6795n	M1-88-1400_01	ULM1	−11.3	9.6	1.0
ACL-6797a	M1-88-1400_01	ULM1	−16.5	6.1	21.0
ACL-6797b	M1-88-1400_01	ULM1	−16.5	6.1	20.2
ACL-6797c	M1-88-1400_01	ULM1	−16.6	6.1	19.5
ACL-6797d	M1-88-1400_01	ULM1	NA	NA	18.7
ACL-6797e	M1-88-1400_01	ULM1	NA	NA	17.9
ACL-6797f	M1-88-1400_01	ULM1	NA	NA	17.1
ACL-6797g	M1-88-1400_01	ULM1	NA	NA	16.3
ACL-6797h	M1-88-1400_01	ULM1	NA	NA	15.6
ACL-6797i	M1-88-1400_01	ULM1	NA	NA	14.8
ACL-6797j	M1-88-1400_01	ULM1	NA	NA	14.0
ACL-6797k	M1-88-1400_01	ULM1	NA	NA	12.2
ACL-6797l	M1-88-1400_01	ULM1	−15.1	6.0	10.3
ACL-6797m	M1-88-1400_01	ULM1	−15.5	5.7	8.5
ACL-6875a	M1-95-271032_01	LRM1	−14.6	5.7	1.0
ACL-6875b	M1-95-271032_01	LRM1	−14.4	5.8	NA
ACL-6875c	M1-95-271032_01	LRM1	−14.2	6.1	NA
ACL-6875d	M1-95-271032_01	LRM1	−13.9	5.9	NA
ACL-6875e	M1-95-271032_01	LRM1	−13.5	6.2	NA
ACL-6875f	M1-95-271032_01	LRM1	−13.9	6.0	NA
ACL-6875g	M1-95-271032_01	LRM1	−14.5	6.2	NA
ACL-6875h	M1-95-271032_01	LRM1	−14.2	6.3	NA
ACL-6875i	M1-95-271032_01	LRM1	−14.3	6.3	NA
ACL-6875j	M1-95-271032_01	LRM1	−14.4	6.2	NA
ACL-6875k	M1-95-271032_01	LRM1	−14.7	6.3	9.0
ACL-6877a	M1-95-271032_01	LRM1	−15.5	5.7	21.0
ACL-6877b	M1-95-271032_01	LRM1	−15.3	5.9	20.3
ACL-6877c	M1-95-271032_01	LRM1	−14.6	6.2	19.6
ACL-6877d	M1-95-271032_01	LRM1	−14.4	6.4	18.9
ACL-6877e	M1-95-271032_01	LRM1	−14.4	6.8	18.2
ACL-6877f	M1-95-271032_01	LRM1	−14.0	6.8	17.5
ACL-6877g	M1-95-271032_01	LRM1	−13.3	6.2	16.8
ACL-6877h	M1-95-271032_01	LRM1	−13.9	5.6	16.1
ACL-6877i	M1-95-271032_01	LRM1	NA	NA	15.4
ACL-6877j	M1-95-271032_01	LRM1	−14.9	4.9	14.7
ACL-6877k	M1-95-271032_01	LRM1	−15.6	4.7	14.0

(*continued*)

Table 6.2 (*continued*)

Laboratory number	Specimen or tomb number	Sample type	δ¹³C collagen (VPDB) (‰)	δ¹⁵N collagen (AIR) (‰)	Serial Section age (y)
ACL-6877l	M1-95-271032_01	LRM1	−14.6	5.3	8.5
ACL-6893a	M1-95-303022_01	LLM1	−13.9	6.4	9.0
ACL-6893b	M1-95-303022_01	LLM1	−13.4	6.3	8.5
ACL-6893c	M1-95-303022_01	LLM1	−13.4	5.8	8.0
ACL-6893d	M1-95-303022_01	LLM1	−12.7	5.8	7.5
ACL-6893e	M1-95-303022_01	LLM1	−13.5	5.6	7.0
ACL-6893f	M1-95-303022_01	LLM1	−13.3	5.7	6.5
ACL-6893g	M1-95-303022_01	LLM1	−12.6	6.0	6.0
ACL-6893h	M1-95-303022_01	LLM1	−12.5	6.0	5.5
ACL-6893i	M1-95-303022_01	LLM1	−12.2	6.3	5.0
ACL-6893j	M1-95-303022_01	LLM1	−11.5	7.1	4.0
ACL-6893k	M1-95-303022_01	LLM1	−12.1	8.1	3.0
ACL-6893l	M1-95-303022_01	LLM1	−12.9	NA	2.5
ACL-6893m	M1-95-303022_01	LLM1	−13.0	NA	2.0
ACL-6893n	M1-95-303022_01	LLM1	−13.6	NA	1.5
ACL-6893o	M1-95-303022_01	LLM1	−12.6	NA	1.0
ACL-6895a	M1-95-303022_03	LLM3	−13.2	7.5	21.0
ACL-6895b	M1-95-303022_03	LLM3	−12.7	7.3	20.2
ACL-6895c	M1-95-303022_03	LLM3	−13.5	7.2	19.5
ACL-6895d	M1-95-303022_03	LLM3	NA	NA	18.7
ACL-6895e	M1-95-303022_03	LLM3	NA	NA	17.9
ACL-6895f	M1-95-303022_03	LLM3	NA	NA	17.1
ACL-6895g	M1-95-303022_03	LLM3	NA	NA	16.3
ACL-6895h	M1-95-303022_03	LLM3	NA	NA	15.6
ACL-6895i	M1-95-303022_03	LLM3	NA	NA	14.8
ACL-6895j	M1-95-303022_03	LLM3	−13.1	7.4	14.0
ACL-6920a	M1-02-026_01	ULM1	−13.6	8.2	9.0
ACL-6920b	M1-02-026_01	ULM1	−11.3	8.1	8.4
ACL-6920c	M1-02-026_01	ULM1	−13.6	7.2	7.8
ACL-6920d	M1-02-026_01	ULM1	−13.2	7.3	7.2
ACL-6920e	M1-02-026_01	ULM1	−13.0	7.4	6.6
ACL-6920f	M1-02-026_01	ULM1	−13.1	7.3	6.0
ACL-6920g	M1-02-026_01	ULM1	−14.5	7.3	5.4
ACL-6920h	M1-02-026_01	ULM1	−12.9	8.0	4.8
ACL-6920i	M1-02-026_01	ULM1	−12.9	7.9	4.2
ACL-6920j	M1-02-026_01	ULM1	−11.9	8.3	3.6
ACL-6920k	M1-02-026_01	ULM1	−12.8	8.5	3.0
ACL-6920l	M1-02-026_01	ULM1	−13.1	9.2	2.5
ACL-6920m	M1-02-026_01	ULM1	−11.5	10.1	2.0
ACL-6920n	M1-02-026_01	ULM1	−12.0	10.0	1.5

(*continued*)

Table 6.2 (*continued*)

Laboratory number	Specimen or tomb number	Sample type	$\delta^{13}C$ collagen (VPDB) (‰)	$\delta^{15}N$ collagen (AIR) (‰)	Serial Section age (y)
ACL-6920o	M1-02-026_01	ULM1	−12.2	10.4	1.0
ACL-6922a	M1-02-026_03	ULM3	−10.6	10.1	20.0
ACL-6922b	M1-02-026_03	ULM3	−11.9	9.5	19.3
ACL-6922c	M1-02-026_03	ULM3	−12.0	9.0	18.5
ACL-6922d	M1-02-026_03	ULM3	NA	NA	17.8
ACL-6922e	M1-02-026_03	ULM3	NA	NA	17.0
ACL-6922f	M1-02-026_03	ULM3	NA	NA	16.3
ACL-6922g	M1-02-026_03	ULM3	NA	NA	15.5
ACL-6922h	M1-02-026_03	ULM3	NA	NA	14.8
ACL-6922i	M1-02-026_03	ULM3	NA	NA	14.0
ACL-6922j	M1-02-026_03	ULM3	−12.4	12.4	11.3
ACL-6922k	M1-02-026_03	ULM3	−12.7	8.4	8.5
ACL-6998a	M1-02-712_01	LRM1	−16.6	5.9	8.0
ACL-6998b	M1-02-712_01	LRM1	−17.3	6.0	7.5
ACL-6998c	M1-02-712_01	LRM1	−16.3	6.1	7.0
ACL-6998d	M1-02-712_01	LRM1	−16.2	5.8	6.0
ACL-6998e	M1-02-712_01	LRM1	−16.4	5.9	5.5
ACL-6998f	M1-02-712_01	LRM1	−16.1	5.8	5.0
ACL-6998g	M1-02-712_01	LRM1	−16.1	5.9	4.0
ACL-6998h	M1-02-712_01	LRM1	−16.4	6.0	3.0
ACL-6998i	M1-02-712_01	LRM1	−14.7	6.0	2.5
ACL-6998j	M1-02-712_01	LRM1	−14.7	6.0	2.0
ACL-6998k	M1-02-712_01	LRM1	−15.0	6.0	1.0
ACL-6998l	M1-02-712_01	LRM1	−14.5	8.2	0.3
ACL-7000a	M1-02-712_03	LRM3	−14.5	6.8	21.0
ACL-7000b	M1-02-712_03	LRM3	−14.0	7.0	20.1
ACL-7000c	M1-02-712_03	LRM3	−14.7	6.8	19.3
ACL-7000d	M1-02-712_03	LRM3	−17.0	6.5	18.4
ACL-7000e	M1-02-712_03	LRM3	−15.1	6.5	17.5
ACL-7000f	M1-02-712_03	LRM3	−15.9	6.5	16.6
ACL-7000g	M1-02-712_03	LRM3	−15.2	6.3	15.8
ACL-7000h	M1-02-712_03	LRM3	−16.6	6.5	14.9
ACL-7000i	M1-02-712_03	LRM3	−15.9	7.1	14.0
ACL-7000j	M1-02-712_03	LRM3	−15.0	7.4	11.3
ACL-7000k	M1-02-712_03	LRM3	−15.3	6.8	8.5

Note: NA = not available.

with acceptable collagen preservation and lack of diagenetic contamination (C:N = 2.9–3.6; DeNiro 1985).

Isotopic data generated through serial sampling, as well as published bulk collagen data, were analyzed using MixSIAR to reconstruct diet (Parnell et al. 2013). The MixSIAR model is a nondeterministic, isotopic mixing model software package that uses a Bayesian multivariate approach to reconstruct the diet of whole populations. Using Mix-SIAR, individual samples are treated as random samples pulled from the underlying population. In this study, using the previously constructed South Central Andean foodweb, MixSIAR allowed us to more effectively model dietary reconstruction and to identify inter- and intraindividual variability by creating likelihood distributions for the inclusion of each resource in the overall makeup of diet (Parnell et al. 2013). Here, we rely on the substantial body of literature on Andean paleodiet through carbon and nitrogen isotopes to create a foodweb of isotopic values of various resources in the region. Our comparative foodweb data set was based on published data of both archaeological and modern flora and fauna samples (Berryman 2010; DeNiro and Hastorf 1985; Marsteller, Zolotova, and Knudson 2017; Miller, Capriles, and Hastorf 2010; Miller 2005; Szpak et al. 2013; Thornton et al. 2011; Tieszen and Chapman 1992; Tung and Knudson 2018). Finally, we also apply MixSIAR modeling to published bone collagen data from the Tiwanaku-affiliated Moquegua Valley sites of Omo M10, Rio Muerto M43, and Rio Muerto M70 to further contextualize the isotopic data from Chen Chen and provide additional paleodietary information from the Moquegua Valley (Somerville et al. 2015, Sandness 1992, Tomczak 2001).

CARBON AND NITROGEN ISOTOPE RESULTS

At Chen Chen the mean $\delta^{13}C_{bone\ collagen(V\text{-}PDB)}$ = –13.5‰ ± 1.3‰ (n = 101, 1σ), with a range from $\delta^{13}C_{bone\ collagen(V\text{-}PDB)}$ = –18.9‰ to $\delta^{13}C_{bone\ collagen(V\text{-}PDB)}$ = –10.2‰ (table 6.1). At Chen Chen, mean $\delta^{15}N_{bone\ collagen(AIR)}$ = 7.1‰ ± 3.2‰ (n = 101, 1σ), with a range of $\delta^{15}N_{bone\ collagen(AIR)}$ = 4.4‰ to $\delta^{15}N_{bone\ collagen(AIR)}$ = 20.6‰. The results from the serial samples obtained from six individuals are presented in table 6.2 and exhibit mean $\delta^{13}C_{dentinal\ collagen(VPDB)}$ = –14.6‰ ± 2.0‰ (n = 123, 1σ) and mean $\delta^{15}N_{dentinal\ collagen(AIR)}$ = 7.5‰ ± 2.0‰ (n = 123, 1σ; table 6.2).

DIETARY RECONSTRUCTION
IN THE MOQUEGUA VALLEY

The Moquegua Valley Tiwanaku-affiliated settlements were very likely colonies established to produce maize for the Tiwanaku heartland, which was located in the high-altitude Lake Titicaca Basin. Therefore, we could expect that the individuals buried at Chen Chen consumed predominately C_4 resources, particularly maize. Based on geography alone, we would not expect any individuals from these inland sites to consume large amounts of marine products. Finally, based on faunal data from excavations, we would expect some consumption of terrestrial herbivores but little freshwater fish consumption. Below, we detail actual diets as inferred through carbon and nitrogen isotopic data and MixSIAR dietary modeling.

At all sites analyzed in the Moquegua Valley, individuals consumed a mixture of terrestrial herbivores, C_4 and C_3 plants, legumes, and some freshwater fish (figs. 6.1–6.4). However, these broad trends in paleodietary reconstruction mask interesting site-based trends in the isotopic data. At Chen Chen and Rio Muerto M43, for example, almost half of the diet was probably C_4 plants and legumes, with much smaller amounts of C_3 plants, terrestrial herbivores, freshwater fish, and marine mammals (figs 6.1, 6.2). In contrast, at Omo and Rio Muerto M70, smaller quantities of C_4 plants and legumes were consumed with larger quantities of freshwater fish (figs 6.3, 6.4). Interestingly, fish bones or scales or river shrimp remains are not present in large quantities at these sites (Susan deFrance, personal communication), which illustrates the complexities, and necessity, of using multiple lines of evidence to infer paleodiet. Even sites located on the banks of Lake Titicaca show little freshwater fish consumption, which may be indicative of larger patterns in the South Central Andes (Miller et al., this volume). We hope that future baseline data sets include larger numbers of modern freshwater fish and shrimp to help resolve this issue for future dietary reconstruction using MixSIAR.

At all Moquegua Valley sites, the relatively high proportion of the diet dedicated to legumes was surprising, as legumes are not commonly discussed in the Andean paleodiet literature. However, Andean agriculturalists cultivated a variety of legumes that thrive in marginal soil quality and whose nutrient-rich seeds are extremely high in proteins and lipids

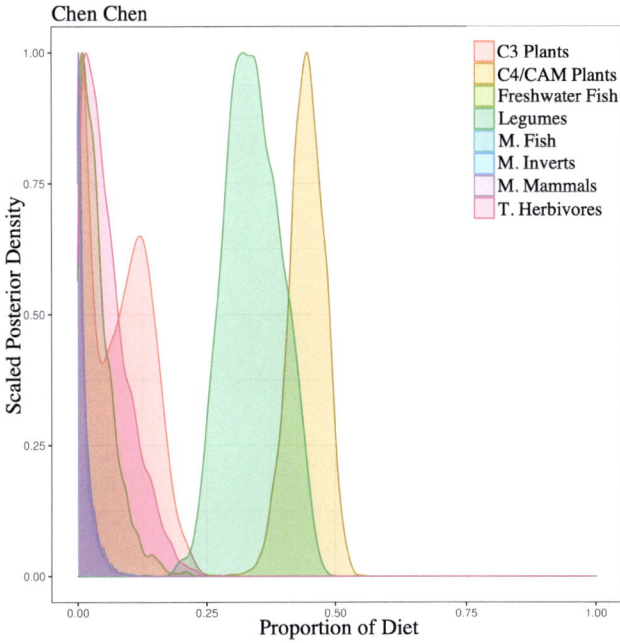

Figure 6.1 Dietary inferences and proportions of different resources consumed at Chen Chen based on MixSIAR modeling. Image by Marcos de la Rosa-Martinez.

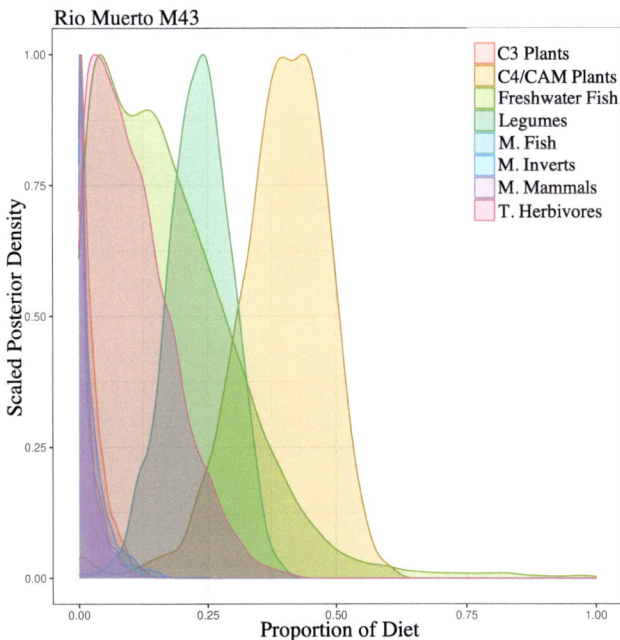

Figure 6.2 Dietary inferences and proportions of different resources consumed at Rio Muerto M43 based on MixSIAR modeling. Image by Marcos de la Rosa-Martinez.

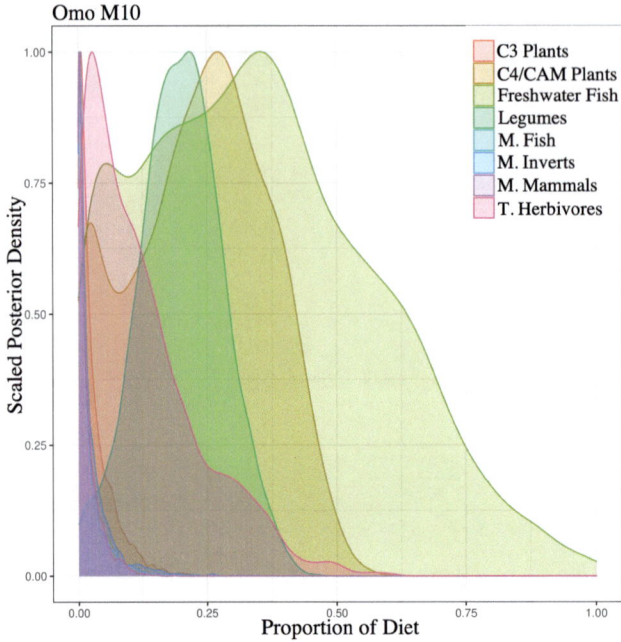

Omo M10

Legend:
- C3 Plants
- C4/CAM Plants
- Freshwater Fish
- Legumes
- M. Fish
- M. Inverts
- M. Mammals
- T. Herbivores

Figure 6.3 Dietary inferences and proportions of different resources consumed at Omo M10 based on MixSIAR modeling. Image by Marcos de la Rosa-Martinez.

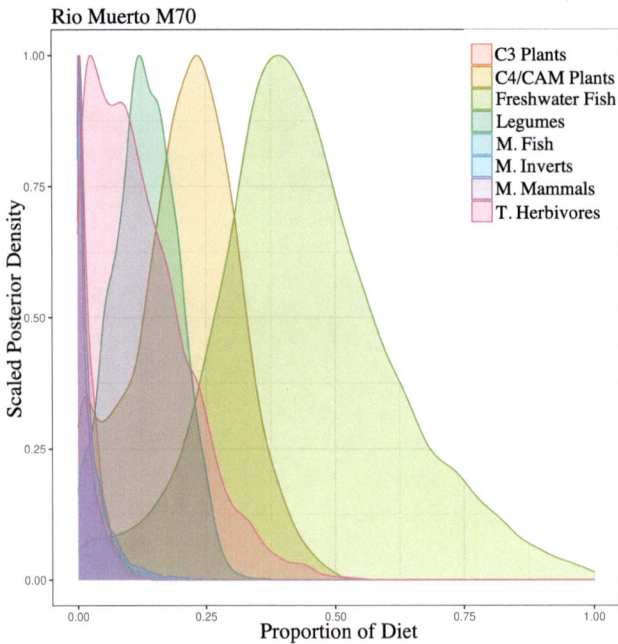

Rio Muerto M70

Legend:
- C3 Plants
- C4/CAM Plants
- Freshwater Fish
- Legumes
- M. Fish
- M. Inverts
- M. Mammals
- T. Herbivores

Figure 6.4 Dietary inferences and proportions of different resources consumed at Rio Muerto M70 based on MixSIAR modeling. Image by Marcos de la Rosa-Martinez.

(Biwer, Alaica, and Quiñonez Cuzcano, this volume; Healy 1996; Trucchi et al. 2021; Wright, Hastorf, and Lennstrom 2003). For example, *tarwi* (*Lupinus mutabilis*) grows well at high altitudes, while common beans (*Phaseolus* sp.) and peanuts (*Arachis hypogea*) grow well at lower altitudes in the Andes and are commonly found at low-altitude archaeological sites. At Tiwanaku, macrobotanical studies demonstrated that legumes (particularly *tarwi*) are scarce in the archaeobotanical record, but this may result from differential preservation, as legumes' high lipid content makes them prone to decomposition when prepared for consumption (Wright, Hastorf, and Lennstrom 2003). In contrast, the exceptional preservation at lower-altitude sites ensures that both bean and peanut macroremains are found at Moquegua Valley sites. While peanuts and beans do not grow well at high altitudes, they would have grown well in the Moquegua Valley and could account for the large amount of legume consumption. The ubiquity of environmentally resilient legumes in the MixSIAR models from Tiwanaku-affiliated sites implies that legumes could have been important in the past.

In addition to inferring diet in the years before death through bulk bone collagen samples, multiple isotopic samples from one individual can also be used to reconstruct dietary changes over the lifetime (e.g., Scaffidi, Vang, and Tung, this volume). The examination of dietary variability during the lifetimes of six individuals buried in Chen Chen show a general dietary pattern focused on C_4 plants and legumes, with much smaller amounts of C_3 plants, terrestrial herbivores, freshwater fish, and marine mammals, as seen in the bulk collagen samples. The analysis of the sequential data shows that some individuals exhibited little change in carbon and nitrogen isotope values over the first 20 years of their lives (e.g., individuals with specimen numbers M1-02-712 and M1-02-026). However, other individuals changed their consumption patterns over their lives (table 6.2). For example, the individual from burial A-228 (specimen number M1-88-0235_01; fig. 6.5) shows relatively stable consumption of primarily terrestrial herbivores and legumes across the observed life course. However, between the ages of 14–20 years, higher carbon isotope values imply that the consumption of C_4 resources increased, while lower nitrogen isotope values indicate a decrease in the already low consumption of higher-trophic-level foods like fish or marine products.

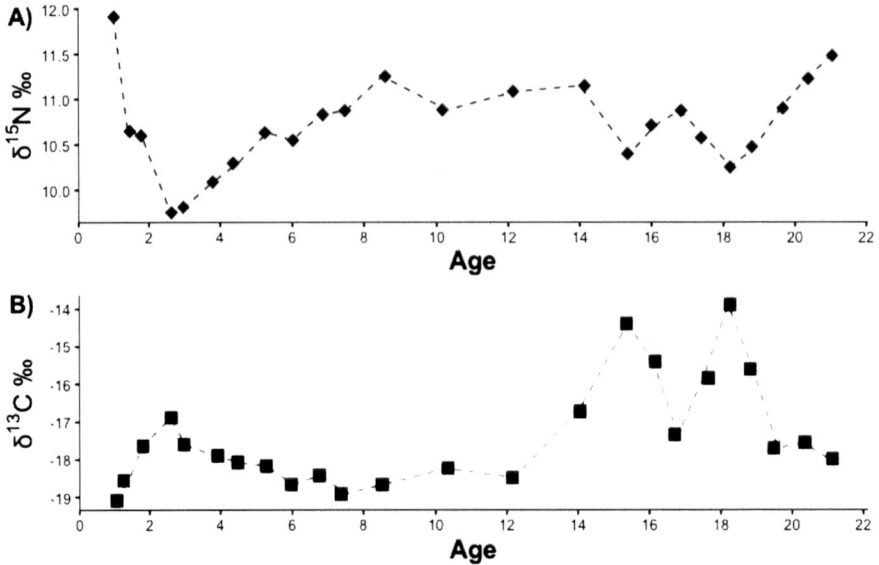

Figure 6.5 Nitrogen (*A*) and carbon (*B*) isotopes values in sequential dentine samples from the individual interred in burial A-228 and assigned specimen number M1-88-0235_01 at Chen Chen. Image by Marcos de la Rosa-Martinez.

DIETARY CHOICES AND SOCIAL IDENTITIES IN THE MOQUEGUA VALLEY

In the previous section, we provided dietary reconstructions of individuals buried in Tiwanaku-affiliated sites in the Moquegua Valley. There are broad patterns of consumption based on a combination of C_4 and C_3 plants and legumes, with some terrestrial herbivores and freshwater fish. However, these general trends mask variability at the site level. At both Chen Chen and Rio Muerto M43, almost half of the diet was probably C_4 plants and legumes. This implies that the maize agriculturalists buried at these sites were in fact consuming large amounts of maize rather than only growing it for export. In contrast, at Omo and Rio Muerto M70, also in the Moquegua Valley, smaller quantities of C_4 plants and legumes were consumed (figs. 6.3, 6.4). Interestingly, Rio Muerto M70 had the highest amount of terrestrial herbivore consumption (fig. 6.4), which may reflect the emphasis on camelid pastoralism in this Omo-style cemetery. Terrestrial herbivore consumption was much lower at

Chen Chen and Rio Muerto M43 (figs. 6.1, 6.2), and intermediate at Omo (fig. 6.3). In this way, community or occupational identities as agriculturalists versus pastoralists may be reflected in dietary choices when looking at site-level data.

It is also interesting to note that while maize could have made up half of the diet at Chen Chen and Rio Muerto M43, the isotopic data alone cannot distinguish between maize imbibed as chicha and maize consumed in other ways. The paleobotanical data and ceramic assemblages at the Moquegua Valley sites show that maize could have been consumed as fresh cobs, or roasted, boiled, or cooked into stews or porridges in addition to being fermented and imbibed as chicha (Goldstein 2005). Peanuts could also have been imbibed as *chicha de maní*, which is made today in Peru and Bolivia, as well as consumed whole, roasted, or cooked in stews. However, since at least some maize was imbibed as chicha at the Moquegua Valley sites, feasting events were probably important in creating and maintaining Tiwanaku community identities and political authority in the colonies as seen at Tiwanaku itself (Berryman and Blom, this volume).

Within each site complex, and each site complex's community-level identity, we also looked at the impact of gender identities on diet in the Moquegua Valley. Of the adult individuals with skeletal sex data who were buried at Chen Chen, there are no differences in adult diet as evidenced by bone collagen carbon and nitrogen isotope values. At Chen Chen, for adult females, mean $\delta^{13}C_{bone\ collagen(V-PDB)}$ = −13.7‰ ± 1.1‰ (n = 27, 1σ) and mean $\delta^{15}N_{bone\ collagen(AIR)}$ = 7.0‰ ± 3.6‰ (n = 27, 1σ), while for adult males, mean $\delta^{13}C_{bone\ collagen(V-PDB)}$ = −13.5‰ ± 1.5‰ (n = 13, 1σ) and mean $\delta^{15}N_{bone\ collagen(AIR)}$ = 6.9‰ ± 1.6‰ (n = 13, 1σ). At Chen Chen, gender identities do not seem to have a substantial impact on dietary choices, and Berryman and Blom (this volume) also did not see gendered diets in the Lake Titicaca Basin.

Gender identities at the sites of Omo and Rio Muerto (M43 and M70) also did not seem to have a substantial impact on paleodiet, as individuals skeletally sexed as male or female did not have substantial differences in carbon and nitrogen isotopes values (Somerville et al. 2015). Interestingly, Somerville et al. (2015) argued that while maize consumption was similar between males and females, males consumed more protein from maize, which may have been because males had access to more chicha. While we don't yet have carbonate data to understand protein sources versus whole-diet carbon at Chen Chen, as Somerville and colleagues (2015) did, we look forward to future work that combines these lines of evidence.

Since diet did not vary substantially based on gender identities, did age identities or constructs such as "child" ensure different diets? The bone collagen data from individuals who died before approximately 15 years of age exhibits mean $\delta^{13}C_{\text{bone collagen(V-PDB)}} = -13.4‰ \pm 1.2‰$ ($n = 28, 1\sigma$) and mean $\delta^{15}N_{\text{bone collagen(AIR)}} = 7.1‰ \pm 3.5‰$ ($n = 38, 1\sigma$), which was not distinct from bone collagen data from those who died as adults. This implies that the diets of people buried at Chen Chen did not differ substantially for people with different age identities. However, bone collagen data shows diet in the last years of life, and it is possible that the diets of people who died as infants and children were different during childhood compared to the childhood diets of those who survived to adulthood. Here we use serial samples to provide data on dietary choices during the first 20 years of six individual's lives; all six individuals were adults when they died. For these individuals, there are no clear dietary patterns based on age that are present in all individuals. While some individuals exhibited very consistent dietary patterns during their early lives, others (like Burial A-228; specimen number M1-88-0235) did exhibit an increase in maize consumption in their teen years.

In conclusion, we have presented bone collagen data based on bulk collagen samples from 101 individuals and 123 sequential samples from dentinal collagen from six individuals buried at the Tiwanaku-affiliated site of Chen Chen. When interpreted in concert with the isotopic admixture modeling, our data show both inter- and intraindividual variation in dietary choices between AD 500 and AD 1000. The most substantial dietary differences in the Moquegua Valley seem to be based on occupational or community identities rather than individual-level social identities such as age or gender identities. Based on these data, occupational identity and an individual's role as an agriculturalist or a pastoralist has the most significant impact on dietary choices during both childhood and adulthood for both females and males. More broadly, when contextualized with published isotopic values from other Tiwanaku-affiliated sites in the Moquegua Valley, it is clear that subsistence and consumption patterns varied widely within the Tiwanaku polity.

ACKNOWLEDGMENTS

We very gratefully acknowledge funding from the National Science Foundation (BCS-0202329, SBR-9708001), the University of Vermont's College of Arts and Sciences Dean's Fund for Faculty Development, the Wenner-Gren Foundation (grant 5863), the School of Human Evolution and Social Change Doctoral Pilot Research Funding Program, and the Center for Evolution and Medicine at Arizona State University. The authors would like to thank especially the Centro de Investigaciones Arqueológicas Antropológicas y Administración de Tiwanaku (CIAAAT), Unidad de Arqueología y Museos (UDAM), Ministerio de Culturas y Turismo de Bolivia, Proyecto Wila Jawira, Proyecto Jach'a Marka, our project codirector, Luis Callisaya Medina, and project members Ruth Fontenla, Raquel Moscoso, Mabel Ramirez, Sara Becker, Genesis Morales, Carrie Anne Berryman, Cesar and Marta Callisaya, Delia and Aurora Medina, Anna Renzi, Richard Witting, and Gina Palefsky. We also gratefully acknowledge the assistance of technicians in the Archaeological Chemistry Laboratory, particularly Allisen Dahlstedt, Sofia Pacheco-Fores, Sarah Hall, and Jessica Rothwell, and the faculty and staff in the Metals, Environmental and Terrestrial Analytical Laboratory (METAL), both at Arizona State University. We thank the organizers, Marta Alfonso-Durruty and Deborah Blom, and the participants of the Society for American Archaeology (SAA) symposium and the SAA-Amerind Foundation Advanced Seminar for inviting us to participate in truly insightful and productive discussions about the Andean past and present.

REFERENCES

Berryman, Carrie Anne. 2010. "Food, Feasts, and the Construction of Identity and Power in Ancient Tiwanaku: A Bioarchaeological Perspective." PhD diss., Vanderbilt University.

Blom, Deborah E., Benedikt Hallgrimsson, Linda Keng, Maria C. Lozada Cerna, and Jane E. Buikstra. 1998. "Tiwanaku 'Colonization': Bioarchaeological Implications for Migration in the Moquegua Valley, Peru." *World Archaeology* 30 (2): 238–61. https://doi.org/10.1080/00438243.1998.9980409.

Buikstra, Jane E., and Rachel E. Scott. 2009. "Key Concepts in Identity Studies." In *Bioarchaeology and Identity in the Americas*, edited by Kelly J. Knudson and Christopher M. Stojanowski, 24–55. Gainesville: University Press of Florida.

DeNiro, Michael J. 1985. "Postmortem Preservation and Alteration of *in vivo* Bone Collagen Isotope Ratios in Relation to Paleodietary Reconstruction." *Nature* 317:806–9. https://doi.org/10.1038/317806a0.

DeNiro, Michael J., and Christine A. Hastorf. 1985. "Alteration of ^{15}N/^{14}N and ^{13}C/^{12}C Ratios of Plant Matter During the Initial Stages of Diagenesis: Studies Utilizing Archaeological Specimens from Peru." *Geochimica et Cosmochimica Acta* 49 (1): 97–115. https://doi.org/10.1016/0016-7037(85)90194-2.

Díaz-Andreu, Margarita, Sam Lucy, Stasia Babic, and David N. Edwards, eds. 2005. *The Archaeology of Identity: Approaches to Gender, Age, Status, Ethnicity, and Religion.* London: Routledge.

Goldstein, Paul S. 1992. "Tiwanaku Temples and State Expansion." *Latin American Antiquity* 4:22–47. https://doi.org/10.2307/972135.

Goldstein, Paul S. 2005. *Andean Diaspora: The Tiwanaku Colonies and the Origins of South America Empire.* Gainesville: University Press of Florida.

Healy, Kevin. 1996. "Ethnodevelopment of Indigenous Bolivian Communities: Emerging Paradigms." In *Tiwanaku and Its Hinterland: Archaeology and Paleoecology of an Andean Civilization.* Vol. 1, *Agroecology,* edited by Alan L. Kolata, 241–64. Washington, D.C.: Smithsonian Institution Press.

Hillson, Simon. 1986. *Teeth.* Cambridge: Cambridge University Press.

Hillson, Simon. 1996. *Dental Anthropology.* Cambridge: Cambridge University Press.

Janusek, John Wayne. 2004. *Identity and Power in the Ancient Andes: Tiwanaku Cities Through Time.* London: Routledge.

Janusek, John Wayne. 2008. *Ancient Tiwanaku.* Cambridge: Cambridge University Press.

Knudson, Kelly J. 2004. "Tiwanaku Residential Mobility in the South Central Andes: Identifying Archaeological Human Migration Through Strontium Isotope Analysis." PhD diss., University of Wisconsin–Madison.

Knudson, Kelly J. 2008. "Tiwanaku Influence in the South Central Andes: Strontium Isotope Analysis and Middle Horizon Migration." *Latin American Antiquity* 19 (1): 3–23. https://doi.org/10.1017/S104566350000763X.

Knudson, Kelly J., Paul S. Goldstein, Allisen Dahlstedt, Andrew Somerville, and Margaret J. Schoeninger. 2014. "Paleomobility in the Tiwanaku Diaspora: Biogeochemical Analyses at Rio Muerto, Moquegua, Peru." *American Journal of Physical Anthropology* 155 (3): 405–21. https://doi.org/10.1002/ajpa.22584.

Knudson, Kelly J., and Christopher M. Stojanowski. 2009. "The Bioarchaeology of Identity." In *Bioarchaeology and Identity in the Americas,* edited by Kelly J. Knudson and Christopher M. Stojanowski, 1–23. Gainesville: University Press of Florida.

Kolata, Alan L. 1993. *The Tiwanaku: Portrait of an Andean Civilization.* Oxford: Blackwell.

Kolata, Alan L., ed. 1996. *Tiwanaku and Its Hinterland: Archaeology and Paleoecology of an Andean Civilization.* Vol. 1, *Agroecology.* Washington, D.C.: Smithsonian Institution Press.

Kolata, Alan L., ed. 2003. *Tiwanaku and Its Hinterland: Archaeology and Paleoecology of an Andean Civilization.* Vol. 2, *Urban and Rural Archaeology.* Washington, D.C.: Smithsonian Institution Press.

Lewis, Cecil M., Jr., Jane E. Buikstra, and Anne C. Stone. 2007. "Ancient DNA and Genetic Continuity in the South Central Andes." *Latin American Antiquity* 18 (2): 145–60. https://doi.org/10.2307/25063101.

Marsteller, Sara J., Natalya Zolotova, and Kelly J. Knudson. 2017. "Investigating Economic Specialization on the Central Peruvian Coast: A Reconstruction of Late Intermediate Period Ychsma Diet Using Stable Isotopes." *American Journal of Physical Anthropology* 162 (2): 300–17. https://doi.org/10.1002/ajpa.23117.

Miller, Melanie J. 2005. "What's In That Pot? Using Stable Isotope Analysis to Understand Cuisines of the Taraco Peninsula, Bolivia, 1500 BC–AD 1000." Senior honors thesis, University of California, Berkeley.

Miller, Melanie J., José M. Capriles, and Christine A. Hastorf. 2010. "The Fish of Lake Titicaca: Implications for Archaeology and Changing Ecology Through Stable Isotope Analysis." *Journal of Archaeological Science* 37 (2): 317–27. https://doi.org/10.1016/j.jas.2009.09.043.

Owen, Bruce. 1997. *Informe de Investigaciones en los Sectores Mortuorios de Chen Chen.* Internal Report submitted to Museo Contisuyo.

Parnell, Andrew C., Donald L. Phillips, Stuart Bearhop, Brice X. Semmens, Eric J. Ward, Jonathan W. Moore, Andrew L. Jackson, Jonathan Grey, David J. Kelly, and Richard Inger. 2013. "Bayesian Stable Isotope Mixing Models." *Environmetrics* 24:387–99. https://doi.org/10.1002/env.2221.

Sandness, Karin. 1992. "Temporal and Spatial Dietary Variability in the Osmore Drainage, Southern Peru: The Isotope Evidence." Master's thesis, University of Nebraska–Lincoln.

Somerville, Andrew D., Paul S. Goldstein, Sarah I. Baitzel, Karin L. Bruwelheide, Allisen C. Dahlstedt, Linda Yzurdiaga, Sarah Raubenheimer, Kelly J. Knudson, and Margaret J. Schoeninger. 2015. "Diet and Gender in the Tiwanaku Colonies: Stable Isotope Analysis of Human Bone Collagen and Apatite from Moquegua, Peru." *American Journal of Physical Anthropology* 158 (3): 408–22. https://doi.org/10.1002/ajpa.22795.

Szpak, Paul, Christine D. White, Fred J. Longstaffe, Jean-François Millaire, and Víctor F. Vásquez Sánchez. 2013. "Carbon and Nitrogen Isotopic Survey of Northern Peruvian Plants: Baselines for Paleodietary and Paleoecological Studies." *PLoS One* 8 (1): e53763. https://doi.org/10.1371/journal.pone.0053763.

Thornton, Erin K., Susan D. deFrance, John S. Krigbaum, and Patrick Ryan Williams. 2011. "Isotopic Evidence for Middle Horizon to 16th Century Camelid

Herding in the Osmore Valley, Peru." *International Journal of Osteoarchaeology*
21 (5): 544–67. https://doi.org/10.1002/oa.1157.

Tieszen, Larry L., and Michael Chapman. 1992. "Carbon and Nitrogen Isotopic
Status of the Major Marine and Terrestrial Resources in the Atacama Desert
of Northern Chile." In *Proceedings of the First World Congress on Mummy
Studies*, 409–25. Tenerife: Museo Arqueológico y Etnográfico de Tenerife.

Tomczak, Paula. 2001. "Prehistoric Socio-economic Relations and Population
Organization in the Lower Osmore Valley of Southern Peru." PhD diss.,
University of Chicago.

Torres-Rouff, Christina. 2008. "The Influence of Tiwanaku on Life in the Chilean Atacama: Mortuary and Bodily Perspectives." *American Anthropologist*
110 (3): 325–37. https://doi.org/10.1111/j.1548-1433.2008.00042.x.

Torres-Rouff, Christina. 2011. "Hiding Inequality Beneath Prosperity: Patterns
of Cranial Injury in Middle Period San Pedro de Atacama, Northern Chile."
American Journal of Physical Anthropology 146 (1): 28–37. https://doi.org/10
.1002/ajpa.21536.

Torres-Rouff, Christina, and Kelly J. Knudson. 2017. "Integrating Identities: An
Innovative Bioarchaeological and Biogeochemical Approach to Analyzing
the Multiplicity of Identities in the Mortuary Record." *Current Anthropology*
58 (3): 381–409. https://doi.org/10.1086/692026.

Trucchi, Emiliano, Andrea Benazzo, Martina Lari, Alice Iob, Stefania Vai, Laura
Nanni, Elisa Bellucci, et al. 2021. "Ancient Genomes Reveal Early Andean
Farmers Selected Common Beans While Preserving Diversity." *Nature Plants*
7 (2): 123–28. https://doi.org/10.1038/s41477-021-00848-7.

Tung, Tiffiny A., and Kelly J. Knudson. 2018. "Stable Isotope Analysis of a Pre-
Hispanic Andean Community: Reconstructing Pre-Wari and Wari Era Diets
in the Hinterland of the Wari Empire, Peru." *American Journal of Physical
Anthropology* 165 (1): 149–72. https://doi.org/10.1002/ajpa.23339.

Tung, Tiffiny A., Rick W. A. Smith, Nicole Creanza, Cara Monroe, Deborah A.
Bolnick, and Brian M. Kemp. 2019. "Constrained Agency While Negotiating Spanish Colonialism: A Bioarchaeological, Isotopic, and Ancient DNA
Study of the Vinchos Cave Mummies, Ayacucho, Peru." *Bioarchaeology International* 3 (3): 187–217. https://doi.org/10.5744/bi.2019.1013.

Turner, Bethany L., Parker VanValkenburgh, Kristina E. Lee, and Benjamin J.
Schaefer. 2019. "Palaeodiet Inferred from Pre-Hispanic and Early Colonial
Human Remains from Carrizales, Zaña Valley, Peru." *International Journal of
Osteoarchaeology* 29 (4): 560–73. https://doi.org/10.1002/oa.2752.

Vargas V., Bertha. 1994. *Informe Sobre Tumbas Intactas (334) Excavadas Durante
el Proyecto "Rescate Arqueológico en el Cementerio de Chen Chen, Moquegua."*
Manuscript on file at Museo Contisuyo, Moquegua, Perú.

Velasco, Matthew C., and Tiffiny A. Tung. 2021. "Shaping Dietary Histories:
Exploring the Relationship Between Cranial Modification and Childhood
Feeding in a High-Altitude Andean Population (1100–1450 CE)." *Journal*

of Anthropological Archaeology 62: 101298. https://doi.org/10.1016/j.jaa.2021
.101298.

Williams, Patrick Ryan, and Donna J. Nash. 2021. "Consuming Kero: Molle
Beer and Wari Social Identity in Andean Peru." *Journal of Anthropological
Archaeology* 63: 101327. https://doi.org/10.1016/j.jaa.2021.101327.

Wright, Melanie F., Christine A. Hastorf, and Heidi A. Lennstrom. 2003. "Pre-
Hispanic Agriculture and Plant Use at Tiwanaku: Social and Political Impli-
cations." In *Tiwanaku and Its Hinterland: Archaeology and Paleoecology of an
Andean Civilization*. Vol. 2, *Urban and Rural Archaeology*, edited by Alan L.
Kolata, 384–403. Washington, D.C.: Smithsonian Institution Press.

7

Private Dinners and Public Feasts

Food as Political Action in Middle Horizon Cusco

Véronique Bélisle, Aleksa K. Alaica, and Matthew T. Brown

Commensality, the act of eating and drinking together, is a necessarily social form of political action ("gastro-politics") that can act both as a unifying and a dividing force (Appadurai 1981; see also Alconini, this volume; Dietler 2001; Weismantel 2009). By bringing people together, food unites individuals under a shared identity and acts as a channel of social solidarity and community (Appadurai 1981, 507). Whether uniting a few family members during a daily meal or an entire community during an annual event, sharing food emphasizes social cohesion and common group membership. Food might also serve to homogenize subgroups that might not otherwise meet, for example, in the contemporary Peruvian *Inti Raymi* celebration. The common identity fostered by commensality can be deep and long-lasting or superficial and ephemeral, and food sharing is often repeated to maintain and reinforce bonds.

Despite its ability to unify and include, food can be equally dividing and exclusive (Appadurai 1981; Curet and Pestle 2010; Dietler and Hayden 2001; Jennings and Bowser 2009). Food and beverage sharing is often imbued with relationships of power, and they are used to display and negotiate status, manipulate social relationships, or resist against and protest social hierarchy (Biwer, Alaica, and Quiñonez Cuzcano, and Berryman and Blom, this volume). In this case, food is heterogenizing and emphasizes difference and distance (Appadurai 1981). Certain types of feasts, for example, are notoriously competitive or ostentatious (Dietler 2001). In these cases, an individual or group actively displays their status by offering a large volume of food or by serving prized or exotic items to an impressive number of guests. The fact that few individuals (if any) can reciprocate these feasts further reinforces inequality "for generosity is, by its very nature, an exercise of power" (Weismantel 2009, 269). Food further creates boundaries by prescribing where individuals of a particular status or gender can sit during those feasts and what and how they are served, if invited at all (e.g., Chicoine 2011; Dietler 2001).

In this chapter we examine faunal remains, ceramic vessels, and the contexts of food consumption at the local center of Ak'awillay in the Cusco region of southern Peru to understand how political action was enacted through commensal events. We compare consumption activities in the private contexts of houses with those in public spaces to evaluate power dynamics in Cusco during the Middle Horizon (600–1000 CE). While research on communal feasts can shed light on local and regional political dynamics (e.g., Bray 2003a; Dietler and Hayden 2001), the study of smaller meals and everyday consumption is equally important to understand how people related to one another. After all, as Monica Smith (2006, 481) aptly observed, "households cannot survive on feasts alone." The use of multiple lines of archaeological evidence from large-scale excavations constitutes a holistic view that reveals that politics were played in both private and public contexts and that food was used simultaneously to unify and divide the members of the community. Before presenting the evidence, we discuss how commensal politics can be identified through the analysis of excavated items and spaces.

COMMENSAL POLITICS IN THE ARCHAEOLOGICAL RECORD

Several types of archaeological clues can be used to shed light on commensal politics; here we focus on three. First, food remains recovered in excavated contexts provide important data on the ingredients ingested at commensal events. The selection of foods and beverages served at these meals is not random, as food choices result from economic, social, and symbolic factors (Harris 1985; Smith 2006). For example, elites sometimes pick fancy, rare, or exotic food items to display access to long-distance trade goods (Curet and Pestle 2010; Gumerman 1997). In some instances, ordinary ingredients are transformed into haute cuisine or luxurious foods through special preparation or transformation (Hastorf 2003; Hastorf and Johannessen 1993; Jennings and Duke 2018). In other cases, it is not the quality but the quantity of food served that characterizes a special meal or a feast (e.g., Halstead 2015). In the ancient Andes, meat and *chicha*, a fermented beverage made from maize or other plants, were two important items served in large quantities at feasts. Chicha required a lengthy and labor-intensive process of transformation (Hastorf 2003).

Second, how hosts presented foods and beverages using particular pottery vessels is an important element of commensal politics that is particularly well studied in Andean archaeology (e.g., Bray 2003b; Hastorf 2015; Vaughn 2009). Ceramics' shapes and residues can reveal what was served, while their motifs can signal certain ideologies or connections to deities and other groups. The overall quality of pottery is a further indication of access to resources, labor, and trade networks. Like food, pottery can thus simultaneously be inclusive and exclusive by emphasizing a common cosmology while at the same time displaying the elevated status of hosts and their privileged relationships with sacred beings.

Finally, the consumption setting is particularly important (Gumerman 1997; Halstead 2015; Hastorf 2015). Because of their sacred or prestigious character, special places such as temples or elite houses can transform an ordinary meal into an extraordinary one. In addition, what is served in public and what is kept in the private domain of houses often differ, shedding light on local dynamics, larger sociopolitical processes, and the intersection of the two. In the following sections, we examine ingredients, serving wares, and private and public commensal settings at the center of Ak'awillay. We start with a brief introduction to the Cusco region.

MIDDLE HORIZON CUSCO AND THE LOCAL CENTER OF AK'AWILLAY

Wari colonists arrived in the Cusco region of southern Peru at the beginning of the Middle Horizon (ca. 600–650 CE) and built large settlements in the Lucre Basin (Pikillaqta) and Huaro Valley (map 7.1; Glowacki 2002; McEwan 2005; Skidmore 2014; Zapata 1997). Additionally, regional systematic surveys covering >2,000 km^2 indicate strong continuity in settlement patterns between the Early Intermediate Period (EIP, 200–600 CE) and the Middle Horizon (Bauer 2004; Bélisle 2014; Covey 2006, 2014; Covey et al. 2013). During the EIP, sites shifted to lower altitudes close to valley floors, a key location for maize cultivation. At this time, a few settlements in the Cusco Basin, the Xaquixaguana plain (west of Cusco), and the Lucre Basin (east of Cusco) emerged as

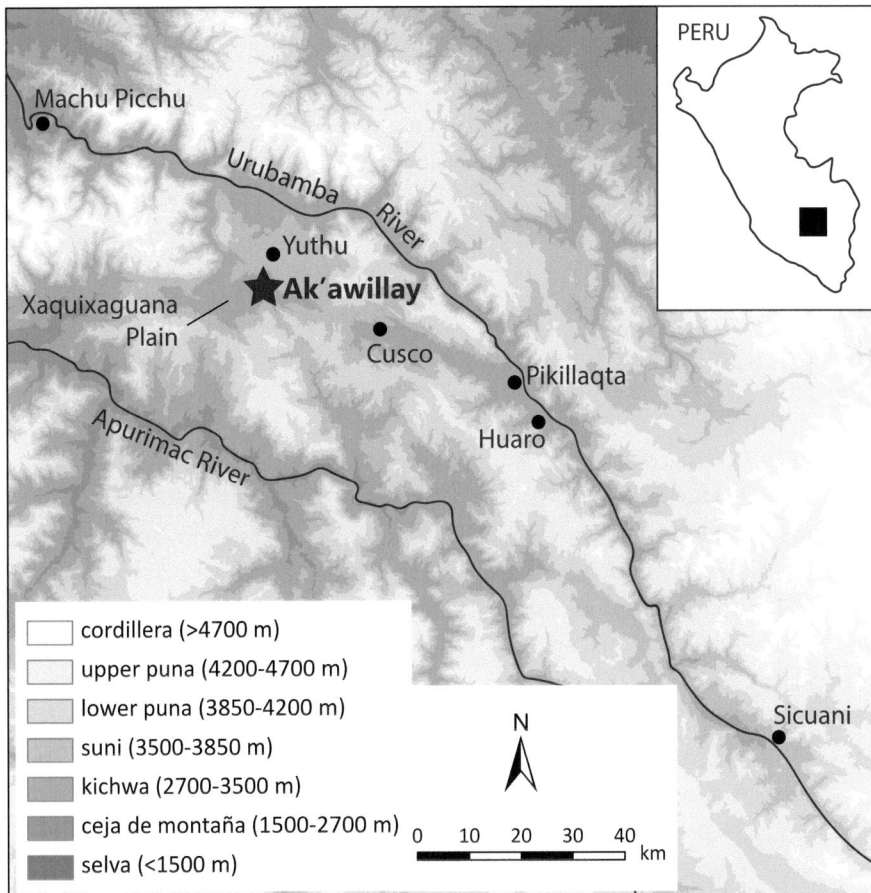

Map 7.1 Map of the Cusco region with the location of Ak'awillay and other sites mentioned in the text. Illustration by Véronique Bélisle.

local centers at the head of small regional polities. During the Middle Horizon, most sites continued to be occupied, and surveys revealed no changes in the distribution of local pottery, site location, hierarchy, or clustering. Wari pottery appears in small numbers at local sites closest to the Lucre Basin and declines sharply in areas farther away. Regional settlement patterns suggest that Wari influence in Cusco was strongest in the area immediately surrounding the Wari sites.

Recent large-scale excavations at the local center of Ak'awillay lead us to reassess the penetration of the Wari state in the Cusco region (Bélisle

2015, 2019; Bélisle and Bauer 2020; Bélisle et al. 2020). Located north-west of the city of Cusco in the Xaquixaguana (Anta) plain, Ak'awillay was established around 150 BCE (Late Formative) and continued to be occupied through the Middle Horizon. At 10 ha, it was one of the largest local settlements in the Cusco area. Work at Ak'awillay included the excavation of 632 m² of Late Formative, EIP, and Middle Horizon contexts. Fieldwork documented several domestic and public spaces; here we focus on those dating to the Middle Horizon.

PRIVATE AND PUBLIC SPACES AT AK'AWILLAY

Private spaces at Ak'awillay are defined as houses and their adjacent features and spaces, such as outdoor pits and patios (fig. 7.1*A*). The seven Middle Horizon houses that we excavated had circular stone foundations and measured between 4.5 and 7 m in diameter (16–38.5 m²). These spaces were associated with hearths, ash lenses, storage pits, and numerous artifacts, including pottery, stone and bone tools, grinding stones, and fired clay objects. The presence of similar features and artifacts in the patios attached to these houses suggests that similar household activities took place there. Since houses were relatively small, the number of guests that could have been invited to share meals in houses was lower than in the patios, which could have been used for larger events.

Excavations at Ak'awillay also uncovered a circular building (11 m in diameter) dating to the Middle Horizon (fig. 7.1*B*). We interpret this space as a public building where the people of Ak'awillay or select individuals periodically gathered. Larger than any of the houses, and lacking domestic features such as hearths, ash lenses, and storage pits, the building was not used for household activities. Based on area (~95 m²), approximately one hundred people could have assembled in this space.

MEAT CONSUMPTION

The analysis of vertebrate faunal remains from Ak'awillay is based on an assemblage of 15,970 fragments of animal bone, with 3,202 (20.1%) specimens identified by genus and species. The results presented below focus on the analysis of taxa, meat portions, and evidence for charring and burning in both private and public contexts. We acknowledge that

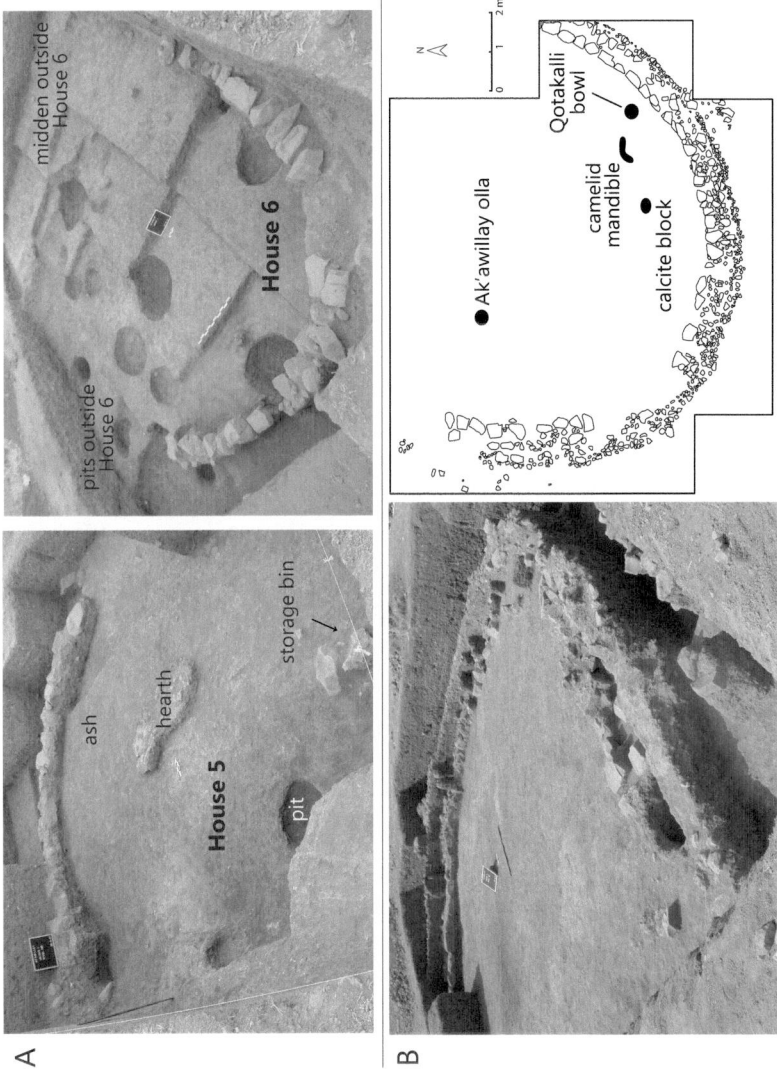

Figure 7.1 Private and public contexts at Ak'awillay. *A*, houses 5 and 6. *B*, public building. Illustration by Véronique Bélisle.

there may have been distinct processes influencing the accumulation of faunal remains in private and public spaces, and taphonomic factors may have differentially affected fragmentation rates among these assemblages (Reitz and Wing 2008). Domestic spaces were used daily, while the public context was probably used less often. Therefore, a denser palimpsest of remains was amassed in the house groups than in the public building. Since it is not possible to separate these cumulated assemblages, we are cautious in our interpretations of differences between these contexts. Here we report on the individual count of bone (Number of Identified Specimens [NISP]) to make fauna more comparable to pottery data presented in the next section.

SPECIES DISTRIBUTION

Sixteen species were identified in Middle Horizon contexts at Ak'awillay (table 7.1). Houses are species rich, with 14 of these 16 taxa present. The most common taxa in houses include camelids (*Lama* sp., *Vicugna* sp.), guinea pigs (*Cavia porcellus*), and deer (*Odocoileus virginianus, Hippocamelus antisensis*), all of which were available locally. Birds such as ducks, swans, and geese could have originated from lakes around Ak'awillay. Apart from these local taxa, private spaces include a few nonlocal species such as sea lion (*Otaria* sp.), penguin (*Spheniscus humboldti*), and cormorant (*Phalacrocorax* sp.), all of which are marine animals native to the coast. The bones of these nonlocal animals appeared on floors or in middens, suggesting that they were consumed, probably in a dried or salted state. In contrast, the public building has 9 identified taxa. The assemblage is largely dominated by camelids, with 93.2% of faunal remains corresponding to either llama or alpaca. The public building has some guinea pigs and deer along with a few bird species; sea lion is the only nonlocal taxa. One sea lion long bone was recovered in a midden, while a metapodial was associated with a nearly complete decorated ceramic cup in an abandonment offering.

The fauna sample shows statistically significant differences in species distribution between private and public contexts. Houses contain significantly more guinea pig remains ($\chi^2 = 47.3$, df = 1, $p < .001$) and deer bones ($\chi^2 = 9.6$, df = 1, $p < .001$) than the Public Building, while the latter includes substantially more camelid remains than the houses ($\chi^2 = 66.031$,

Table 7.1 Species distribution in private and public contexts at Ak'awillay

Taxa	Private[a]		Public[b]	
	NISP	%	NISP	%
Local				
Anas sp. (duck)	18	0.8	3	0.3
Anser sp. (goose)	2	0.1	1	0.1
Gavia sp. (loon)	2	0.1	0	0.0
Strix sp. (owl)	1	0.04	0	0.0
Columbina sp. (dove)	1	0.04	0	0.0
Cygnus sp. (swan)	1	0.04	0	0.0
Larus sp. (gull)	1	0.04	0	0.0
Cavia porcellus (guinea pig)	234	10.2	26	2.9
Felis sp. (cat)	0	0.0	1	0.1
Canis familiaris (dog)	23	1.0	2	0.2
Lycalopex sp. (fox)	0	0.0	2	0.2
Odocoileus virginianus, Hippocamelus antisensis (deer)	121	5.3	25	2.7
Lama sp., *Vicugna* sp. (camelid)	1876	81.9	849	93.2
Total local taxa	2280	99.5	909	99.8
Nonlocal				
Spheniscus humboldti (penguin)	4	0.2	0	0.0
Phalacrocorax sp. (cormorant)	1	0.04	0	0.0
Otaria sp. (sea lion)	6	0.3	2	0.2
Total nonlocal taxa	11	0.5	2	0.2
	2,291	100.0	911	100.0

[a] Private contexts include house floors and adjacent patios, pits, and middens.
[b] Public contexts correspond to the public building.

df = 1, $p < .001$). In fact, the public building fauna is more uniform than that of the houses, and private spaces are characterized by more variety. Moreover, houses include more nonlocal fauna than the public building, although this difference is not statistically significant.

CAMELID MEAT CUTS

Camelids were an important part of the Ak'awillay diet in both private and public spaces, so we focused on the skeletal portions present in each context (table 7.2). The most abundant part of the camelid skeleton recovered in houses is the thorax region (vertebrae and ribs). In fact,

Table 7.2 Distribution of camelid meat cuts in private and public contexts at Ak'awillay

Cut	Private		Public	
	No.	**%**	**No.**	**%**
Cranial	293	15.6	83	9.8
Thorax	589	31.4	210	24.7
Total axial	882	47.0	293	34.5
Front limb	306	16.3	131	15.4
Hind limb	463	24.7	364	42.9
Extremities (feet)	225	12.0	61	7.2
Total appendicular	994	53.0	556	65.5
Total	1,876	100.0	849	100.0

houses contain significantly more camelid meat from the thorax than the public building ($\chi^2 = 37.3$, df $= 1$, $p < .001$). This is a meaty portion of the camelid body that can be portioned into smaller food packages by butchering the ribs into sections that are distributed among participants in daily meals or larger events. Cranial remains ($\chi^2 = 16.8$, df $= 1$, $p < .001$) and extremities ($\chi^2 = 14.4$, df $= 1$, $p < .001$) are also more common in the houses than in public contexts. In contrast, camelid remains in the public building are dominated by hind limb portions, which are significantly more abundant than in the private contexts ($\chi^2 = 23.6$, df $= 1$, $p < .001$). The hind limb includes the femur, which has a large portion of meat that could have provided a substantial amount of food to share in feasting activities.

COOKING AND BURNING

Evidence for charring and burning can provide information on cooking methods. Discoloration of bone results from direct exposure to heat: lower temperatures discolor bones to a dark brown color, while higher temperatures and long exposures produce calcined white bones. For this study, burning was recorded in five gradations (table 7.3; Stiner et al. 1995). Charred bone (grades 1–3) is generally indicative of roasting, while bone becomes calcined (grades 4–5) when discarded into hearths after consumption or when offerings are burned. The Ak'awillay sample

Table 7.3 Distribution of burning gradations among camelid remains in private and public contexts at Ak'awillay

	Private		Public	
Burning gradations	**No.**	**%**	**No.**	**%**
Grade 1 (slightly burned, <half carbonized)	52	5.1	0	0
Grade 2 (lightly burned, >half carbonized)	96	9.4	2	4.3
Grade 3 (fully carbonized, completely black)	689	67.6	43	91.4
Total charred	837	82.1	45	95.7
Grade 4 (locally calcined, hues of blue)	151	14.8	2	4.3
Grade 5 (calcined, completely white)	31	3.1	0	0
Total calcined	182	17.9	2	4.3
Total	1019	100.0	47	100.0

includes evidence for both charred and calcined bone. The houses contain more calcined bone than expected, while the public building has more charred bone than the private contexts (χ^2 = 5.8, df = 1, p = .016). The sample also includes a large proportion of bones from both private and public contexts that are not burnt but heavily bleached and almost glassy, suggesting that camelid meat was often boiled in soups or stews.

POTTERY VESSELS

The analysis of the large Ak'awillay pottery assemblage focused on vessel rims recovered from the occupation floors and associated features and patios of private and public contexts. For each of the 4,443 rim fragments, we assessed vessel shape, diameter, presence or absence of decoration, and other attributes not discussed here. Only fragments larger than a Peruvian sol coin are included.

Several vessel shapes are present in the sample (table 7.4). The houses and the public building are dominated by bowls, suggesting that the serving and consumption of foods and beverages were important activities in both spaces. Bowls represent more than 40% of the sample and fall into two sizes. Small bowls (5–16 cm in diameter; mean = 12 cm) were most likely used for individual servings of food and beverages. Large bowls (17–48 cm in diameter; mean = 25 cm) are open vessels more appropriate for the sharing of solid foods among several individuals. Houses have a

Table 7.4 Distribution of pottery (rims) in private and public contexts at Ak'awillay

	Private		Public	
Vessel	**No.**	**%**	**No.**	**%**
Shape				
Bowls	1,678	43.8	269	43.9
Jars	599	15.6	134	21.9
Cooking pots	718	18.8	113	18.5
Neckless vessels	348	9.1	43	7.0
Other	488	12.7	53	8.7
Total	3831	100.0	612	100.0
Bowls*				
Small bowls (mean = 12 cm)	782	49.3	171	65.3
Large bowls (mean = 25 cm)	803	50.7	91	34.7
Total	1,585	100.0	262	100.0
Decoration				
Decorated vessels	1,504	39.3	215	35.1
Undecorated vessels	2,327	60.7	397	64.9
Total	3,831	100.0	612	100.0

*Includes bowls with known diameter only.

fairly equal distribution of small (49.3%) and large (50.7%) bowls, while the public building has significantly more small bowls (65.3%) than the houses (χ^2 = 22.8, df = 1, p < .0001). The public building also contains a higher proportion of jars compared to houses (χ^2 = 15.0, df = 1, p = .0001). Other vessel shapes have similar proportions in private and public settings.

Decoration on Ak'awillay vessels consists of painted or incised motifs, pattern burnishing, punctations, modeled applications, or a combination of these techniques (fig. 7.2). Decoration appears on the interior and exterior surfaces of bowls and on the exterior wall surfaces of jars, neckless vessels, and, more rarely, cooking pots. In both private and public contexts, over half of the vessels are undecorated (table 7.4). Private spaces contain more decorated pottery than the public building (χ^2 = 3.79, df = 1, p = .05). This difference is mostly due to one domestic sector of the site (houses 9–12), which has significantly more decorated vessels than the other houses (χ^2 = 50.5, df = 1, p < .0001). Other lines of evidence suggest that this sector comprised the houses of high-status individuals

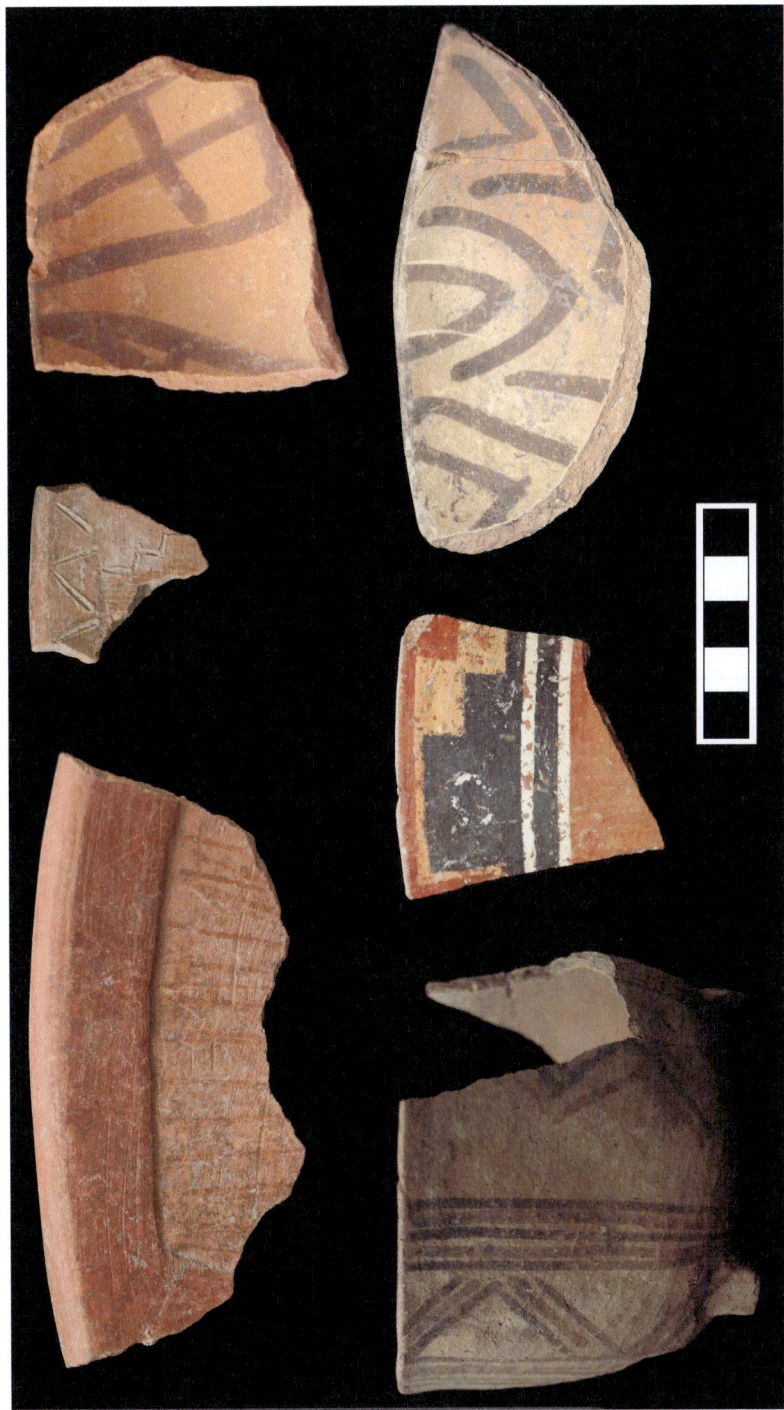

Figure 7.2 Decorated bowls from Ak'awillay: Derived Chanapata and Ak'awillay styles (*upper row*); Qotakalli, Muyu Urqu, and Waru styles (*lower row*). Illustration by Véronique Bélisle.

at Ak'awillay, including the significantly higher number of exotic goods, large storage vessels, and items related to food production and processing compared to other houses.

DISCUSSION

COMPARISON BETWEEN PRIVATE AND PUBLIC SPACES AT AK'AWILLAY

Faunal and pottery data suggest that houses and public spaces at Ak'awillay were associated with different food practices. While material assemblages possibly accumulate at different rates in private and public contexts, their comparison reveals differences in the presence of specific food items. Rare species obtained directly or indirectly from the coast appear to have been reserved for private meals in houses, while public feasts focused on a narrow range of species. This difference in species diversity could be due to the greater number of meals taking place in houses over time compared to the public building. However, given that private and public spaces differ across multiple lines of evidence, it is possible that the divergence in species diversity is not due to palimpsest alone. The sea lion bone in the offering from the public building further points to ritual use of exotic animals, and feasts in the public contexts might have occasionally included offerings of coastal animals that traveled with stories about creatures and places experienced by few (Newman 2016).

The distribution of camelid remains suggests further differences in meat-sharing strategies between private and public spaces. The prevalence of cranial bones and extremities in private contexts suggests that individual families prepared food in houses and associated patios whether it was for a small home meal or a large public feast in the public building. In the houses, the higher proportion of camelid thorax bones facilitated the portioning of ribs into small meat packages that were distributed to a relatively low number of guests. In the public building, the higher proportion of hind limbs indicates that large meaty segments were preferred in a context where the wider community and possibly outside guests were engaged in feasting and exchange.

Finally, data on camelid bone burning suggest that roasted meat, although abundant in both types of contexts, was more often consumed in the public building. These results coincide with other studies that have shown roasting to be the preferred way to prepare meat for feasts in the Andes (Hastorf 2015). The prevalence of calcined bone in houses could reflect a practice where bones were discarded into hearths to clean spaces after cooking and consumption, something that rarely occurred in the public building because of the absence of hearths. Alternatively, since calcined bone can also be indicative of burnt offerings, our data could point to the home as the main locale for such rituals.

Evidence from pottery further illustrates important differences between private and public contexts at Ak'awillay. The higher proportion of small bowls and jars in the public building suggests that beverages such as chicha were more commonly served and consumed in public spaces. Another possibility, which does not exclude the former, is that food in the public building was served in individual portions instead of being shared among several individuals in large bowls. Moreover, the paucity of decorated vessels in the public building could indicate that these fancy ceramics were not stored or discarded there; instead, feast participants could have brought those bowls back home after the events (e.g., Vaughn 2009). Alternatively, public feasts might have provided large amounts of food and drink in vessels considered disposable compared to fancy decorated ones.

Similarities between private and public contexts are also informative. Despite the absence of hearths in the public building, this space and the houses have a comparable proportion of cooking vessels and neckless vessels, which were used for cooking and storage. These data suggest that food was brought to public feasts in cooking pots, not in serving vessels, and then portioned out to guests. This further indicates that all food, no matter the occasion, was prepared in the houses. Carrying large quantities of food from specific houses to the public building might have served as an additional way to display status. Some food served in public feasts could also have been prepared near the public building in earth ovens (*watiya* or *pachamanca*; Alconini, this volume).

THE IMPORTANCE OF MAIZE IN COMMENSAL ACTIVITIES

Several findings point to the important role of maize chicha in Middle Horizon commensal activities at Ak'awillay and in Cusco in general. This

marks a change from the Late Formative in Cusco, which was characterized by sites located in areas ideal for mixed agropastoral economies focusing on the cultivation of quinoa and tubers and the herding of camelids
(Davis 2014). At the Late Formative village of Yuthu (400–100 BCE),
maize represents a small proportion (8.8%) of crops grown (Davis 2011,
14), and isotope data from human remains confirm a preference for C_3
protein and C_3 energy sources such as quinoa, tubers, legumes, and meat
from terrestrial animals who consumed C_3 forage (Turner et al. 2018).
In contrast, Early Intermediate Period (EIP) and Middle Horizon sites
were established in areas ideal for maize cultivation, and isotope data from
Ak'awillay skeletons from the Middle Horizon show mixed C_3-C_4 protein
sources and mixed C_3-C_4 energy sources, including C_4 foods such as maize
and meat from animals consuming C_4 forage (Turner et al. 2018, 145).

Evidence from pottery vessels also reveals the growing importance of
maize in Cusco through the EIP and Middle Horizon. At Yuthu and in
Late Formative contexts at Ak'awillay, serving vessels correspond to the
large family-sized open bowls (Bélisle 2015; Davis 2011). At the end of the
Late Formative and beginning of the EIP, the people of Ak'awillay started
to consume some of their food and beverages in small bowls and cups.
During the Middle Horizon, more than half of the bowls from Ak'awillay
were small individual vessels. This suggests that starting in the EIP, food
was prepared differently, allowing for more liquid meals (like soups) and
beverages such as chicha (Bélisle 2015). Although absent in Yuthu (Davis
2011), jars are common at Ak'awillay (18% of the sample), where they
could have been used for the fermentation, storage, and serving of chicha.

The evidence from the Cusco region shows that maize's importance
increased in the Middle Horizon in relation to the EIP. The presence of
small bowls in both private and public spaces at Ak'awillay suggests that
the consumption of chicha was a central element of both small dinners
and larger feasts. However, since small bowls are significantly more common in the public building, chicha might have been more important in
that context.

LAVISH DINNERS AND ORDINARY FEASTS

House meals included diverse ingredients, the occasional exotic resources,
and decorated serving ware. Compared to locally available items, the

procurement of rare and nonlocal animals was probably time consuming, and their preparation possibly involved more labor or higher levels of difficulty than the more common ingredients from the area (e.g., Jennings and Duke 2018). In contrast, feasts in the public building relied on a large quantity of a limited set of ingredients, mainly camelid meat and chicha served in vessels that were most often undecorated. The use of meat from large, local, and familiar animals might have reduced both the amount of time required for meat procurement and the level of difficulty of its preparation, which could have been key to balancing the much larger amounts of meat and chicha needed for public feasts. Thus, the people of Ak'awillay consumed fancier meals in the home and simpler meals in the public building.

Feasts in public contexts at Ak'awillay illustrate the contradiction at the heart of commensality. Public meals did not emphasize the display of rare items and fancy wares but focused on common ingredients and ceramic vessels that blurred inequality in favor of community unity, identity, and solidarity. The choice of ingredients might have responded to a social consensus about food preferences, furthering the expression of common group membership (Smith 2006). At the same time, feasts are necessarily political, and their very organization displays the economic and symbolic capital of the host (e.g., Dietler 2001), especially if guests cannot reciprocate. By provisioning food and beverages for these public feasts, the elites living in houses 9–12 were probably able to publicize emerging social inequalities (see Alconini, this volume). The setting of the public building and the number of guests attending a feast in that space would have further transformed what seems like an ordinary meal into an extraordinary one.

Meals in the home also represent the inclusive and exclusive character of foodways at Ak'awillay. The smaller size of houses compared to public spaces suggests that home resources were shared more exclusively among kin groups or with a limited number of guests. These meals could have reinforced family ties and celebrated a hierarchy of tastes that was not shared by the community at large. Unlike the consensus food preferences in public events, private meals allowed some individuals to consume foods that were not appreciated by or accessible to other members of the community. Fancier home meals could have been used to impress regional leaders or trading partners invited to local houses, forging and negotiating alliances between local and nonlocal interests. These private events would have excluded most community members. The incipient elites at Ak'awillay could thus have used their home to compete and overtly display their status to a selected number of guests, while the events of the public building seemingly focused on group solidarity. To use a modern analogy, house meals at Ak'awillay are akin to dining at the prime minister's home with a few high-ranking guests, while feasts in the public building are more comparable to eating at the Parliament with a large number of undifferentiated guests. At Ak'awillay, different types of politics were played in the private and public spheres, and commensal events taking place in both contexts simultaneously unified and divided people.

CONCLUSIONS

Faunal and ceramic evidence from Ak'awillay suggests that the way in which local elites were sharing food and beverages in public spaces during large consumption events was a mechanism for maintaining community cohesion. The emphasis on large quantities of camelid meat and maize chicha fostered collective solidarity, the importance of which probably increased as Wari colonists arrived in the Cusco region at the beginning of the Middle Horizon. By organizing these feasts, local leaders simultaneously displayed (or even legitimized) their status and possibly manipulated social relationships, thereby presenting themselves as distinct members of the community. This public impression was paired with private house meals that involved a variety of resources, exotic species, and more decorated serving ware. These smaller events fostered the development of alliances and the maintenance of privileged relationships with a limited number of people, excluding most community members and possibly encouraging competition between households.

Data from private and public spaces at Ak'awillay reveal the unifying and dividing character of commensality that shaped community dynamics and politics during the Middle Horizon. This study illustrates the importance of using multiple lines of evidence and considering different contexts, from the private house meal to the larger public feast. Both types of events were key places for political action that fostered common identity while also emphasizing difference. These events were different from the large-scale feasts organized at the Wari site of Pikillaqta, and future research in Cusco should investigate the tension between local and Wari patterns of commensality.

REFERENCES

Appadurai, Arjun. 1981. "Gastro-politics in Hindu South Asia." *American Ethnologist* 8 (3): 494–511. https://doi.org/10.1525/ae.1981.8.3.02a00050.

Bauer, Brian S. 2004. *Ancient Cuzco: Heartland of the Inca.* Austin: University of Texas Press.

Bélisle, Véronique. 2014. "Early Intermediate Period and Middle Horizon Settlement Patterns in the Xaquixaguana Region." In *Regional Archaeology in the Inca Heartland: The Hanan Cuzco Surveys,* edited by R. A. Covey, 77–91. Ann Arbor: University of Michigan Museum of Anthropology.

Bélisle, Véronique. 2015. "Understanding Wari State Expansion: A 'Bottom-Up' Approach at the Village of Ak'awillay, Cusco, Peru." *Latin American Antiquity* 26 (2): 180–99. https://doi.org/10.7183/1045-6635.26.2.180.

Bélisle, Véronique. 2019. "Hallucinogens and Altered States of Consciousness in Cusco, Peru: A Path to Local Power During Wari State Expansion." *Cambridge Archaeological Journal* 29 (3): 375–91. https://doi.org/10.1017/S095977 4319000015.

Bélisle, Véronique, and Brian S. Bauer. 2020. "Local Trade and Pottery Production in the Cusco Region Before and During the Wari Expansion." *Ñawpa Pacha* 40 (1): 1–20. https://doi.org/10.1080/00776297.2020.1712097.

Bélisle, Véronique, Hubert Quispe-Bustamante, Thomas J. Hardy, Allison R. Davis, Elder Antezana Condori, Carlos Delgado González, José Victor Gonzales Avendaño, David A. Reid, and Patrick Ryan Williams. 2020. "Wari Impact on Regional Trade Networks: Patterns of Obsidian Exchange in Cusco, Peru." *Journal of Archaeological Science: Reports* 32:102439. https://doi.org/10 .1016/j.jasrep.2020.102439.

Bray, Tamara L., ed. 2003a. *The Archaeology and Politics of Food and Feasting in Early States and Empires.* New York: Kluwer Academic; Plenum.

Bray, Tamara L. 2003b. "Inka Pottery as Culinary Equipment: Food, Feasting, and Gender in Imperial State Design." *Latin American Antiquity* 14 (1): 3–28. https://doi.org/10.2307/972232.

Chicoine, David. 2011. "Feasting Landscapes and Political Economy at the Early Horizon Center of Huambacho, Nepeña Valley, Peru." *Journal of Anthropological Archaeology* 30:432–53. https://doi.org/10.1016/j.jaa.2011.06.003.

Covey, R. Alan. 2006. *How the Incas Built Their Heartland: State Formation and the Innovation of Imperial Strategies in the Sacred Valley, Peru.* Ann Arbor: University of Michigan Press.

Covey, R. Alan. 2014. "Local Developments in the Sacred Valley and Responses to Wari Colonization." In *Regional Archaeology in the Inca Heartland: The*

Hanan Cuzco Surveys, edited by R. A. Covey, 93–108. Ann Arbor: University of Michigan Museum of Anthropology.

Covey, R. Alan, Brian S. Bauer, Véronique Bélisle, and Lia Tsesmeli. 2013. "Regional Perspectives on Wari State Influence in Cusco, Peru (c. AD 600–1000)." *Journal of Anthropological Archaeology* 32:538–52. https://doi.org/10.1016/j.jaa.2013.09.001.

Curet, L. Antonio, and William J. Pestle. 2010. "Identifying High-Status Foods in the Archeological Record." *Journal of Anthropological Archaeology* 29:413–31. https://doi.org/10.1016/j.jaa.2010.08.003.

Davis, Allison R. 2011. *Yuthu: Community and Ritual in an Early Andean Village.* Ann Arbor: University of Michigan Museum of Anthropology.

Davis, Allison R. 2014. "Formative Period Settlement Patterns in the Xaquixaguana Region." In *Regional Archaeology in the Inca Heartland: The Hanan Cuzco Surveys*, edited by R. A. Covey, 53–64. Ann Arbor: University of Michigan Museum of Anthropology.

Dietler, Michael. 2001. "Theorizing the Feast: Rituals of Consumption, Commensal Politics, and Power in African Contexts." In *Feasts: Archaeological and Ethnographic Perspectives on Food, Politics, and Power*, edited by M. Dietler and B. Hayden, 65–114. Tuscaloosa: University of Alabama Press.

Dietler, Michael, and Brian Hayden, eds. 2001. *Feasts: Archaeological and Ethnographic Perspectives on Food, Politics, and Power.* Tuscaloosa: University of Alabama Press.

Glowacki, Mary. 2002. "The Huaro Archaeological Site Complex: Rethinking the Huari Occupation of Cuzco." In *Andean Archaeology I: Variations of Sociopolitical Organization*, edited by W. H. Isbell and H. Silverman, 267–85. New York: Kluwer Academic.

Gumerman IV, George. 1997. "Food and Complex Societies." *Journal of Archaeological Method and Theory* 4 (2): 105–39.

Halstead, Paul. 2015. "Feast, Food and Fodder in Neolithic-Bronze Age Greece: Commensality and the Construction of Value." In *Between Feasts and Daily Meals: Towards an Archaeology of Commensal Spaces*, edited by S. Pollock, 29–61. Berlin: Edition Topoi.

Harris, Marvin. 1985. *Good to Eat: Riddles of Food and Culture.* Long Grove, Ill.: Waveland Press.

Hastorf, Christine A. 2003. "Andean Luxury Foods: Special Food for the Ancestors, Deities and the Élite." *Antiquity* 77 (297): 545–54. https://doi.org/10.1017/S0003598X00092607.

Hastorf, Christine A. 2015. "Steamed or Boiled: Identity and Value in Food Preparation." In *Between Feasts and Daily Meals: Towards an Archaeology of Commensal Spaces*, edited by S. Pollock, 243–75. Berlin: Edition Topoi.

Hastorf, Christine A., and Sissel Johannessen. 1993. "Pre-Hispanic Political Change and the Role of Maize in the Central Andes of Peru." *American Anthropologist* 95 (1): 115–38. https://doi.org/10.1525/aa.1993.95.1.02a00060.

Jennings, Justin, and Brenda J. Bowser. 2009. "Drink, Power, and Society in the Andes: An Introduction." In *Drink, Power, and Society in the Andes*, edited by J. Jennings and B. J. Bowser, 1–27. Gainesville: University Press of Florida.

Jennings, Justin, and Guy Duke. 2018. "Making the Typical Exceptional: The Elevation of Inca Cuisine." In *The Oxford Handbook of the Incas*, edited by S. Alconini and R. A. Covey, 303–21. New York: Oxford University Press.

McEwan, Gordon F., ed. 2005. *Pikillacta: The Wari Empire in Cuzco*. Iowa City: University of Iowa Press.

Newman, Sarah E. 2016. "Sharks in the Jungle: Real and Imagined Sea Monsters of the Maya." *Antiquity* 90 (354): 1522–36. https://doi.org/10.15184/aqy.2016.218.

Reitz, Elizabeth, and Elizabeth Wing. 2008. *Zooarchaeology*. Cambridge: Cambridge University Press.

Skidmore, Maeve. 2014. "Wari Power, Wari People: Building Critical Perspectives on State Expansion at Hatun Cotuyoc, Huaro, Peru." PhD diss., Southern Methodist University.

Smith, Monica. 2006. "The Archaeology of Food Preference." *American Anthropologist* 108 (3): 480–93. https://doi.org/10.1525/aa.2006.108.3.480.

Stiner, Mary C., Steven L. Kuhn, Stephen Zeiner, and Ofer Bar-Yosef. 1995. "Differentiating Burning, Recrystallization, and Fragmentation of Archaeological Bone." *Journal of Archaeological Science* 22:223–37. https://doi.org/10.1006/jasc.1995.0024.

Turner, Bethany L., Véronique Bélisle, Allison R. Davis, Maeve Skidmore, Sara L. Juengst, Benjamin J. Schaefer, R. Alan Covey, and Brian S. Bauer. 2018. "Diet and Foodways Across Five Millennia in the Cusco Region of Peru." *Journal of Archaeological Science* 98:137–48. https://doi.org/10.1016/j.jas.2018.07.013.

Vaughn, Kevin J. 2009. *The Ancient Andean Village: Marcaya in Prehispanic Nasca*. Tucson: University of Arizona Press.

Weismantel, Mary. 2009. "Have a Drink: Chicha, Performance, and Politics." In *Drink, Power, and Society in the Andes*, edited by J. Jennings and B. J. Bowser, 257–77. Gainesville: University Press of Florida.

Zapata Rodríguez, Julinho. 1997. "Arquitectura y Contextos Funerarios Wari en Batan Urqu, Cusco." In *La Muerte en el Antiguo Perú: Contextos y Conceptos Funerarios*, edited by P. Kaulicke, 165–206. Lima: Fondo Editorial de la Pontificia Universidad Católica del Perú.

8

Extraordinary Meals in the Wari Empire

Zooarchaeological and Paleoethnobotanical Evidence
from the Site of Quilcapampa La Antigua

Matthew E. Biwer, Aleksa K. Alaica, and
Patricia Quiñonez Cuzcano

Beyond nutrition, producing, processing, and consuming meals encodes food and associated activities with social, economic, and political messages (Appadurai 1981; Bray, this volume; Goody 1982; Hastorf 2017; Weismantel 1988). Mary Douglas (1984) conceptualizes cuisine not only as ingredients but as a series of patterned rules, choices, methods of preparation, and flavors that structure meals. For archaeologists, the patterned residues of these activities link food production and processing to politics and social realities enacted through daily meals and special events.

Extraordinary meals often include feasts, theatrical commensal events involving the consumption of food and drink that are distinct from daily meals in several ways (Dietler 2001; Hayden 2001). Feasts are often politically and socially charged public events that reify asymmetrical institutions of power. Feasts may contain foods that are rare or labor intensive to produce and larger quantities of food items, be they common or rare. Other visible archaeological indicators for feasts may include unusual types, quantities, or numbers of ceramics; expansive food preparation facilities; large deposits of animal bone or plant refuse; special locations; associated prestige items; ritual paraphernalia; or other evidence for aggrandizing (Dietler 2001; Gumerman 1997; Hayden 2001; Klarich 2010). Finally, as opposed to daily meals, feasts connect people that might normally not eat together, which can widen social circles (Pollock 2012).

In Wari's political economy, extraordinary meals were central to political and socioeconomic relationships (e.g., Cook and Glowacki 2003; Moseley et al. 2005; Nash and deFrance 2019). And although feasts probably served many functions, their primary outcome was the creation and maintenance of status-based differences and of social connections that served to bind host and guest together through commensality and the reciprocal exchange of guest's and host's contributions in the form of food and labor (Allen 1988; Kerner, Chou, and Warmind 2015; Weismantel 1988). In this chapter, we present an integrated analysis of animal and plant food remains from Quilcapampa La Antigua to define and describe the co-creation of extraordinary commensal meals in the Wari Empire. Mutual input of food and labor served as a method for Wari-local interaction. Wari-affiliated elites hosted feasts within patio groups steeped in symbols, sounds, smells, and experiences representative of their own cultural affiliation (Biwer et al. 2022; Cook and Glowacki 2003; Nash and deFrance 2019), but both hosts and guests contributed to the meal.

BACKGROUND

The Wari Empire rose during the Middle Horizon period (AD 600–1000) in the south-central Peruvian Andes. Wari-affiliated communities constructed numerous sites throughout the south-central coast and highlands, expanding regional social, economic, and political connections and facilitating the movement of people, ideas, and resources (e.g., Jennings, Biwer, and Conlee 2022; Rosenfeld, Jordan, and Street 2021; Williams, Dussubieux, and Nash 2012). Agents affiliated with the Wari Empire interacted with Indigenous local groups via numerous colonial encounters negotiated by both sides (e.g., Bélisle 2015; Williams and Nash 2016). But by ~AD 1000, the interaction network broke down, and Wari sites were subsequently abandoned (Jennings, Biwer, and Conlee 2022; Isbell 2008).

Quilcapampa is located in the hyperarid *yunga* region of the middle Sihuas Valley (~1,600 masl) in the province of Arequipa, Peru (map 8.1). Wari-affiliated persons established the site as a roadside outpost overlooking the Rio Sihuas during the early ninth century (Jennings, Yépez Álvarez, and Bautista 2021). The site allowed the Wari-aligned group to strategically control access to an ancient trade route that crossed the valley. Quilcapampa was ritually abandoned in the mid-ninth century, making the occupation relatively short lived. One of the final events included an extraordinary meal at the center of the site that marked the end of Wari occupation (Alaica, Quiñonez Cuzcano, and González La Rosa 2021; Biwer and Melton 2021).

Our analysis focuses on materials recovered from 17 excavated units from Sector A. Sector A is divided into two areas: the core area and the

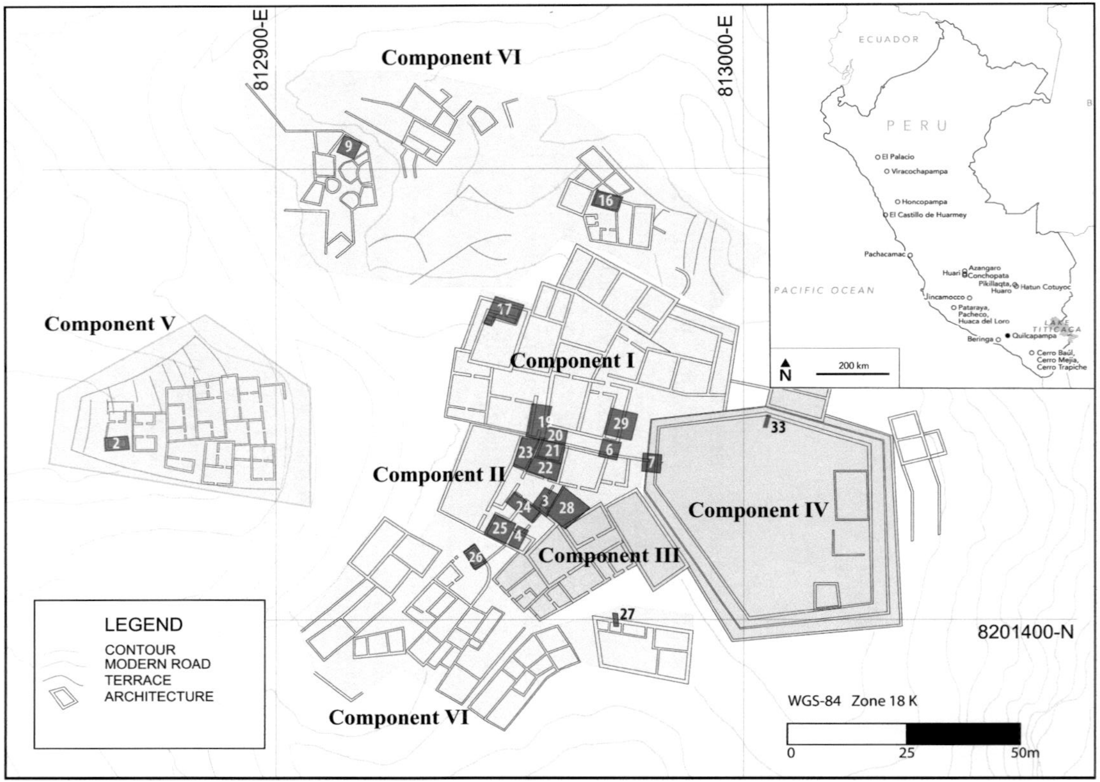

Map 8.1 Map of Quilcapampa Sector A noting architectural components and excavated units. Illustration by Matthew Biwer.

outlying area, each with distinct architectural components that housed culturally distinct groups (González La Rosa et al. 2021, 134). Dividing the site architecture into components allows analysts to group artifacts and the residues of activities by space to illustrate site-level differences in behavior and movement patterns. Orderly walls similar to other Wari sites in the south-central Andes outline the boundaries of the core area, which are divided into architectural Components I, II, III, and IV. The perimeter walls of the planned core area were laid out first, and then internal walls were constructed later on (González La Rosa et al. 2021, 136). Excavations in this area revealed a large plaza, a number of patio groups, and associated side rooms where Wari-style ceramics were recovered in high quantities, suggesting that Wari-affiliated peoples occupied these spaces.

The outlying area reveals a construction style and assemblage that are distinct from that of the core area. Buildings in the outlying area are grouped into Components V and VI. These components are made up of a series of buildings built on terraces that lack planning and coordination, appearing to be ad hoc and hastily built, in comparison to the core. Wari-style ceramics are almost completely absent from the outlying area, suggesting the occupants were culturally distinct from the core residents, possibly being locally affiliated (see Huamán López, Jennings, and Yépez Álvarez, 2021; González La Rosa et al. 2021, 161).

ZOOARCHAEOLOGICAL ANALYSIS

A total of 4,344 fragments of animal bone were recovered representing at least 20 individual animals (table 8.1; Alaica, Quiñonez Cuzcano, and González La Rosa 2021). Vertebrate remains at Quilcapampa include eight species. Considering the count of individual faunal specimens (Number of Individual Specimens [NISP]) and the estimated number of individuals that are needed to be present to accumulate the assemblage (Minimum Number of Individuals [MNI]; Gifford-González 2018; Reitz and Wing 2008), llama (*Lama glama*) and alpaca (*Vicugna pacos*) are the most common remains (NISP = 20.0%, MNI = 20.0%, weight = 79.1%). Other vertebrate remains include local duck (*Anas* sp.), rodents such as guinea pig (*Cavia porcellus*), and coastal species like cormorant (*Phalacrocorax* sp.).

Table 8.1 Number of Individual Specimens (NISP), Minimum Number of Individuals (MNI), and weight of the zooar-chaeological remains recovered from Quilcapampa

Class	Taxon	Common name	NISP	NISP (%)	MNI	MNI (%)	Weight (g)	Weight (%)
Reptilia	Lacertilia	Lizard	7	0.2	1	5.3	0.8	0.01
Aves	Bird	Bird	4	0.1	0	0.0	3.6	0.04
	Large bird	Large bird	5	0.1	1	5.3	4.0	0.04
	Medium bird	Medium bird	3	0.1	0	0.0	2.1	0.02
	Anas sp.	Duck	3	0.1	1	5.3	2.2	0.02
	Anser sp.	Goose	3	0.1	2	10.5	0.8	0.01
	Phalacrocorax carbo	Cormorant	7	0.2	1	5.3	25.0	0.3
Mammalia	Microfauna	Microfauna	39	0.9	0	0.0	0.9	0.01
	Muridae	Rodent	205	4.7	3	15.8	10	0.1
	Cavia porcellus	Guinea pig (*cuy*)	65	1.5	2	10.5	44.2	0.5
	Small mammal	Small mammal	6	0.1	0	0.0	4.4	0.05
	Canidae	Fox/dog	12	0.3	1	5.3	3.4	0.04
	Mammal	Mammal	554	12.8	0	0.0	73.8	0.8
	Large mammal	Large mammal	2323	53.5	0	0.0	1317.3	13.6
	Artiodactyl	Cervid/camelid	236	5.4	2	10.5	492.1	5.1
	Odocoileus virginianus	White-tailed deer	5	0.1	1	5.3	35.4	0.4
	Lama sp. / *Vicugna* sp.	Camelid	867	20.0	4	21.1	7636.4	79.1
	Vertebrate total		4344	100.0	19	100.0	9656.4	100.0

Bivalvia	Bivalve	Bivalve shell	12	2.4	2	2.3	11.1	1.5
	Aulacomya ater.	Ribbed mussel	28	5.6	7	8.0	22.9	3.0
	Choromytilus chorus	Choro mussel	248	49.6	20	23.0	335.8	44.1
	Concholepas concholepas	Abalone	1	0.2	1	1.1	2.2	0.3
	Mesodesma donacium	Macha clam	20	4	7	8.0	22.9	3.0
	Protothaca thaca	Pacific littleneck clam	39	7.8	9	10.3	68.5	9.0
	Semele solida	Brownish clam	4	0.8	1	1.1	18.7	2.5
	Spondylidae	Spondylus	1	0.2	1	1.1	6.2	0.8
	Spondylus calcifer	Spiny oyster	2	0.4	1	1.1	0.5	0.1
	Spondylus princeps	Spiny oyster	2	0.4	1	1.1	3	0.4
Gastropoda	Gastropod	Gastropod	19	3.8	11	12.6	19.2	2.5
	Oliva sp.	Olive shell	1	0.2	1	1.1	1.9	0.2
	Oliva peruviana	Peruvian olive shell	101	20.2	20	23.0	171.6	22.5
	Stramonita chocolate	Red-mouthed rock shell	22	4.4	5	5.7	76.9	10.1
	Invertebrate total		500	100.0	87	100.0	761.4	100.0

In addition, 500 fragments of shell were also recovered representing 87 individual mollusks (table 8.1). All identified invertebrate species are from shallow marine waters. Fish or riverine prawns, which would have been locally available in the adjacent Sihuas River, were not identified in the assemblage. The most common shells are from the Choro mussel (*Choromytilus chorus*) (NISP = 49.6%) and the Peruvian olive (*Oliva peruviana*), a sea snail (NISP = 20.2%). Other significant mollusk taxa that were recovered include spondylus (*Spondylus princeps*, *Spondylus calcifer*), or spiny oyster.

MACROBOTANICAL ANALYSIS

A total of 1,448,776 botanical remains were identified representing 20 genera (table 8.2) (Biwer and Melton 2021). Molle (*Schinus molle*) drupes are the most abundant plant remain, followed by quinoa and maize. Chili pepper (*Capsicum* spp.), peanut (*Arachis hypogaea*), common bean (*Phaseolus vulgaris*), and potato (*Solanum tuberosum*) are also present but make up a smaller percentage of the total plant assemblage. Locally available fruits and tended plants such as cactus fruit (*Echinocereus* sp., *Echinopsis* sp.), lucuma (*Pouteria lucuma*), and pacay (*Inga feuillei*) were also recovered.

INTEGRATING THE PLANT AND ANIMAL DATA

FOOD ABUNDANCE AND PROCESSING

The core and outlying areas differ in several ways. Faunal remains were recovered from all units and areas of the site, though the majority were recovered from the core area, specifically Component II (core; NISP = 1,497). Component II also exhibits the highest species diversity, with 15 of 17 vertebrate taxa and 9 of the 14 invertebrate taxa identified, and some are exclusive to it (e.g., duck and goose). In the outlying areas, camelid remains were the most common species identified with a few remains of deer, guinea pig, and marine shell.

Minimum Animal Unit (MAU) and Food Utility Index (FUI) were used to measure the primary food value of different skeletal parts (Mengoni Goñalons 1991). The MAU is calculated by dividing the total number of elements by the occurrence of each skeletal portion per species. The FAU is calculated by examining the correlation between the food utility of each skeletal element and MAU. In the outlying area of Quilcapampa, the camelid assemblage is dominated by metapodial fragments and extremities, including carpals, tarsals, metacarpals, metatarsals, and phalanges, which are lower ranked because they have smaller amounts of meat compared to other cuts (table 8.3; fig. 8.1*a*). In the core area, however, we find greater frequencies of more highly ranked camelid portions with more meat, including greater quantities of femur, humerus, and thorax (ribs and vertebrae).

Cutmark analyses show distinct differences in the processing of meat at the site (fig 8.1*b*). Specifically, meaty portions of the camelids, which include portions of the thorax area, are most associated with the core. In the outlying areas, cutmarks appear predominantly on hind limbs and extremities, which have a lower caloric ranking. The differences in cutmarks on faunal remains at the site align with some of the skeletal element distribution patterns, suggesting that access to certain meat cuts was potentially highly regulated.

There are also differences in terms of plant abundance and processing. Comparing the density of maize, molle, and quinoa remains between the core and outlying areas demonstrates that these taxa exhibit higher densities in the core than the outlying area (fig. 8.2). The higher density of molle in the core area, the majority of which shows signs of morphological alteration consistent with soaking and/or boiling (see Sayre et al. 2012), suggests intensive brewing activities. The core area has a greater amount of molle than the outlying area even when a pit filled ~1.2 million molle seeds from Component II is excluded from the analysis.

Maize processing also differs between the two areas. The ratio of kernel to cupule is higher in the core (.36) than the outlying area (.12), suggesting maize processing was more intense in the outlying area. The higher counts of maize, molle, quinoa, and other plants in the core area could represent greater amounts of cooking activities and/or the inclusion of these foods in the brewing process of *chicha* (Weber and Young, this volume). It was at the core, specifically Component II, that a set of food-related practices well outside the realm of normal domestic behaviors took place.

Table 8.2 Count and weight of paleoethnobotanical remains recovered from Quilcapampa

Family	Taxon	Common name	Count	Weight (g)
Amaranthaceae	*Chenopodium quinoa*	Quinoa	25,186	36.28
	Chenopodium quinoa cf.	Quinoa cf.	5	0.05
	Chenopodium/Amaranthus sp.	Quinoa/Kiwicha	17	0.08
	Amaranthus sp.	Kiwicha	338	0.16
Anacardiaceae	*Schinus molle*	Molle	1,400,361	6,130.73
	Schinus molle cf.	Molle cf.	4	0.36
Cactaceae	*Echinopsis* sp.	Cactus	61	0.33
	Echinocereus sp.	Cactus	23	4.23
	Cactaceae	Cactus family	22	0.1
Cannaceae	*Canna indica*	Achira	10	2.06
Cucurbitaceae	*Lagenaria* sp.	Bottle gourd	218	24.35
	Lagenaria sp. cf.	Bottle gourd cf.	26	0.58
	Cucurbita maxima	Zapallo	12	0.18
	Cucurbitaceae	Squash family	65	4.55
	Cucurbitaceae cf.	Squash/gourd cf.	13	0.07
Cyperaceae	Cyperaceae	Sedge family	9	0.08
Erythroxylaceae	*Erythroxylum coca*	Coca	8	0.12
	Erythroxylum coca cf.	Coca cf.	141	0.12
Fabaceae	*Inga feuillei*	Pacay	1,326	162.29
	Inga feuillei cf.	Pacay	105	40.61
	Anadenanthera colubrina	Wilka	16	1.26
	Fabaceae	Bean family	162	1.2
	Fabaceae cf.	Bean family cf.	46	0.67

Family	Taxon	Common name	Count	%
	Phaseolus vulgaris	Common bean	351	22.12
	Arachis hypogaea	Peanut	349	8.69
	Arachis hypogaea cf.	Peanut cf.	8	0.04
Malvaceae	*Gossypium barbadense*	Cotton	181	2.27
	Gossypium barbadense cf.	Cotton Seed cf.	4	0.2
Rosaceae	*Prunus* sp. cf.	Wild plum/cherry cf.	7	0.06
Sapotaceae	*Pouteria lucuma*	Lucuma	295	30.96
	Pouteria lucuma cf.	Lucuma cf.	83	0.04
Solanaceae	*Solanum tuberosum*	Potato	369	79.8
	Solanum tuberosum cf.	Potato cf.	263	5.79
	Capsicum sp.	Chili pepper	2,111	6.27
	Capsicum sp. cf.	Chili pepper cf.	7	0.03
	Physalis sp.	Aguaymanto	176	2.37
Poaceae	*Poaceae*	Grass family	31	0.13
	Zea mays	Maize	14,848	439.26
	Zea mays cf.	Maize cf.	184	17.15
UID			729	40.28
UID seed			488	1.26
Unidentifiable			118	2.54

Note: number of samples = 76; wood weight (g) = 154.62; total liters of soil = 405; total plant count = 1,448,776.

Table 8.3 Food Utility Index (FUI), Minimum Number of Elements (MNE), and Minimum Animal Unit (MAU) counts and percentages in the core and outlying areas

Element	FUI	Elements/skeleton	MNE		MAU		%MAU	
			Core	Outlying	Core	Outlying	Core	Outlying
Skull	14.75	1	2	0	2	0	5.8	0
Mandible	9.95	1	2	0	2	0	5.8	0
Cervical	64.15	7	12	3	1.7	0.4	4.9	4.5
Thoracic	61.75	12	9	1	0.8	0.1	2.2	0.9
Lumbar	77.97	7	13	0	1.9	0	5.4	0
Rib	100	24	13	2	0.5	0.1	1.6	0.9
Scapula	41.66	2	3	0	1.5	0	4.3	0
Humerus	36.68	2	4	1	2	0.5	5.8	5.2
Radio-ulna	23	2	7	1	3.5	0.5	10.1	5.2
Carpal	11.76	14	22	2	1.6	0.1	4.5	1.5
Metacarpal	9	2	8	3	4	1.5	11.5	15.6
Pelvis	40.18	2	6	1	3	0.5	8.7	5.2
Femur	75.94	2	7	1	3.5	0.5	10.1	5.2
Tibia	43.04	2	4	0	2	0	5.8	0
Astragalus	21.88	2	0	1	0	0.5	0	5.2
Calcaneus	21.88	2	3	2	1.5	1	4.3	10.4
Tarsal	21.88	12	2	8	0.2	0.7	0.5	6.9
Metatarsal	9	2	2	2	1	1	2.9	10.4
Metapodial	9	4	3	6	0.8	1.5	2.2	15.6
Phalanx	4.78	24	31	17	1.3	0.7	3.7	7.4

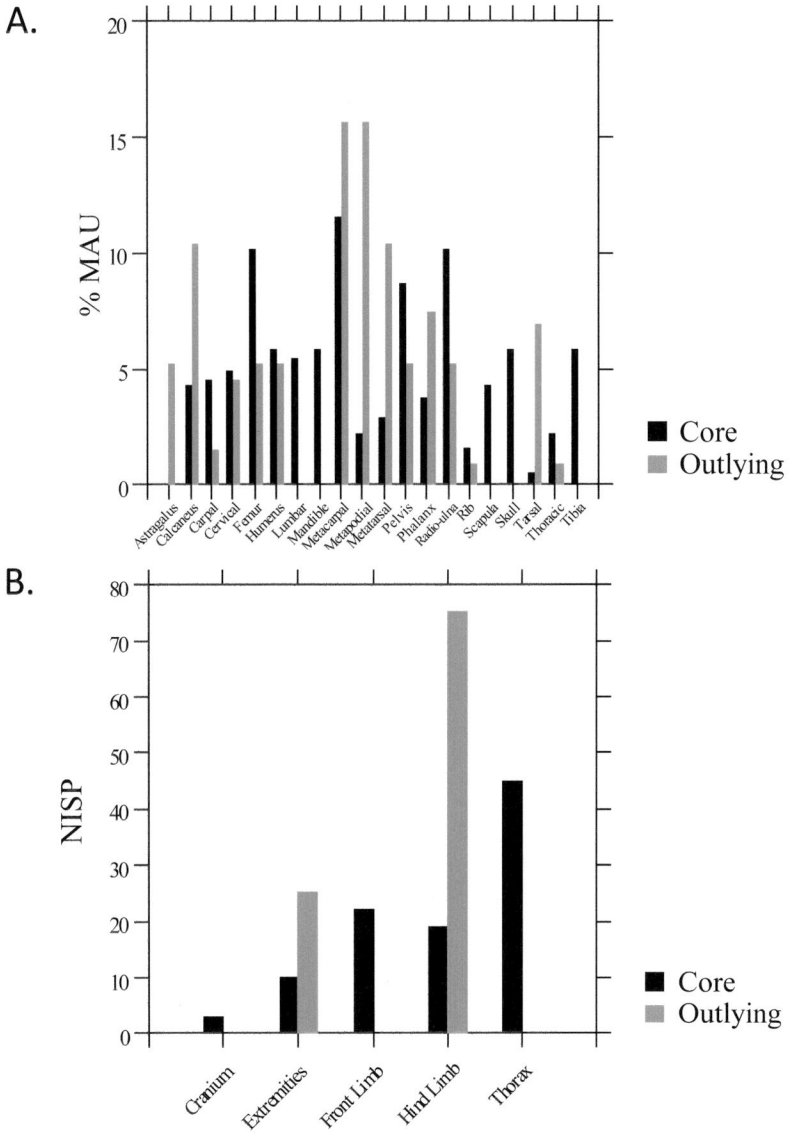

Figure 8.1 Comparison of camelid faunal remains from the core and outlying areas at Quilcapampa. *A*, percent of Minimum Animal Unit (MAU). *B*, distribution of cut marks by part segment (meaty–thorax, front limb, hind limb; lacking meat–cranium and extremities). Image by Matthew Biwer.

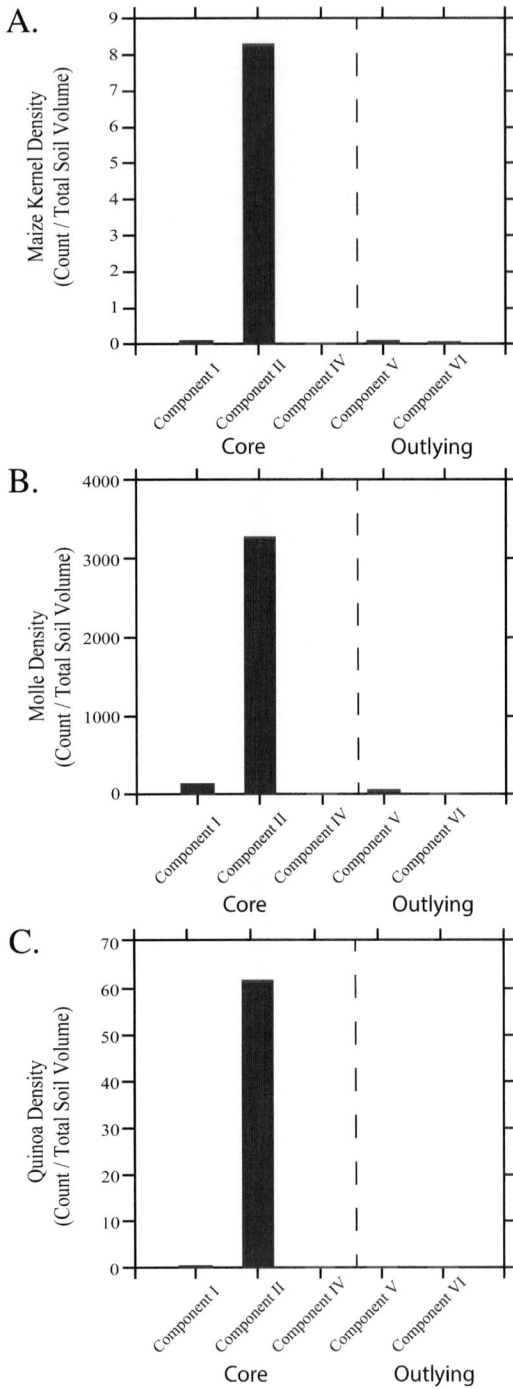

Figure 8.2 Density of plant remains in core and outlying components at Quilcapampa. *A*, maize. *B*, molle. *C*, quinoa. Image by Matthew Biwer.

UBIQUITY

Ubiquity is the percentage of the analyzed samples that contain a particular taxon over the total number of samples (Popper 1988). Animal and plant ubiquity was calculated in all the excavated contexts from Quilcapampa to characterize the extent of use of the more abundant taxa (table 8.4). Llama- and alpaca-size camelids and molle exhibit 100% ubiquity, making these taxa the most prevalent at the site. Choro mussel, olive snail, chili pepper, maize kernel, lucuma, and peanut are also well distributed, and bottle gourd ubiquity is high (76%). The gourds, however, were probably used as cups, bowls, or containers. Most site residents had access to these foods, and they were probably used in a variety of cooking activities. Although far from the coast, Quilcapampa residents had access to marine mussels (76%), ribbed mussels (41%), clams (47%), and snails (53%).

The low ubiquity of guinea pig remains at Quilcapampa (18%) is noteworthy because they are more ubiquitous at other Wari sites (e.g., deFrance 2014; Rosenfeld 2012). Common bean, *wilka* (*Anadenanthera colubrina*), and potato also have low ubiquity scores (18%; table 8.4) and are exclusively recovered from the core area. Wild bird remains, including duck, goose, and cormorant, are the least ubiquitous animals, with scores ≤12%.

Table 8.4 Ubiquity of botanical and faunal remains from Quilcapampa

Faunal		Botanical	
Taxa	**Ubiquity score (%)**	**Taxa**	**Ubiquity score (%)**
Camelid	100	Molle	100
Mussel	76	Chili pepper	88
Peruvian olive snail	53	Maize kernel	82
Clam	47	Bottle gourd	76
Ribbed mussel	41	Quinoa	76
Spondylus	24	Pacay	71
Deer	18	Lucuma	53
Guinea pig	18	Peanut	41
Duck	12	Common bean	24
Goose	12	Wilka	18
Cormorant	6	Potato	18

DISCUSSION AND CONCLUSION

The residents of Quilcapampa had access to a number of domesticated and wild resources. Camelid meat, molle, maize, chili pepper, quinoa, bottle gourd, and pacay dominate the assemblage in terms of abundance and extent of use, suggesting they were part of quotidian meals. Cultigens such as common bean, potato, and peanut are less widespread and dense, suggesting that they were a lesser, but perhaps no less important, part of foodways at the site. Locally available hunted and gathered wild foods and gathered or tended fruits such as pacay, lucuma, and cactus fruit also appear in the assemblage and were probably common additions to meals. Wild small mammals and local waterfowl (including duck and geese) are found in small amounts, suggesting their contribution to daily meals was relatively minor through opportunistic acquisition.

There are clear differences associated with processing labor and the abundance of food between the core and the outlying area. Camelid meat was a somewhat regular ingredient in daily meals throughout the site, though the portions accessible to the residents varied. The greater abundance of high-calorie cuts of camelid meat in the core and the high incidence of cutmarks on low-ranked hind limb extremities in the out-lying areas demonstrate that meat and food processing labor were not equitably distributed. Further, maize processing was more common in the outlying area. While these patterns suggest status-related differences in diet breadth, faunal and botanical data indicate that processing and cooking were emphasized in the outlying area, whereas discard (and probably consumption) were most common in the core area.

Component II, in the core, has the highest density of maize kernel and molle of all components in the site. The relationship is notewor-thy because maize was a staple of many complex societies in the Andes throughout history (e.g., Alfonso-Durruty et al. 2016; Cutright 2015; Goldstein 2003). The high abundance of maize recovered from Component II points to this area as the location of cooking or possibly con-sumption practices that far exceed those of other areas of the site.

The high density of molle recovered from Component II also falls outside normal discard patterns. The majority of the molle drupes recov-ered from Component II, and the site in general, shows signs of being used for brewing *chicha de molle* (see Biwer and Melton 2021). *Chicha de molle* was produced and consumed as part of public political and ritual feasts as well as in more private events in the Wari Empire (see Biwer et al. 2022; Goldstein, Goldstein, and Williams 2009; Nash and deFrance 2019; Sayre et al. 2012). While not a formal brewery like the one at the southern Wari colony at Cerro Baúl (see Moseley et al. 2005), the large number of molle drupes associated with Component II suggest large amounts of chicha brewing by the Wari-affiliated occupants.

Two considerations should be made concerning the plant and animal data at Quilcapampa. First, 69 of the total 76 soil samples come from the core area. Thus, some analyses, such as density and kernel-to-cupule ratios, may be skewed to more heavily emphasize core activities. Second, while the majority of faunal remains come from the core area of the site, all recovered faunal remains were analyzed. Taking these two considerations together, we suggest that higher absolute counts of plant and animal remains in the core relative to the outlying area reflect differences in occupation and/or food-related activities. While sample size may be a factor, the broad distribution of excavation units was selected to capture site-level variation. Thus, it is more likely that the lower taxa counts in the outlying area result from less intensive occupation of the outlying area of Sector A compared to the core.

Given the large amounts of food remains recovered, the molle pit, the high rate of cutmarks, and the cooking of cuts of camelid meat, we suggest that it is likely that Component II was the location of extraordinary commensal meals that included large amounts of staple foods such as camelid meat, maize, and quinoa. Exotic ingredients, such as wilka, may have been added to chicha for a hallucinogenic effect (Biwer et al. 2022). Within this space, both Wari-affiliated occupants of the core area and possible Sihuas locals from the outlying area would have come together to participate in commensal politics surrounding the communal consumption of food. Local guests to these extraordinary meals would have taken in a variety of both familiar and new sensory details, including sights, sounds, smells, and feelings. These sensory aspects to feasting shaped the types of power structures guiding the choices of hosts and guests.

Michael Dietler (2001) identifies three principal types of feasts: empowering, diacritical, and patron-client feasts. Empowering feasts create political and social power through displays of hospitality where reciprocal

obligations are required. Commonly known as work feasts in the Andes (see Allen 1988, 116–18; Isbell 1978), these events allow the host
to acquire social and political capital to influence community decision
making, or the ability to call on neighbors for aid in various projects (e.g.,
planting a field or constructing a canal). Diacritical feasts are used to
signal elite status and often rely on large amounts of exotic foods or other
hard-to-obtain resources (Dietler 2001). These types of feasts demonstrate differences in status, rank, and a social order where the emphasis
is placed not on the quantity of food but on style and taste (Bourdieu
1984; Goody 1982). Finally, patron-client (or alliance building) feasts
tend to provide typical food and drink in high quantities (Dietler 2001,
82–83; Hastorf 2017, 199). These events emphasize the hospitality of the
host while strengthening institutionalized relations of power for social,
economic, or political gain.

Both diacritical and patron-client feasts are documented at Wari-
associated settlements (see Biwer et al. 2022; Cook and Glowacki 2003;
Nash 2010; Nash and deFrance 2019; Rosenfeld 2012). We argue the
evidence from the Component II assemblage is more in line with patron-
client feasts. At Quilcapampa, locals from the outlying area of the site
and beyond were served camelid meat, maize, quinoa, bean, and other
staple foods in quantities that far exceeded daily meals. Copious amounts
of chicha, a transformed food made from molle, maize, or other ingredients, brewed by Wari-affiliated hosts would have flowed. Exotic ingredients, such as wilka, were added to the chicha to provide a hallucinogenic
effect. Such a gathering would have functioned as a powerful political
tool for Wari-affiliated groups who could bring local guests into the Wari
core compounds of Quilcapampa from the outlying area and beyond
(Jennings, Alaica, and Biwer, forthcoming).

Locals invited into this space feasted on vast quantities of staple foods.
They experienced ingredients, methods of preparation, serving, and consumption that were somewhat different from their own, but they were
not completely unfamiliar. Locals added provisions to the feast by re-
moving maize kernels from the cob and butchering camelids, with choice
cuts being delivered to the core. Commensality in the core was thus not
strictly defined by Wari hosts providing food, drink, and experiences to
guests but instead, it was an extraordinary meal of mutual construction.
The inclusion of labor and/or foods prepared by locals for communal

consumption would have been a powerful statement for building guests-hosts social bonds. Such a relationship would have been paramount for gaining local support for Wari projects; creating and maintaining social, political, and economic relationships; or possibly pacifying local community anxiety as a result of Wari incursion. Whatever their goals may have been, extraordinary commensal meals appear to have been integral to Wari politics and society.

The provisioning of food and alcoholic beverages by both Wari hosts and local guests would have forged a community bond, a connection desired by Wari-affiliated leaders. The co-construction of the meal with elements contributed by both Wari and local guests was a physical enactment of bonding. As the meal was assembled, cooked, and consumed, using diverse ingredients and methods, the inclusion of culinary identities from all participants would have been a powerful statement of connectedness whereby cultural ideals were shared and literally consumed by all. Wari hosts may have aggrandized by hosting the feast and providing hallucinogenic chicha, but locals seemingly also participated in provisioning and processing the foods to make the meal. The participation of both guest and host in the construction of this extraordinary meal was part of the diverse range of experiences at Wari sites.

REFERENCES

Alaica, Aleksa K., P. Quiñonez Cuzcano, and L. M. González La Rosa. 2021. "Eating and Feasting: Vertebrate and Invertebrate Remains from Quilcapampa." In *Quilcapampa: A Wari Colony in a Networked Horizon*, edited by J. Jennings, W. Y. Álvarez, and S. Bautista, 353–93. Tallahassee: University Press of Florida.

Alfonso-Durruty, Marta, Andrés Troncoso, Pablo Larach, Cristian Becker, and Nicole Misarti. 2016. "Maize (*Zea mays*) Consumption in the Southern Andes (30°–31° S. Lat): Stable Isotope Evidence (2000 BCE–1540 CE)." *American Journal of Physical Anthropology* 164:148–62. https://doi.org/10.1002/ajpa.23263.

Allen, Catharine J. 1988. *The Hold Life Has: Coca and Cultural Identity in an Andean Community*. Washington D.C.: Smithsonian Institution Press.

Appadurai, Arjun. 1981. "Gastro-Politics in Hindu South Asia." *American Ethnologist* 8 (3): 494–511. https://doi.org/10.1525/ae.1981.8.3.02a00050.

Bélisle, Veronique. 2015. "Understanding Wari State Expansion: A 'Bottom-Up' Approach at the Village of Ak'awillay, Cusco, Peru." *Latin American Antiquity* 26 (2): 180–99. https://doi.org/10.7183/1045-6635.26.2.180.

Biwer, Matthew E., and Mallory A. Melton. 2021. "Plant Use at Quilcapampa."
    In *Quilcapampa: A Wari Colony in a Networked Horizon*, edited by J. Jennings,
    W. Y. Álvarez, and S. Bautista, 310–52. Tallahassee: University Press of Florida.
Biwer, Matthew E., Willey Yépez Álvarez, Stefanie Bautista, and Justin Jen-
    nings. 2022. "Hallucinogens, Alcohol, and Shifting Leadership Strategies in
    the Ancient Peruvian Andes." *Antiquity* 96 (385): 142–58. https://doi.org/10
    .15184/aqy.2021.177.
Bourdieu, Pierre. 1984. *Distinction: A Social Critique of the Judgement of Taste.*
    Cambridge, Mass.: Harvard University Press.
Cook, Anita, and Mary Glowacki. 2003. "Pots, Politics, and Power: Huari Ce-
    ramic Assemblages and Imperial Administration." In *The Archaeology and
    Politics of Food and Feasting in Early States and Empires*, edited by T. L. Bray,
    173–202. New York: Springer.
Cutright, Robyn. 2015. "Eating Empire in the Jequetepeque: A Local View of
    Chimú Expansion on the North Coast of Peru." *Latin American Antiquity*
    26:64–86. https://doi.org/10.7183/1045-6635.26.1.64.
deFrance, Susan D. 2014. "The Luxury of Variety: Animals and Social Distinc-
    tion at the Wari Site of Cerro Baúl, Southern Peru." In *Animals and Inequality
    in the Ancient World*, edited by B. S. Arbuckle and S. A. McCarthy, 63–84.
    Boulder: University Press of Colorado.
Dietler, Michael. 2001. "Theorizing the Feast: Rituals of Consumption, Com-
    mensal Politics, and Power in African Contexts." In *Feasts: Archaeological and
    Ethnographic Perspectives on Food, Politics, and Power*, edited by M. Dietler
    and B. Hayden, 65–114. Washington, D.C.: Smithsonian Institution Press.
Douglas, Mary. 1984. *Food in the Social Order: Studies of Food and Festivities in
    Three American Communities*. New York: Routledge.
Gifford-González, Diane. 2018. *An Introduction to Zooarchaeology*. Cham: Springer.
Goldstein, David John, Robin Coleman Goldstein, and Patrick Ryan Wil-
    liams. 2009. "You Are What You Drink: A Sociocultural Reconstruction of
    Pre-Hispanic Fermented Beverage Use at Cerra Baúl, Moquegua, Peru." In
    Drink, Power, and Society in the Andes, edited by Justin Jennings and Brenda
    Bowser, 133–66. Gainesville: University Press of Florida.
Goldstein, Paul S. 2003. "From Stew-Eaters to Maize-Drinkers: The Chicha
    Economy and the Tiwanaku Expansion." In *The Archaeology and Politics of
    Food and Feasting in Early States and Empires*, edited by T. L. Bray, 143–72.
    New York: Kluwer Academic; Plenum.
González La Rosa, Luis Manuel, Justin Jennings, Giles Spence Morrow, and
    Willy Yépez Álvarez. 2021. "Settling Quilcapampa: Plan and Adaptation."
    In *Quilcapampa: A Wari Enclave in Southern Peru*, edited by J. Jennings,
    W. Yépez Álvarez, and S. Bautista, 131–67. Tallahassee: University Press
    of Florida.
Goody, Jack. 1982. *Cooking, Cuisine and Class: A Study in Comparative Sociology.*
    Cambridge: Cambridge University Press.

Gumerman, George J., IV. 1997. "Food and Complex Societies." *Journal of Archaeological Method and Theory* 4:105–39. https://doi.org/10.1007/BF02428056.

Hastorf, Christine A. 2017. *The Social Archaeology of Food: Thinking About Eating from Prehistory to the Present*. New York: Cambridge University Press.

Hayden, Brian. 2001. "Fabulous Feasts: A Prolegomenon to the Importance of Feasting." In *Feasts: Archaeological and Ethnographic Perspectives on Food, Politics, and Power*, edited by M. Dietler and B. Hayden, 23–64. Tuscaloosa: University of Alabama Press.

Huamán López, Oscar, Justin Jennings, and Willy Yépez Álvarez. 2021. "Quilcapampa's Ceramics: Imperial Styles and Local Traditions." In *Quilcapampa: A Wari Enclave in Southern Peru*, edited by Justin J. Jennings, W. Yépez Álvarez, and S. Bautista, 209–57. Tallahassee: University Press of Florida.

Isbell, Billy Jean. 1978. *To Defend Ourselves: Ecology and Ritual in an Andean Village*. Austin: University of Texas Press.

Isbell, William H. 2008. "Wari and Tiwanaku: International Identities in the Central Andean Middle Horizon." In *Handbook of South American Archaeology*, edited by H. Silverman and W. H. Isbell, 731–59. New York: Springer.

Jennings, Justin, Aleksa K. Alaica, and Matthew E. Biwer. Forthcoming. "Beer, Drugs, and Meat: A Reconsideration of Early Wari Feasting and Statecraft." *Archaeology of Food and Foodways*.

Jennings, Justin, Matthew E. Biwer, and Christina Conlee. 2022. "Assembling the Early Expansionary State: Wari and the Southern Peruvian Coast." *Journal of Anthropological Archaeology* 65:101395. https://doi.org/10.1016/j.jaa.2022.101395.

Jennings, Justin, Willy Yépez Álvarez, and Stefanie Bautista, ed. 2021. *Quilcapampa: A Wari Colony in a Networked Horizon*. Gainesville: University Press of Florida.

Kerner, Suzanne, Cynthia Chou, and Morten Warmind, ed. 2015. *Commensality: From Everyday Food to Feast*. New York: Bloomsbury.

Klarich, Elizabeth A. 2010. "Behind the Scenes and into the Kitchen: New Directions for the Study of Prehistoric Meals." In *Inside Ancient Kitchens: New Directions in the Study of Daily Meals and Feasts*, edited by E. Klarich, 1–15. Boulder: University Press of Colorado.

Mengoni Goñalons, Guillermo. 1991. "La Llama y sus Productos Primarios." *Arqueología: Revista de la Sección Prehistoria, Universidad de Buenos Aires, Instituto de Ciencias Antropológicas* 1:179–96.

Moseley, Michael E., Donna J. Nash, Patrick Ryan Williams, Susan D. deFrance, Ana Miranda, and Mario Ruales. 2005. "Burning Down the Brewery: Establishing and Evacuating an Ancient Imperial Colony at Cerro Baúl, Peru." *Proceedings of the National Academy of Sciences* 102 (48): 17264–71. https://doi.org/10.1073/pnas.0508673102.

Nash, Donna J. 2010. "Fine Dining and Fabulous Atmosphere: Feasting Facilities and Political Interaction in the Wari Realm." In *Inside Ancient Kitchens:*

New Directions in the Study of Daily Meals and Feasting Events, edited by E. Klarich, 83–110. Boulder: University Press of Colorado.

Nash, Donna J., and Susan deFrance. 2019. "Plotting Abandonment: Excavating a Ritual Deposit at the Wari Site of Cerro Baúl." *Journal of Anthropological Archaeology* 53:112–32. https://doi.org/10.1016/j.jaa.2018.12.002.

Pollock, Susan. 2012. "Towards an Archaeology of Commensal Spaces: An Introduction." In *Between Feasts and Daily Meals*, edited by Susan Pollock, 7–28. Berlin: Edition Topoi.

Popper, Virginia S. 1988. "Selecting Quantitative Measurements in Paleoethnobotany." In *Current Paleoethnobotany: Analytical Methods and Cultural Interpretations of Archaeological Plant Remains*, edited by C. A. Hastorf and V. S. Popper, 53–71. Chicago: University of Chicago Press.

Reitz, Elizabeth J., and Elizabeth S. Wing. 2008. *Zooarchaeology*, 2nd ed. Cambridge: Cambridge University Press.

Rosenfeld, Silvana A. 2012. "Animal Wealth and Local Power in the Huari Empire." *Ñawpa Pacha* 32 (1): 131–64. https://doi.org/10.1179/naw.2012.32.1.131.

Rosenfeld, Silvana, Brennan T. Jordan, and Megan E. Street. 2021. "Beyond Exotic Goods: Wari Elites and Regional Interaction in the Andes During the Middle Horizon (AD 600–1000)." *Antiquity* 95 (380): 400–16. https://doi.org/10.15184/aqy.2020.250.

Sayre, Matthew, David Goldstein, William Whitehead, and Patrick Ryan Williams. 2012. "A Marked Preference." *Ñawpa Pacha* 32 (2): 231–82. https://doi.org/10.1179/naw.2012.32.2.231.

Weismantel, Mary. 1988. *Food, Gender, and Poverty in the Ecuadorian Andes*. Philadelphia: University of Pennsylvania Press.

Williams, Patrick Ryan, Laure Dussubieux, and Donna J Nash. 2012. "Provenance of Peruvian Wari Obsidian: Comparing INAA, LA-ICP-MS, and Portable XRF." In *Obsidian and Ancient Manufactured Glasses*, edited I. Liritzis and C. Stevenson, 75–96. Albuquerque: University of New Mexico Press.

Williams, Patrick Ryan, and Donna J. Nash. 2016. "Religious Ritual and State Expansion." In *Religious Ritual and Archaic States*, edited by J. M. A. Murphy, 131–56. Gainesville: University Press of Florida.

PART III

FOOD DURING TIMES OF TROUBLE:
CONFLICT, INSTABILITY, AND
COLLAPSE

9

Maize as a Marker

An Isotopic Perspective on Childhood Diets and the Constitutive Power of Food in the Lower Majes Valley, Peru

Beth K. Scaffidi, Natasha P. Vang, and Tiffiny A. Tung

Subsistence practices are borne of more than necessity and availability. As described in this volume, food procurement, preparation, and consumption can be conscious choices that define aspects of individual and communal identity. The foods present on a household or communal table can be a keyhole into the social relationships and exchange networks through which we can read a community's geopolitical positioning, as well as individuals' relative positions and roles.

Since Levi-Strauss (1963) recognized food as "good to think with," anthropologists have conceptualized food as a window into social relationships (Dietler and Hayden 2001; Gumerman 1997; Hastorf 2016; Smith 2006). Much scholarship has focused on understanding meals and feasts as socially stratifying events that reify differentiation between social groups (Dietler and Hayden 2001; Gumerman 1997; Klarich 2010). Eating enables people to perform and contest aspects of identities like social status, occupation, ethnicity, gender, and age.

However, as Bray (this volume) contends, food is not merely symbolic but has material and mutable qualities that transform corporeal bodies. Daily and ritual eating and food abstention all generate bodies of like kinds. Allen (2002) and Sillar (2009), among others, have examined how Andean ontologies view food as agentive and vital to reciprocal feeding relationships between living and dead or natural and supernatural. As the animating essence of food is transferred to the consumer, both are transformed and (re)made.

Ethnographic and archaeological evidence demonstrates the transformative potential of animated foods in South American groups. For example, some Amazonian groups abstain from meat eating before a hunt to avoid the vengeful essences of dead prey (e.g., Conklin 2001;

Fausto et al. 2007; Uzendoski 2004). Similarly, Hastorf (2003, 551) interprets a famous Moche ceramic scene as demonstrating animated plates of food walking toward the festival chief. These brief examples highlight the animacy and generative potential of foods and also how they can be reserved for certain individuals.

MAIZE AS A PRESTIGE FOOD IN THE PRE-HISPANIC ANDES

The consumption of prestige foods often connotes high-status social groups. Prestige foods are either rare and exotic (Hastorf 2003, 545) or they can be everyday foods consumed by commoners in ritual or special occasions (Hastorf 2016; Hastorf and Johannessen 1993). Mundane foods can also become special when imported from afar (Hastorf 2003) or when lavished on guests in great quantities at feasts (Dietler and Hayden 2001; Gumerman 1997).

As others in this volume demonstrate (Alconini; Belisle et al.; Biwer, Alaica, and Quiñonez Cuzcano; Berryman and Blom; Bray), maize and maize beer (*chicha*) were some of the paramount prestige foods used in commensal feasting in the pre-Hispanic Andes (Hastorf 2003; Hastorf and Johannessen 1993). Because maize does not grow reliably at the highest elevations in the Andes, the presence of maize can indicate exchange between high- and lower-elevation communities (see Baitzel et al. this volume). Particularly in places where it was rarer, maize and maize chicha were sometimes restricted to elites with access to political and ritual dining and drinking activities. Even at sites where maize consumption was common, such as sites on the north coast of Peru, maize cobs from foreign locations found in high-status burials show how access to exotic strains set the elite apart from commoners (Gumerman, Johannessen, and Hastorf 1994; Hastorf 2003; Hastorf and Johannessen 1993).

In this chapter we explore the animated and generative capacities of maize through stable isotope analysis of tooth enamel formed throughout early life. We investigate how maize consumption differed between burials from Uraca, in the Lower Majes Valley of Arequipa, Peru, and how differential maize consumption throughout distinct childhood phases constituted, and was constituted by (sensu Giddens 1984), male identity and violence. This allows us to explore how maize consumption transformed identity throughout life and how it structured the risk for violence and violent postmortem dismemberment later in life for injured adult males.

SPECIALIZED DIETS AND CONSUMPTIVE IDENTITIES THROUGHOUT THE LIFE COURSE

As Weismantel (1995, 695) observed in modern Quechua households, familial and communal identities are generated through eating. Children "who eat together in the same household share the same flesh"; they are literally "made of the same stuff." For some Amazonian groups, food is also "a device for producing related bodies" (Fausto et al. 2007, 500). Because people are generated by the foods they consume, understanding how food consumption changed throughout early life can show how children ate their way into adulthood identities.

STABLE ISOTOPES OF CARBON ($\Delta^{13}C$) AND EARLY-LIFE ISOBIOGRAPHIES

As other authors in this volume explain (e.g., Berryman and Blom, Knudson et al., Miller et al.), the ratio of stable carbon isotopes ($^{13}C/^{12}C$, expressed as $\delta^{13}C$) in tooth enamel shows whether C_3 or C_4 foods were more dominant during the juvenile enamel development period. Because plants utilize different photosynthetic pathways, we can discriminate between Andean C_3 plants (e.g., potatoes, beans, squash, quinoa) with low $\delta^{13}C$ (mean = −26.8‰), and C_4 plants like maize and amaranth (*kiwicha*) with high $\delta^{13}C$ (mean = −13.9‰; Cadwallader et al. 2012). After correcting for diet-body fractionation of approximately 12.0‰, pure C_3 feeders have carbonate values around −14.5‰, while pure C_4 feeders have values around −0.5‰, with mixed feeders falling in between (Tykot 2006; van der Merwe 1982).

Stable isotope studies have demonstrated how sex-based patterns in diet can emerge in early life and persist (Miller et al. 2020), or diets can be similar between boys and girls throughout early life (Tung and Knudson 2018). Here, we use tooth enamel from two or three early-life development phases per individual to explore early-life dietary change. To complement bioarchaeological scholarship on osteobiographies and to avoid conflation with the ecological concept of life history, we follow Eerkens and colleagues (2018) in using *isobiography* to describe isotopic variability of samples from sequential developmental phases.

ARCHAEOLOGICAL CONTEXT

URACA, A BURIAL GROUND FOR PRESTIGIOUS COMBATANTS

Uraca is located in the Lower Majes Valley of modern-day Arequipa, between the Nasca region and the Wari imperial heartland (map 9.1). According to AMS dates, the cemetery was used between approximately 200 and 750 CE (Scaffidi 2018; Scaffidi and Tung 2020). This dates Uraca to the late Early Intermediate Period (ca. 200 BCE–750 CE) and early Middle Horizon (ca. 600–1000 CE).

Endemic Violence for Uracans

The mid-first millennium was a time of endemic violence in the Lower Majes, which some males leveraged to augment their social status. Grave goods and cranial trauma analysis suggest Uraca was used as a burial ground for combatants (and perhaps their affines) who achieved prestige through violent raiding or warfare (Scaffidi and Tung 2020). Among the 165 individuals recovered, there were twice as many males as females, and most individuals died in young or middle adulthood (Scaffidi and Tung 2020). This demographic pattern suggests either that the community was ravaged by intergroup conflict where mostly adult males were targeted or that this burial location was reserved for combatants.

This sample shows the highest cranial trauma rate among contemporaneous or semi-contemporaneous sites in southern Peru—67% of adults exhibit cranial trauma (Scaffidi and Tung 2020). Over 60% of the Uraca adults show multiple injuries, mostly on the anterior cranium, but the posterior, lateral, and superior cranium are also affected. Lethal injuries were documented on five males (Scaffidi and Tung 2020). Four of these also had healed cranial wounds, showing they were injured in at least two episodes (Scaffidi and Tung 2020). This multiple, repetitive, sometimes lethal, and nonfocal cranial trauma pattern suggests Uracans participated

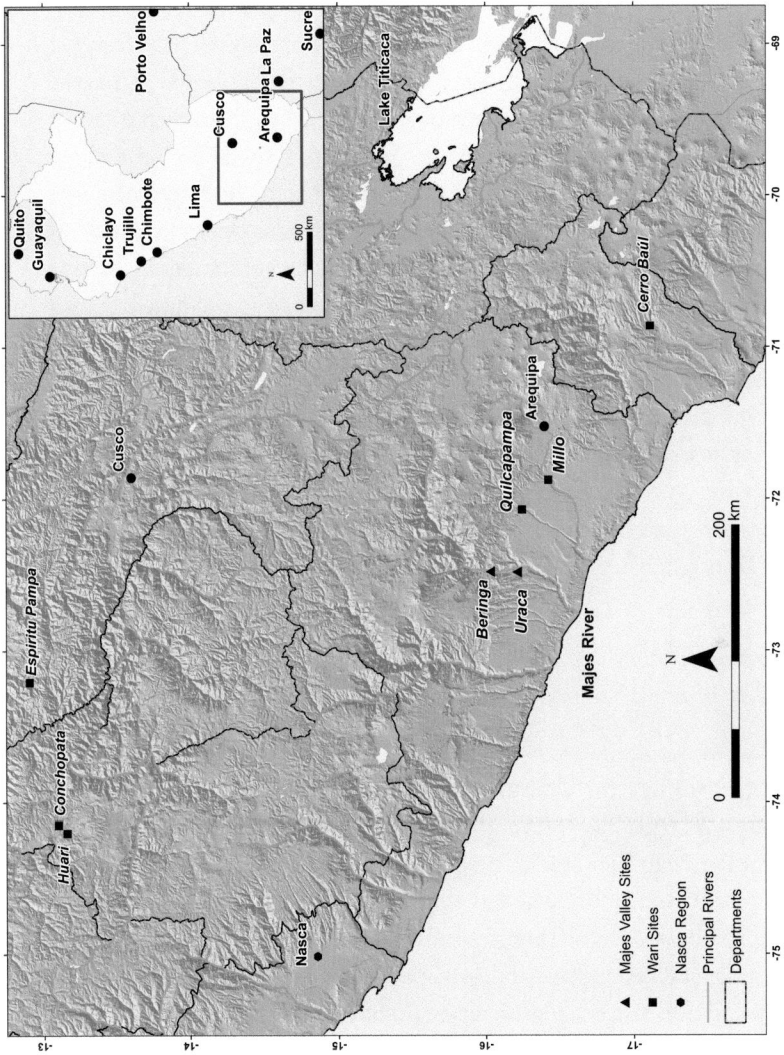

Map 9.1 Location of the Uraca cemetery and the village of Beringa (mentioned in the text) relative to Early Intermediate Period (Nasca) and Middle Horizon (Wari) centers. The reference grid is in latitude/longitude (WGS 1984). Images by Beth K. Scaffidi.

in cyclical episodes of raiding and intergroup warfare—sometimes as victims and other times as perpetrators (Scaffidi and Tung 2020).

Adult Male Trophy Heads at Uraca

Additional evidence of endemic violence at Uraca comes from twelve decapitated and violently mutilated adult male trophy heads and eight defleshed mandibles which were probably also taken from teen or adult males. All show healed trauma, while four of twelve (33.3%) also show perimortem trauma (Scaffidi 2018, 2020b). All were violently dismembered adult males, suggesting trophy taking and making were related to intergroup conflict where men were the primary combatants and victims. Combined with the cranial trauma evidence from the non-trophies (Scaffidi and Tung 2020), it is likely that trophy heads were taken during raids against neighboring groups (Scaffidi 2018, 2020a). While the cranial trauma rate was similar between the trophies (12/12 = 100%) and non-trophy males (52/65 = 80.0%; Fisher's exact, df = 1, $n = 77, p = .201$), injuries were more lethal for trophies (4/12 or 33.3% had perimortem trauma) compared to non-trophy males (5/60 = 8.3%; Fisher's exact, df = 1, $n = 77, p = .029$).

Exploring Early-Life Dietary Differences Based on Adult Violence

Based on this cumulative evidence, we have argued that combat was an avenue to prestige for Uracans (Scaffidi and Tung 2020; Scaffidi 2018, 2020a), similar to paths to high status for Wari military agents in the Central Peruvian highlands (Tung 2012). Given the greater lethality for the trophies, we explore whether they had early-life dietary experiences similar to non-trophies. Then, to limit potentially confounding variables such as skeletal sex and age at death, we compare early-life diets between trophy and non-trophy adult males: Did boys who became trophy heads or who later exhibited cranial trauma have distinct diets from boys who subsequently showed no cranial trauma? Did boys who later presented lethal injuries consume different diets from those who survived their injuries? To address these questions, we compare Uraca early childhood isobiographies ($\delta^{13}C$).

FOODS CONSUMED IN THE MAJES VALLEY

The best evidence of Majes Valley diets comes from isotopic and paleo-botanical data from the village of Beringa, 20 km north of Uraca. Beringa people consumed animal proteins from camelids, guinea pigs, river shrimp from the Majes River, and some seafood from the coast (Tung and Knudson 2018; Tung 2007). Plants recovered included maize, squash, beans, *camote* (sweet potato), peanuts, *lucuma* (stone fruit), yuca, and *molle* (pink peppercorn—consumed fermented as chicha; Tung 2007). Stable isotope analysis shows Beringa individuals consumed mixed C_3/C_4 diets with a relatively low proportion of C_4 foods relative to the maize-centric Wari heartland and coastal agriculturalists (Tung and Knudson 2018).

We lack domestic contexts at Uraca for direct comparison, but paleo-botanical materials deposited in the Uraca tombs show that many of the same foods were used in Uraca funerary rites. We recovered uncharred camelid remains (suggesting they were not consumed in funerary settings) as well as guinea pig, shellfish, and river shrimp. Like at Beringa, we recovered peanuts, beans, *lucuma*, and maize cobs as well as *ají* (peppers) and *pacay* (a leguminous fruit). Amaranth, a common Andean C_4 food, was not recovered from Beringa or Uraca, so maize was probably the main C_4 food in the Majes Valley. While the abundance of maize shows it was important in funerary contexts, it is unclear whether maize was widely consumed during life, and if so, whether maize consumption differed between social groups.

MATERIALS AND METHODS

Here we present $\delta^{13}C$ from trophies ($n = 19$) and non-trophies ($n = 60$), making up 48.2% (79/164) of individuals excavated. We analyzed 286 enamel samples from 176 teeth.

STABLE ISOTOPE ANALYSIS

We prepared enamel carbonates in the Bioarchaeological and Stable Isotope Research Laboratory (BSIRL) at Vanderbilt University, assigning each sample to its corresponding enamel development phase according to Hillson (1986, 1996). We cleaned teeth with ultrapure water, abraded surface enamel to remove potential contaminants, and collected 10 mg of enamel powder per sample with a rotary multispeed tool. Whenever possible, we drilled serial sections from the occlusal wall of the crown (forming earlier in life) and approximately 1–2 mm from the cemento-enamel junction (forming later in life). When serial samples could not be drilled, we drilled bulk enamel powder opportunistically. We removed inorganic contaminates with a 30% hydrogen peroxide soak and subsequent ultrapure water rinses. We removed exogenous carbonates with a 0.1 M acetic acid soak and several ultrapure water rinses. We then rinsed samples in methanol before desiccation and shipment to stable isotope analysis facilities.

Stable Isotope Facilities at Yale University and the University of Wyoming analyzed samples for $^{13}C/^{12}C$ measurements. At Yale, samples were analyzed on a Thermo MAT253 with KIEL IV carbonate device with an analytical precision of ±0.1‰ and long-term standard reproducibility of $\delta^{13}C$ = ±0.2‰. At Wyoming, samples were analyzed on a Thermo Gasbench coupled to a Thermo Delta Plus XL IRMS with a long-term standard reproducibility of $\delta^{13}C$ = ±0.3‰. We report $\delta^{13}C$ relative to Vienna Pee Dee Belemnite (VPDB) in standard per mill (‰) notation (Coplen 1994). Carbonate diagenesis is unlikely given the biogenic elemental concentration data from radiogenic isotope analysis from Uraca has not detected postdepositional contamination. Although Pestle and colleagues (2014) analyzed inter- and intralaboratory differences in $\delta^{13}C$ from bone carbonates, and our study is based on enamel carbonates, we nonetheless apply Pestle and colleagues' threshold of $\delta^{13}C_{carbonate}$ > 1.2‰ as the minimum meaningful difference (MMD) between samples required for discerning between actual dietary differences and mere inter- and intralaboratory error. Duplicate ($n = 14$) and triplicate ($n = 1$) samples analyzed as BSIRL process replicates yielded good analytical precision with standard deviations from 0.0–0.9‰ (mean sd = 0.1‰).

STATISTICAL ANALYSIS

We completed statistical tests without first averaging serially sampled $\delta^{13}C$ measurements, although we averaged replicates before compiling summary statistics or conducting statistical tests. For individuals with serial sections ($n = 72$), the early-life range = absolute value (maximum

$\delta^{13}C$ – minimum $\delta^{13}C$). Since $\delta^{13}C$ is nonnormally distributed (Shapiro-Wilk $W(286) = .796$, $p < .001$, $n = 287$), we used Mann-Whitney U to compare subgroup median ranks.

RESULTS

DIETARY DISTINCTION IN EARLY LIFE

At Uraca, distinctions can be detected in the early childhood diets of those whose remains were transformed into trophy heads when compared to those who were interred with their bodies intact. Trophy head enamel from all age phases shows a different median $\delta^{13}C$ compared to non-trophies (Mann-Whitney $U(286) = 2{,}294.5$, $z = -8.9$, $p < .001$; table 9.1). The difference between the two subgroups exceeds the 1.2‰ MMD attributable to inter- and intralaboratory error (Pestle, Crowley, and Weirauch 2014).

Higher median $\delta^{13}C$ for trophies persists from infancy through adolescence for tooth enamel formed during infancy and early childhood (IEC) (Mann-Whitney $U(105) = 280$, $z = -5.4$, $p < .001$; table 9.1, fig. 9.1*a*), middle childhood (MC) (Mann-Whitney U, $U(115) = 44.0$, $z = -5.0$, $p < .001$; table 9.1, fig. 9.1*b*), and adolescence/teen years (T) (Mann-Whitney U, $U(66) = 101.0$, $z = -5.1$, $p < .001$; table 9.1, fig. 9.1*c*). Differences between subgroups in each development phase are >1.2‰ MMD.

To examine relationships between childhood diet and adult violence, we focused subsequent analyses on adult males. Trophy head median $\delta^{13}C$ is greater (by >1.2‰ MMD) than non-trophy males (Mann-Whitney $U(222) = 1{,}748.5$, $z = -8.1$, $p < .001$; table 9.2).

Median trophy $\delta^{13}C$ is higher than non-trophy adult males for IEC (Mann-Whitney, $U(72) = 194.0$, $z = -4.6$, $p < .001$; fig. 9.2*a*), MC (Mann-Whitney $U(93) = 329.0$, $z = -4.6$, $p < .001$; fig. 9.2*b*), and T samples (Mann-Whitney $U(57) = 86.5$, $z = -4.8$, $p < .001$; fig. 9.2*c*) (>1.2‰ MMD).

DIETARY SIMILARITIES IN EARLY LIFE

We next compared childhood $\delta^{13}C_{enamel}$ among non-trophy males who had different adulthood experiences with violence (table 9.2). Median $\delta^{13}C$ of adults with and without injuries (table 9.2) (Mann-Whitney

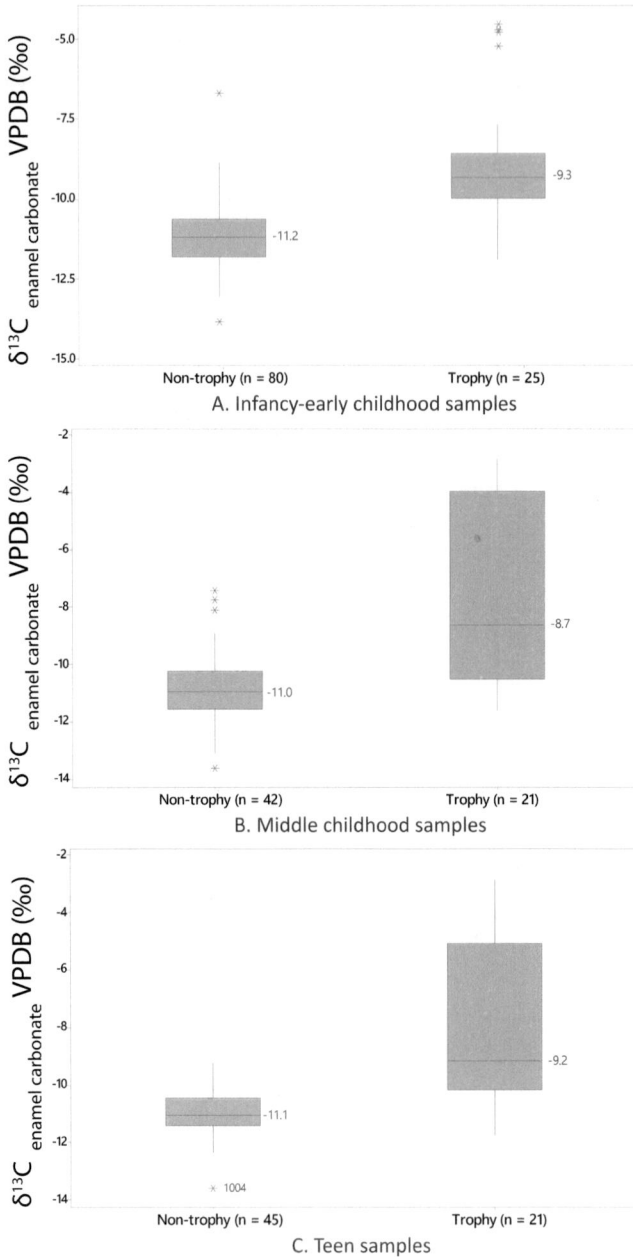

Figure 9.1 Boxplots of trophy versus non-trophy median $\delta^{13}C_{enamel}$ for tooth enamel development phases. *A*, infancy and early childhood. *B*, middle childhood. *C*, adolescence. Images by Beth K. Scaffidi.

Table 9.1 Summary statistics for $\delta^{13}C$ of trophies vs. non-trophies from Uraca

Subgroup	Number of samples	Mean $\delta^{13}C$ (VPDB‰)	Median $\delta^{13}C$ (VPDB‰)	sd $\delta^{13}C$	Minimum $\delta^{13}C$ (VPDB‰)	Maximum $\delta^{13}C$ (VPDB‰)
All trophies (n = 19)	72	–8.2	–9.2	2.7	–11.9	–2.8
All non-trophies (n = 60)	214	–11.0	–11.1	1.0	–13.8	–6.7

Table 9.2 Summary statistics for $\delta^{13}C$ (VPDB‰) from Uraca non-trophy male subgroups

Subgroup	Number of samples	Mean $\delta^{13}C$ (VPDB‰)	Median $\delta^{13}C$ (VPDB‰)	sd $\delta^{13}C$	Minimum $\delta^{13}C$ (VPDB‰)	Maximum $\delta^{13}C$ (VPDB‰)
All non-trophy adult males (n = 38)	150	–10.8	–11.0	0.9	–13.1	–6.7
Non-trophy adult males with cranial trauma (n = 29)	113	–10.8	–11.1	0.9	–12.2	–6.7
Non-trophy adult males without cranial trauma (n = 9)	37	–11.0	–11.0	1.1	–13.1	–7.8
Non-trophy adult males with perimortem trauma (n = 5)	26	–10.7	–10.6	0.9	–11.9	–9.0
Non-trophy adult males with antemortem cranial trauma (n = 24)	87	–10.8	–11.0	0.9	–12.2	–6.7

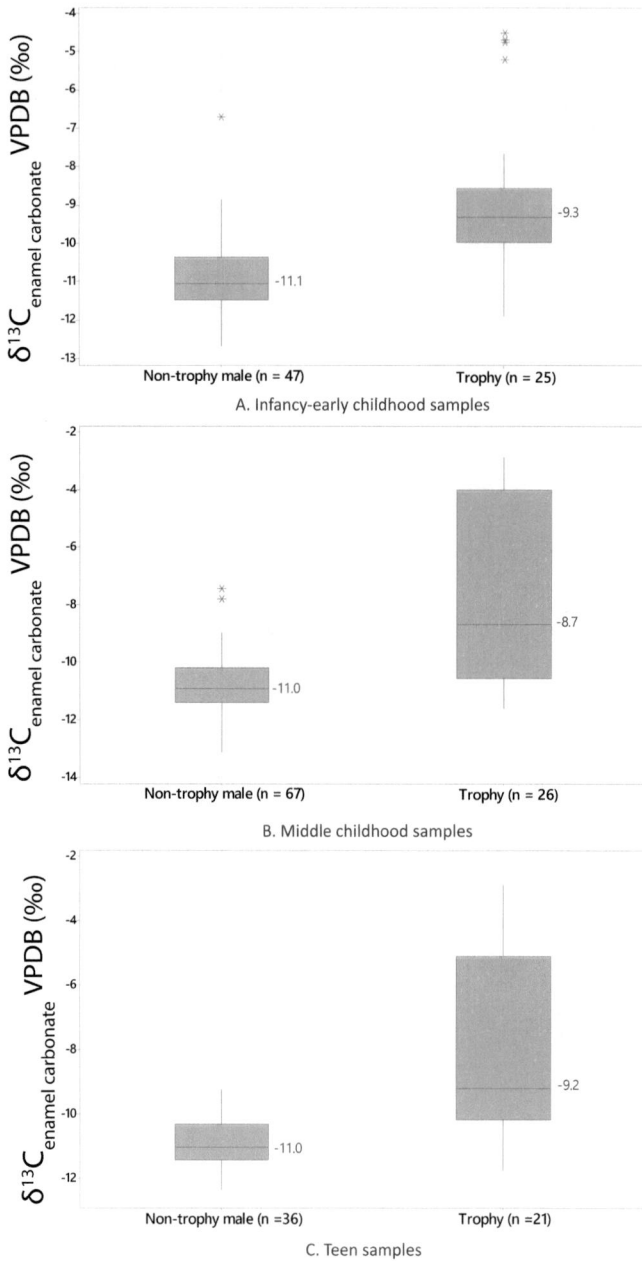

Figure 9.2 Boxplots of trophy versus non-trophy male median $\delta^{13}C_{enamel}$. *A*, infancy–early childhood. *B*, middle childhood. *C*, adolescence. Images by Beth K. Scaffidi.

$U(150) = 1,920.0, z = -.74 \ p = .460$; fig. 9.3*a*) and with lethal versus sublethal injuries were similar (Mann-Whitney $U(150) = 1,344.0, z = -1.3, p = .184$; fig. 9.3*b*).

DISCUSSION

MAIZE AS A MARKER OF DIFFERENCE

Relative to non-trophy males, females, and subadults, the trophy head victims consumed a greater relative proportion of C_4 foods from infancy throughout childhood and adolescence. This could reflect reliance on C_4-consuming proteins like seafood and maize-foddered camelids. None-theless, the paleobotanical evidence from Majes Valley sites and skeletal $\delta^{13}C$ data from the Majes Valley (Tung and Knudson 2018) suggest maize and maize chicha were the C_4 foods consumed.

The distinct childhood foodways of the trophy victims throughout early life suggests that the social differentiation leading to their violent deaths and decapitation began as children and followed them throughout their lives. Access to and consumption of special food and drink may have been required for the various preparations that combatants carried out before organized war or raiding, or during postcombat celebrations or mourning. While there are limited ethnographic accounts of raid-ing in the Andes, comparative data from lowland Amazonian groups show that participants in raids (primarily young and adult males) often consumed alcohol such as manioc beer and Ayahuasca-based *natéma* to prepare for battle or raids (see summaries in Redmond 1994). Similarly, feasting and drinking are essential to the violent, combat fiestas known as *tinkuy* (Chacon, Chacon, and Guandinango 2007; Abercrombie 1998; Topic and Topic 2009) still practiced in the Andes today. Participating in these violence-related rituals may have given trophy takers (and eventual trophy victims) repeated opportunities to consume large quantities of maize foods throughout their lifetimes.

MAIZE AND SHARED CHILDHOOD EXPERIENCES

Uraca non-trophy males had similar C_3/C_4 plant consumption as children whether they were killed as adults, survived cranial injuries, or avoided

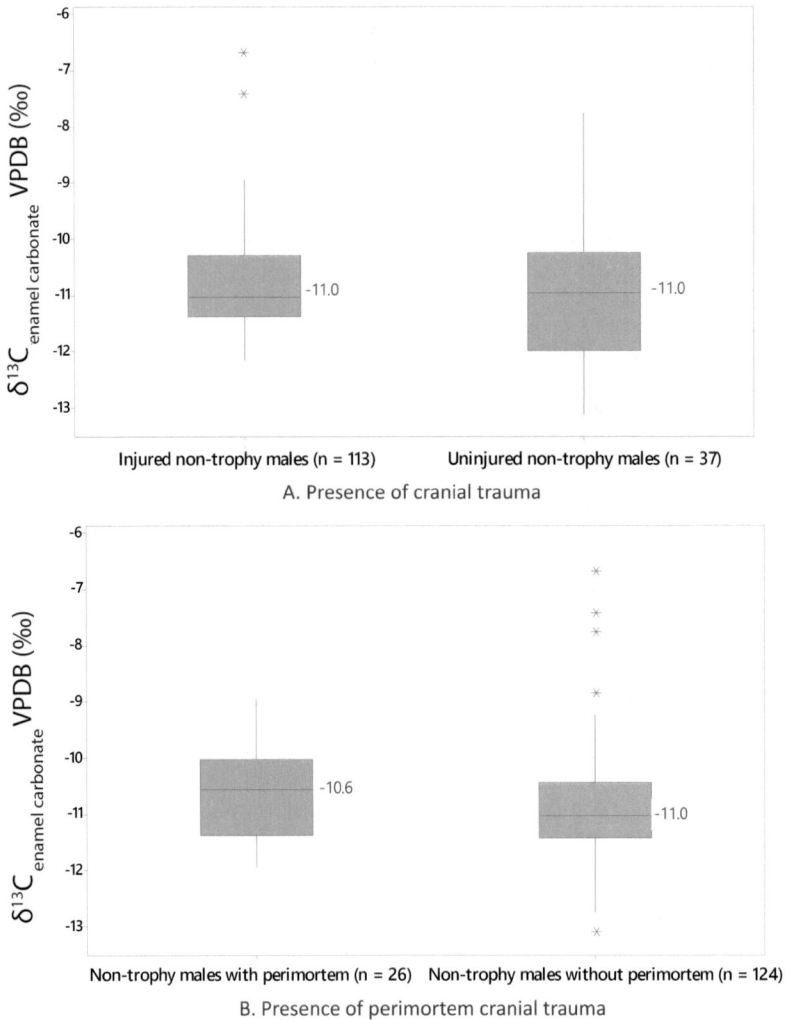

Figure 9.3 Boxplots of non-trophy male δ¹³C median and cranial injuries. *A*, injured versus uninjured. *B*, lethal versus sublethal injuries. Images by Beth K. Scaffidi.

injuries altogether. Uraca's infant boys (and for preweaning teeth, the women who nursed them) consumed similar plant foods throughout early life. This familiarity of shared foodways among boys and the nursing women at Uraca may have contributed to a sense of community belonging and shared identity in this village.

As Dietler and Hayden (2001) note, eating constitutes individual and communal senses of identity and how those identities are perceived by outsiders. Sharing foods—at home, in communal spaces, or sacred ritual places—can shape and cement identities as insiders or outsiders. Andean studies emphasize how commensal politics and feasting unify people, create community, mark difference, and enable the performance of distinctive identities within and between villages and/or cultural regions (Bray 2003a; Bray 2003b; Hastorf 2016; Swenson 2006; Sutherland et al. 2020). In the Andes, "you are what you eat" can be understood metaphorically as "you become what you eat." As Hastorf contends (2015, 244), "*how* one consumes is related to *who one is*, as one's identity is embedded within a tradition that is reinvented with every meal" (emphasis ours). Eating or being fed certain foods with certain groups of people and in distinct sociopolitical settings simultaneously reflects who someone is, who they aspire to be, and who they are being crafted into by communities, caregivers, and the transformative essences of the foods they consume. This way of "making and marking" identity and belonging through food also shows the powerful effects of social, political, and gender norms in structuring what people eat, denaturalizing notions about what is appropriate to eat and drink (Tung 2021).

CONCLUSIONS

The data presented here show there were key differences in early-childhood diets between Uraca trophies and non-trophies, which began at birth and persisted through adolescence. Consuming high-maize diets may have been one mechanism for enculturating social differences among the boys who were eventually killed and transformed into trophy heads. These boys may have been socially marked by consuming prestigious and powerful maize foods throughout their early lives. Of course, part of that becoming may have also been informed by preexisting ideas about their standing (and their families' standing) in their communities. If, for example, they were children of elite families with more consistent access to maize, then the consumption of that valued food source could have been used to mark that social difference while simultaneously making them into certain kinds of persons within the community. Examining dietary isobiographies through an Andean ontological perspective enables us to understand how dietary aspects of social identities changed throughout life and how food preparation, consumption, and abstention both literally and figuratively created different kinds of people and communities in the pre-Hispanic Andes.

ACKNOWLEDGMENTS

Excavation and laboratory analyses were supported by the Wenner-Gren Dissertation Fieldwork Fellowship (award 8680), permitted by the Peruvian Ministry of Culture (resoluciónes #082-2014, #067-2015-VMPCIC-MC, and #212-2018-VMPCIC-MC). Stable isotope analysis was supported by a Vanderbilt College of Arts and Science grant to Tung, the Nell I. Mondy Fellowship of the Graduate Women in Science to Scaffidi, and the National Science Foundation SBE Postdoctoral Fellowship to Scaffidi (award 1809470). Natasha Vang at the Vanderbilt University Bioarchaeology and Stable Isotope Research Lab (BSIRL) directed chemical preparation. We thank student lab workers at BSIRL for drilling teeth, Matt Biwer for macrobotanical identification, and colleagues in Arequipa for assisting with excavation and material management (Manuel Mamaní, Mirza del Castillo Salazar, Departments of Anthropology and History, and the Centro de Investigaciones Ciencias Sociales of the Universidad Nacional de San Agustín). Finally, we thank the editors and Susan deFrance for their feedback.

REFERENCES

Abercrombie, Thomas Alan. 1998. *Pathways of Memory and Power: Ethnography and History Among an Andean People.* Madison: University of Wisconsin Press.

Allen, Catherine J. 2002. *The Hold Life Has: Coca and Cultural Identity in an Andean Community.* 2nd ed. Washington, D.C.: Smithsonian Institution Press.

Bray, Tamara L. 2003a. *The Archaeology and Politics of Food and Feasting in Early States and Empires.* New York: Kluwer Academic; Plenum.

Bray, Tamara L. 2003b. "The Commensal Politics of Early States and Empires." In *The Archaeology and Politics of Food and Feasting in Early States and Empires,* edited by Tamara L. Bray, 1–13. Boston: Springer.

Cadwallader, Lauren, David G. Beresford-Jones, Oliver Q. Whaley, and Tamsin C. O'Connell. 2012. "The Signs of Maize? A Reconsideration of What $\delta^{13}C$ Values Say About Palaeodiet in the Andean Region." *Human Ecology* 40 (4): 487–509. https://doi.org/10.1007/s10745-012-9509-0.

Chacon, Richard J., Yamilette Chacon, and Angel Guandinango. 2007. "The Inti Raymi Festival Among the Cotacachi and Otavalo of Highland Ecuador: Blood for the Earth." In *Latin American Indigenous Warfare and Ritual Violence*, edited by Richard J. Chacon and Ruben G. Mendoza, 116–41. Tucson: University of Arizona Press.

Conklin, Beth A. 2001. *Consuming Grief: Compassionate Cannibalism in an Amazonian Society*. Austin: University of Texas Press.

Coplen, Tyler B. 1994. "Reporting of Stable Hydrogen, Carbon, and Oxygen Isotopic Abundances (Technical Report)." *Journal of Pure Applied Chemistry* 66 (2): 273–76. https://doi.org/10.1351/pac199466020273.

Dietler, Michael, and Brian Hayden. 2001. *Feasts: Archaeological and Ethnographic Perspectives on Food, Politics, and Power*. Washington, D.C.: Smithsonian Institution Press.

Eerkens, Jelmer W., Alex De Voogt, Tosha L. Dupras, Vincent Francigny, and Alexandra M. Greenwald. 2018. "Early Childhood Diets on the Nile: δ^{13}C and δ^{15}N in Serial Samples of Permanent First Molars in an Elite Meroitic Population from Sai Island, Sudan." *International Journal of Osteoarchaeology* 28:552–562. https://doi.org/10.1002/oa.2679.

Fausto, Carlos, Kaj Århem, Dimitri Karadimas, Eduardo Kohn, Els Lagrou, E. Jean Langdon, Morten Axel Pedersen, Laura Rival, Virginie Vaté, and Rane Willerslev. 2007. "Feasting on People: Eating Animals and Humans in Amazonia." *Current Anthropology* 48 (4): 497–530. https://www.journals.uchicago.edu/doi/10.1086/518298.

Giddens, Anthony. 1984. *The Constitution of Society*. Berkley: University of California Press.

Gumerman, George. 1997. "Food and Complex Societies." *Journal of Archaeological Method and Theory* 4 (2): 105–39. https://doi.org/10.1007/BF02428056.

Gumerman, George, S. Johannessen, and Christine A. Hastorf. 1994. "Corn for the Dead: The Significance of *Zea mays* in Moche Burial Offerings." In *Corn and Culture in the Prehistoric New World*, edited by Sissel Johannessen and Christine A. Hastorf, 399–410. Boulder, Colo.: Westview Press.

Hastorf, Christine A. 2003. "Andean Luxury Foods: Special Food for the Ancestors, Deities and the Élite." *Antiquity* 77 (297): 545–54. https://doi.org/10.1017/S0003598X00092607.

Hastorf, Christine A. 2015. "Steamed or Boiled: Identity and Value in Food Preparation." In *Between Feasts and Daily Meals*, edited by Susan Pollock, 243–76. Berlin: Berlin Studies of the Ancient World.

Hastorf, Christine A. 2016. *The Social Archaeology of Food: Thinking About Eating from Prehistory to the Present*. New York: Cambridge University Press.

Hastorf, Christine A., and Sissel Johannessen. 1993. "Pre-Hispanic Political Change and the Role of Maize in the Central Andes of Peru." *American Anthropologist* 95 (1): 115–38. https://doi.org/10.1525/aa.1993.95.1.02a00060.

Hillson, Simon. 1986. *Teeth*. Cambridge: Cambridge University Press.

Hillson, Simon. 1996. *Dental Anthropology*. Cambridge: Cambridge University Press.

Klarich, Elizabeth, ed. 2010. *Inside Ancient Kitchens: New Directions in the Study of Daily Meals and Feasts*. Boulder: University Press of Colorado.

Lévi-Strauss, Claude. 1963. *Totemism*. Boston: Beacon.

Miller, Melanie J., Yu Dong, Kate Pechenkina, Wenquan Fan, and Siân E. Halcrow. 2020. "Raising Girls and Boys in Early China: Stable Isotope Data Reveal Sex Differences in Weaning and Childhood Diets During the Eastern Zhou Era." *American Journal of Physical Anthropology* 172:567–585. https://doi .org/10.1002/ajpa.24033.

Pestle, William J., Brooke E. Crowley, and Matthew T. Weirauch. 2014. "Quantifying Inter-Laboratory Variability in Stable Isotope Analysis of Ancient Skeletal Remains." *PLoS One* 9 (7): e102844. https://doi.org/10.1371/journal .pone.0102844.

Redmond, Elsa M. 1994. *Tribal and Chiefly Warfare in South America*. Ann Arbor: University of Michigan Museum of Anthropology.

Scaffidi, Beth K. 2018. "Networks of Violence: Bioarchaeological and Spatial Perspectives on Structural and Physical Violence in the Pre- and Early-Wari Era in the Lower Majes Valley, Arequipa, Peru." PhD diss., Vanderbilt University.

Scaffidi, Beth K. 2020a. "Bioarchaeological Approaches to Understanding Conflict and Collaboration: The Circulation of Violence as a Heterarchical Structure." In *Cooperative Bodies: Bioarchaeologists Address Non-Ranked Societies*, edited by Sara Becker and Sara Juengst, 924–29. *American Anthropologist* 122 (4): 891–940.

Scaffidi, Beth K. 2020b. "Power, Mediation, and Transformation: Dismembered Heads from Uraca (Majes Valley, Peru) and the Andean Feline-Hunter Myth." In *The Poetics of Processing: Memory Formation, Cosmology and the Handling of the Dead*, edited by Anna Osterholtz, 15–40. Boulder: University Press of Colorado.

Scaffidi, Beth K., and Tiffiny A. Tung. 2020. "Endemic Violence in a Pre-Hispanic Andean Community: A Bioarchaeological Study of Cranial Trauma from the Majes Valley, Peru." *American Journal of Physical Anthropology* 172:246–69. https://doi.org/10.1002/ajpa.24005.

Sillar, Bill. 2009. "The Social Agency of Things? Animism and Materiality in the Andes." *Cambridge Archaeological Journal* 19 (3): 367–77. https://doi.org /10.1017/S0959774309000559.

Smith, Monica L. 2006. "The Archaeology of Food Preference." *American Anthropologist* 108 (3): 480–93.

Sutherland, Kenneth, David Chicoine, Matthew Helmer, and Hugo C. Ikehara. 2020. "Pots Speak Volumes: Commensal Politics and Kitchenwares in Early Horizon Nepeña, Peru." *Ñawpa Pacha* 40 (1): 101–17. https://doi.org/10.1080 /00776297.2020.1712022.

Swenson, Edward R. 2006. "Competitive Feasting, Religious Pluralism and De-centralized Power in the Late Moche Period." In *Andean Archaeology III*, edited by William H. Isbell and Helaine Silverman, 112–42. Boston: Springer.

Topic, Theresa, and John Topic. 2009. "Variation in the Practice of Prehispanic Warfare on the North Coast of Peru." In *Warfare in Cultural Context: Practice, Agency, and the Archaeology of Violence*, edited by Axel Nielsen and William Walker, 17–55. Tucson: University of Arizona Press.

Tung, Tiffiny A. 2007. "The Village of Beringa at the Periphery of the Wari Empire: A Site Overview and New Radiocarbon Dates." *Andean Past* 8:253–86. https://digitalcommons.library.umaine.edu/andean_past/vol8/iss1/18.

Tung, Tiffiny A. 2012. *Violence, Ritual, and the Wari Empire: A Social Bioarchaeology of Imperialism in the Ancient Andes*. Gainesville: University Press of Florida.

Tung, Tiffiny A. 2021. "Making and Marking Maleness and Valorizing Violence: A Bioarchaeological Analysis of Embodiment in the Andean Past." *Current Anthropology* 62 (S23): S125–S44. https://www.journals.uchicago.edu/doi/full/10.1086/712305.

Tung, Tiffiny A., and Kelly J. Knudson. 2018. "Stable Isotope Analysis of a Pre-Hispanic Andean Community: Reconstructing Pre-Wari and Wari Era Diets in the Hinterland of the Wari Empire, Peru." *American Journal of Physical Anthropology* 165 (1): 149–72. https://doi.org/10.1002/ajpa.23339.

Tykot, Robert H. 2006. "Isotope Analyses and the Histories of Maize." In *Histories of Maize: Multidisciplinary Approaches to the Prehistory, Linguistics, Biogeography, Domestication, and Evolution of Maize*, edited by John Staller, Robert Tykot, and Bruce Benz, 131–42. New York: Routledge.

Uzendoski, Michael A. 2004. "Manioc Beer and Meat: Value, Reproduction and Cosmic Substance Among the Napo Runa of the Ecuadorian Amazon." *Journal of the Royal Anthropological Institute* 10 (4): 883–902. https://doi.org/10.1111/j.1467-9655.2004.00216.x.

van der Merwe, Nikolaas J. 1982. "Carbon Isotopes, Photosynthesis, and Archaeology: Different Pathways of Photosynthesis Cause Characteristic Changes in Carbon Isotope Ratios That Make Possible the Study of Prehistoric Human Diets." *American Scientist* 70 (6): 596–606.

Weismantel, Mary. 1995. "Making Kin: Kinship Theory and Zumbagua Adoptions." *American Ethnologist* 22 (4): 685–704. https://doi.org/10.1525/ae.1995.22.4.02a00010.

10

Diasporic Foodways and the Transformation of Andean Agropastoralism in the Wake of Tiwanaku Collapse (11th–12th Century CE) at Los Batanes, Sama Valley

Sarah I. Baitzel, Maureen E. Folk, Lucia M. Diaz, Kurt M. Wilson, Arturo F. Rivera Infante, and BrieAnna S. Langlie

As communities develop alternative strategies to ensure resource availability and access, knowledge of distant resources, places, and people may incentivize migration. For migrants, food is not just about sustenance; it is also constitutive of social identity as cuisine, taste, and commensality maintain memories and a sense of belonging in the diaspora (Hastorf 2016). Modern diasporic foodways comprise the transformation of traditional cuisines into new constellations of familiar (yet distant) and exotic (yet nearby) ingredients (Tookes 2015). In the ancient Andes, diasporic foodways emerged in the context of increasing aridity and state collapse. In contrast to farmers for whom crises constrained food availability and access (Chiou, this volume), agropastoralists in the south-central Andes relied on expansive food environments that afforded food security and incorporated traditional and new ingredients in the wake of Tiwanaku state collapse. Our case study examines diasporic foodways of agropastoralists in the coastal desert of southern Peru during the eleventh and twelfth centuries CE. Paleoethnobotanical and zooarchaeological assemblages and stable isotopic analyses show how residents of the site of Los Batanes, a Tiwanaku-descendant Cabuza community located in a coastal-highland ecotone, exploited local and distant ecological niches. They maintained familiar foodways in the form of highland resources while their cuisine came to include lowland crops and marine resources. The juxtaposition of familiar and exotic resources characterizes the diasporic transformation of agropastoral foodways.

AGROPASTORALISM AND THE TIWANAKU STATE

Herders routinely pack up their worldly possessions and move to seasonal pastures. Andean pastoralism developed as a multiresource strategy to manage the risks associated with ecologically diverse but often marginal Andean highlands (Browman 1974). Transhumance provided access to different ecological niches that supported small-scale foraging, hunting, fishing, and horticulture or agriculture. Andean agropastoral settlements are commonly located between highland pastures and lower-elevation fields (Parsons, Hastings, and Matos Mendieta 1997). Vertical trans-humance also facilitated direct access and exchange of complementary resources with the coast: fiber, salt, and *charki* (dried llama meat) were traded for maize, chili peppers, and guano (Murra 1975). As a result, herders maintained extensive social networks with knowledge of and access to diverse food environments, an advantage for dealing with the challenges of migration and collapse.

Agropastoralism supported the emergence and expansion of the Tiwanaku state during the Middle Horizon between 400 and 1000 CE in the south-central Andean highlands (Browman 1984). Camelid populations provided food, fuel, and fiber for Tiwanaku's urban populations (Vallières 2016), and llama caravans mobilized regional exchange of key resources (Janusek 2008). Tuber and cereal cultivation—along with fishing, hunt-ing, and foraging—complemented pastoral foodways across the region (Miller et al., this volume). By the eighth century CE, maize imported from Tiwanaku's lowland colonies formed a cornerstone of the city's diet and ritual economy (Knudson et al. and Berryman and Blom, this volume; Wright, Hastorf, and Lennstrom 2003). Together, this indicates Tiwan-aku people maintained spatially extensive and economically diverse food networks characterized by a taste for highland and lowland resources.

Nonetheless, Tiwanaku's economic and political systems were not immune to the climatic and political changes of the eleventh century CE. Colder temperatures and prolonged drought led to a shift toward rain-fed terrace agriculture and mobile camelid pastoralism (Abbott et al. 1997; Langlie 2018). Across the region, warfare dominated life in the highlands (Arkush 2011). Trade networks broke down, and Altiplano populations relied solely on locally produced foodstuffs, including quinoa and potatoes. Maize imports ceased completely (Langlie 2020; Langlie and Arkush 2016). Tiwanaku-descendant communities in the western Andean valleys dispersed to smaller, more defensive settlements (Owen 2005). Ritual and material culture continuity characterizes Tiwanaku's diasporic communities. Colonial foodways supplemented highland crops (quinoa, potato, and oca) and camelids with lowland guinea pig, maize, beans, gourds, lucuma, and peanuts (deFrance 2016,127; Goldstein 2005). As trade networks and demand for maize declined, Tiwanaku-descendant communities in the lowlands relied more on locally available resources of grains other than maize, tubers, and legumes, and they consumed lesser quantities of animal meat (Quispe Vilcahuaman 2018).

Postcollapse resettlement near the coast reshaped diasporic foodways. Tiwanaku-descendant communities near the Pacific coast farmed the valley bottom for maize, beans, peanuts, and so forth; they kept small camelid herds, foraged *lomas*, or exploited marine and littoral resources depending on seasonal availability (Owen 2005). This diaspora, which extends from the far south coast of Peru to northern Chile, receives its name, Cabuza, from its distinctive Tiwanaku-derived material culture (Owen 2005, 72). In the Ilo and Azapa valleys where these post-Tiwanaku traditions were first identified, there is clear evidence for an earlier presence of Tiwanaku-affiliated settlers in the valley. In contrast, the Sama Valley, located between Ilo and Azapa, shows evidence of Cabuza settlement without prior Tiwanaku colonization.

THE ARCHAEOLOGY AND ENVIRONMENT OF LOS BATANES

The agropastoral Cabuza settlement of Los Batanes (500 masl) is located in the hyperarid lower Sama Valley. Architectural debris, subfloor storage, trash pits, and grinding stones that litter the surface attest to a multitude of economic activities. Residential compounds point to a year-round occupation, whereas open spaces may have accommodated seasonal encampments of herders. Clusters of burials found throughout Los Batanes substantiate the site's use as a permanent homestead. Terminal Middle Horizon–style material culture and ritual practices indicate affinity with or descent from Tiwanaku. Research on the origins of these Cabuza migrants is ongoing to determine whether members of this

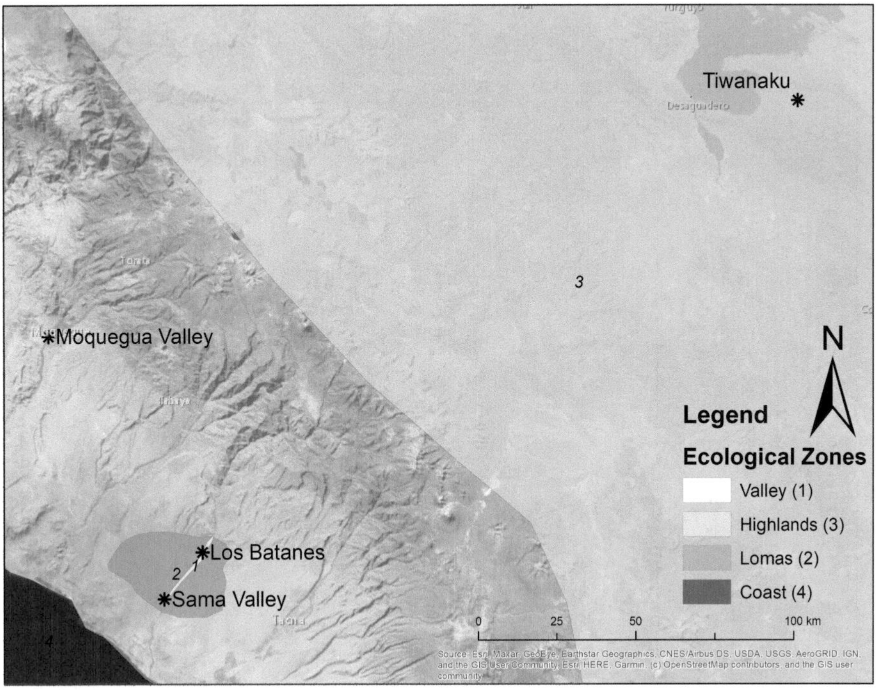

Map 10.1 Map of the South Central Andes with site locations and eco-zones. Image by S. Baitzel/Esri.

Cabuza community emigrated directly from the highlands or were part of Tiwanaku's lowland diaspora from regions like Moquegua. Certainly their settlement in this valley required knowledge of and adaptation to different landscapes and resources.

Los Batanes is located at an ecological nexus (map 10.1). The site overlooks the Sama Valley, a narrow stretch of arable land flanking the nonperennial Sama River. Temperate climate, soil salinity, and water alkalinity favor hardy crops such as maize, onions, and chili peppers. Desert plains surrounding the valley support seasonal *lomas* vegetation during the austral winter, when dense coastal fogs provide sparse precipitation. The herbaceous *lomas* attract and sustain rodents, foxes, and until recently camelids seeking pasture during the highland dry season (Masuda 1985). A day's walk west of Los Batanes, the Pacific littoral offers fish and marine mammals, shellfish, birds, and algae. Toward the east, the Sama Valley ascends into the highlands, where within a few days' walk one reaches the intermontane Tarata Valley, where tubers and maize grow, and beyond it lies the Altiplano, the natal habitat of wild and domesticated camelids.

To characterize the food environment of Los Batanes, we undertook macrobotanical, zooarchaeological, and human and camelid isotopic analyses of materials recovered from excavations in 2018 and 2019. Materials included in this analysis were collected from house floors, storage and trash pits, middens, patio surfaces, and burials. While the sample sizes are relatively small, materials preserve exceedingly well in the arid coastal desert, and the diversity of contexts sampled offer solid insights into food-related activities at Los Batanes.

CULTIVATING REGIONAL CONNECTIONS: RESULTS FROM PALEOETHNOBOTANICAL ANALYSIS

Macrobotanical analysis of desiccated and charred seeds elucidates evidence of food consumption, refuse, and natural intrusion from the local environment. Following standard paleoethnobotanical methods, 2-L samples were taken where possible (Lennstrom and Hastorf 1992), and all contents of vessels were collected (Pearsall 2015). Paleoethnobotanical samples from 21 contexts at Los Batanes were completely sorted. Based on gross morphology under lower-power binocular microscopy, a number of wild and domesticated food plants were identified (table 10.1). We employed various descriptive statistics to illustrate plant use at the site (Popper 1988). While the identified plants could have been locally grown, highland-adapted plants were found alongside typical lowland cultivars.

LOCAL CROPS AND WILD FOOD PLANTS

The most abundant food crop was maize (*Zea mays*). Fragments of cobs, cupules, and kernels indicate maize was processed, stored, and consumed on site. Maize could have been consumed as *chicha*, a sometimes-fermented beverage commonly drunk in the Andes. Or it could have been used in stews, as flour, or dried and stored. Chicha consumption was deeply embedded in Tiwanaku ceremonies to incorporate relationships of reciprocity (Janusek 2008). The ubiquity of maize at Los Batanes indicates that it was frequently consumed and played a role in burial rituals, as well. Chili

Table 10.1 Counts and ubiquity of plant taxa from Los Batanes ($n = 21$)

Taxon	Count	Ubiquity (%)
Cactaceae	101	47.6
Chenopod (Chenopodium quinoa)	131	71.4
Chili pepper fruit (*Capsicum baccatum*)	20	—
Chili pepper seed (*Capsicum baccatum*)	12	19
Maize cob (*Zea mays*)	962	—
Maize cupule (*Zea mays*)	134	61.9
Maize kernel (*Zea mays*)	38	61.9
Parenchyma	16	28.6
Portulaca	13	28.6
Solanaceae	38	52.4

peppers (*ají*) were also found in burials at Los Batanes. Ají consumption probably played a ritual role at Los Batanes based on its inclusion in burials. Chili peppers may have also been used as an anti-inflammatory (Zimmer et al. 2012). Today in the Sama Valley local varieties of ají are cultivated, including orange, red, and black.

Identified wild-plant remains could have entered the site through natural means, but they have documented human uses. Cactus seeds appear to come from the sweet fruits of the *Echinopsis* genus. Similarly, *Portulaca* sp. seeds point to the possible consumption of *Portulaca* (purslane) which can be eaten raw or cooked, or the seeds can be ground into flour (Irawan, Hariyadi, and Wijaya 2003). This plant may have grown in the nearby *lomas*.

HIGHLAND CROPS

The second most abundant food-plant remains found at Los Batanes were chenopod seeds, which are generally considered highland crops most likely domesticated in the Altiplano (Planella, López, and Bruno 2015). Two species of chenopods were domesticated for their culinary qualities in the highlands, quinoa (*Chenopodium quinoa*) and kañawa (*Chenopodium pallidicaule*), which are toasted, added to soups, ground into flour, or dried and stored. Based on gross morphology, the chenopod seeds recovered appear to be quinoa, which has been cultivated for more than 7000 years in the Andes and has long been appreciated for its high protein content and exceptional nutritional value (Bruno 2014). The authors observed that Sama farmers who are first- or second-generation immigrants from the Altiplano cultivate quinoa in the valley, where the plant usually does not exceed a height of about one meter, a notable size reduction compared to the highland variants grown today. Perhaps Los Batanes settlers brought quinoa with them from the highlands, or they locally cultivated the crop in their new homeland. Farmers have long been growing quinoa varieties on the coast of central and southern Chile (Bazile et al. 2015, 404). Ancient Sama residents could have also grown a coastal variety. Future paleoethnobotanical research may elucidate this issue.

Low numbers of Solanaceae seeds and parenchyma fragments were recovered. While countless Solanaceae species grew in the Andes, the identification of parenchyma that resembles tubers makes it plausible that Los Batanes residents consumed potatoes, one of the most abundant Solanaceae crops in the Andes. Tubers are boiled or mashed in preparation for consumption. The dense water content of tubers means that they also rarely carbonize wholly like grains (Pearsall 2015, 157). As such, archaeobotanists only expect to find small quantities of parenchyma. The quantities we found could reflect low importance in the diet or simply poor preservation. While they are primarily a highland crop, today, Sama farmers grow a variety of potatoes, proving they can be grown locally. Like quinoa, it is possible that Los Batanes settlers locally cultivated potatoes, or they procured them from the highlands.

Overall, the paleobotanical analysis reveals that residents of Los Batanes maintained familiar foodways through the consumption of highland resources while their diet also expanded to include more local crops (fig. 10.1). We see the maintenance of familiar foodways most strongly with the consumption of highland crops, quinoa, maize, and possibly potatoes along with the expansion of the diet in local cacti and chili peppers. Whether this Cabuza community descended from Altiplano populations or migrated from a lowland Tiwanaku colony, they brought with them highland agricultural goods and practices.

CAMELIDS AND MOLLUSKS: RESULTS FROM ZOOARCHAEOLOGICAL ANALYSIS

Zooarchaeological remains from six contexts were recovered using ¼ inch and 2 mm mesh screens. Because of the small size of this sample, these

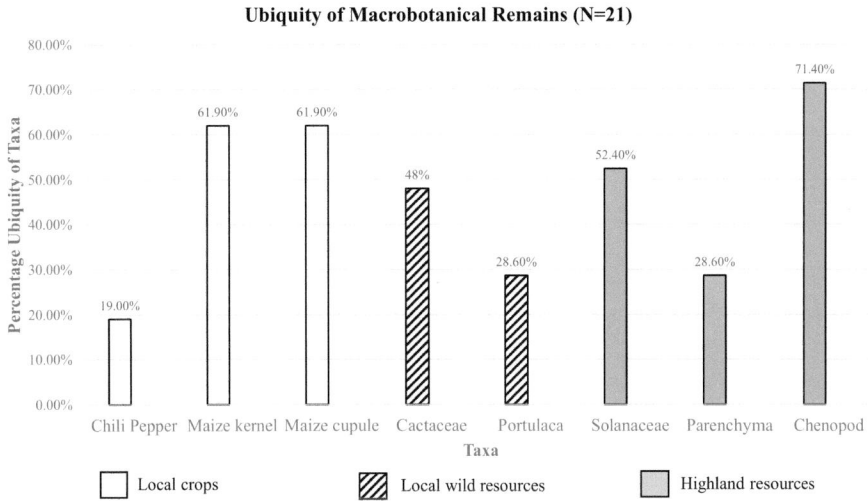

Figure 10.1 Ubiquity of macrobotanical remains from Los Batanes ($n = 21$). Image by S. Baitzel.

data prohibit a meaningful quantitative comparison. Nonetheless, the diversity of contexts sampled reveals the breadth of animal resources used by the site's residents as shaped by natural availability, anthropogenic access, and desirability. At the most basic interpretative level, the seven terrestrial faunal and nine marine taxa identified in the samples from Los Batanes (table 10.2) represent local faunal and coastal exploitation as well as highland-derived taxa.

ANIMALS CLOSE TO HOME

Four of the identified taxa (rodents, dogs, amphibians, and birds) occur naturally near Los Batanes. Dogs and guinea pigs probably co-resided with humans at the site as shown by guinea pig dung found in various contexts. Guinea pigs in the Andes are raised as domestic livestock for household consumption. Dogs are known hunting companions of Andean people and were rarely eaten. Food production, processing, and storage at the site would have attracted commensal rodents. The Sama River and its wetlands sustain seasonal crayfish populations, amphibians (frogs, lizards), and birds that the site's residents may have gathered.

Table 10.2 Fauna Number of Individual Specimens (NISP) and Minimum Number of Individuals (MNI), analyzed from selected contexts at Los Batanes ($n = 6$)

Taxon	NISP (n)	NISP (%)	MNI
Mammalia			
Camelidae	954	77.8	9
Canidae	17	1.4	4
Rodentia—*Cavia* sp.	126	10.3	12
Rodentia—other	18	1.5	3
Bird	3	0.2	1
Fish	9	0.7	3
Amphibian	100	8.1	5

COASTAL ANIMALS

The Pacific littoral and ocean, a day's walk from the site, offer diverse resources. The intertidal rocky coastline harbors a plethora of edible marine species, including bivalves (*Choromytilus* sp., *Perumytilus* sp.), sea snails (*Concholepas concholepa, Fissurella peruviana, Oliva* sp.), and sea urchins (*Echinoidea* sp.). Chitons (*Tonicia chilensis*) inhabit the coastal beaches. Deep ocean waters offer an abundance of fish species that can be extracted with net and line fishing.

The predominance of mussels, sea snails, and chitons in our sample points to the exploitation of the littoral rather than open waters. We recovered no fishing implements during excavations. The site's residents may have acquired coastal resources indirectly through exchange, but the focus on accessible shoreline resources supports direct procurement through shoreline gathering. Other resources that have historically attracted highland populations to the coast, such as guano and seaweed, have not been recovered at Los Batanes but may also have been desirable to agropastoralists.

HIGHLAND ANIMALS

Camelid (alpaca or llama) make up the largest portion of the zooarchaeological samples (table 10.2). They are highland species that forage on bunchgrasses but may have been raised locally on lomas or fallow fields (Santana-Sagredo et al., this volume). The ubiquity of camelid dung and

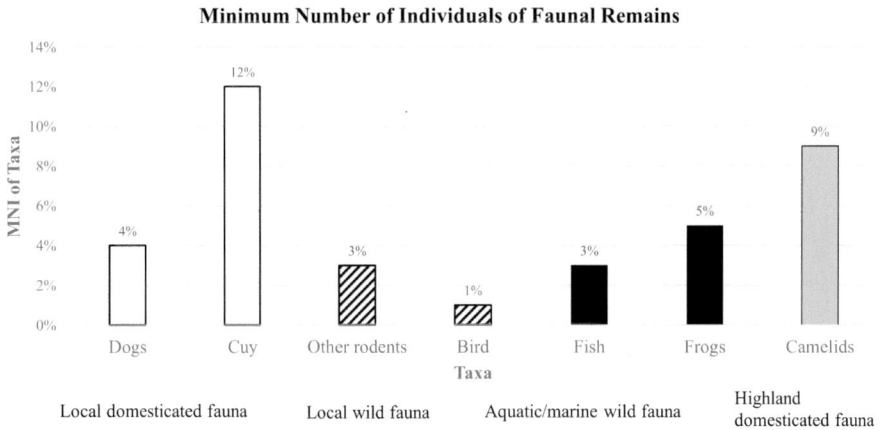

Figure 10.2 Taxonomic diversity of faunal remains at Los Batanes. Image by S. Baitzel.

fiber at Los Batanes indicates that animals were kept near or at the site to facilitate easy access to fuel and weaving materials. Less than 10% of the analyzed sample showed breaking or burning from human processing. Although limb bones account for two-thirds of the camelid assemblage, head and axial elements were also present. This supports the hypothesis that camelids were a local resource and processed in full at the site, rather than imported as fresh or freeze-dried meat.

Zooarchaeological remains from Los Batanes speak to exploitation of distinct ecotopes near the site (valley, lomas, coast) as well as at some distance (highlands) for food and nondietary purposes (fig. 10.2). Although we are unable at this point to establish the relative dietary contributions from each of these environments, taxonomic diversity of faunal evidence from the site suggests that its residents counteracted the constraints of their marginal surroundings by exploiting a range of locally available domesticated and wild edible fauna. Mobility played a key role in providing access to nonlocal resources from the highlands and coast.

INCORPORATING NEW ENVIRONMENTS: RESULTS FROM STABLE ISOTOPE ANALYSIS

Paleodietary reconstruction using stable isotopic analysis presents an additional dimension for studying foodways because it discriminates between availability and actual consumption of food resources. Human and animal paleodiet reconstructions at Los Batanes were derived from the stable carbon and nitrogen isotopic values from human (rib) and camelid (mandible) bone. Bone collagen samples were prepared following a modified method by Richards and Hedges (1999) at the Laboratory for the Analysis of Early Food-Webs at Washington University in St. Louis. Measurement uncertainty was monitored using in-house standards, and precision and accuracy were determined using standards by Szpak, Metcalfe, and Macdonald (2017).

Collagen was extracted by demineralizing ~500 mg of bone in 0.5 M HCL, which was then rinsed with deionized water. Samples were submerged in pH3 water, heated at 75°C, and then freeze-dried. Collagen samples were analyzed either in replicate or duplicate using a Flash2000 EA coupled to a Thermo Fisher Scientific Delta V Plus continuous-flow IRMS through a ConFlo IV interface (Bradley Lab, Washington University in St. Louis). Stable carbon and nitrogen isotope compositions were calibrated to VPDB and AIR with USGS 40 ($\delta^{13}C$ = −26.39‰, $\delta^{15}N$ = −4.52‰) and USGS 41 (glutamic acid, accepted $\delta^{13}C$ = +37.63‰, $\delta^{15}N$ = +47.57‰).

Measurement uncertainty was monitored using two in-house standards with well-characterized compositions: IRM-1 (IU acetanilide, $\delta^{13}C$ = −29.53‰ ± 0.16‰, $\delta^{15}N$ = 1.18‰ ± 0.07‰) and IRM-2 (protein, $\delta^{13}C$ = −26.98‰ ± 0.12‰, $\delta^{15}N$ = 5.94‰ ± 0.12‰). Precision (u(Rw)) was determined to be ±0.12‰ for $\delta^{13}C$ and ±0.29‰ for $\delta^{15}N$. Accuracy or systematic error (u(bias)) was determined to be ±0.24‰ for $\delta^{13}C$ and ±0.18‰ for $\delta^{15}N$, based on the difference between the observed and known δ values of the check standards and the long-term standard deviations of these check standards (Szpak, Metcalfe, and Macdonald 2017). Total analytical uncertainty was estimated to be ±0.26‰ for $\delta^{13}C$ and ±0.34‰ for $\delta^{15}N$ (Szpak, Metcalfe, and Macdonald 2017, app. F).

Results from five samples were deemed to be of good quality according to the following criteria: atomic C:N ratio of 2.9 to 3.6 (DeNiro 1985), collagen yield of >1% by mass, final carbon yields of >13%, and final nitrogen yields of >4.8% (Ambrose 1990). Although our sample is too small to be representative of human and animal populations from Los Batanes, the analysis to date complements other lines of evidence of Cabuza diet.

Isotopic compositions of bone collagen from two camelid specimens have similar mean $\delta^{15}N$ values but different $\delta^{13}C$ values, reflecting diverse grazing or feeding practices (table 10.3). The carbon isotopic values

Table 10.3 Stable carbon and nitrogen isotopic values from human and camelid specimens

Taxa	Specimen	Context	Age/sex	Lab ID	δ¹³C (‰ VPDB)	δ¹⁵N (‰ Air)	C:N	Mean C	Mean N
Human*	S45 = 601	U:4, ENT–9	17–19 y/M	V12	−13.8	17.3	3.4	−13.6	16.3
				V1a	−13.4	16	3.3		
				V1	−13.5	15.7	3.1		
	S45 = 588	U:6, ENT–8	25–35 y/F	V2a	−16.5	12.5	3.2	−16.5	12.2
				V2	−16.6	12.2	3.1		
				V3	−16.3	12	3.1		
	S45 = 403*	U:6, ENT–6	4–7 y/–	V13	−13.1	15.7	3.3	−13	15.3
				V13a	−13.1	15.6	3.3		
				V4	−12.9	14.6	3.1		
Camelid	S45 = 150_17	U:2, C:3	adult/–	V18	−18.6	8	3.3	−18.4	7.9
				V18a	−18.6	8	3.3		
				V8	−18.1	7.8	3.2		
	S45 = 150_18	U:2, C:3	juv/–	V16	−15.7	8	3.3	−15.7	7.9
				V16a	−15.7	7.9	3.3		

*Three samples were not included because of poor quality.

are congruent with high-altitude grazing (Santana-Sagredo et al., this volume; Thornton et al. 2011). The elevated $\delta^{13}C$ value in one camelid may indicate dietary contributions from C_4 plants such as maize either as fodder or pasture on harvested fields. Pasturing on wild lowland C_4 grasses or seasonal lomas may also raise $\delta^{13}C$ signatures.

All three human individuals (ENT–6, ENT–8, ENT–9) were buried with Cabuza-style vessels and textiles. To interpret their stable isotopic data, we refer to previously published paleodietary data from south-central Andean Altiplano agropastoralists, mid-valley Tiwanaku-affiliated maize agriculturalists, and coastal maize-farming and marine-fishing populations (fig. 10.3; see Knudson et al. and Berryman and Blom, this volume).

Mean $\delta^{13}C$ values are consistent with a mixed C_3/C_4 marine diet (Tieszen and Chapman 1992). Individual ENT–8 has carbon isotopic values similar to highland agropastoralists, whereas individuals ENT–6 and ENT–9 have enriched carbon isotopic values similar to mid-valley maize agriculturalists or coastal maize-farming and marine-fishing populations (fig. 10.3). Mean $\delta^{15}N$ values exceed the expected trophic-level offset of >4‰–8‰ between humans and camelids at Los Batanes (DeNiro and Epstein 1981). Instead, they signal consumption of marine resources or crops grown in arid environments (fig. 10.3). Together, stable carbon and nitrogen isotopic values of humans from Los Batanes are characteristic of terrestrial and marine fauna and C_3/C_4 plant consumption.

Paleodietary reconstruction confirms that the foods identified by paleoethnobotanical and zooarchaeological analyses variably contributed to a diet of highland grasses, tubers, and maize, with substantial contributions from highland and lowland-pastured camelids and some marine resources. Despite the small sample size, dietary heterogeneity of humans and animals requires further investigations of site-wide diet and mobility.

DISCUSSION

Intersecting archaeological methods in this study capture the variability in subsistence strategies that constituted the Cabuza food environment at Los Batanes. Despite small sample sizes and the nascent state of this research, we identified a diversity of wild and domesticated taxa of local

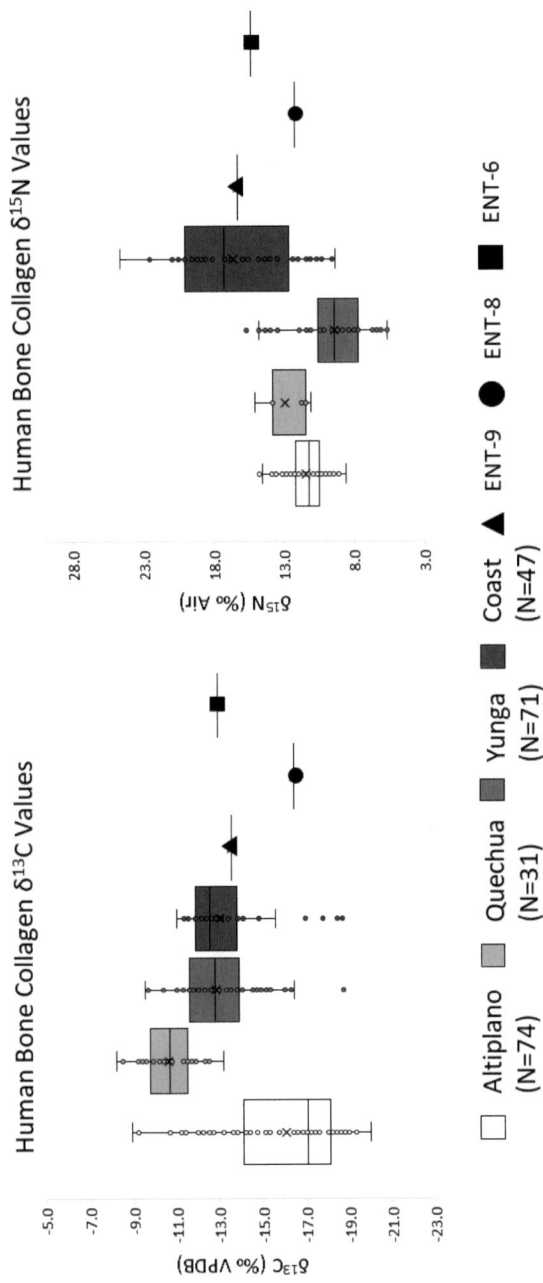

Figure 10.3 Stable carbon (*left*) and nitrogen (*right*) isotopic values from Los Batanes compared to data sets from different ecozones (Berryman and Blom, this volume; Finucane, Agurto, and Isbell 2006; Knudson, Aufderheide, and Buikstra 2007; Sandness 1992; Somerville et al. 2015). Image by Lucia Diaz.

and distant origins that reflects how this diasporic community forged its identity by integrating new ingredients into established foodways.

The site's proximity to multiple ecozones ensured year-round availability of resources that can be cultivated in the valley or foraged from nearby lomas or along the coast. The prevalence of maize throughout the site and the human (and possibly camelid) paleodiet highlight its continued desirability as a legacy of Tiwanaku. Whether the Cabuza community at Los Batanes hailed from the highlands or a lowland Tiwanaku colony, they brought with them the knowledge to produce the crop and a taste for maize-based foods and drinks that embodied relationships between the living and their ancestors. The Los Batanes community also seized the opportunity to cultivate chili peppers, a valued exotic foodstuff to highlanders. The social importance of chili peppers is emphasized in their use as burial offerings, likening it to maize as food for the dead.

Wild animal species reflect the customary agropastoral hunting and foraging of earlier times (Miller et al., this volume). The pasturing of camelids on seasonal lomas as indicated by stable isotopic data supports awareness of changing food environments. In fact, this short-lived but vibrant ecosystem offered sustenance to humans and animals en route to the Pacific coast, and it may have given the initial impetus to agropastoralists in search of a new home. The littoral is located far enough from the site to require some travel yet near enough to be reliable and sustainable. The emphasis on littoral species in the Los Batanes assemblage indicates a preference for accessible resources that did not require seafaring technologies, which were unlikely to be part of the agropastoral subsistence "package."

The ubiquity of highland resources at Los Batanes indicates a spatially extensive food environment. Although it is possible to grow and keep quinoa, tubers, and camelids at the site based on modern observations, the arid conditions of the lower Sama Valley are not ideal for these species and would have posed a challenge to their sustained use as reliable foodstuffs. The emergence of local variants of highland crops because of migration into the lowlands is a possibility that remains to be investigated. It is more probable that some highland resources were acquired directly or via exchange from the highlands with the help of camelid caravans, using familiar routes and social networks. Although Altiplano trade networks broke down during this time, coastal communities such as Los Batanes maintained trade and exchange with the highlands. We look forward to carrying out further analyses that may shed light on this matter, including radiogenic and stable isotopes on human and animal bones, morphological analysis of seeds, and possible ancient DNA analysis on flora and fauna samples.

Even though highland crops and animal resources were essential foodstuffs in the everyday meals of the Los Batanes community, they also subsisted on local foods, such as maize, shellfish, wild plants, and animals. The exclusive cultivation of maize and chili peppers at Los Batanes contrasts with the diversity of local plant cultivars found at Tiwanaku-descendant communities in Moquegua, where archaeologists also found chili peppers, squash, cotton, lucuma, beans, and other crops (Gaggio 2014). These findings point to different strategies being employed within the Tiwanaku diaspora. More specifically though, they suggests that Los Batanes agropastoralists did not invest in a broad agricultural subsistence base. Instead, the Sama Valley tells a unique story of migration, adaptation, and foodways different from that of diasporic Tiwanaku communities in other regions of the south-central Andes. Cabuza peoples in Sama seem to have maintained mobility networks that provided access to familiar highland foodstuffs. Maize, chili peppers, and shellfish in Los Batanes cooking pots and burials embody the transformation of highland agropastoral foodways into a diasporic cuisine. This incorporation of the local "exotic" into the familiar-but-hard-to-get may reflect both the desire for something new in the wake of Tiwanaku's collapse as well as the need to adapt subsistence strategies as regional drought conditions persisted.

CONCLUSION

The economic and dietary variety at Los Batanes as implied by the results of paleoethnobotanical, zooarchaeology, and stable isotopic analyses provides an exciting first step toward understanding agropastoralist agency through foods in the wake of sociopolitical collapse and climate change in the south-central Andes. The multimethodological approach used in this study will be essential to increasing the temporal resolution of different data sets and connecting them with regional dynamics of culture and climate change in the south-central Andes during the Late Intermediate Period. Many of the data sets on which we base our interpretations need to be expanded into more robust sample sizes to address questions of intrasite variability at Los Batanes.

The ecological niches exploited by the Cabuza formed a shifting mosaic of seasonally productive and complementary food sources. Evidence for farming, herding, hunting, and foraging at Los Batanes align with the diverse multiresource strategies of Andean highland agropastoralists. Counter to archaeological narratives of the early Late Intermediate as a period of hardship conditioned by increasing aridity, social conflict, and population dispersals, the case of Los Batanes exemplifies how mobile pastoralists are uniquely positioned to succeed as migrants. Our findings highlight the locally contingent and diverse economic strategies of the Tiwanaku diaspora. At Los Batanes, diasporic identities emerged through foodways that fused distant homelands and new homesteads.

REFERENCES

Abbott, Mark B., Michael W. Binford, Mark Brenner, and Kerry R. Kelts. 1997. "A 3500^{14}C yr High-Resolution Record of Water-Level Changes in Lake Titicaca, Bolivia/Peru." *Quaternary Research* 47 (1): 169–80. https://doi.org/10.1006/qres.1997.1881.

Ambrose, Stanley H. 1990. "Preparation and Characterization of Bone and Tooth Collagen for Isotopic Analysis." *Journal of Archaeological Science* 17:431–51. https://doi.org/10.1016/0305-4403(90)90007-R.

Arkush, Elizabeth N. 2011. *Hillforts of the Ancient Andes: Colla Warfare, Society, and Landscape.* Gainesville: University Press of Florida.

Bazile, Didier, Enrique A. Martínez, Francisco F. Fuentes, Eduardo Chia, Mina Namdar-Irani, Pablo Olguín, Constanza Saa, Max Thomet, and Alejandra B. Vidal. 2015. "Quinoa Crops in Andean Countries: Chile." In *State of the Art Report on Quinoa Around the World in 2013*, edited by Didier Bazile, Daniel Bertero, and Carlos Nieto, 401–21. Rome: Food and Agriculture Organization of the United Nations.

Browman, David L. 1974. "Pastoral Nomadism in the Andes." *Current Anthropology* 15 (2): 188–96. https://doi.org/10.1086/201455.

Browman, David L. 1984. "Tiwanaku: Development of Interzonal Trade and Economic Expansion in the Altiplano." In *Social and Economic Organization in the Prehispanic Andes*, edited by David L. Browman, Richard L. Burger, and Mario A. Rivera, 117–42. Oxford: BAR International.

Bruno, Maria C. 2014. "Beyond Raised Fields: Exploring Farming Practices and Processes of Agricultural Change in the Ancient Lake Titicaca Basin of the Andes." *American Anthropologist* 116 (1):130–45. https://doi.org/10.1111/aman.12066.

deFrance, Susan D. 2016. "Pastoralism Through Time in Southern Peru." In *The Archaeology of Andean Pastoralism*, edited by José M. Capriles and Nicholas Tripcevich, 119–38. Albuquerque: University of New Mexico Press.

DeNiro, Michael J. 1985. "Postmortem Preservation and Alteration of In Vivo Bone Collagen Isotope Ratios in Relation to Palaeodietary Reconstruction." *Nature* 317: 806–09. https://doi.org/10.1038/317806a0.

DeNiro, Michael J., and Samuel Epstein. 1981. "Influence of Diet on the Distribution of Nitrogen Isotopes in Animals." *Geochimica et Cosmochimica Acta* 45 (3):341–51. https://doi.org/10.1016/0016-7037(81)90244-1.

Finucane, Brian, Patricia Maita Agurto, and William H. Isbell. 2006. "Human and Animal Diet at Conchopata, Peru: Stable Isotope Evidence for Maize Agriculture and Animal Management Practices During the Middle Horizon." *Journal of Archaeological Science* 33 (12): 1766–76. https://doi.org/10.1016/j.jas.2006.03.012.

Gaggio, Giacomo. 2014. "Ceremonies and Activities in a Tiwanaku Temple: Results of a Paleoethnobotanical Analysis of the Site of Omo M10A, Moquegua, Peru." Master's thesis, University of California, San Diego.

Goldstein, Paul S. 2005. *Andean Diaspora: The Tiwanaku Colonies and the Origins of South American Empire*. Gainesville: University Press of Florida.

Hastorf, Christine A. 2016. *The Social Archaeology of Food: Thinking about Eating from Prehistory to the Present*. New York: Cambridge University Press.

Irawan, Daisy, Purwiyatno Hariyadi, and Hanny Wijaya. 2003. "The Potency of Krokot (*Portulaca oleracea*) as Functional Food Ingredients." *Indonesian Food and Nutrition Progress* 10 (1): 1–12. https://humaniora.journal.ugm.ac.id/ifnp/article/view/15198/0.

Janusek, John Wayne. 2008. *Ancient Tiwanaku*. New York: Cambridge University Press.

Knudson, Kelly J., Arthur E. Aufderheide, and Jane E. Buikstra. 2007. "Seasonality and Paleodiet in the Chiribaya Polity of Southern Peru." *Journal of Archaeological Science* 34 (3): 451–62. https://doi.org/10.1016/j.jas.2006.07.003.

Langlie, BrieAnna S. 2018. "Building Ecological Resistance: Late Intermediate Period Farming in the South-Central Highland Andes (A.D. 1100–1450)." *Journal of Anthropological Archaeology* 52:167–79. https://doi.org/10.1016/j.jaa.2018.06.005.

Langlie, BrieAnna S. 2020. "Late Intermediate Period Plant Use at a Colla Hillfort, Puno, Peru (AD 1300–1450)." *Latin American Antiquity* 31 (4): 702–19. https://doi.org/10.1017/laq.2020.28.

Langlie, BrieAnna S., and Elizabeth N. Arkush. 2016. "Managing Mayhem: Conflict, Environment, and Subsistence in the Andean Late Intermediate Period, Puno, Peru." In *The Archaeology of Food and Warfare*, edited by Amber M. VanDerwarker and Gregory D. Wilson, 259–89. New York: Springer.

Lennstrom, Heidi A., and Christine A. Hastorf. 1992. "Testing Old Wives' Tales in Palaeoethnobotany: A Comparison of Bulk and Scatter Sampling Schemes from Pancan, Peru." *Journal of Archaeological Science* 19 (2): 205–29. https://doi.org/10.1016/0305-4403(92)90050-D.

Masuda, Shozo. 1985. "Algae Collectors and Lomas." In *Andean Ecology and Civilization*, edited by Shozo Masuda, Izumi Shimada, and Craig Morris, 233–50. Tokyo: University of Tokyo Press.

Murra, John V. 1975. "El 'Control Vertical' de un Máximo de Pisos Ecológicos en la Economía de las Sociedades Andinas (1972)." In *Formaciones Económicas y Políticas del Mundo Andino*, edited by John V. Murra, 59–115. Lima: Instituto de Estudios Peruanos.

Owen, Bruce D. 2005. "Distant Colonies and Explosive Collapse: The Two Stages of the Tiwanaku Diaspora in the Osmore Drainage." *Latin American Antiquity* 16 (1): 45–80. https://doi.org/10.2307/30042486.

Parsons, Jeffrey R., Charles M. Hastings, and Ramiro Matos Mendieta. 1997. "Rebuilding the State in Highland Peru: Herder-Cultivator Interaction During the Late Intermediate Period in the Tarama-Chinchaycocha Region." *Latin American Antiquity* 8 (4): 317–41. https://doi.org/10.2307/972106.

Pearsall, Deborah M. 2015. *Paleoethnobotany: A Handbook of Procedures*. San Diego, Calif.: Academic Press.

Planella, María Teresa, María Laura López, and María C. Bruno. 2015. "Domestication and Prehistoric Distribution." In *State of the Art Report on Quinoa Around the World in 2013*, edited by Didier Bazile, Daniel Bertero, and Carlos Nieto, 29–41. Rome: Food and Agriculture Organization of the United Nations.

Popper, Virginia S. 1988. "Selecting Quantitative Measurements in Paleoethnobotany." In *Current Paleoethnobotany: Analytical Methods and Cultural Interpretations of Archaeological Plant Remains*, edited by Virginia S. Popper. and Christine A. Hastorf, 53–71. Chicago: University of Chicago Press.

Quispe Vilcahuaman, Bredy. 2018. "Investigating Paleodiet and Mobility Through Stable Isotope Analysis at the Site of Tumilaca la Chimba, Moquegua, Peru." Senior honors thesis, Georgia State University.

Richards, Michael P., and Robert E. M. Hedges. 1999. "Stable Isotope Evidence for Similarities in the Types of Marine Foods Used by Late Mesolithic Humans at Sites Along the Atlantic Coast of Europe." *Journal of Archaeological Science* 26 (6): 717–22. https://doi.org/10.1006/jasc.1998.0387.

Sandness, Karen. 1992. "Temporal and Spatial Dietary Variability in the Prehistoric Lower and Middle Osmore Drainage: The Carbon and Nitrogen Isotope Evidence." Master's thesis, University of Nebraska, Lincoln.

Somerville, Andrew D., Paul S. Goldstein, Sarah I. Baitzel, Karin L. Bruwelheide, Allisen C. Dahlstedt, Linda Yzurdiaga, Sarah Raubenheimer, Kelly J. Knudson, and Margaret J. Schoeninger. 2015. "Diet and Gender in the Tiwanaku Colonies: Stable Isotope Analysis of Human Bone Collagen and Apatite from Moquegua, Peru." *American Journal of Physical Anthropology* 158 (3): 408–22. https://doi.org/10.1002/ajpa.22795.

Szpak, Paul, Jessica Z. Metcalfe, and Rebecca A. Macdonald. 2017. "Best Practices for Calibrating and Reporting Stable Isotope Measurements in Archaeology." *Journal of Archaeological Science: Reports* 13:609–16. https://doi.org/10.1016/j.jasrep.2017.05.007.

Thornton, Erin K., Susan D. deFrance, John Krigbaum, and Patrick R. Williams. 2011. "Isotopic Evidence for Middle Horizon to 16th Century Camelid Herding in the Osmore Valley, Peru." *International Journal of Osteoarchaeology* 21 (5): 544–67. https://doi.org/10.1002/oa.1157.

Tieszen, Larry L., and Michael Chapman. 1992. "Carbon and Nitrogen Isotopic Status of the Major Marine and Terrestrial Resources in the Atacama Desert of Northern Chile." In *Actas del I Congreso Internacional de Estudios Sobre Momias/Proceedings of the I World Congress on Mummy Studies*, edited by World Congress on Mummy Studies, 409–41. Santa Cruz de Tenerife, Canary Islands: Museo Arqueológico y Etnográfico de Tenerife, Organismo Autónomo de Museos y Centros.

Tookes, Jennifer Sweeney. 2015. "'The Food Represents': Barbadian Foodways in the Diaspora." *Appetite* 90:65–73. https://doi.org/10.1016/j.appet.2015.02.011.

Vallières, Claudine. 2016. "Camelid Pastoralism at Ancient Tiwanaku: Urban Provisioning in the Highlands of Bolivia." In *The Archaeology of Andean Pastoralism*, edited by Nico Tripcevich and Jose M. Capriles Flores, 67–85. Albuquerque: University of New Mexico.

Wright, Melanie F., Christine A. Hastorf, and Heidi A. Lennstrom. 2003. "Pre-Hispanic Agriculture and Plant Use at Tiwanaku: Social and Political Implications." In *Tiwanaku and Its Hinterland: Archaeology and Paleoecology of an Andean Civilization*. Vol. 2, *Urban and Rural Archaeology*, edited by Alan L. Kolata, 384–403. Washington, D.C.: Smithsonian Institution Press.

Zimmer, Aline Rigon, Bianca Leonardi, Diogo Miron, Elfrides Schapoval, Jarbas Rodrigues de Oliveira, and Grace Gosmann. 2012. "Antioxidant and Anti-inflammatory Properties of *Capsicum baccatum*: From Traditional Use to Scientific Approach." *Journal of Ethnopharmacology* 139 (1): 228–33. https://doi.org/10.1016/j.jep.2011.11.005.

11

Inside the Moche House

Uncovering Peasant Foodways in the Andean Past

Katherine L. Chiou

In the past, at home by the hearth, meals were prepared and shared, sustaining people through both good times and turbulent times. Through memory, continuity, and tradition, knowledge about foods was passed down from generation to generation, situating individuals in the world through a sense of place (terroir) and self. Foodways that are marginal, rural, daily, and/or common are often intimately connected to feelings of nostalgia and comfort in the collective consciousness. Today, these "low" foods are commonly used as a source of inspiration for—and as a contrast to—the crafting of meaning in haute, or high, cuisine. Memories tied to sustenance and hardship can be particularly poignant, quietly shaping and modifying the food-related practices of cultures over the *longue durée* (Anderson 2017; Holtzman 2006; Mannur 2007). The low foods and dishes associated with peasant cookery are the products of generations of creativity and resourcefulness in the face of—at times—grim realities. The banality of the day-to-day culinary routine is thus a worthy topic of archaeological inquiry with the potential to unveil subtle details about past social relations and lived experiences (Atalay and Hastorf 2006).

Food memories linked to times of scarcity are often particularly emotive. When catastrophe strikes—whether the culprit is disease, climate changes, or war—production and supply chains are commonly disrupted (Koren and Bagozzi 2016). Many are left vulnerable as the impacts of food shortages reverberate throughout society. Although those with less material wealth and social, economic, and political capital have always coped with insecurity and uncertainty on multiple fronts, in moments of crisis, stress is intensified. Meanwhile, the underlying social tensions stemming from inequality are suddenly exposed and magnified, threatening the stability of the existing order.

In this chapter I approach the theme of low cuisine from an Andean perspective by visiting an archaeological case study involving the Moche people of the desert north coast of Peru. The Moche, a highly complex and stratified political group, experienced societal decline and unrest in the Late Moche Period (AD 600–800), a time that was punctuated by repeated episodes of severe drought that probably affected local food-ways. During these tense times, fortified hillside and hilltop settlements with an emphasis on security, such as the site of Cerro Chepén in the Jequetepeque Valley, were hastily constructed near prime agricultural land. Given the evidence for social stress, Cerro Chepén provides an opportunity to probe the impact of social, environmental, and political upheaval on daily life. By analyzing the spatial distribution of food re-mains within commoner living spaces, I highlight the humble ingredients that Moche commoners ate and the practices they adopted to put food on the table in lean times.

THE MOCHE OF THE NORTH COAST OF PERU

The Moche flourished from roughly AD 100 to AD 850. Organized as a series of valley-based polities, the Moche were supported by the organization of labor and the expansion of large networks of irrigation canals that converted swaths of desert into arable land. The data in this paper comes from the Late Moche Period, a time of increasing political fragmentation, social upheaval, internecine warfare, and possible foreign incursions that led to the end of the Moche as a political entity (Castillo 2001; La Lone 2000; Rosas Rintel 2010; Sutter and Castillo 2015).

The Moche resided in the northern region of the desertic coast of modern-day Peru, an area that features a tropical-dry climate. The region only receives, on average, 75 mm of rainfall each year. These conditions create an inhospitable environment that is highly dependent on the avail-ability of water; as such, environmental fluctuations affecting rainfall in the Andes have pronounced effects on the coast. Because of the con-struction of expansive irrigation networks, the north coast landscape is defined by barren pampas transversed by green, fertile valleys—it is in these locales that the Moche exercised their sovereignty (Bawden 1996; Benson 1972; Billman 2002; Stanish 2001).

Between the fifth and seventh centuries AD, the Moche embarked on a period of decline (Bourget 2006). Between AD 570 and AD 620, an extended period of drought was punctuated with mega–El Niño storms that brought massive floods. These floods were followed by a La Niña period that devastated the Moche and prompted a major restructuring of north coast societies (e.g., see Bawden 1996; Shimada 1994; Shimada et al. 1991). Nevertheless, despite continued attempts to recuperate, the Moche polity itself did not survive beyond the eighth century AD.

INSECURITY IN THE BUILT ENVIRONMENT: LATE MOCHE PERIOD FORTIFICATIONS IN THE JEQUETEPEQUE VALLEY

During the Late Moche Period (~AD 600), the Jequetepeque Valley experienced significant social and political transformations (map 11.1*A*). At the ritual center of San José de Moro, the disparity between socio-economic strata in Moche society grew (Chiou 2017; Johnson and Zori 2011). Furthermore, an increased focus on marine themes in iconographic representations likely reflects concerns related to the El Niño events (McClelland 1990; McClelland, McClelland, and Donnan 2007; Shimada et al. 1991).

In the Jequetepeque Valley, large shifts in settlement patterns suggest the Late Moche Period was a time of political decentralization (Swenson 2006). Autonomous, fortified communities built along hillsides and hilltops indicate the primacy of safety and security and the rising level of factionalization and social stress (Castillo 2010; Dillehay 2001; Johnson 2008; Swenson 2006). Regional ideological innovations that promoted resistance to dominant, elite ideologies also arose (Swenson 2007). The greater presence of foreign goods from highland groups such as the Wari and Cajamarca suggest that invasions from exogenous groups precipitated the Moche collapse, although the evidence for this interpretation is weak (see Rosas Rintel 2010, 209–218). Nevertheless, occasional conflicts or skirmishes may have taken place between highland and coastal groups, particularly during a time when resources were scarcer. All of these sources of social, political, and economic strife would potentially have been present in the lives of the Cerro Chepén individuals that are the focus of this study (map 11.1*B*).

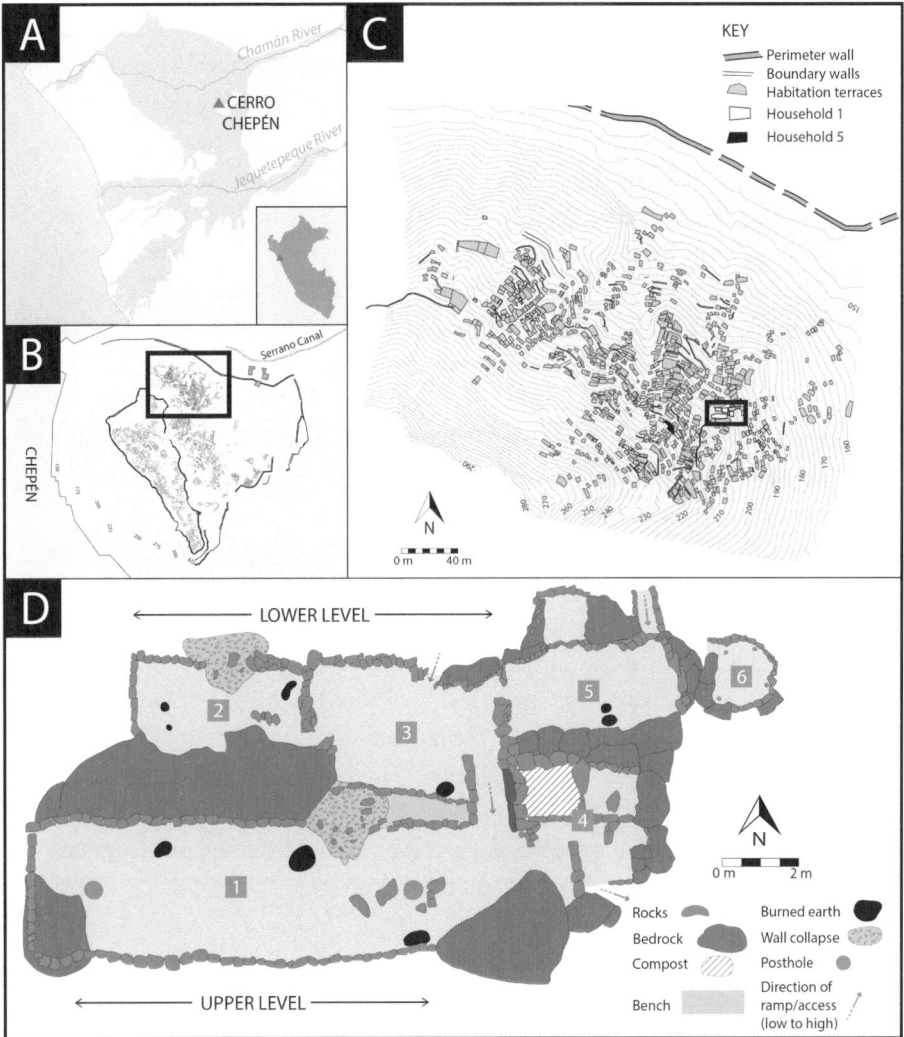

Map 11.1 *A*, Jequetepeque Valley, showing the location of Cerro Chepén. *B*, settlement of Cerro Chepén with a box surrounding the Hillside Community. *C*, Hillside Community with the location of households mentioned in this chapter and a box surrounding Household 1. *D*, Household 1, with room number designations. Image courtesy of Katherine L. Chiou.

Cerro Chepén, the second-largest Late Moche site in the Jequetepeque Valley (40 ha), is located on the northern projection of the Cerros
de Chepén hill chain. Surrounded by vast expanses of fertile, agricultural
land, Cerro Chepén boasts the most elaborate defensive works in the entire region and holds a privileged central position in the northern branch
of the lower valley (Rosas Rintel 2010, 331). Cerro Chepén is split into
two primary occupational sectors delineated by peripheral walls that in
this chapter are referred to as Hilltop Community and Hillside Community. Those of high status seem to have lived in the Hilltop Community,
which is comprised primarily of monumental buildings and residences of
the elite. This sector is protected by a massive, continuous stone wall that
features towers, platforms, and large piles of slingshot stones. The Hilltop
Community is only accessible through three formal entrances (Rosas
Rintel 2010, 4). The location of the Hilltop Community (~400 masl)
afforded its residents an excellent view of the surrounding area, aiding in
the early detection of unwanted local or foreign intrusions.

The Hillside Community, located on the northeastern slopes of Chepén
hill, has over 700 constructed terraces and platforms that provided leveled surfaces for habitation (Cusicanqui Marsano 2010). These terraces
are smaller than those in the Hilltop Community and are surrounded
by a defensive wall that starts just south of the Hilltop Community
(map 11.1*C*). Compared to the formal and well-planned architecture at
the Hilltop Community, the Hillside Community construction is more
irregular and haphazard. Nevertheless, living in the Hillside Community
would have afforded residents easy access to water from the nearby canals
as well as the surrounding agricultural fields where many of the residents
probably worked.

The data discussed in this chapter comes primarily from 2011 excavations conducted in Household 1 in the Hillside Community (map 11.1*D*;
Chiou 2017). The complete (100%) excavation of Household 1 is one of
a small handful of archaeological research projects in the hillside sector
(see also Cusicanqui Marsano 2010 and Rosas Rintel 2010). This project
employed a single-context excavation strategy and blanket sampling that
involved the collection of 10-L samples from each defined locus. Dirt
that was not collected in sediment samples was screened through ¼ in
mesh (6.35 mm) for the systematic recovery of small objects and ecofacts.
Samples were evenly divided with the use of a riffle-type sample splitter,

and each subsample was processed through either machine-assisted water flotation or dry-sieving in a methodological test designed to assess recovery rates of archaeobotanical material (Chiou 2013, 2017). The samples were exported to the McCown Archaeobotany Laboratory at the University of California, Berkeley, where they were sorted for plant and animal remains with the use of a low-powered stereo microscope.

At Cerro Chepén, maize (*Zea mays* L.) and *algarrobo* (*Prosopis pallida* L.) were the most abundant cultivated plants. Camelid and guinea pig bones dominate the faunal assemblages and appeared to have been boiled, a cooking method that is commonly associated with Andean daily meals; roasting, on the other hand, appears to be associated with feasting events in the Andes (see Bélisle, Alaica, and Brown, this volume; Chiou 2017; Hastorf 2012). Unlike Late Moche elite contexts (e.g., San José de Moro and the Hilltop Community), the ingredients consumed by Household 1 residents were very limited in terms of the number of taxa present and the density of remains recovered (Chiou 2017; Rosas Rintel 2010), and the ubiquity of cultivated plants as a whole is comparatively low (i.e., 28% in Household 1 vs. 100% in a feast preparation area at San José de Moro).

The food remains in Household 1 are heavily concentrated in two locations, only one of which is a primary deposit. In one of the hearths, carbonized maize kernels and *algarrobo* seeds—two staple foods—were found in large quantities. These maize kernels did not exhibit evidence of germination, indicating that they probably weren't used for *chicha* brewing (Chiou 2017). The other context is a compost bin—a secondary deposit—located on the eastern side of the structure that was completely filled with camelid and guinea pig dung mixed with desiccated food refuse.

When viewed three-dimensionally in a kernel density map, the discrete distribution of food-plant remains is even starker (fig. 11.1*A*). A limited, almost negligible amount of food-plant material was recovered throughout the house, although the major peaks concentrate in the compost pit and Room 1 on the upper level. The lack of extensive plant patterning, however, may also relate to notions of cleanliness. The compost bin contained, unsurprisingly, the highest density of food-related refuse and camelid dung (fig. 11.1*B*). In this unique context, the food plants, as green waste, were in the process of becoming plant food, decomposing over the course of weeks or months into a usable, nutrient-rich humus.

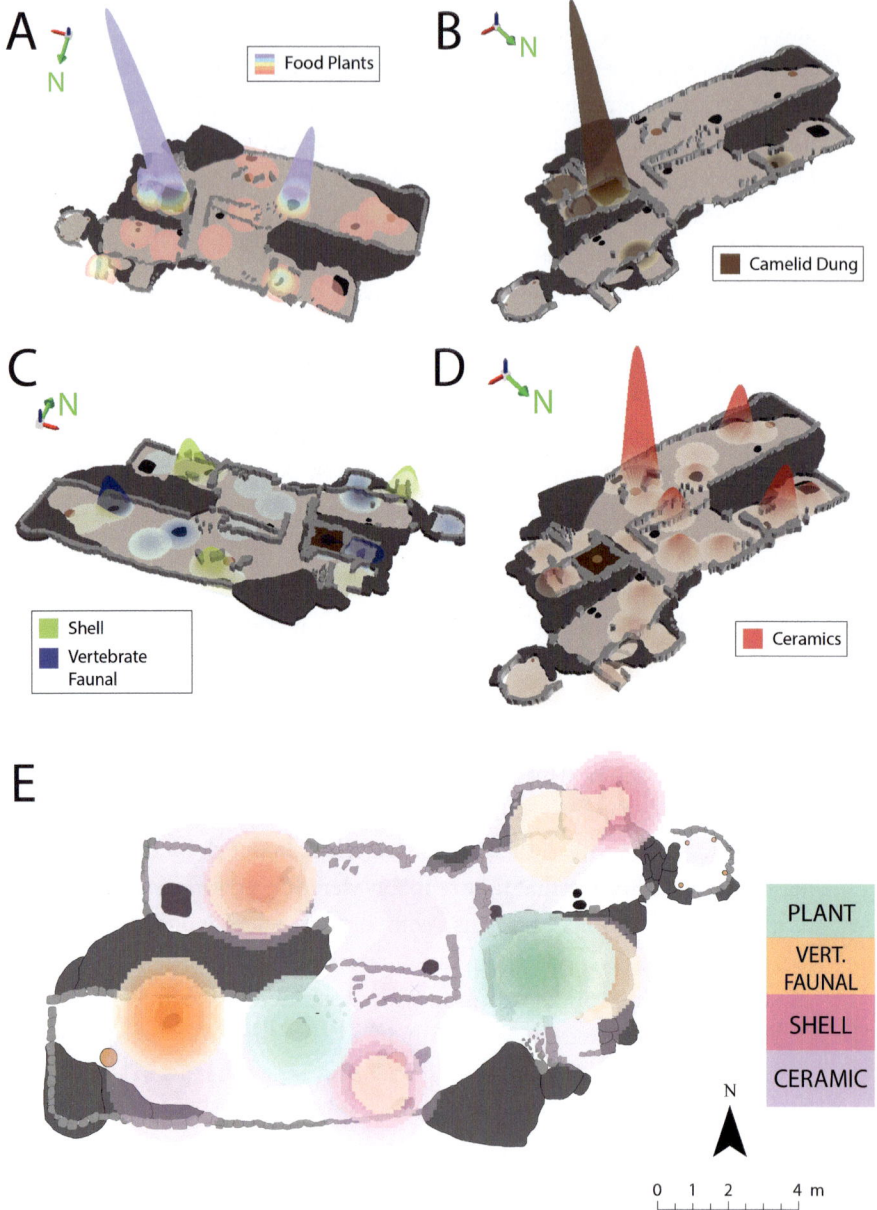

Figure 11.1 Kernel densities of various assemblages in Household 1 including food-plant remains (*A*), camelid dung (*B*), shell and vertebrate faunal remains (*C*), ceramics (*D*), and food-related assemblages layered on top of one another in Household 1 (*E*). Image courtesy of Katherine L. Chiou.

The vertebrate faunal and shell data, however, do not follow the spatial patterning of the food plants (fig. 11.1C). The highest density of vertebrate remains was recovered in a hearth located on the western side of Room 1 followed by the space located to the east of the compost bin in Room 4. In contrast, shell remains were recovered from contexts adjacent to areas with concentrations of vertebrate remains. These data suggest that activities related to the processing, cooking, and consumption of shell and vertebrate protein did not take place in the same location, although they were spatially related. In contrast to the plant data, the faunal data indicate that, at least in terms of food, activities took place throughout the household. Similarly, ceramic sherds (from cooking pots, jars, bottles, and bowls), although found throughout Household 1, show greatest densities in Rooms 1 and 2 (fig. 11.1D), spaces that were closely tied with cooking activities, consumption, and discard.

When viewed together in two dimensions (fig. 11.1E), it appears that a range of food activities was taking place in different areas of the household. The large room on the upper level of the house seems to be a particularly busy area where food tasks were being completed. In fact, the compost bin in Room 4 is especially dense in plant and vertebrate faunal remains but not shell. The lower level of the house was also an area where food was prepared or eaten, albeit primarily dishes involving animal protein. Shells were dense around one of the ramp entrances located on the northern end of the house, although whether this represents food debitage or a natural death assemblage of land snails that lived on the hill remains unclear.

Taken together, the botanical, faunal, and ceramic data impart a view of *taskscapes*; the socially constructed and spatially bound spaces of human activity (Ingold 1993). As anticipated, the largest room is particularly well used. Moving from west to east, the room begins with some evidence for cooking and/or processing of meat; toward the center of the room, a dish involving maize and *algarrobo* was being prepared. To the southeast of this context, a discrete area outlined with rocks surrounding another hearth contains evidence of a dish involving meat and land snails. In between these two loci, a grinding stone (*chungo*) suggests this room served the main processing and cooking functions in the structure. Because of its small size, the occupants of Household 1 also may have shared meals there or engaged in other activities related to household production.

The northwestern room with a hearth located on the lower level was associated with the meat and shellfish cooking and maize processing (because maize cupules outnumber maize kernels; see Scarry and Steponaitis 1997; VanDerwarker 2005). The square room on the second level was primarily used for composting, although attempts to compartmentalize the space suggest that it was meant for other purposes such as storage. The small, northernmost rectilinear room may have been relegated to a similar function. Both the western, rectangular room on the lower level and the adjacent circular room on the westernmost extent of the house remain somewhat of a mystery. The rectangular room contains evidence of small fires that did not yield much in the way of food remains. These small burning events may have been related to other activities including household ritual, although there is no clear evidence of such (for examples, see Ringberg 2008 and Cutright 2013).

FOOD IN CONFLICT TIMES

All people, and particularly people with lesser means, are concerned with how to ensure a constant food supply, especially during times of famine, disaster, war and conflict, and political strife (Cuellar 2013; Morell-Hart 2012; Woodward 2000). In the Late Moche Period, the degree to which war was present is unknown (see Arkush and Tung 2013, 329; Verano 1986, 2013). In the coastal valleys, however, the proliferation of defensible settlements with high walls, parapets, and slingshot stone piles in the Late Moche Period suggests that attacks aimed at raiding for stores or captives, eliminating enemies, or driving residents from desirable lands were a looming possibility (Castillo 2010; Dillehay 2001).

Along with this existing or perceived threat, drought in the Late Moche Period most probably complicated people's access to food in the Jequetepeque Valley, especially for the rural poor. Environmental fluctuations have profound effects on foodways: crop failure and diminished yields, food shortages, and worst of all, starvation. Food insecurity leads to conflict, although the reverse relationship is also true (Collinson and Macbeth 2014). The residents of Household 1 probably adopted strategies to cope with uncertain times. The compost bin, for example, is an example of the "waste not, want not" mindset. Floors in Household 1 were kept, for the most part, meticulously clean of food refuse, further suggesting that food was not meant to be squandered.

Other peoples, at other times and places in the Andes, have faced scarcity and instability. In the highlands of Lake Titicaca during the Late Intermediate Period (AD 1100–1450), people nucleated into large settlements, exacerbating the stress over local resources (Arkush 2011; Langlie and Arkush 2016). At the site of Ayawiri, residents intensified agriculture and grazing near the site, thereby reducing the threat of camelid theft or violent encounters with outsiders. Ayawiri's peoples prioritized the amelioration of intergroup over intragroup stress, increasing social tension at the site (Langlie and Arkush 2016, 282). At the Mantaro Valley, during the Wanka II phase (Late Intermediate Period), warring polities and relocation affected people's food strategies. As the Sausa moved upslope to aggregated walled communities, they shifted their focus to upland species and camelids, foregoing lowland species growing in vulnerable locales down the slope (Hastorf 1993).

At Cerro Chepén's Hillside Community, residents employed a similar strategy to diminish the risk of attack. The constrained nature of the Household 1 diet based heavily on staple crops shows a reluctance to traverse diverse ecologies and thus risk greater exposure to ambush. Furthermore, the internal location of the compost bin in Household 1 in the least accessible room in the structure may represent a physical manifestation of increased wariness toward other residents on the hillside.

Thus, while people at Cerro Chepén may have lived with insecurity, the evidence suggests that when the time came to leave, they looked back at their temporary residence with fondness. Excavations at Household 5, just west of Household 1, have revealed that household members took the time to formally end their house's life history (fig. 11.2). A plain, well-used cooking pot, for example, was carefully left behind and buried in the kitchen next to the hearth. On the other side of the house, a pit was filled with large ceramic sherds and dirt and carefully covered with a layer of flat rocks. This may have been another way to symbolically close off the house's occupation.

What happened to the residents of Household 1 and Cerro Chepén at large? Although it is unclear whether Cerro Chepén was ever under attack, at some point, the site was abandoned. While population mobility

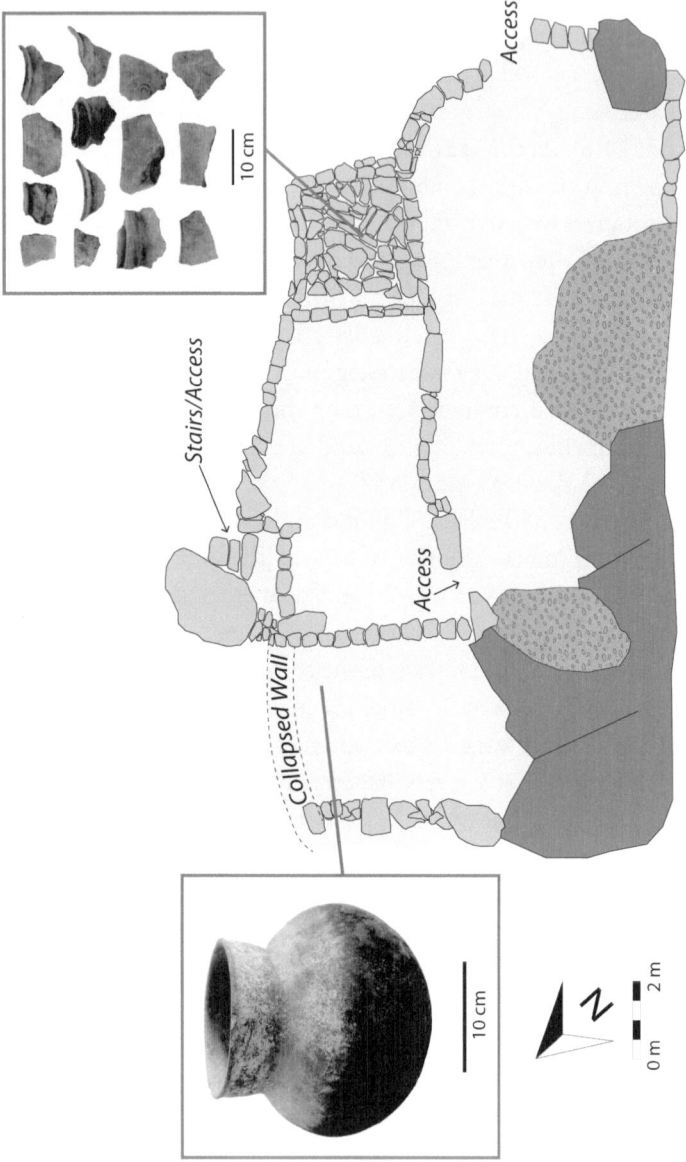

Figure 11.2 Plan of Household 5 showing the location of the intact and buried cooking vessel and examples of the potsherds found in the covered pit. Image courtesy of Katherine L. Chiou.

in the Jequetepeque Valley was a normal occurrence (e.g., White et al. 2009), the Late Moche Period was anything but normal. Did the threats subside, allowing people to move back of their own accord to their original lands? Most probably not given the impending "collapse" of the Moche ~AD 800 and the intense political reorganization of the following Transitional period. Were they driven out, forced to give up access to their nearby fields? Did they move to higher elevations up the valley to seek out more productive lands as a result of prolonged drought? These are questions that require further investigation.

CONCLUDING THOUGHTS

The household archaeology of common folk is not, as of yet, a prolific pursuit in the north coast of Peru. Regardless, what the study of contexts like Household 1 reveals is that an examination of the people who made up the bulk of the population in complex societies can contribute to the greater discussion about social and political organization. The residents of the Cerro Chepén Hillside Community were interacting with the larger, overarching structure of society, being both constrained by it and shaping it through their everyday actions. Unlike other research areas where only a segment of the population can be investigated (e.g., elite funerary objects), food studies can address people of all backgrounds in the past. Everyone eats; therefore, every individual has the potential to leave something behind. An exploration of the use of Moche everyday space vis-à-vis the plant and faunal data can reveal hidden truths that cannot be found in the contexts of the rich and powerful.

While the residents of Household 1 may have lived under the constant, looming threat of warfare, life persisted. Residents did not waste food resources, a type of strategy often implemented by women who play a large role in mitigating food insecurity (Page-Reeves 2014). Residents looked after their animals, keeping guinea pigs inside the house and camelids in corrals. They regularly trekked down the hillslope to nearby canals and fields to manage and maintain their crops, bringing water and food back up the hill. They relied on staple foods in their day-to-day lives. They consumed maize as part of the core of their meals. They did not have access to special, exotic, or luxury goods such as coca, even though coca can be conveniently used to stave off hunger pains (Bolton

1979). They collected wild plants from around the agricultural areas and incorporated them into their meals. They foraged for land snails (*Scutalus proteus* [Broderip]) that could be found on cacti growing right on the Chepén hill, eating—in the true sense of the word—locally. They took the remains of their food and composted them, possibly creating fertilizer to enhance their agricultural yields. Nevertheless, despite the necessity of routine, life was probably not like it was before.

Contemporaneous data of feast settings from the nearby ritual center of San José de Moro serve as an intriguing foil to Cerro Chepén. Feasts in San José de Moro were dominated by the presence of fruits and marine fauna (both vertebrates and invertebrates). Staple foods such as maize and *algarrobo* were also recovered in great densities, with the bulk of the former relegated to use in chicha brewing. The elite feasting signature is also distinguished by the presence of plants with psychoactive properties such as coca (*Erythroxylum novogranatense* var. *truxillense* [Rusby] E. Machado), San Pedro (*Trichocereus pachanoi* Britton & Rose), and *Guarea* sp. L., the possible *ulluchu* plant depicted in Moche iconographic representations of elite rituals (Bussmann and Sharon 2009). Some of these hallucinogenic plants may have been ingredients in chicha recipes, allowing people to enter altered states of consciousness. While elites ate wild foods such as amaranth (*Amaranthus* sp. L.), wild tomato (*Solanum pimpinellifolium* Mill. ex. Donal), and purslane (*Portulaca* sp. L.), they made up a very small proportion of the food-plant assemblage (Chiou 2017).

When the ingredients in the commoner domestic cuisine of Cerro Chepén and the haute cuisine of San José de Moro are shown together, scaled roughly according to abundance, we get a visual sense of how social inequality can be manifested at the microscale (fig. 11.3). While the elite individuals at San José de Moro participated in celebrations marked by the consumption of copious amounts of food and drink and the presence of luxury foods and substances, the commoner household at Cerro Chepén had access to less. Although the settings of the food events at both sites differ (i.e., public display feasts at San José de Moro vs. intimate meals in Household 1), food data representing meals within elite residences of the Hilltop Community at Cerro Chepén suggest that these basic distinctions between social classes hold regardless of setting (see Bélisle, Alaica, and Brown, this volume, for a discussion of public feasting versus private, everyday consumption at Ak'awillay, and Biwer,

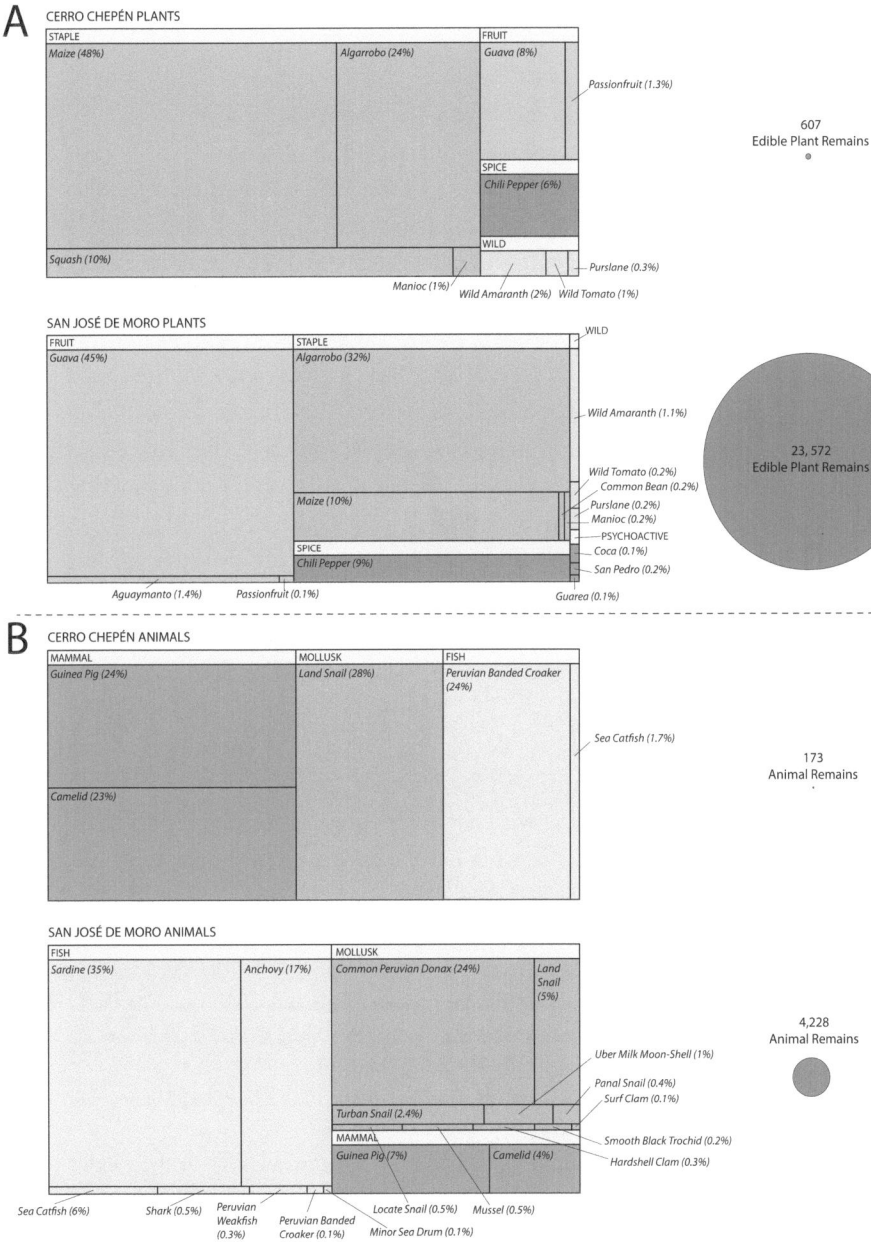

Figure 11.3 Treemaps of the identified plant (*A*) and faunal (*B*) ingredients found at Cerro Chepén and San José de Moro. Areas associated with categories and subcategories are displayed in proportion to quantities. The gray circles on the right provide a comparative visualization of the relative number of identified specimens in each data set. Image courtesy of Katherine L. Chiou.

Alaica, and Patricia Quiñonez Cuzcano, this volume, for a discussion of everyday and extraordinary meals at Quilcapampa).

Such stark differences are reminiscent of periods of hardship and unrest, much like the U.S. Great Depression in the 1930s. While many in the United States were suffering from the fallout of economic collapse, high-society members were engaging in even more elaborate displays of conspicuous consumption. For many, the Depression was a time of frugality that was reflected in the creation of filling meals made of simple and few ingredients (Ziegelman and Coe 2016). The rich pageantry of the social elite was difficult to stomach. "Poor little rich girl" and heiress to the Woolworth fortune Barbara Hutton, for example, was forced to flee Europe to escape the press after coming under intense scrutiny and criticism when she was given an elaborate debutante ball in 1930 (Erenberg 1986). These class-based distinctions can lead, as we have repeatedly seen throughout history, to social unrest and uprisings, such as the Women's March on Versailles precipitated by the price of bread during the reign of Louis XVI, the food riots during the Irish Potato Famine, and the Southern Riots over food shortages during the Civil War (Chesson 1984; Garrioch 1999; Kelly 2017). In the case of the Moche, the limited food data that we have thus far reveals vast disparities in food access. These inequities may have fueled resentment and, along with environmental catastrophe and warfare, contributed to the Moche's downfall at the end of the eighth century.

REFERENCES

Anderson, David. 2017. "Consuming Memories: Food and Childhood in Post-bellum Plantation Memoirs and Reminiscences." *Food, Culture, & Society* 20 (3): 443–61. https://doi.org/10.1080/15528014.2017.1288800.

Arkush, Elizabeth. 2011. *Hillforts of the Ancient Andes: Colla Warfare, Society, and Landscape.* Gainesville: University Press of Florida.

Arkush, Elizabeth, and Tiffiny A. Tung. 2013. "Patterns of War in the Andes from the Archaic to the Late Horizon: Insights from Settlement Patterns and Cranial Trauma." *Journal of Archaeological Research* 21:307–69. https://doi.org /10.1007/s10814-013-9065-1.

Atalay, Sonya, and Christine A. Hastorf. 2006. "Food, Meals, and Daily Activities: Food Habitus at Neolithic Çatalhöyük." *American Antiquity* 71 (2): 283–319. https://doi.org/10.2307/40035906.

Bawden, Garth. 1996. *The Moche.* New York: Wiley-Blackwell.

Benson, Elizabeth P. 1972. *The Mochica: A Culture of Peru.* New York: Praeger.

Billman, Brian R. 2002. "Irrigation and the Origins of the Southern Moche State on the North Coast of Peru." *Latin American Antiquity* 13 (4): 371–400. https://doi.org/10.2307/972222.

Bolton, Ralph. 1979. "On Coca Chewing and High-Altitude Stress." *Current Anthropology* 20 (2): 418–20. https://doi.org/10.1086/202294.

Bourget, Steve. 2006. *Sex, Death, and Sacrifice in Moche Religion and Visual Culture.* Austin: University of Texas Press.

Bussmann, Rainer W., and Douglas Sharon. 2009. "Naming a Phantom: The Quest to Find the Identity of *Ulluchu*, An Unidentified Ceremonial Plant of the Moche Culture in Northern Peru." *Journal of Ethnobiology and Ethnomedicine* 5: art. no. 8. https://doi.org/10.1186/1746-4269-5-8.

Castillo, Luis Jaime. 2001. "The Last of the Mochicas." In *Moche Art and Archaeology in Ancient Peru*, edited by Joanne Pillsbury, 307–32. New Haven, Conn.: National Gallery of Art and Yale University Press.

Castillo, Luis Jaime. 2010. "Moche Politics in the Jequetepeque Valley: A Case for Political Opportunism." In *New Perspectives in Moche Political Organization*, edited by Luis Jaime Castillo and Jeffrey Quilter, 83–109. Washington, D.C.: Dumbarton Oaks.

Chesson, Michael B. 1984. "Harlots or Heroines? A New Look at the Richmond Bread Riot." *Virginia Magazine of History and Biography* 92 (2): 131–75. http://www.jstor.org/stable/4248710.

Chiou, Katherine L. 2013. "Flotation Versus Dry Sieving Archaeobotanical Remains: A Case History from the Middle Horizon Southern Coast of Peru." *Journal of Field Archaeology* 38 (1): 38–53. https://doi.org/10.1179/0093469012Z.00000000035.

Chiou, Katherine L. 2017. "Common Meals, Noble Feasts: An Archaeological Investigation of Moche Food and Cuisine in the Jequetepeque Valley, Peru, AD 600–800." PhD diss., University of California, Berkeley.

Collinson, Paul, and Helen Macbeth. 2014. Introduction to *Food in Zones of Conflict: Cross-Disciplinary Perspectives*, edited by Paul Collinson and Helen Macbeth, 1–26. New York: Berghahn Books.

Cuellar, Andrea M. 2013. "The Archaeology of Food and Social Inequality in the Andes." *Journal of Archaeological Research* 21:123–74. https://doi.org/10.1007/s10814-012-9061-x.

Cusicanqui Marsano, Solsiré. 2010. "Prospecciones en los Sitios Arqueológicos Cerro Chepén y San Ildefonso." In *Programa Arqueológico San José de Moro, Informe de Excavaciones, Temporada 2009*, edited by Luis Jaime Castillo, 46–74. Lima: Pontificia Universidad Católica del Perú. http://sanjosedemoro.pucp.cdu.pc/dcscargas/rcportcs/INFORME2009.pdf.

Cutright, Robyn E. 2013. "Household Ofrendas and Community Feasts: Ritual at a Late Intermediate Period Village in the Jequetepeque Valley, Peru." *Journal of Andean Archaeology* 33 (1): 1–21. https://doi.org/10.1179/0077629713Z.0000000001.

Dillehay, Tom D. 2001. "Town and Country in Late Moche Times: A View from Two Northern Valleys." *Studies in the History of Art* 63:258–83. https://www.jstor.org/stable/42622325.

Erenberg, Lewis A. 1986. "From New York to Middletown: Repeal and the Legitimization of Nightlife in the Great Depression." *American Quarterly* 38 (5): 761–78. https://doi.org/10.2307/2712822.

Garrioch, David. 1999. "The Everyday Lives of Parisian Women and the October Days of 1789." *Social History* 24 (3): 231–49. https://doi.org/10.1080/0307102 9908568067.

Hastorf, Christine A. 1993. *Agriculture and the Onset of Political Inequality Before the Inca.* Cambridge: Cambridge University Press.

Hastorf, Christine A. 2012. "Steamed or Boiled: Identity and Value in Food Preparation." *Journal for Ancient Studies* 2:243–76. http://dx.doi.org/10.17169 /refubium-21678.

Holtzman, Jon D. 2006. "Food and Memory." *Annual Review of Anthropology* 35:361–78. https://doi.org/10.1146/annurev.anthro.35.081705.123220.

Ingold, Timothy. 1993. "The Temporality of the Landscape." *World Archaeology* 25 (2): 152–74. https://doi.org/10.1080/00438243.1993.9980235.

Johnson, Ilana. 2008. "Daily Life and Political Organization at the Hinterland Site of Portachuelo de Charcape." In *Arqueología Mochica: Nuevos Enfoques*, edited by Luis Jaime Castillo, Hélène Bernier, Gregory Lockard, and Julio Rucabado Yong, 261–74. Lima: Pontificia Universidad Católica del Perú and Instituto Francés de Estudios Andinos.

Johnson, Ilana, and Colleen M. Zori. 2011. "Introduction: State and Empire in the Jequetepeque Valley." In *From State to Empire in the Prehistoric Jequetepeque Valley, Peru*, edited by Colleen M. Zori and Ilana Johnson, 1–32. Oxford: BAR.

Kelly, James. 2017. *Food Rioting in Ireland in the Eighteenth and Nineteenth Centuries: The "Moral Economy" and the Irish Crowd.* Dublin: Four Courts Press.

Koren, Ore, and Benjamin E. Bagozzi. 2016. "From Global to Local, Food Insecurity Is Associated with Contemporary Armed Conflicts." *Food Security* 8:999–1010. https://doi.org/10.1007/s12571-016-0610-x.

La Lone, Darrell. 2000. "Rise, Fall, and Semiperipheral Development in the Andean World-System." *Journal of World-Systems Research* 6 (1): 67–98. https://doi.org/10.5195/jwsr.2000.231.

Langlie, BrieAnna S., and Elizabeth N. Arkush. 2016. "Managing Mayhem: Conflict, Environment, and Subsistence in the Andean Late Intermediate Period, Puno, Peru." In *The Archaeology of Food and Warfare*, edited by Amber M. VanDerwarker and Gregory D. Wilson, 259–90. New York: Springer.

Mannur, Anita. 2007. "Culinary Nostalgia: Authenticity, Nationalism, and Diaspora." *MELUS* 32 (4): 11–31. https://doi.org/10.1093/melus/32.4.11.

McClelland, Donna. 1990. "A Maritime Passage from Moche to Chimú." In *The Northern Dynasties: Kingship and Statecraft in Chimor*, edited by Michael E.

Moseley and Alana Cordy-Collins, 75–106. Washington, D.C.: Dumbarton Oaks.

McClelland, Donna, Donald McClelland, and Christopher B. Donnan. 2007. *Moche Fineline Painting from San José de Moro*. Los Angeles: Cotsen Institute of Archaeology, University of California, Los Angeles.

Morell-Hart, Shanti. 2012. "Foodways and Resilience Under Apocalyptic Conditions." *Culture, Agriculture, Food, and Environment* (2): 161–71. https://doi.org/10.1111/j.2153-9561.2012.01075.x.

Page-Reeves, Janet, ed. 2014. *Women Redefining the Experience of Food Insecurity: Life off the Edge of the Table*. London: Lexington Books.

Ringberg, Jennifer E. 2008. "Figurines, Household Rituals, and the Use of Domestic Space in a Middle Moche Rural Community." In *Arqueología Mochica: Nuevos Enfoques*, edited by Luis Jaime Castillo, Hélène Bernier, Gregory Lockard, and Julio Rucabado Yong, 341–58. Lima: Pontificia Universidad Católica del Perú and Instituto Francés de Estudios Andinos.

Rosas Rintel, Marco. 2010. "Cerro Chepén and the Late Moche Collapse in the Jequetepeque Valley, North Coast of Peru." PhD diss., University of New Mexico.

Scarry, C. Margaret, and Vincas P. Steponaitis. 1997. "Between Farmstead and Center: The Natural and Social Landscape of Moundville." In *People, Plants, and Landscapes: Studies in Paleoethnobotany*, edited by Kristen J. Gremillion, 107–22. Tuscaloosa: University of Alabama Press.

Shimada, Izumi. 1994. *Pampa Grande and the Mochica Culture*. Austin: University of Texas Press.

Shimada, Izumi, Crystal B. Schaaf, Lonnie G. Thompson, and Ellen Moseley-Thompson. 1991. "Cultural Impacts of Severe Droughts in the Prehistoric Andes: Application of a 1,500-Year Ice Core Precipitation Record." *World Archaeology* 22 (3): 247–70. https://doi.org/10.1080/00438243.1991.9980145.

Stanish, Charles. 2001. "The Origins of State Societies in South America." *Annual Review of Anthropology* 30:41–64. https://doi.org/10.1146/annurev.anthro.30.1.41.

Sutter, Richard C., and Luis Jaime Castillo. 2015. "Population Structure During the Demise of the Moche (550–850 A.D.): Comparative Phenetic Analyses of Tooth Trait Data from San José de Moro, Perú." *Current Anthropology* 56 (5): 762–71. https://doi.org/10.1086/683269.

Swenson, Edward R. 2006. "Competitive Feasting, Religious Pluralism, and Decentralized Power in the Late Moche Period." In *Andean Archaeology III: North and South*, edited by William H. Isbell and Helaine Silverman, 112–42. New York: Springer.

Swenson, Edward R. 2007. "Adaptive Strategies or Ideological Innovations? Interpreting Sociopolitical Developments in the Jequetepeque Valley of Peru During the Late Moche Period." *Journal of Anthropological Archaeology* 26 (2): 253–82. https://doi.org/10.1016/j.jaa.2006.11.001.

VanDerwarker, Amber M. 2005. "Field Cultivation and Tree Management in Tropical Agriculture: A View from Gulf Coastal Mexico." *World Archaeology* 37 (2): 275–89. https://doi.org/10.1080/00438240500095298.

Verano, John W. 1986. "A Mass Burial of Mutilated Individuals at Pacatnamu." In *The Pacatnamu Papers*, edited by Christopher B. Donnan and Guillermo A. Cock, 1:117–38. Los Angeles: Cotsen Institute of Archaeology, University of California, Los Angeles.

Verano, John W. 2013. "Warfare, Human Sacrifice and Mortuary Practices of the Elite in Late Pre-Hispanic Northern Peru." In *The Routledge Handbook of the Bioarchaeology of Human Conflict*, edited by Christopher Knüsel and Martin J. Smith, 355–70. New York: Routledge.

White, Christine D., Andrew J. Nelson, Fred J. Longstaffe, Gisela Grupe, and A. Jung. 2009. "Landscape Bioarchaeology at Pacatnamu, Peru: Inferring Mobility from δ^{13}C and δ^{15}N Values of Hair." *Journal of Archaeological Science* 36 (7): 1527–37. https://doi.org/10.1016/j.jas.2009.03.008.

Woodward, Michelle R. 2000. "Considering Household Food Security and Diet at the Classic Period Village of Cerén, El Salvador (A.D. 600)." *Mayab* 13:22–33. https://dialnet.unirioja.es/descarga/articulo/2774887.pdf.

Ziegelman, Jane, and Andrew Coe. 2016. *A Square Meal: A Culinary History of the Great Depression*. New York: Harper Collins.

12

Camelids in the Oasis

New Evidence from the Pica 8 Cemetery, Atacama Desert, Northern Chile (AD 900–1450)

Francisca Santana-Sagredo, Anahí Maturana-Fernández, Cecilia Lemp, Petrus le Roux, Chris Harrod, and Mauricio Uribe

Because camelids today are found almost exclusively in the South American highlands (*puna*), archaeologists originally assumed that they largely inhabited that ecosystem in pre-Colonial times (Murra 1972; Núñez 1984; Núñez and Dillehay [1978] 1995). However, we now know that lowland camelid herds were either killed by Spanish conquerors or died from diseases introduced by European animals (deFrance 2016; Latcham 1922). Stable isotope analyses have recently corroborated Shimada and Shimada's (1985) proposal that camelids may have lived on the northern coast of Peru (Dufour et al. 2014, 2020; Szpak et al. 2014; Szpak et al. 2020; Santana-Sagredo et al. 2020; Vásquez et al. 2020), and similar observations have been made for southern Peru (Thornton et al. 2011) and northern Chile (Gayo et al. 2020; López et al. 2017; Szpak and Valenzuela 2020). Here, we advance knowledge of camelid residence patterns and their sociocultural implications during the Late Intermediate Period (AD 900–1450) in the northern Chilean Tarapacá region.

For decades, South American camelids were studied in relation to mobility as part of llama caravans that crossed the desert from the altiplano to the coast and that were managed by highland specialists and societies who controlled the trade and exchange of the products they carried (Núñez and Dillehay [1978] 1995). This highland-centric model has recently been debated as new studies highlight the relevance of locally maintained camelids in the South Central Andean lowlands (Nielsen, Berenguer, and Pimentel 2019; Pimentel et al. 2017; Santana-Sagredo and Uribe 2019). Moving beyond models of highland-controlled caravans allows us to investigate the impact of local herding on sociocultural and symbolic aspects of lowland societies, as important sources of food (camelid meat), raw materials (leather, wool, and bone), and dung (fertilizer [*guano*] and fuel) as well as beasts of burden (Bonavia 2008; Nielsen 2009; Núñez 1984).

During the Late Intermediate Period (LIP), complex societies resided in the Andean lowlands from the coast to the precordillera (Albarracín 1996; Uribe 2006). While we know some lowland LIP groups brought camelids from the highlands (Baitzel et al., this volume), these autonomous and segmentary societies could have certainly managed their own camelid herds independent of highland caravans and altiplano groups. To test this hypothesis, we analyzed camelid stable carbon and nitrogen and radiogenic strontium isotopes from the LIP Pica 8 cemetery located in the oasis settlement of Matilla in the Atacama Desert. By evaluating the diet and mobility of Pica 8 camelids, we determine whether the animals were herded locally or originated in the highlands.

THE PICA 8 CEMETERY

The Pica 8 cemetery in the lowlands of the Tarapacá is close to the small modern-day town of Pica (20°S, 69°W), 90 km from the coast at an altitude of 1,325 masl (map 12.1). The cemetery dates to AD 991–1414 (Núñez 1976; Santana-Sagredo et al. 2017; Uribe, Sanhueza, and Bahamondes 2007) and is associated with the LIP Pica-Tarapacá Cultural Complex (Agüero 2015; Múñoz, Agüero and Valenzuela 2016; Núñez 1984). This cultural complex is characterized by the presence of autonomous and highly hierarchical agropastoral societies as well as an absence of states and empires. The varied offerings of the 246 burials excavated at the cemetery (Núñez 1984; Zlatar 1984) include camelid remains such as bones and mummified heads. The camelid fibers and woolen textiles from Pica 8 (Agüero 1998; Delpino 2020) present a unique opportunity for evaluating whether camelids were inhabiting the oases or if they were brought from somewhere else.

PREVIOUS ISOTOPIC ANALYSIS ON CAMELIDS IN ANCIENT PERU AND NORTHERN CHILE

Recent studies use stable isotope analyses of camelid diets to characterize herding behaviors. Highland environments (*puna*, >3,800 masl) contain *bofedales* ideal for camelid pasture (Dufour et al. 2014; Fernández

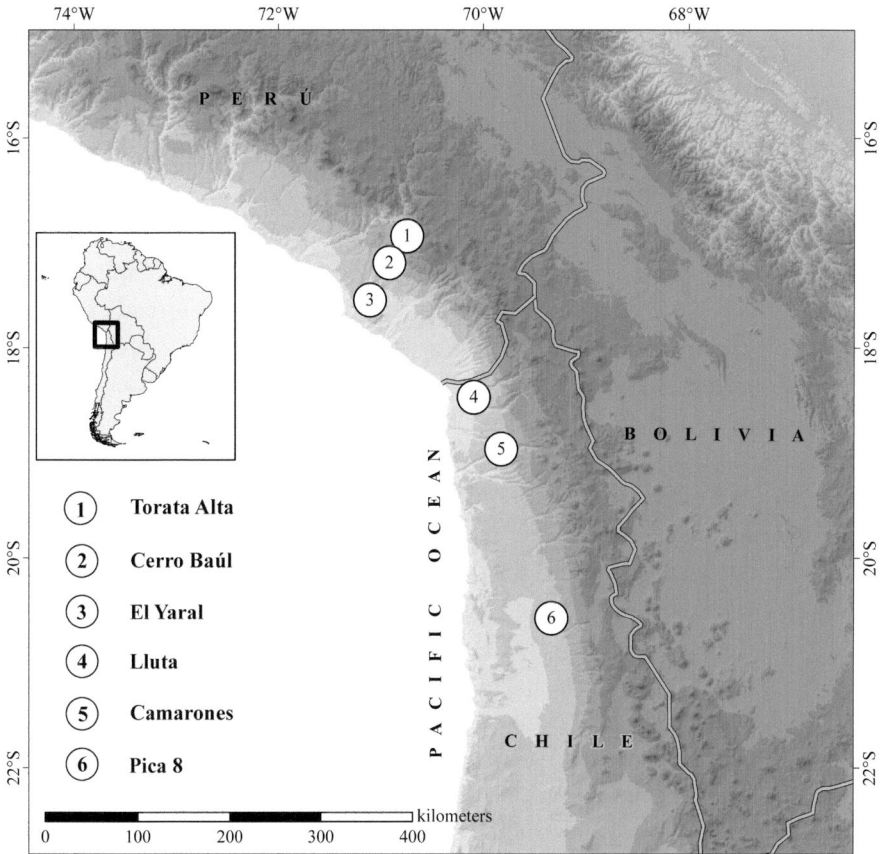

Map 12.1 Map of northern Chile. The approximate location of the sites discussed in the text is presented in numbers. Images by F. Santana Sagredo.

and Panarello 1999–2001; Szpak et al. 2014) and are almost exclusively dominated by C_3 plants (Szpak et al. 2013; Tieszen and Chapman 1995). Thus, camelids that feed in the *puna* display lower values of $\delta^{13}C$ and $\delta^{15}N$ (DeNiro 1988; Dufour et al. 2014; Fernández and Panarello 1999–2001; Szpak et al. 2014; Yacobaccio, Morales, and Samec 2009). In the hyperarid coastal and lowland habitats of Peru and northern Chile, C_3 plants dominate as well, but camelids also graze on wild C_4 plants, such as *Distichlis spicata* and *Atrixplex* sp., resulting in enriched compositions in ^{13}C and ^{15}N (Díaz et al. 2016; Dufour et al. 2014; Ehleringer et al. 1998; Evans and Ehleringer 1994; Gayo et al. 2020; Szpak et al. 2013;

Szpak et al. 2014; Thornton et al. 2011). In the Atacama Desert, where precipitation is low (<1 mm per year; Gayo et al. 2012) and springs are the main source of water (Aravena 1995; Magaritz et al. 1990), grazing resources can be limited. Therefore, supplementation with fodder may have been necessary, such as with the leaves and stalks of maize, a C_4 plant commonly cultivated in the lowlands (Finucane, Agurto, and Isbell 2006; Núñez 1984).

Lowland dietary signatures have been found in camelids from sites such as La Chilca (DeNiro 1988), La Paloma (DeNiro 1988), and Pacatnamu (Verano and DeNiro 1993), as well as several sites in the Osmore Valley (Thornton et al. 2011). In the Northern Chilean Camarones and Lluta Valleys, carbon and nitrogen isotope results indicate that the most likely origin of these camelids is the Chilean northern *puna* (Szpak and Valenzuela 2020). However, some textile samples showed higher $\delta^{13}C$ and $\delta^{15}N$ values, suggesting that a small proportion of camelids were kept in the lowland valleys during the LIP and Late Horizon (AD 1450–1600). This is not surprising because camelids are thought to have occupied the Northern Chilean coastal valleys of Vitor as early as the Late Archaic and Early Formative Periods (Gayo et al. 2020). Given previous studies, we expect that camelids in the Pica lowlands had access to wild C_4 plants enriched in ^{15}N because of the aridity of the Atacama Desert. Additionally, considering the reliance on agriculture in the Pica oasis, camelid diets could have included cultivated plants, in particular maize, the most abundant domestic plant in Pica 8 (Núñez 1984).

MATERIALS AND METHODS

Eighteen samples from various sectors of the Pica 8 cemetery were gathered from the archaeological collections of the Departamento de Antropología of the Universidad de Chile and the Instituto de Investigaciones Antropológicas of the Universidad de Antofagasta (table 12.1). Two fiber samples were collected from the fur of mummified camelids, and sixteen samples were selected from textiles, including tunics, bags, and loincloths, that had camelid fibers as raw material (Lemp, Benavente, and Sepúlveda 2018; Sepúlveda et al. 2021). While zooarchaeological analyses have not been carried out to identify species, the color of the camelid fibers used in the textiles indicates that at least some of the camelids were domesticated

(Frank et al. 2006). All samples were used for carbon and nitrogen isotopic analyses; four were also analyzed for $^{87}Sr/^{86}Sr$ composition.

STABLE ISOTOPE ANALYSIS

Carbon and nitrogen stable isotope analyses were conducted at the Universidad de Antofagasta Stable Isotope Facility (UASIF). Samples were pretreated following the protocol of O'Connell and Hedges (1999). Samples were weighed in 8 × 5 mm pressed standard weight tin capsules using a high-precision (repeatability = 0.0008 mg) microbalance (model XS 3DU, Mettler Toledo, Greifensee, Switzerland).

Analyses were carried out using an EA-IRMS by Elementar. Calibration and estimation of analytical errors were conducted using different international standards in each batch run in Elementar's ionOS software package. Certified reference materials USGS40 and USGS41 were used. Stable isotope ratios are expressed in δ units relative to Vienna Pee Dee Belemnite for carbon and atmospheric air for nitrogen. Repeated analysis of standards showed that analytical errors (±1 sd) were ±0.05‰ for $\delta^{13}C$ and ±0.1‰ for $\delta^{15}N$. An in-house standard (rainbow trout) was used to correct for machine drift. All samples produced adequate C/N ratios for hair keratin, indicating good preservation (O'Connell and Hedges 1999).

RADIOGENIC STRONTIUM ISOTOPES

Radiogenic strontium isotope analyses were undertaken in the Department of Geological Sciences, University of Cape Town, South Africa. Samples were ashed in the clean chemistry laboratory at 800°C overnight, starting at 300°C and ramping by 100°C/hour, and digested in concentrated HNO_3 for 48 hours at 140°C in closed Teflon beakers. After sample dissolution, Sr elemental separation followed Pin et al. (1994).

Isolated strontium fractions were analyzed as 200 ppb Sr solutions in 0.2% HNO_3. The strontium isotope analyses were performed on a Nu Instruments NuPlasma HR in the MC-ICP-MS facility (Copeland et al. 2008). All $^{87}Sr/^{86}Sr$ data were referenced to a value of 0.710255 for SRM987 and corrected for Rb interference on mass 87 using the measured ^{85}Rb signal and the natural $^{85}Rb/^{87}Rb$ ratio. Instrumental mass fractionation was corrected using the exponential law and the accepted

Table 12.1 Stable carbon and nitrogen isotope results and $^{87}Sr/^{86}Sr$ results for textiles and fibers of the Pica 8 cemetery

Sample type	Lab number	Context information	δ ^{13}C	δ ^{15}N	C/N	$^{87}Sr/^{86}Sr$	±2sd	Reference
Tunic (dyed by tights)	P18-TX1	T1-SD/A05749	−19.4	12.3	3.9	0.706686	12	—
Tunic	P18-TX2	T55-SI/A05761	—	—	—	0.707540	12	—
Bag	P18-TX3	T3-SE/A05730	—	—	—	0.707913	13	—
Tunic	P18-TX5	SB-T3/A05681	—	—	—	0.707288	10	—
Blanket	P18-TX12	T47-SD/A05787	−16.1	9.6	3.5	—	—	—
Bag	P18-TX31	T32-SI, Zlatar 1059, B0438	−18.5	8.9	3.3	—	—	—
Camelid fiber (camelid head)	P18-TX37	T5-SG	−13.6	9.8	3.5	—	—	—
Camelid fiber from mummified individual	P18-TX43	T13-SA	−8.1	19.01	3.5	—	—	—
Bag	P18-TX46	T24-SA, Zlatar 0168, B0457	−20.0	7.7	3.6	—	—	—
Bag (wayuña)	P18-TX48	T9-SI, Zlatar 0917	−20.9	5.9	3.5	—	—	—
Bag	P18-TX49	T3-SF, Zlatar 0717	−20.0	12.8	3.3	—	—	—
Tunic	P18-TX52	A03827	−14.2	13	3.8	—	—	Santana-Sagredo et al. 2017
Bag	P18-TX53	B0415 sector D	−17.5	8.6	3.4	—	—	Santana-Sagredo et al. 2017
Tunic	P18-TX54	A03829	−16.2	9.6	3.7	—	—	Santana-Sagredo et al. 2017
Bag	P18-TX55	A03830	−19.4	9.9	3.8	—	—	Santana-Sagredo et al. 2017
Bag	P18-TX56	B0420 sector E	−12.8	16.5	3.8	—	—	Santana-Sagredo et al. 2017
Tunic	P18-TX57	B0444 sector F	−16.3	9.3	3.5	—	—	Santana-Sagredo et al. 2017
Hair bundle	P18-TX58	A03839	−11.4	18.6	3.8	—	—	Santana-Sagredo et al. 2017
Loincloth	P18-TX59	B0455 sector I	−17	11.4	3.6	—	—	Santana-Sagredo et al. 2017
Tunic	P18-TX60	A03834	−17.6	8.9	3.5	—	—	Santana-Sagredo et al. 2017
Tunic	P18-TX61	A03825	−11.5	10.4	4	—	—	Santana-Sagredo et al. 2017

value of 0.1194 for ^{86}Sr/^{88}Sr. Although there are no bioavailable baselines
published for the Tarapacá region, salt concentrations in the Tarapacá ra-
vine (1,000–1,400 masl; ~100 km north of Pica) display ^{87}Sr/^{86}Sr values of
0.7075–0.7078 (Cosentino and Jordan 2017). Additional ^{87}Sr/^{86}Sr ratios
from the Isluga and Irruputuncu volcanoes in the altiplano of Tarapacá
are 0.7059–0.7060 and 0.7053–0.7058, respectively (Mamani, Tassara,
and Wörner 2008; Mamani, Wörner, and Sempera 2010).

STATISTICAL ANALYSIS

The δ^{13}C and δ^{15}N centroids were compared with similar camelid data
from sites in southern Peru (Thornton et al. 2011) and extreme northern
Chile (Szpak and Valenzuela 2020), using a permutation (n = 9,999)
based nonparametric MANOVA test, or PERMANOVA (Anderson
2001). PERMANOVA was based on Euclidean distances and conducted
in the R package *vegan* (Oksanen et al. 2016), with post hoc tests (corrected for false discovery rates) conducted using the R package *RVAide-
Memoire* (Hervé 2019). All statistical analyses were undertaken using The
R Project for Statistical Computing.[1]

RESULTS

The data from the Pica 8 camelid fiber and textiles displayed high variability in both δ^{13}C (−20.9‰ to −8.1‰) and δ^{15}N (5.9‰ to 19.0‰)
(table 12.1; fig. 12.1). Mean values measured −16.1‰ ± 3.5‰ for δ^{13}C
and 11.2‰ ± 3.6‰ for δ^{15}N. Of the 18 samples analyzed, at least nine
(carbon) and nine (nitrogen) values were isotopically heavy. Strontium
isotope ratios range between ^{87}Sr/^{86}Sr of 0.7067 to 0.7079 with an average
of 0.7074 ± 0.0005.

We first compared δ^{15}N–δ^{13}C centroids for camelid textiles from LIP
and Late Horizon (LH) contexts in the Camarones and Lluta Valleys
of northern Chile (Szpak and Valenzuela 2020) to the Pica 8 textile and
fiber data (fig. 12.2a). Significant differences were found overall (pseudo-
$F_{5,81}$ = 4.64, p =.0019), and post hoc PERMANOVA tests (adjusted for
the false discovery rate) demonstrated significant differences in δ^{13}C and

---

1. https://www.R-project.org/.

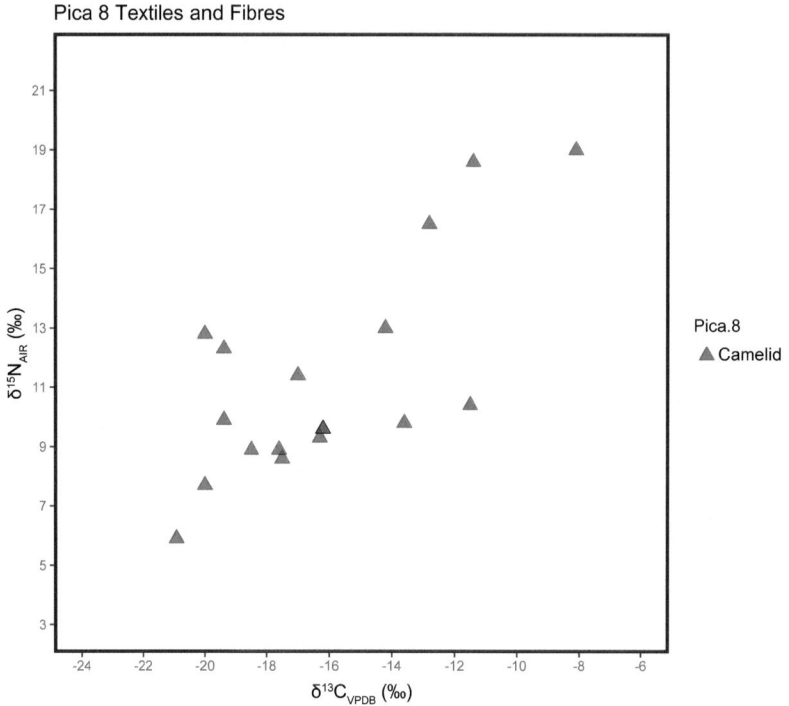

Figure 12.1 Bivariate plot showing δ13C and δ15N values for textiles and fibers of camelids from the Pica 8 cemetery. Images by F. Santana-Sagredo.

$\delta^{15}N$ values between Pica 8 and LIP Camarones (p =.006) and LH Lluta (p = 0.046) contexts. In contrast, no significant differences were found between Pica 8 and LIP Lluta and the LH Camarones contexts.

We then compared the Pica 8 textile and fiber data with bone collagen data from camelids from LIP and LH contexts in the Lluta Valley and three sites in the southern Peruvian Osmore drainage: the Middle Horizon, Wari-affiliated site of Cerro Baúl (AD 600–1000, 2,500 masl), the LIP site of Yaral (AD 1000–1200, 1,000 masl), and the sixteenth-seventeenth century site of Torata Alta (2,500 masl) (fig. 12.2*B*). To properly compare the textile and fiber data with bone collagen data, textile and fiber values were adjusted by +1.3‰ (Szpak et al. 2014). Significant differences in $\delta^{13}C$ and $\delta^{15}N$ were identified between Pica 8 and the Lluta Valley and southern Peru samples (pseudo-$F_{5,67}$ = 4.53, p =.0000). Pica 8 values differed significantly from both the Lluta Valley LIP (p = .006)

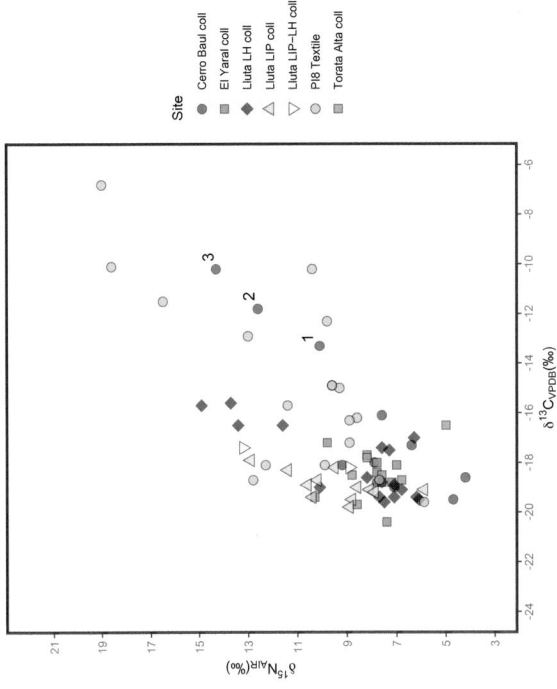

B. Comparison Textiles and Fibres with bone collagen

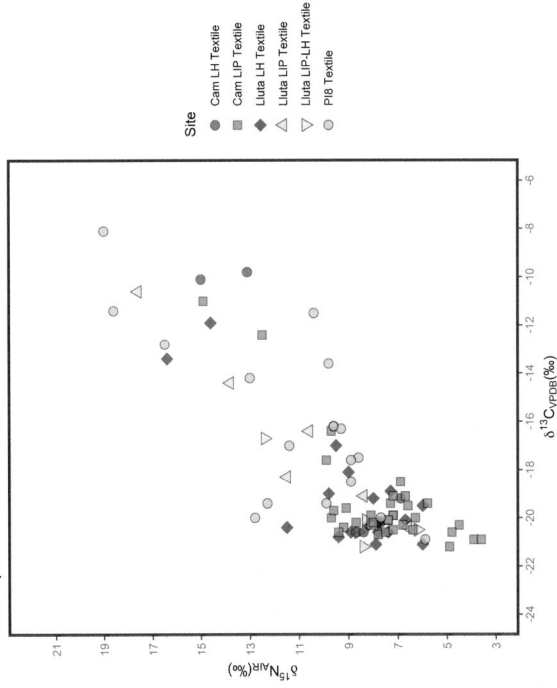

A. Comparison Textiles and Fibres

Figure 12.2 Bivariate plots. *A*, δ¹⁵N and δ¹³C values for fibers and textiles from Pica 8 compared to textile samples from Lluta and Camarones Valley Late Intermediate Period (LIP) and Late Horizon (LH) contexts (Szpak and Valenzuela 2020). *B*, δ¹⁵N and δ¹³C values for fibers and textiles from Pica 8 compared to bone collagen samples from the Lluta Valley LIP and LH contexts (Szpak and Valenzuela 2020) as well as from the sites from southern Peru, Torata Alta, El Yaral and Cerro Baúl (Thornton et al. 2011). The three outliers from Cerro Baúl are indicated with numbers (*1, 2,* and *3*). Images by F. Santana-Sagredo.

and LH (p = .008) bone collagen samples (a result distinct from the Lluta Valley textile data, in which the LIP sample did not differ significantly from Pica). Significant differences were also seen between Pica 8 and the southern Peruvian sites of Torata Alta (p = .0356) and El Yaral (p =.039); whereas Pica 8 and Cerro Baúl values were not significantly different.

DISCUSSION

The high variability in carbon and nitrogen stable isotope values from Pica 8 is consistent with heterogeneity reported previously for camelid diets in southern and northern Peru (Dufour et al. 2014, 2020; Santana-Sagredo et al. 2020; Szpak et al. 2014, 2020; Thornton et al. 2011). Camelid herding practices probably varied at the site level, with some individuals being locally herded while others were kept in the highlands. Social differences were common among the segmentary and autonomous groups of the LIP (Uribe 2006), and decisions on how they managed camelids, such as whether to keep them in the lowlands or bring them from the highlands, were surely based on a complex set of social, political, and cultural factors.

The ^{13}C- and ^{15}N-enriched stable isotope compositions from Pica strongly suggest that approximately a third of the camelids (eight or nine of the samples) from Pica resided in the oasis of the Atacama Desert. Other individuals, with lower δ^{13}C and δ^{15}N, probably came from the highlands. Carbon isotope results suggest some camelids consumed a diet with considerable input from C_4 plants. Given the high quantities of maize cobs and leaves, as well as popcorn, found in Pica 8 burials (Nuñez 1984; Zlatar 1984), this suggests that camelids were foddered with maize, as has been proposed for camelids in Conchopata-Ayacucho (Finucane, Agurto, and Isbell 2006).

The high δ^{15}N levels in the camelid may be the result of various factors, such as consumption of marine macroalgae (DeNiro 1988) or ^{15}N-enriched *lomas* vegetation (Thornton et al. 2011). Since marine algae's δ^{15}N values are lower than those observed in *lomas* vegetation (Szpak et al. 2013, 2014), macroalgae consumption is unlikely. The consumption of fertilized crops can also increase δ^{15}N values and are an important consideration for our study.

Fertilizers such as llama dung or seabird guano increase crop δ^{15}N values by 2‰–4‰ and 11‰ respectively (Szpak et al. 2012). Thus, camelids showing very high $\delta^{15}N$ values probably consumed plants fertilized with seabird guano, while camelids with lower $\delta^{15}N$ values and high $\delta^{13}C$ values consumed crops, in particular maize, fertilized with llama dung. The individuals in our sample with $\delta^{15}N$ values ~12‰–13‰ have lower $\delta^{13}C$ values (–20‰ to –18‰), indicating consumption of fertilized C_3 crops such as squash and chili peppers, both of which were found at Pica 8 (Núñez 1984). More recently we have learned that the $\delta^{15}N$ values observed from the human remains of Pica 8 were not indicative of marine resources but instead were a consequence of consuming crops fertilized with seabird guano as well as the consumption of the meat of camelids, which were probably enriched in ^{15}N (Julien 1985; Santana-Sagredo et al. 2017, 2021). This new line of evidence strongly supports the hypothesis that at least eight or nine camelids of Pica 8 (ca. 30% of the total samples analyzed here) were herded locally. However, we cannot discard the possibility that these camelids ate wild local C_4 grasses such as *Atriplex* sp. It must be noted that in other areas of the Andes, crops given to animals (and consumed by humans) were not fertilized and did not lead to enriched ^{15}N compositions (DeNiro 1988; Thornton et al. 2011; Verano and DeNiro 1993).

When comparing the $^{87}Sr/^{86}Sr$ values from the four textile samples interred in the Pica 8 cemetery to the values from salt concentrations from the Tarapacá lowlands (Cosentino and Jordan 2017) and altiplano volcanoes (Mamani, Tassara, and Wörner 2008; Mamani, Wörner, and Sempera 2010), results show that at least three of the samples fall close to the range expected for the Tarapacá lowlands. A fourth textile contained wool from a camelid whose range falls midway between Tarapacá lowland and altiplano ranges. This information indicates some textiles were made from camelids that had rather limited mobility, living primarily in the lowlands, for the period of time reflected in the fiber. This has important implications for herding as well as textile production, which probably occurred locally.

Comparative data from northern Chile and southern Peru allow additional insights. The carbon and nitrogen isotopic signatures of the Pica 8 camelids were significantly different from those from the Peruvian sites of Torata Alta and El Yaral, which were dominated by *puna* camelids (Thornton et al. 2011). Noteworthy, the stomach contents of the El Yaral camelids included lowland vegetation, suggesting they were probably based in the valleys for only a short time before their death. Surprisingly, the Pica 8 samples were not significantly different from those from the Middle Horizon site Cerro Baúl. It has been suggested that these Cerro Baúl camelids ($n = 3$) probably consumed *lomas* vegetation from the coastal valleys (Thornton et al. 2011).

Significant differences were also seen between Pica 8 and samples from Camarones and Lluta, in northern Chile. Researchers have concluded that the Camarones and Lluta camelid bone collagen and textile data point to LIP and LH camelids that originated in the *puna* and textiles that were made from highland camelids (Szpak and Valenzuela 2020). However, these authors have proposed that some individuals (based on their textile isotope composition) would have been locally herded in the western lowlands.

Clearly, Pica 8 generally differentiates from highland bone collagen and textile samples from the Camarones and Lluta Valleys, indicating that at least some Pica 8 camelids were from the lowlands. Perhaps this situation is part of the important variability and heterogeneity reported previously for camelid diets in southern and northern Peru (Dufour et al. 2014; 2020; Santana-Sagredo et al. 2020; Szpak et al. 2014, 2020; Szpak and Valenzuela 2020; Thornton et al. 2011). Camelid herding practices probably differed at the site level, with some individuals being locally herded but others being kept in the highlands. The decisions on whether to keep the camelids in the lowlands or bring them from the highlands were probably related to social, political, and cultural aspects by the local groups. Considering they were segmentary and autonomous groups with social diversity (Uribe 2006), there are different ways in which they could have managed camelids. In addition, the evidence strongly suggests that textile manufacture and raw material acquisition occurred locally.

CONCLUSIONS

With a few exceptions, our data strongly suggest that the Pica camelids were herded locally, where they consumed lowland agricultural products and vegetation affected by the aridity effect characteristic of the Atacama Desert, fertilization, or both. This has important repercussions for human dietary reconstruction since the ingestion of camelids enriched in ^{15}N can be easily confused with the consumption of marine resources.

In addition, $^{87}Sr/^{86}Sr$ on a small sample of textiles indicates that textile production occurred locally and supports the conclusion that camelids probably stayed on the oasis and did not travel to the *puna* or other high-altitude places. Larger-scale studies, zooarchaeological analyses, and investigation of other isotopes such as oxygen are needed to complement our $^{87}Sr/^{86}Sr$ data.

Our results have important implications for the local archaeology of Tarapacá and the Atacama Desert and for the understanding of camelid use in prehistory. Our results challenge the long-held assumption that camelids were exclusively highland animals and that their presence in the lowlands would have necessarily been related to highland caravan activity or importation of highland products, such as dry meat (*charki*), fibers, textiles, or leather. (Berenguer 2004; Núñez 1984; Núñez and Dillehay [1978] 1995). In the lowlands of Tarapacá, communities sustained small groups of local camelids through intensive agricultural activities, a situation, we propose, that is generalizable to the lowlands of southern Peru and northern Chile (Rostworowski 1986). In addition to providing an alternative view and calling for a reevaluation of old models, our results open important new lines of research for understanding camelid husbandry, textile production, and human and camelid diets in arid regions.

ACKNOWLEDGMENTS

We would like to thank FONDECYT Projects N°3180317, 1181829, 1191452, 1221166. We are also grateful to the Departamento de Antropología–Universidad de Chile and Instituto de Investigaciones Antropológicas–Universidad de Antofagasta for allowing access to their collections. We thank Nicole Barraux and Agustín Llagostera for their help.

REFERENCES

Agüero, Carolina. 1998. "Tradiciones Textiles de Atacama y Tarapacá Presentes en Quillagua Durante los Períodos Intermedio Tardío y Tardío." *Boletín del Comité Nacional de Conservación Textil* 3:103–28.

Agüero, Carolina. 2015. *Vestuario y Sociedad Andina: Desarrollo del Complejo Pica Tarapacá (800–1400 DC)*. San Pedro de Atacama: Universidad Católica del Norte.

Albarracín, Juan. 1996. *Tiwanaku: Arqueología Regional y Dinámica Segmentaria*. La Paz: Editorial Plural.

Anderson, M. J. 2001. "A New Method for Non-Parametric Multivariate Analysis of Variance." *Austral Ecology* 26 (1): 32–46. https://doi.org/10.1111/j.1442 -9993.2001.01070.pp.x.

Aravena, Ramón. 1995. "Isotope Hydrology and Geochemistry of Northern Chile Groundwaters." *Bulletin de l'Institut Français d'Études Andines* 24 (3): 495–503.

Berenguer, José. 2004. *Caravanas, Interacción y Cambio en el Desierto de Atacama.* Santiago: Sirawi Ediciones.

Bonavia, Duccio. 2008. *The South American Camelids.* Los Angeles: Cotsen Institute of Archaeology.

Copeland, Sandy. R., Matt Sponheimer, Petrus J. Le Roux, Vaughan Grimes, Julia A. Lee-Thorp, D. J. de Ruiter, and Michael P. Richards. 2008. "Strontium Isotope Ratios ($^{87}Sr/^{86}Sr$) of Tooth Enamel: A Comparison of Solution and Laser Ablation Multicollector Inductively Coupled Plasma Mass Spectrometry Methods." *Rapid Communications in Mass Spectrometry* 22 (20): 3187–94. https://doi.org/10.1002/rcm.3717.

Cosentino Nicolás, and Teresa Jordan. 2017. "$^{87}Sr/^{86}Sr$ of Calcium Sulfate in Ancient Soils of Hyperarid Settings as a Paleoaltitude Proxy: Pliocene to Quaternary Constraints for Northern Chile (19.5–21.7°S)." *Tectonics* 36: 137– 62. https://doi.org/10.1002/2016TC004185.

deFrance, Susan. D. 2016. "Pastoralism Through Time in Southern Peru." In *The Archaeology of Andean Pastoralism*, edited by José M Capriles and Nicolas Tripcevich, 119–38. Albuquerque: University of New Mexico Press.

Delpino, Doris. 2020. "Selección, Uso y Procesamiento de la Materia Prima Fibra en las Túnicas del Cementerio Pica-8 (Período Intermedio Tardío de la Región de Tarapacá, Norte de Chile)." Undergraduate diss., Universidad de Chile.

DeNiro, Michael. J. 1988. "Marine Food Sources for Prehistoric Coastal Peruvian Camelids: Isotopic Evidence and Implications." In *Economic Prehistory of the Central Andes*, edited by Elizabeth S. Wing and Jane C. Wheeler, BAR International Series 427, 119–28. Oxford: BAR.

Díaz, Francisca P., Matías Frugone, Rodrigo A. Gutiérrez, and Claudio Latorre. 2016. "Nitrogen Cycling in an Extreme Hyperarid Environment Inferred from $\delta^{15}N$ Analyses of Plants, Soils and Herbivore Diet." *Scientific Reports* 6: art. no. 22226. https://doi.org/10.1038/srep22226.

Dufour, Elise, Nicolas Goepfert, Belkys Gutiérrez Léon, Clause Chauchat, Régulo F. Jordán, and Segundo Vásquez Sánchez. 2014. "Pastoralism in Northern Peru During Pre-Hispanic Times: Insights from the Mochica Period (100–800 AD) Based on Stable Isotopic Analysis of Domestic Camelids." *PLoS One* 9 (1): e87559. https://doi.org/10.1371/journal.pone.0087559.

Dufour, Elise, Nicolas Goepfert, Manon Le Neün, Gabriel Prieto, and John W. Verano. 2020. "Life History and Origin of the Camelids Provisioning a Mass Killing Sacrifice During the Chimú Period: Insight from Stable Isotopes."

Environmental Archaeology 25 (3): 310–24. https://doi.org/10.1080/14614103 .2018.1498165.

Ehleringer, James, Philip Rundel, Beatriz Palma, and Harold A. Mooney. 1998. "Carbon Isotope Ratios of Atacama Desert Plants Reflect Hyperaridity of Region in Northern Chile." *Revista Chilena de Historia Natural* 71:79–86.

Evans, Richard D., and James R. Ehleringer. 1994. "Plant δ^{15}N Values Along a Fog Gradient in the Atacama Desert, Chile." *Journal of Arid Environments* 28 (3): 189–93. https://doi.org/10.1016/S0140-1963(05)80056-4.

Fernández, Jorge, and Héctor O. Panarello. 1999–2001. "Isótopos del Carbono en la Dieta de Herbívoros y Carnívoros de los Andes Jujeños." *Xama (Mendoza, Argentina)* 12–14:71–85. https://www.researchgate.net/profile/Hector -Panarello/publication/283123419_Isotopos_del_carbono_en_la_dieta_de _herbivoros_y_carnivoros_de_los_Andes_Jujenos/links/562bed3408ae22b 170337553/Isotopos-del-carbono-en-la-dieta-de-herbivoros-y-carnivoros-de -los-Andes-Jujenos.pdf.

Finucane, Brian, Patricia M. Agurto, and William H. Isbell. 2006. "Human and Animal Diet at Conchopata, Peru: Stable Isotope Evidence for Maize Agriculture and Animal Management Practices During the Middle Horizon." *Journal of Archaeological Science* 33 (12): 1766–76. https://doi.org/10.1016/j.jas .2006.03.012.

Frank, Eduardo, Michel Victor Hick, C. Gauna, Hugo Lamas, Carlo Renieri, and Marco Antonini. 2006. "Phenotypic and Genetic Description of Fibre Traits in South American Domestic Camelids (Llamas and Alpacas)." *Small Ruminant Research* 61 (2/3): 113–29. https://doi.org/10.1016/j.smallrumres .2005.07.003.

Gayo, Eugenia M., Claudio Latorre, Teresa Jordan, Peter L. Nester, Sergio A. Estay, Karla F. Ojeda, and Calogero M. Santoro. 2012. "Late Quaternary Hydrological and Ecological Changes in the Hyperarid Core of the Northern Atacama Desert (~21°S)." *Earth-Science Reviews* 113 (3/4): 120–40. https:// doi.org/10.1016/j.earscirev.2012.04.003.

Gayo, Eugenia M., Tracy Martens, Hillary Stuart-Williams, Jack Fenner, Calogero M. Santoro, Christopher Carter, and Judith Cameron. 2020. "Procurement of Camelid Fiber in the Hyperarid Atacama Desert Coast: Insights from Stable Isotopes." *Quaternary International* 548: 71–83. https://doi.org /10.1016/j.quaint.2019.12.008.

Herve, Maxime. 2019. *Package "RVAideMemoire," Diverse Basic Statistical and Graphical Functions (Version 0.9-52).* Vienna: R Foundation for Statistical Computing. https://cran.r-project.org/web/packages/RVAideMemoire /index.html.

Julien, Catherine. 1985. "Guano and Resource Control in Sixteenth-Century Arequipa." In *Andean Ecology and Civilization: An Interdisciplinary Perspective on Andean Ecological Complementarity*, edited by Shozo Masuda, Izumi Shimada, and Craig Morris, 185–231. Tokyo: University of Tokyo Press.

Latcham, Ricardo E. 1922. *Los Animales Domésticos de la América Precolombiana.* Santiago: Imprenta Cervantes.

Lemp, Cecilia, María Antonia Benavente, and Marcela Sepúlveda. 2018. "Fibras: Entre lo Vegetal, lo Animal y lo Humano." In *Vistiendo la Vida y la Muerte en Tarapacá: Período Formativo e Intermedio Tardío,* edited by Cecilia Lemp, 34–39. Santiago: Salviat.

López, Patricio, Isabel Cartajena, Rodrigo Loyola, Lautaro Núñez, and Carlos Carrasco. 2017. "The Use of Hunting and Herding Spaces: Stable Isotope Analysis of Late Archaic and Early Formative Camelids in the Tulan Transect (Puna de Atacama, Chile)." *International Journal of Osteoarchaeology* 27 (6): 1059–69. https://doi.org/10.1002/oa.2631.

Magaritz, Mordeckai, Ramón Aravena, Humberto Peña, Osamu Suzuki, and Alejandro Grilli. 1990. "Source of Ground Water in the Deserts of Northern Chile: Evidence of Deep Circulation of Ground Water from the Andes." *Groundwater* 28 (4): 513–17. https://doi.org/10.1111/j.1745-6584.1990.tb01706.x.

Mamani, Mirian, Andrés Tassara, and Gerhard Wörner. 2008. "Composition and Structural Control of Crustal Domains in the Central Andes." *Geochemistry, Geophysics, Geosystems* 9 (3): art. no. Q03006. https://doi.org/10.1029/2007GC001925.

Mamani, Mirian, G. Wörner, and Thierry Sempera. 2010. "Geochemical Variations in Igneous Rocks of the Central Andean Orocline (13°S to 18°S): Tracking Crustal Thickening and Magma Generation Through Time and Space." *Geological Society of America Bulletin* 122 (1/2): 162–82. https://doi.org/10.1130/B26538.1.

Múñoz, Iván, Carolina Agüero, and Daniela Valenzuela. 2016. "Poblaciones Prehispánicas de los Valles Occidentales del norte de Chile: Desde el Período Formativo al Intermedio Tardío (ca. 1000 años a.C. a 1400 años d.C.)." In *Prehistoria en Chile Desde sus Primeros Habitantes Hasta los Incas,* edited by Fernanda Falabella, Mauricio Uribe, Lorena Sanhueza, Carlos Aldunate, and Jorge Hidalgo, 181–238. Santiago: Editorial Universitaria.

Murra, John V. 1972. "El 'Control Vertical' de un Máximo de Pisos Ecológicos en la Economía de las Sociedades Andinas." In *Visita a la Provincia de León de Huánuco (1562),* 429–72. Huánuco: Universidad Hermilio Valdizan.

Nielsen, Axel. 2009. "Pastoralism and the Non-Pastoral World in the Late Pre-Columbian History of the Southern Andes (1000–1535)." *Nomadic People* 13 (2): 17–35. https://doi.org/10.3167/np.2009.130202.

Nielsen, Axel, José Berenguer, and Gonzalo Pimentel. 2019. "Inter-nodal Archaeology, Mobility, and Circulation in the Andes of Capricorn During the Late Intermediate Period (AD 1000–1450.)." *Quaternary International* 533:48–65. http://dx.doi.org/10.1016/j.quaint.2018.09.044.

Núñez, Lautaro. 1976. "Registro Regional de Fechas Radiocarbónicas del Norte de Chile." *Estudios Atacameños* 4:69–111.

Núñez, Lautaro. 1984. "Tráfico de Complementariedad de Recursos Entre las Tierras Altas y el Pacífico en el área centro-sur Andina." PhD diss., University of Tokyo.

Núñez, Lautaro, and Tom. D. Dillehay. (1978) 1995. *Movilidad Giratoria, Armonía Social y Desarrollo en los Andes Meridionales: Patrones de Tráfico e Interacción Económica; Ensayo*. Antofagasta: Universidad Católica del Norte.

O'Connell, Tamsin C., and Robert E. M. Hedges. 1999. "Investigations into the Effect of Diet on Modern Human Hair Isotopic Values." *American Journal of Physical Anthropology* 108 (4): 409–25. https://doi.org/10.1002/(sici)1096 -8644(199904)108:4%3C409::aid-ajpa3%3E3.0.co;2-e.

Oksanen, Jari, Guillaume Blanchet, Michael Friendly, and Roeland Kindt. 2016. *Vegan: Community Ecology Package. R package version 2.4-3.* Vienna: R Foundation for Statistical Computing. https://cran.r-project.org/web/packages /vegan/vegan.pdf.

Pimentel, Gonzalo, Mariana Ugarte, José Blanco, Christina Torres-Rouff, and William J. Pestle. 2017. "Calate: De Lugar Desnudo a Laboratorio Arqueológico de la Movilidad y el Tráfico Intercultural Prehispánico en el Desierto de Atacama (ca. 7000 AP–550 AP)." *Estudios Atacameños* 56:21–56.

Pin, Christian, Danielle Briot, Chantal Bassin, and Franck Poitrasson. 1994. "Concomitant Separation of Strontium and Samarium-Neodymium for Isotopic Analysis in Silicate Samples, based on Specific Extraction Chromatography." *Analytica Chimica Acta* 298:209–17.

Rostworowski, María. 1986. "La Región del Colesuyu." *Chungará Revista Chilena de Antropología* 16/17:127–35.

Santana-Sagredo, Francisca. 2016. "From the Andes to the Coast: Human Mobility and Diet in the Atacama Desert During the Late Intermediate Period (AD 900–1450)." PhD diss., University of Oxford.

Santana-Sagredo, Francisca, Elise Dufour, Nicolas Goepfert, Antoine Zazzo, Régulo Franco Jordán, and Segundo Vásquez Sánchez. 2020. "New Bioarchaeological Evidence and Radiocarbon Dates from the Lambayeque/Sicán Culture Camelids from the El Brujo Complex (Northern Coast of Peru): Implications for Funerary and Herd Management Practices." *Environmental Archaeology* 25 (3): 333–52. https://doi.org/10.1080/14614103.2018.1556960.

Santana-Sagredo, Francisca, Julia A. Lee-Thorp, Rick Schulting, and Mauricio Uribe. 2015. "Isotopic Evidence for Divergent Diets and Mobility Patterns in the Atacama Desert, Northern Chile, During the Late Intermediate Period (AD 900–1450)." *American Journal of Physical Anthropology* 156 (3): 374–87. http://dx.doi.org/10.1002/ajpa.22663.

Santana-Sagredo, Francisca, Rick Schulting, Julia A. Lee-Thorp, Carolina Agüero, Mauricio Uribe, and Cecilia Lemp. 2017. "Paired Radiocarbon Dating on Human Samples and Camelid Fibers and Textiles from Northern Chile: The Case of Pica 8 (Tarapacá)." *Radiocarbon* 59 (4): 1195–213. http://dx.doi.org /10.1017/RDC.2017.36.

Santana-Sagredo, Francisca, Rick Schulting, Pablo Méndez-Quiros, Ale Vidal-Elgueta, Mauricio Uribe, Rodrigo Loyola, Anahí Maturana-Fernández, et al. 2021. "'White Gold' Guano Fertilizer Drove Agricultural Intensification in the Atacama Desert from AD 1000." *Nature Plants* 7 (2): 152–58. http://dx .doi.org/10.1038/s41477-020-00835-4.

Santana-Sagredo, Francisca, and Mauricio Uribe. 2019. "New Perspectives on Movements of Humans, Animals, and Materials in the South-Central Andes from the Early Peopling to the Inca Empire (11000 BC–AD 1540): A Multidisciplinary Approach." *Quaternary International* 533:1–6. http://dx.doi .org/10.1016/j.quaint.2019.11.047.

Sepúlveda, Marcela, Cecilia Lemp, José Cárcamo-Vega, Edgar Casanova-González, Sebastián Gutiérrez, Miguel Ángel Maynez-Rojas, Benjamín Ballester, and José Luis Ruvalcaba-Sil. 2021. "Colors and Dyes of the Archaeological Textiles from Tarapacá in the Atacama Desert (South Central Andes)." *Heritage Science* 9: art. no. 59. https://doi.org/10.1186/s40494-021-00538-9.

Shimada, Melody, and Izumi Shimada. 1985. "Prehistoric Llama Breeding and Herding on the North Coast of Peru." *American Antiquity* 50 (1): 3–26. https:// doi.org/10.2307/280631.

Szpak, Paul, Jean-François Millaire, Claude Chapdelaine, Christine D. White, and Fred J. Longstaffe. 2020. "An Integrated Isotopic Study of Early Intermediate Period Camelid Husbandry in the Santa Valley, Perú." *Environmental Archaeology* 25 (3): 279–95. https://doi.org/10.1080/14614103.2019.1583302.

Szpak, Paul, Jean-Francois Millaire, Christine D. White, and Fred J. Longstaffe. 2012. "Influence of Seabird Guano and Camelid Dung Fertilization on the Nitrogen Isotopic Composition of Field-Grown Maize (*Zea mays*)." *Journal of Archaeological Science* 39 (12): 3721–40. https://doi.org/10.1016/j.jas.2012 .06.035.

Szpak, Paul, Jean-François Millaire, Christine D. White and Fred J. Longstaffe. 2014. "Small Scale Camelid Husbandry on the North Coast of Peru (Virú Valley): Insight from Stable Isotope Analysis." *Journal of Anthropological Archaeology* 36:110–29. https://doi.org/10.1016/j.jaa.2014.08.005.

Szpak, Paul, and Daniela Valenzuela. 2020. "Camelid Husbandry in the Atacama Desert? A Stable Isotope Study of Camelid Bone Collagen and Textiles from the Lluta and Camarones Valleys, Northern Chile." *PLoS One* 15 (3): e0228332. https://doi.org/10.1371/journal.pone.0228332.

Szpak, Paul, Christine D. White, Fred J. Longstaffe, Jean-Francois Millaire, and Víctor F. Vásquez-Sánchez. 2013. "Carbon and Nitrogen Isotopic Survey of Northern Peruvian Plants: Baselines for Paleodietary and Paleoecological Studies." *PLoS One* 8 (1): e53763. https://doi.org/10.1371/journal.pone.0053763.

Thornton, Erin K., Susan D. deFrance, John Krigbaum, and Patrick R. Williams. 2011. "Isotopic Evidence for Middle Horizon to 16th Century Camelid Herding in the Osmore Valley, Peru." *International Journal of Osteoarchaeology* 21 (5): 544–67. http://dx.doi.org/10.1002/oa.1157.

Tieszen, Larry L., and Michael Chapman. 1995. "Carbon and Nitrogen Isotopic Status of the Major Marine and Terrestrial Resources in the Atacama Desert of Northern Chile." In *Actas del I Congreso Internacional de Estudios Sobre Momias, 1992/Proceedings of the I World Congress on Mummy Studies, 1992*, 2:409–25. [Tenerife]: Museo Arquelógico y Etnográfico de Tenerife, Organismo Autónomo de Museos y Centros.

Uribe, Mauricio. 2006. "Acerca de complejidad, desigualdad social y el complejo cultural Pica-Tarapacá en los Andes Centro-Sur (1000-1450 DC)." *Estudios Atacameños* 31:91–114.

Uribe, Mauricio, Lorena Sanhueza, and Francisco Bahamondes. 2007. "La Cerámica Prehispánica Tardía de Tarapacá, sus Valles Interiores y Costa Desértica, Norte de Chile (ca. 900–1.450 dC): Una Propuesta Tipológica y Cronológica." *Chungará Revista Chilena de Antropología* 39 (2): 143–70. http://dx.doi.org/10.4067/S0717-73562007000200001.

Vásquez, Víctor F., Ramón Redondo, Teresa E. Rosales, Gabriel Dorado, and V. Peiró. 2020. "Osteometric and Isotopic (δ^{13}C and δ^{15}N) Evidence of Pre-Hispanic Camelid-Herd Breeding in Moche Site of 'Huaca de la Luna' (North Coast of Peru)." *Journal of Archaeological Science: Reports* 29: art. no. 102083. https://doi.org/10.1016/j.jasrep.2019.102083.

Verano John W., Michael J. DeNiro. 1993. "Local or Foreigners? Morphological, Biometric and Isotopic Approaches to the Question of Group Affinity in Human Skeletal Remains Recovered from Unusual Archaeological Contexts." In *Investigations of Ancient Human Tissue: Chemical Analysis in Anthropology*, edited by Mary K. Sandford, 261–386. Langhorne: Gordon and Breach.

Yacobaccio, Hugo D., Marcelo R. Morales, and Celeste T. Samec. 2009. "Towards an Isotopic Ecology of Herbivory in the Puna Ecosystem: New Results and Patterns on *Lama Glama*." *International Journal of Osteoarchaeology* 19 (2): 144–55. https://doi.org/10.1002/oa.1050.

Zlatar, Vjera. 1984. *Cementerio Prehispánico Pica-8*. Antofagasta: Universidad de Antofagasta.

PART IV

BUILDING THE INKA EMPIRE WITH SACRED AND HIGH-STATUS FOODS

13

The Dietary Impact of the Inka's Political Strategies in the Semi-Arid Region (30°–31° S. Lat) of Northern Chile

Marta Alfonso-Durruty, Nicole Misarti, and Andrés Troncoso

The role of food in political dynamics as well as in the construction, expression, and negotiation of identity and power can be unveiled through the analysis of stable isotopes. Within the Inka state, food and feasting played relevant noncoercive roles in imperial political strategies that aimed to establish meaningful relationships with local communities. The importance of political commensalism is apparent in the provinces of the Tawantinsuyu, where Inka culinary equipment and vessels (especially *aryballos* for *chicha*) signaled the incorporation of local elites into the Inka's political and symbolic sphere (Dillehay 2002; Bray 2003a, 2003b; Cuéllar 2013; Giovannetti 2015).

The Inka conquest, however, required the implementation of different political strategies that emerged from the entanglement of local histories, the particularities of the Inka's strategic expansion, and the unique political relations established between the state and the local communities (Alconini and Malpass 2010; D'Altroy 2005; Hayashida, Troncoso, and Salazar 2022; Kosiba 2018; Malpass and Alconini 2010). Thus, while the Inka conquest commonly led to an intensification of maize production, the variable political strategies resulted in a heterogeneous productive landscape where people in some provinces experienced a decline in maize production and consumption (Falabella, Planella, and Tykot 2008). Considering the above, this chapter assesses the impact of the Inka in the Semi-Arid Region of Northern Chile (SARNC), one of the southernmost provinces of the Tawantinsuyu.

The SARNC (29°–33°; map 13.1) is an arid strip of land where precipitations oscillate interannually and increase from north to south (~25–400 mm/year; Jenny et al. 2002; Maldonado et al. 2016; Maldonado and Villagrán 2002, 2006; Veit 1996). The drastic drop in altitude from east (Andean Mountains) to west (Pacific Ocean), means that the SARNC's lands and rivers descend quickly through a landscape that changes dramatically from highlands into valleys and the coast. A wide diversity of mammals, birds, and vegetation are present in this area. Historic documents describe the production of large quantities of maize, beans, potatoes, gourds, and quinoa as well as a "wine" made of a mixture of algarroba and maize. Other food items included algarroba, prickly pears, and possibly the fruits of the chañar tree (*Geoffroea decorticans*; de Bibar 1558).

In this study, we examine stable isotope data collected from individuals found at Late Intermediate Period (LIP; Diaguita culture, 1000–1450 CE) and Late Period (LP; Inka-Diaguita culture, 1450–1540 CE) archaeological sites in the inland of the SARNC valleys (map 13.1). During the LIP, the first sedentary agriculturalist groups settled in lands particularly apt for cultivation. These relatively self-sufficient groups, known as Diaguitas, practiced a mixed economy of agriculture (including maize) and the hunting and gathering of inland (e.g., guanaco) and marine resources (Troncoso, Cantarutti, and González 2016). The intervalley variability in material culture suggests the Diaguita were organized as a segmentary society. At the regional level, however, they shared a way of life, modes of production, and a common aesthetic code (Troncoso, Cantarutti, and González 2016; González 2013). The homogeneity of the funeral contexts as well as the household-level production of ceramics reveals low levels of hierarchy or social differentiation (Troncoso, Cantarutti, and González 2016; Ampuero 1994). Some individuals, probably associated with the consumption of hallucinogenic substances, achieved leadership status and were endowed with limited local power (Troncoso, Cantarutti, and González 2016; González 2013).

The SARNC was incorporated into the Tawantinsuyu approximately 1450 CE. The Inka's presence is revealed in the construction of roads, tambos, ceremonial-administrative centers, high-altitude sanctuaries, and sites associated with metallurgic production (Ampuero 1994; Stehberg 1995; Ampuero and Hidalgo 1975). The acculturation process is most visible in the hybridization between the Diaguita and Inka ceramics (Inka-Diaguita), which are found both in domestic and funerary sites (González 2008, 2013). Other changes are also observed in rock art and metallurgic styles (Troncoso, Cantarutti, and González 2016).

The SARNC's incorporation into the Tawantinsuyu was probably operationalized by neighboring groups from northwestern Argentina who

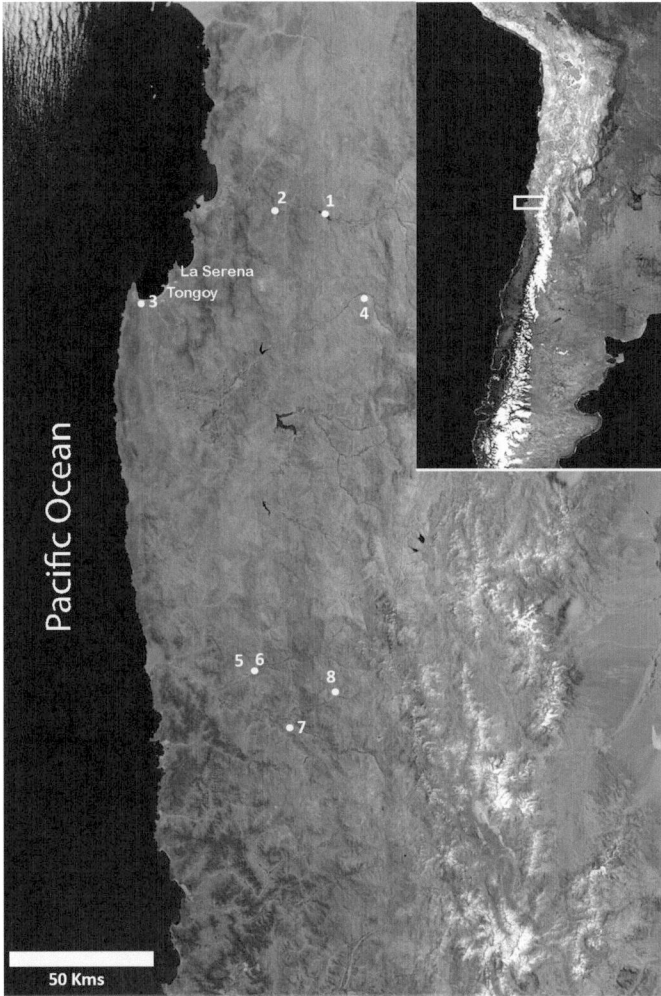

Map 13.1 Map of the SARNC. *1*, Puclaro. *2*, Punta de Piedra. *3*, Los Pozos. *4*, La Turquía. *5*, Independencia–O'Higgins. *6*, Estadio Illapel. *7*, Pisco Control. *8*, Loma El Arenal. Image by Alfonso-Durruty, Misarti, and Troncoso.

established relations with the leaders of the Diaguita groups (Stehberg 1995; Ampuero and Hidalgo 1975; Cantarutti 2004; Troncoso 2018, 2022; Castillo 1998). The absence of pukaras suggests the relation between the Inka and the Diaguita was not openly violent (Ampuero 1994; González 2013; Stehberg 1995). Also, the presence of Diaguita-Inka pottery in central Chile, the Atacama Desert, and central-west Argentina seem to reflect a political alliance between Inkas and Diaguitas (Castillo 1998). Changes in the SARNC, however, suggest (1) an increase in population and individual movements promoted by Inka practices (e.g., *mit-maqkuna*) and facilitated by the construction of roads and tambos (Troncoso, Cantarutti, and González 2016; Uribe and Sánchez 2016; Stehberg 1995; Ampuero and Hidalgo 1975); (2) a complex social situation where a high degree of cultural, and possibly populational, diversity emerged from new relations with, at least, groups in the northwest and center-west regions of Argentina and the circumtiticaca area (González 1995; Cantarutti 2004); and (3) a process of acculturation that was neither harmonious nor egalitarian (Troncoso, Cantarutti, and González 2016; Stehberg 1995; Ampuero and Hidalgo 1975).

While the settlement pattern remained mostly unchanged (Ampuero 1994; Troncoso 2018), agriculture was intensified with a particular emphasis on maize production (González 2013; Llagostera 1976; Troncoso et al. 2009; Cantarutti 2013). However, evidence of ancient agricultural fields in the SARNC is absent because of contemporary agricultural practices. Coastal and mineral resources probably circulated within the established Inka network in the southern Andes. Funerary contexts became richer and included metallic pieces (Cantarutti 2004; Troncoso 2018), while maize consumption rose, possibly because of the state's labor taxation and the popularity of this staple among the Inkas (Ampuero and Hidalgo 1975; Belmar and Quiroz 2006; Troncoso 2004; Troncoso et al. 2009). Along with the Diaguita, small mobile groups lived in the SARNC during the LIP and LP. They buried their ancestors in the summit of hills, probably inhabited rock shelters, and are associated with a the distinctive Molle pottery.

INDIVIDUALS AND METHODS

Bone samples were collected from 39 individuals (table 13.1) found at eight inland archaeological sites (map 13.1). Four sites are ascribed to each period (table 13.2). All individuals were assigned to the LIP or LP based on the archaeological context and radiocarbon dates when available (table 13.1). All LIP individuals are associated with Diaguita sites and/or material culture. All but one (UGAMS 9636) LP individual are associated with Diaguita-Inka sites/material culture or are dated post AD 1450. The exception corresponds to one individual from La Turquia, whose inhumation is related to a mobile group that used Molle pottery and inhabited the SARNC during the sixteenth century.

Thirty-nine samples were analyzed for carbon-13 in apatite ($\delta^{13}C_{ap}$) and collagen ($\delta^{13}C_{col}$) and nitrogen-15 ($\delta^{15}N$). Eight samples were analyzed at the Center for Applied Isotope Studies at the University of Georgia (CAIS; table 13.1).[1] The remaining 31 samples were analyzed at the Alaska Stable Isotope Facility (ASIF; table 13.1) following established procedures (Alfonso-Durruty et al. 2017; Misarti et al. 2009). Stable isotope ratios are expressed in parts per mill. The $\delta^{13}C$ ratios are expressed relative to Vienna Pee Dee Belemnite (VPDB), and those for $\delta^{15}N$ are expressed relative to atmospheric air (N_2 air). Differences in $\delta^{13}C_{apatite}$ and $\delta^{13}C_{collagen}$ ($\Delta^{13}C_{ap-col}$) were calculated for all individuals that had results for both.

Carbon to nitrogen ratios (C/N) were calculated in 38 individuals (table 13.1). Ratios for all but one (01PCS12) of the analyzed samples fall within the acceptable range (2.9–3.6) indicating good preservation (Hedges, Stevens, and Koch 2005; Koch, Fogel, and Tuross 1994; Tuross, Fogel, and Hare 1988). Results obtained from 01PCS12 were excluded from further analyses. The C/N ratio could not be calculated for LEAE25 because of incomplete data. Individual LEAE25's stable isotope results are within the range observed for other individuals and were therefore deemed acceptable for analysis.

Statistical analyses were conducted in SPSS 27.0 and included the calculation of standard descriptive statistics by period and site.[2] Normality was assessed with Kolmogorov-Smirnov tests. Deviations from normality were identified in $\delta^{13}C_{col}$, $\Delta^{13}C_{ap-col}$, and $\delta^{15}N$ ($p < .05$) among individuals from the LP. Thus, parametric t-tests were used in the comparison of $\delta^{13}C_{ap}$ between the periods, whereas nonparametric Mann-Whitney tests were applied to all other variables. An individual with outlier values for $\delta^{15}N$ was identified (Los Pozos UGAMS 9638) and removed from the analysis. After the removal of UGAMS 9638, normality

---

1. The stable isotope methods used at UGAMS are described at http://siel.uga.edu/laboratory-capabilities/animal-analysis.

2. IBM SPSS Statistics for Windows, ver 27.0, 2020.

Table 13.1 Stable isotope results by individual

Period and site	Code	Lab	Burial	Date BP	$\delta^{13}C_{ap}$ (‰)	$\delta^{13}C_{col}$ (‰)	$\Delta^{13}C_{ap}-\delta^{13}C_{col}$ (‰)	$\delta^{15}N$ (‰)	c/n ratio	Reference
Late Intermediate Period (1000–1450 CE)										
Loma El Arenal	21LEAE28	ASIF	28		−7.72	−13.37	5.65	5.57	2.87	Alfonso-Durruty et al. 2017
Loma El Arenal	22LEAE11	ASIF	11		−7.75	−12.84	5.09	5.83	2.88	Alfonso-Durruty et al. 2017
Loma El Arenal	UGAMS 8317	CAIS	9	460±25		−16.50		8.80	3.51	Alfonso-Durruty et al. 2017
Loma El Arenal	UGAMS 8318	CAIS	13	490±25		−12.10		8.00	3.66	Alfonso-Durruty et al. 2017
Loma El Arenal	UGAMS 8316	CAIS	4	560±25		−10.60		7.30	3.66	Alfonso-Durruty et al. 2017
Loma El Arenal	UGAMS 8319	CAIS	24	620±25		−12.20		6.70	3.26	Alfonso-Durruty et al. 2017
Loma El Arenal	LEAE25	CAIS	25	500±30		−11.60		6.50	n/a	Alfonso-Durruty et al. 2017
Loma El Arenal	23LEAE26	ASIF	26		−6.31	−11.45	5.14	8.47	3.07	Alfonso-Durruty et al. 2017
Punta de Piedra	MCH-143	ASIF	6		−5.74	−9.45	3.71	11.50	3.36	
Punta de Piedra	MCH-141	ASIF	13148		−5.88	−9.74	3.85	9.21	3.21	
Punta de Piedra	MCH-140	ASIF	80–1		−5.08	−9.26	4.18	11.39	3.26	
Independencia/ Ohiggins Illapel	MCH-125	ASIF	No number		−5.14	−11.57	6.43	6.54	3.24	
Los Pozos	UGAMS 9638	CAIS	No context	780±20	−5.30	−10.20	4.90	19.40	3.31	Alfonso-Durruty et al. 2017
Late period (1450–1540 CE)										
Pisco Control	14PCS6	ASIF	6		−7.26	−12.46	5.20	8.86	2.91	Alfonso-Durruty et al. 2017
Pisco Control	03PCS15	ASIF	15		−6.40	−12.21	5.81	9.29	3.03	Alfonso-Durruty et al. 2017
Pisco Control	01PCS12	ASIF	12			−11.68		8.17	2.82	Alfonso-Durruty et al. 2017

Group	Lab	Sample		Age (BP)						Reference
Pisco Control	ASIF	13PCS4	4		-6.95	-12.06	5.11	8.38	2.89	Alfonso-Durruty et al. 2017
Pisco Control	ASIF	08PSC111	Individual 1		-7.09	-12.25	5.16	9.80	2.92	Alfonso-Durruty et al. 2017
Pisco Control	ASIF	10PCS13	13		-7.46	-13.32	5.86	8.43	3.08	Alfonso-Durruty et al. 2017
Pisco Control	ASIF	09PSC10	10		-7.56	-13.92	6.36	9.61	3.01	Alfonso-Durruty et al. 2017
Pisco Control	ASIF	20PCS2	2		-7.87	-13.70	5.83	9.30	2.90	Alfonso-Durruty et al. 2017
Pisco Control	ASIF	15PCS15	5		-6.35	-15.15	8.80	8.39	3.56	Alfonso-Durruty et al. 2017
Pisco Control	ASIF	06PCS11	11		-7.60	-12.45	4.85	9.97	2.85	Alfonso-Durruty et al. 2017
Pisco Control	ASIF	05PCS8	8		-8.50	-14.14	5.64	9.72	3.11	Alfonso-Durruty et al. 2017
Pisco Control	ASIF	16PCS7	7		-6.58	-12.45	5.87	9.66	3.08	Alfonso-Durruty et al. 2017
Pisco Control	ASIF	04PCS14	14		-7.09	-12.65	5.56	9.81	3.08	Alfonso-Durruty et al. 2017
Pisco Control	ASIF	02PCsS9	9		-7.30	-13.57	6.27	6.99	3.21	Alfonso-Durruty et al. 2017
Pisco Control	ASIF	12PCS3	3		-5.80	-12.45	6.65	9.61	3.06	Alfonso-Durruty et al. 2017
Puclaro	ASIF	MCH-138	9		-6.10	-11.54	5.44	7.86	3.23	Alfonso-Durruty et al. 2017
Puclaro	ASIF	MCH-137	7a-208		-5.18	-9.37	4.19	9.77	3.21	Alfonso-Durruty et al. 2017
Puclaro	ASIF	MCH-136	7a-208		-6.09	-11.52	5.43	8.44	3.30	Alfonso-Durruty et al. 2017
Puclaro	ASIF	MCH-131	7.2		-7.78	-12.36	4.58	8.31	3.25	Alfonso-Durruty et al. 2017
Puclaro	ASIF	MCH-133	11		-8.27	-11.82	3.54	16.67	3.27	Alfonso-Durruty et al. 2017
Puclaro	ASIF	MCH-127	5		-7.39	-13.06	5.66	8.86	3.23	Alfonso-Durruty et al. 2017
Puclaro	ASIF	MCH-132	14		-8.31	-14.48	6.17	7.20	3.29	Alfonso-Durruty et al. 2017
Puclaro	ASIF	MCH-134	11		-8.45	-16.73	8.27	6.06	3.18	Alfonso-Durruty et al. 2017
Puclaro	ASIF	MCH-139	80-9		-10.21	-17.65	7.44	6.41	3.29	Alfonso-Durruty et al. 2017
La Turquia	CAIS	UGAMS 9636	No number	410±20	-4.00	-12.20	8.20	10.90	3.39	Alfonso-Durruty et al. 2017
Estadio Illapel	CAIS	UGAMS 8315	7	410±25	-7.90			9.10	3.41	Alfonso-Durruty et al. 2017

Note: CAIS, UGAMS = Center for Applied Isotope Studies at the University of Georgia; ASIF = Alaska Stable Isotope Facility.

Kolmogorov-Smirnov tests were run, and no deviation from normality was identified for $\delta^{15}N$. Thus, additional parametric *t*-tests were used to compare $\delta^{15}N$ between the two periods.

Variation within periods was assessed through between-site comparisons. Four of the eight sites (Independencia/O'Higgins/Illapel, Los Pozos, Estadio Illapel, and La Turquía) are represented by a single individual, and Loma El Arenal and Punta de Piedra are represented by only three individuals each. This hindered statistical comparisons between LIP sites. Late Period sites represented by enough individuals to permit comparisons (Pisco Control and Puclaro) were assessed for normality. In Pisco Control, both $\delta^{13}C_{ap}$ and $\delta^{15}N$ showed normal distributions, but $\delta^{13}C_{col}$ and $\Delta^{13}C_{ap\text{-}col}$ did not. Normality tests for Puclaro show all but $\delta^{15}N$ variables to be normally distributed. Thus, all variables, except for $\delta^{15}N$, were compared with nonparametric Mann-Whitney tests. The $\delta^{15}N$ was compared between these two sites using parametric *t*-tests.

The R package simmr 0.4.5 (Parnell and Inger 2021) was used to determine the proportions of each resource in the diets consumed during each period. For the Bayesian math behind mixing models, see Parnell et al. (2013). Initial analyses included all resources, both marine and terrestrial, for which we had regional data (from this study as well as previously published by us and other authors). Based on the initial outcome, a second analysis that included only terrestrial resources was performed.

RESULTS

Results obtained by individual, site, and period are presented in tables 13.1, 13.2, and 13.3, respectively. Both $\delta^{13}C_{ap}$ and $\delta^{13}C_{col}$ appeared more enriched among LIP individuals. The range for both $\delta^{13}C_{ap}$ and $\delta^{13}C_{col}$ is wider among LP individuals than LIP ones. The $\Delta^{13}C_{ap\text{-}col}$ results show that while LIP individuals are, on average, <5.2‰, LP peoples are >5.2‰. Late Period individuals have slightly enriched $\delta^{15}N$ values in relation to LIP ones, which supports the differences identified for $\Delta^{13}C_{ap\text{-}col}$.

Between-period comparisons showed significant differences in $\delta^{13}C_{ap}$ ($t = 2.08$; df = 30; $p < .05$), and $\delta^{13}C_{col}$ ($U = 86.5$, $p < .05$), which resulted from LIP individuals been comparatively enriched (fig. 13.1*A, B*; table 13.2). Comparisons of $\Delta^{13}C_{ap\text{-}col}$ showed significant differences between the periods ($U = 46.0$, $p < .05$; fig. 13.1*C*). No significant differences

Table 13.2 Stable isotope results by site

Period	Site	$\delta^{13}C_{ap}$				$\delta^{13}C_{col}$				$\Delta^{13}C_{ap\text{-}col}$				$\delta^{15}N$			
		n	Mean	sd	Range	n	Mean	sd	Range	n	Mean	sd	Range	n	Mean	sd	Range
Late Intermediate (1000–1450 CE)	Independencia/ O'Higgins/ Illapel	1	−5.1			1	−11.6			1	6.4			1	6.5		
	Loma El Arenal	3	−7.3	0.8	−7.8 to −6.3	8	−12.6	1.8	−16.5 to −10.6	3	5.3	0.3	5.1 to 5.7	8	7.1	1.2	5.6 to 8.8
	Los Pozos	1	−5.3			1	−10.2			1	4.9			1	19.4		
	Punta de Piedra	3	−5.6	0.4	−5.9 to −5.1	3	−9.5	0.2	−9.7 to −9.3	3	3.9	0.2	3.7 to 4.2	3	10.7	1.3	9.2 to 11.5
Late (1450– 1540 CE)	Estadio Illapel	0				1	−7.9			0				1	9.1		
	La Turquia	1	−4.0			1	−12.2			1	8.2			1	10.9		
	Pisco Control	14	−7.1	0.7	−8.5 to −5.8	14	−13.1	0.9	−15.2 to −12.6	14	5.9	1.0	4.9 to 8.8	14	9.1	0.8	7.00 to 10.0
	Puclaro	9	−7.5	1.5	−10.2 to −5.2	9	−13.2	2.7	−17.7 to −9.4	9	5.6	1.5	3.5 to 8.3	9	8.8	3.2	6.1 to 16.7

Note: n = sample size; sd = standard deviation.

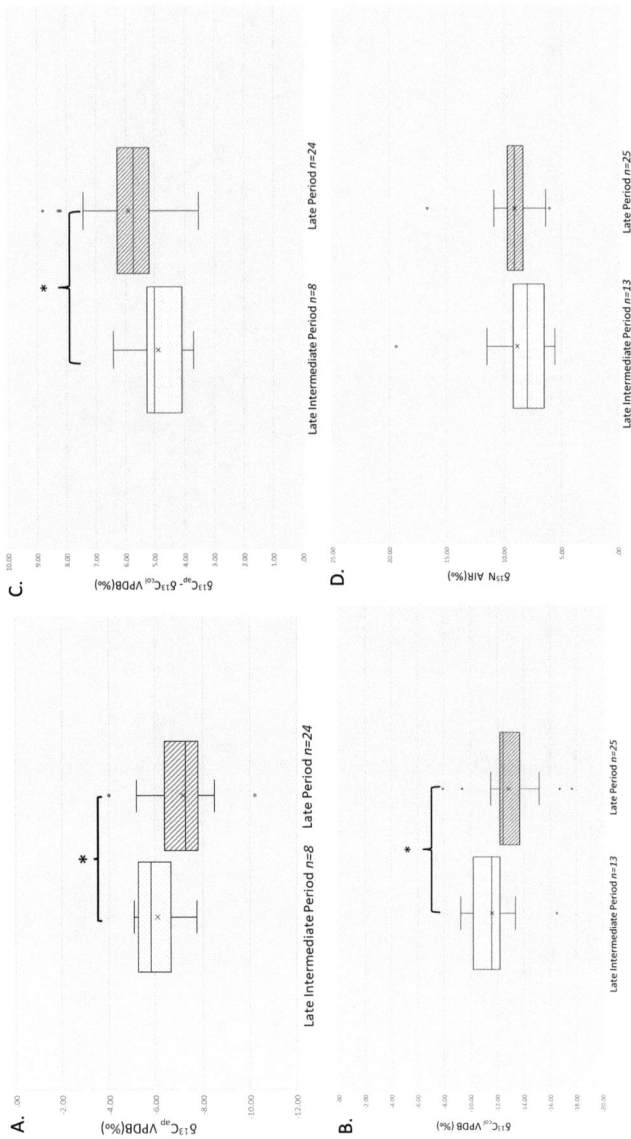

Figure 13.1 Results obtained for the Late Intermediate and Late Period individuals included in this study for (*A*) $\delta^{13}C_{ap}$, (*B*) $\delta^{13}C_{col}$, (*C*) $\Delta 13C_{ap-col}$, and (*D*) $\delta^{15}N$. An asterisk identifies the presence of a statistically significant difference ($p < .05$) between the periods. Image by Alfonso-Durruty, Misarti, and Troncoso.

Table 13.3 Stable isotope results by period

Period	$\delta^{13}C_{ap}$ (‰)					$\delta^{13}C_{col}$ (‰)					$\delta^{13}C_{ap}$ - $\delta^{13}C_{col}$ (‰)					$\delta^{15}N$ (‰)				
	n	X	µ	sd	Range	n	X	µ	sd	Range	n	X	µ	sd	Range	n	X	µ	sd	Range
Late Intermediate (1000–1450 CE)	8	−6.1	−5.8	1.1	−7.8 to −5.1	13	−11.6	−11.6	2.0	−16.5 to −9.3	8	4.9	5.0	0.9	3.7 to 6.4	13	8.9	8.0	3.7	5.6 to 19.4
Late (1450–1540 CE)	24	−7.1	−7.3	1.3	−10.2 to −4.0	25	−12.9	−12.5	2.0	−17.7 to −7.9	24	5.9	5.7	1.3	3.5 to 8.8	25	9.1	9.1	2.0	6.1 to 16.7

Note: n = sample size; X= mean; µ=median; sd = standard deviation.

in $\delta^{15}N$ between the periods were identified ($U = 121.0, p > .05$; fig. 13.1*D*; table 13.2). However, the individual from Los Pozos presents a very high $\delta^{15}N$ compared to all other LIP individuals (table 13.1). When removed from the analysis, the absence of statistically significant differences between the periods remained ($t = -1.6$, df = 35; $p > .5$).

Because of the limited number of individuals, no statistical comparisons between LIP sites were conducted. Results obtained, however, suggest there were some biologically significant variabilities (table 13.3). In particular, the individuals from Loma El Arenal are enriched in their $\delta^{13}C_{ap}$ and $\delta^{13}C_{col}$. Individuals from Independencia/O'Higgins/Illapel and Loma El Arenal show a $\Delta^{13}C_{ap-col}$ that is >5.2‰, whereas the results from Los Pozos and Punta de Piedra are below this threshold. Accordingly, $\delta^{15}N$ is most enriched in the Los Pozos individual, followed by those found at Punta de Piedra. The individual from Independencia/O'Higgins/Illapel presents the lowest value (table 13.3).

During the LP (table 13.3), the individual from La Turquía shows comparatively lower $\delta^{13}C_{ap}$ and higher $\delta^{13}C_{col}$, $\Delta^{13}C_{ap-col}$, and $\delta^{15}N$. These results are coherent with the association of this inhumation to mobile groups inhabiting this territory during the Late Period, who differed from the Diaguita-Inka communities. Individuals from Puclaro and Pisco Control are similar (table 13.3). Comparisons between these two sites showed no significant differences in $\delta^{13}C_{ap}$ ($U = 50.0, p > .05$), $\delta^{13}C_{col}$ ($U = 52.0, p < .05$), $\Delta^{13}C_{ap-col}$ ($U = 50.0, p > .05$), or $\delta^{15}N$ ($t = .33$, df = 21, $p > .05$).

When individual SI values are plotted along with those of all resource data available for this geographic region (fig. 13.2*A*) it is apparent that marine resources did not significantly contribute to the diet of LIP or LP individuals. Because the initial simmr analysis could not clearly distinguish resource proportions for either period, a second analysis that excluded marine resources was conducted. Results revealed (fig. 13.2*B*, *C*) that C_4 plants dominated above all other LIP and LP dietary resource contributions, although they declined from the LIP (~45% of the diet) into the LP (~35% of the diet). Camelids were LIP and LP groups' main source of animal protein. The dietary contribution of camelid resources from the lowlands, highlands, and coast increased from the LIP into the LP (fig. 13.2*B*, *C*). Both LP and LIP peoples consumed terrestrial birds (*Rhea* sp.) of highland origins in small and similar proportions (fig. 13.2*B*, *C*).

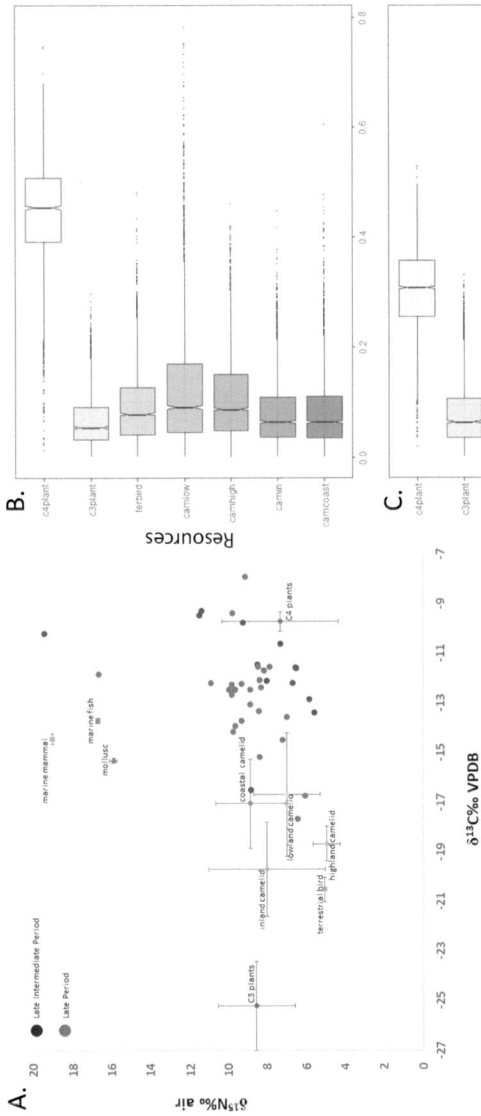

Figure 13.2 Individual carbon and isotope ratios plotted with potential dietary resources (*A*). Notice the absence of marine resources contribution (except for two cases, one for each period). SIMRR-produced boxplot interpretations of the proportions of each resource in group diets during the LIP (*B*) and LP (*C*), without marine resources. *C4plant* = maize; *C3plant* = plants such as quinoa; *terbirds* = terrestrial birds (in this case two species of *Rhea*); *camlow* = lowland camelids; *cambigh* = highland camelids; *camin* = inland camelids; *camcoast* = camelids from coastal areas. Image by Alfonso-Durruty, Misarti, and Troncoso.

The two outliers represent individuals with a higher intake of marine resources. Dated to the LIP, UGAMS 9638 (see table 13.1) showed high consumption of marine mammals (fig. 13.3*A*) and was found at the site of Los Pozos. Los Pozos (map 13.1) is close to the shore, but the archaeological evidence indicates it represents an inland adaptation. The second outlier (MCH133) was found at the site of Puclaro (map 13.1), dates to the LP, and the diet is high in marine mammals and other marine/coastal resources such as marine fish, shellfish, and marine birds (fig. 13.3*B*).

DISCUSSION

The analysis shows that LIP and LP peoples from the SARNC had a similar diet, composed mostly of inland resources, principally maize and camelids. During both periods, the consumption of marine resources is null among most individuals. The intake of rhea is low, and this nonlocal resource may have been accessed in the form of eggs, as documented in Laguna Llancanelo, Argentina (Giardina et al. 2014). LP individuals had lower $\delta^{13}C_{ap}$ and $\delta^{13}C_{col}$ than LIP ones. Biologically, the changes in diet from the LIP to the LP were small, but the $\Delta^{13}C_{ap-col}$ suggests that the LP individuals consumed less protein, although this does not reflect in significant changes in $\delta^{15}N$.

The between-site comparisons for the LIP were hindered by the small sample sizes. However, the differences in the $\Delta^{13}C_{ap-col}$ reveals variability in the amount of protein consumed by individuals interred at these sites. Among LIP individuals, UGAMS9638 from Los Pozos had a unique diet in which marine sources played a significant role. Pisco Control and Puclaro's LP individuals were similar. In contrast, the individual from Estadio Illapel presented an isotopic signature that suggests the consumption of an intertidal diet of shellfish and nearshore fish. The individual from La Turquía also differs from others, as his isotopic signature suggests a diet that can be characterized as herbivore given the $\Delta^{13}C_{ap-col}$, although the $\delta^{15}N$ is comparatively high (table 13.1).

Archaeological studies in the SARNC indicate an intensification of agriculture, including maize, during the LP (González 2013; Llagostera 1976; Troncoso et al. 2009; Cantarutti 2013). However, our results suggest that the maize produced in this area was not preferentially consumed by local peoples, as its intake is lower in the LP than the LIP. The reduction

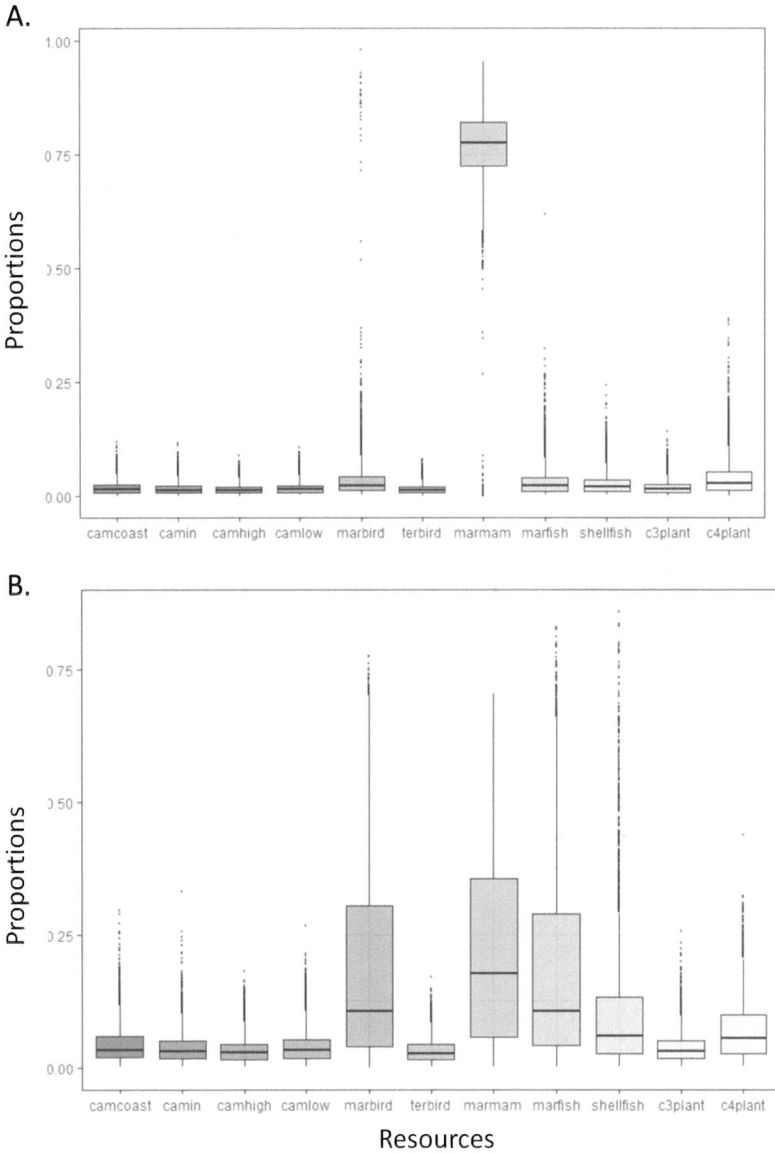

Figure 13.3 A simmr-generated proportion contribution for (*A*) the individual from Los Pozos, UGAMS 9638, and (*B*) the individual from Puclaro, MCH133. *camcoast* = camelid coast; *camin* = camelid inland; *camhigh* = camelid highlands; *camlow* = camelid lowlands; *marbird* = marine birds; *terbird* = terrestrial bird (*Rhea*); *marmam* = marine mammal; *marfish* = marine fish; *shellfish* = shellfish; *C3plant* = plants such as quinoa; *C4plant* = maize. Image by Alfonso-Durruty, Misarti, and Troncoso.

of maize consumption, in a context of agricultural intensification, could result from an Inka political strategy that centered on the movement of resources, in this case maize, to other areas, probably to feed those who participated in the Inka state's redistributing network. Archaeological evidence in the SARNC as well as central-western Argentina suggests the movement of resources (such as fish and shellfish) from the SARNC into the Eastern slopes of the Andes. Similar results have been found in central Chile (Falabella, Planella, and Tykot 2008) as well as western Argentina (Gil et al. 2014). But while maize consumption declined, highland camelid intake increased during the LP. The diversity of camelid origins in the LP is relevant, as it uncovers that the consumption of highland resources during the LP increased in comparison to the LIP. This shift could be linked to the movement of nonlocal resources into the SARNC and the integration of this area into a wider interregional network under the umbrella of the Inka political economy. Thus, although some resources were moved away from the SARNC others became more accessible in the area (Ampuero and Hidalgo 1975; Stehberg 1995; Troncoso, Cantarutti, and González 2016; Uribe and Sánchez 2016).

The larger number of samples in this study accounts for the differences from the ones obtained before (Alfonso-Durruty et al. 2017) and improves our knowledge about maize consumption in SARNC. These new results inform us about a particular sociohistorical context, when the Inka occupation of the SARNC and other provinces resulted in two related processes: (1) an increase in social inequality, which resulted in the differential consumption of foods, especially the main Inka staple of maize (Dillehay 2002; Kosiba 2018; Murra 1978), and (2) a social fragmentation of the territory in which some areas or groups were more heavily influenced by the Inka than others (Llagostera 1976). In combination, these processes created a more heterogeneous dietary landscape that requires further study. In this case, the individual from La Turquia exemplifies the last point, as his diet was clearly different, and the archaeological evidence suggests that the Inka did not influence mobile groups that used Molle pottery in the SARNC.

The results reveal the complexity of the Inka's occupation in the provinces. Although an increase of agricultural production has been recognized, stable isotopes show a decrease of maize consumption and an increase of camelid intake. It is known that Inka imperial strategies of domination varied, that local leaders and intermediate elites were pivotal to them (Alconi and Malpass 2010), and that political negotiations included diverse practices and strategies that expanded well beyond maize (Kosiba 2018). Thus, the political economy of the Inka was a flexible system that emerged from the tension between the state's goals and the political agency of local communities. This situation is nowhere more apparent than in the remote provinces of the Tawantinsuyu, like the SARNC, where the incorporation into the state was mediated by other Inka-influenced groups. Although the study of ancient agricultural fields is hindered by modern agriculture, stable isotope analyses unveil the variability of the Inka's political economy and allow us to discuss the Inka's gastropolitics (Appadurai 1981) in the SARNC.

As mentioned, the absence of pukaras suggests that the relationship between the Inka and the Diaguita was nonviolent. The abundance of ceremonial centers and vessels associated with maize consumption (aryballos and *platos planos*) throughout the SARNC, indicate that feasts were a relevant political strategy for the Inka state. Commensal feasts generated two intertwined political processes in the SARNC. First, the construction of Inka central spaces (ceremonial centers) that promoted Inka experiences related to celebrations in the metropolitan calendar and the use and consumption of Inka material culture (architecture, pottery, and staples). Second, the inclusion in these ceremonies of a selected small number of local subjects (local leaders and other relevant members of the Diaguita community; Troncoso 2022). In this context, the reduction of maize consumption among local communities, despite its importance in political commensalism, was a political tool that marked differences between the Inka state and the local communities at large. At the same time, the select inclusion of local leaders in the feasts promoted their importance and association with the state through maize consumption, the experience of Inka places, and the interaction with Inka material culture. Future studies, with bigger samples, should further evaluate dietary variability of individuals from different archeological sites and regions. This will give us a better understanding of how maize was integrated into the complex political strategies deployed by the Inka state, intermediate elites, and local leaders.

ACKNOWLEDGMENTS

We would like to thank the Museo Nacional de Historia Natural and the Museo de La Serena for granting us access to their collections. Special thanks go to Deborah Blom, whose friendship, observations, and encouraging words have substantially improved this work. We are grateful to all Amerind Seminar participants for their comments and insights. Our heartfelt gratitude to the Amerind Museum and especially to its CEO, Dr. Eric Kaldahl, for this transformative opportunity.

REFERENCES

Alconini, Sonia, and Michael Malpass. 2010. "Toward a Better Understanding of Inka Provincialism." In *Distant Provinces in the Inka Empire: Toward a Deeper Understanding of Inka Imperialism*, edited by Michael Malpass and Sonia Alconini, 279–99. Iowa City: University of Iowa Press.

Alfonso-Durruty, Marta, Andrés Troncoso, Pablo Larach, Cristian Becker, and Nicole Misarti. 2017. "Maize (*Zea mays*) Consumption in the Southern Andes (30°–31° S. Lat): Stable Isotope Evidence (2000 BCE–1540 CE)." *American Journal of Physical Anthropology* 164 (1): 148–62. https://doi.org/10.1002/ajpa.23263.

Ampuero, Gonzalo. 1994. *Cultura Diaguita Chilena. Santiago*. Chile: Ministerio de Educación.

Ampuero, Gonzalo, and Jorge Hidalgo. 1975. "Estructura y Proceso en la Prehistoria y Protohistoria del Norte Chico de Chile." *Chungará Revista Chilena de Antropología*, no. 5, 87–124. http://www.jstor.org/stable/27801701.

Appadurai, Arjun. 1981. "Gastro-Politics in Hindu South Asia." *American Ethnologist* 8 (3): 494–511.

Belmar, Carolina, and Luciana Quiroz. 2006. "Recursos Vegetales de un Asentamiento Inka en el Territorio Diaguita, sitio Loma Los Brujos, Valle Illapel, IV Región." *Anales del Museo de Historia Natural de Valparaíso* 25:79–97.

Bray, Tamara L. 2003a. "Inka Pottery as Culinary Equipment: Food, Feasting, and Gender in Imperial State Design." *Latin American Antiquity* 14 (1): 3–28. https://doi.org/10.2307/972232.

Bray, Tamara L. 2003b. "To Dine Splendidly: Imperial Pottery, Commensal Politics and the Inca State." In *The Archaeology and Politics of Food and Feasting in Early State and Empires*, edited by Tamara L. Bray, 93–142. New York: Kluwer Academic; Plenum.

Cantarutti, Gabriel. 2004. "Estadio fiscal de Ovalle: Redescubrimiento de un Sitio Diaguita-Inka en el Valle del Limarí." Special issue, *Chungará Revista Chilena de Antropología* 36 (2): 833–45. http://dx.doi.org/10.4067/S0717-7356 2004000400024.

Cantarutti, Gabriel. 2013. "Mining Under Inka Rule in North Central Chile: The Los Infieles Complex Mining." In *Mining and Quarrying in the Ancient Andes*, edited by Nicholas Tripcevich and Kevin Vaugh, 185–211. New York: Springer.

Castillo, Gastón. 1998. "Los Períodos Intermedio Tardío y Tardío: Desde la Cultura Copiapó al Dominio Inca." In *Culturas Prehistóricas de Copiapó*, edited by Hans Niemeyer, Miguel Cervellino, and Gastón Castillo, 163–281. Copiapó: Museo Regional de Copiapó.

Cuéllar, Andrea M. 2013. "The Archaeology of Food and Social Inequality in the Andes." *Journal of Archaeological Research* 21 (2): 123–74. http://www.jstor.org/stable/42635578.

D'Altroy, T. 2005. "Remaking the Social Landscape: Colonization in the Inca Empire." In *The Archaeology of Colonial Encounters: Comparative Perspectives*, edited by Gil Stein, pp. 263–96. Santa Fe: SAR Press.

de Bibar, Gerónimo. 1558. *Crónica y Relación Copiosa y Verdadera de Los Reynos de Chile*. Santiago, Chile: Fondo Histórico y Bibliográfico José Torivio Medina.

Dillehay, Tom. 2002. "El Colonialismo Inka, el Consumo de Chicha y los Festines desde una Perspectiva de Banquetes Políticos." *Boletín de Arqueología PUCP* 7:355–63.

Falabella, Fernanda, M. Teresa Planella, and Robert H. Tykot. 2008. "El Maíz (*Zea mays*) en el Mundo Prehispánico de Chile Central." *Latin American Antiquity* 19 (1): 25–46. https://doi.org/10.1017/S1045663500007641.

Giardina, Miguel, Mercedes Corbat, Clara Otaola, Laura Salgán, Andrew Ugan, Gustavo Neme, and Adolfo Gil. 2014. "Recursos y Dietas Humanas en Laguna Llancanelo (Mendoza, Nordpatagonia): Una Discusión Isotópica del Registro Arqueológico." *Magallania (Punta Arenas)* 42 (1): 111–31. https://doi.org/10.4067/S0718-22442014000100007.

Gil, Adolfo, Ricardo Villalba, Andrew Ugan, Valeria Cortegoso, Gustavo Neme, Catalina Teresa Michieli, Paula Novellino, and Víctor Durán. 2014. "Isotopic Evidence on Human Bone for Declining Maize Consumption During the Little Ice Age in Central Western Argentina." *Journal of Archaeological Science* 49:213–27. http://dx.doi.org/10.1016/j.jas.2014.05.009.

Giovannetti, Marcos. 2015. *Fiestas y Ritos Inka en El Shincal de Quimivil: La Presencia del Tawantinsuyu en la Provincia de Catamarca*. Buenos Aires: Punto de Encuentro Editorial.

González, Paola. 1995. "Diseños Cerámicos Diaguita-Inka: Estructura, Simbolismo, Color y Relaciones Culturales." Memoria para optar al título de arqueóloga, Universidad de Chile.

González, Paola. 2008. "Mediating Opposition: On Redefining Diaguita Visual Codes and Their Social Role During the Inca Period." In *Lenguajes Visuales de los Incas*, BAR International Series 1848, edited by Paola González and Tamara Bray, 21–46. Oxford: BAR.

González, Paola. 2013. *Arte y Cultura Diaguita Chilena: Simetría, Simbolismo e Identidad*. Santiago, Chile: Ucayali Editores.

Hayashida, Frances, Andrés Troncoso and Diego Salazar. 2022. "Rethinking the Inka: The View from the South." In *Rethinking the Inka: Community, Landscape, and Empire in the Southern Andes*, edited by Frances Hayashida, Andrés Troncoso, and Diego Salazar, 1–11. Austin: University of Texas Press.

Hedges, R. E. M. 2003. "On Bone Collagen: Apatite-Carbonate Isotopic Relationships." *International Journal of Osteoarchaeology* 13 (1/2): 66–79. https://doi.org/10.1002/oa.660.

Hedges, Robert E. M., Rhiannon E. Stevens, and Paul L. Koch. 2005. "Isotopes in Bones and Teeth." In *Isotopes in Palaeoenvironmental Research*, edited by Melanie J. Leng, 117–45. The Netherlands: Springer.

Hedges, Robert E. M., and Gert J. van Klinken. 2000. "'Consider a Spherical Cow . . .': On Modelling and Diet." In *Biogeochemical Approaches to Paleodietary Analysis*, edited by Stanley H. Ambrose and M. Anne Katzenberg, 211–41. New York: Kluwer Academic; Plenum. https://doi.org/10.1007/0-306-47194-9_11.

Hobson, Keith A., Don M. Schell, Deanne Renouf, and Elizabeth Noseworthy. 1996. "Stable Carbon and Nitrogen Isotopic Fractionation Between Diet and Tissues of Captive Seals: Implications for Dietary Reconstructions Involving Marine Mammals." *Canadian Journal of Fisheries and Aquatic Sciences* 53 (3): 528–33. https://doi.org/10.1139/f95-209.

Hobson, Keith A., John L. Sease, Richard L. Merrick, and John F. Piatt. 1997. "Investigating Trophic Relationships of Pinnipeds in Alaska and Washington Using Stable Isotope Ratios of Nitrogen and Carbon." *Marine Mammal Science* 13 (1): 114–32. https://doi.org/10.1111/j.1748-7692.1997.tb00615.x.

Jenny, Bettina, Blas L. Valero-Garcés, Rodrigo Villa-Martínez, Roberto Urrutia, Mebus Geyh, and Heinz Veit. 2002. "Early to Mid-Holocene Aridity in Central Chile and the Southern Westerlies: The Laguna Aculeo Record (34°S)." *Quaternary Research* 58 (2): 160–70. https://doi.org/10.1006/qres.2002.2370.

Koch, Paul L., Marilyn L. Fogel, and Noreen Tuross. 1994. "Tracing the Diets of Fossil Animals Using Stable Isotopes." In *Stable Isotopes in Ecology and Environmental Sciences*, edited by K. Lajtha, 63–92. London: Blackwell Scientific.

Kosiba, S., 2018. "Cultivating Empire: Inca Intensive Agricultural Strategies." In *The Oxford Handbook of the Incas*, edited by Sonia Alconini and Alan Covey, 227–46. Oxford University Press, Oxford.

Llagostera, Agustín. 1976. "Hipótesis Sobre la Expansión Incaica en la Vertiente Occidental de los Andes Meridionales." In *Homenaje al Dr. Gustavo Le Paige, SJ*, edited by Hans Niemeyer F, 203–38. Antofagasta: Universidad del Norte.

Maldonado, Antonio, María Eugenia de Porras, Andrés Zamora, Marcelo Rivadeneira, and María Abarzúa. 2016. "El Escenario Geográfico y Paleoambiental de Chile." In *Prehistoria en Chile: Desde sus Primeros Habitantes Hasta los Incas*, edited by Fernanda Falabella, Mauricio Uribe, Lorena Sanhueza, Carlos Aldunate, and Jorge Hidalgo, 23–70. Santiago: Editorial Universitaria y Sociedad Chilena de Arqueología.

Maldonado, Antonio, and Carolina Villagrán. 2002. "Paleoenvironmental Changes in the Semiarid Coast of Chile (~32°S) During the Last 6200 Cal Years Inferred from a Swamp-Forest Pollen Record." *Quaternary Research* 58 (2): 130–38. https://doi.org/10.1006/qres.2002.2353.

Maldonado, Antonio, and Carolina Villagrán. 2006. "Climate Variability over the Last 9900 Cal yr BP from a Swamp Forest Pollen Record Along the Semiarid Coast of Chile." *Quaternary Research* 66 (2): 246–58. https://doi.org/10.1016/j.yqres.2006.04.003.

Malpass, Michael, and Sonia Alconini. 2010. "Provincial Inka Studies in the Twenty-First Century." In *Distant Provinces in the Inka Empire: Toward a Deeper Understanding of Inka Imperialism*, edited by Michael Malpass and Sonia Alconini, 1–13. Iowa City: University of Iowa Press.

Misarti, Nicole, Bruce Finney, Herbert Maschner, and Matthew J. Wooller. 2009. "Changes in Northeast Pacific Marine Ecosystems over the Last 4500 Years: Evidence from Stable Isotope Analysis of Bone Collagen from Archeological Middens." *Holocene* 19 (8): 1139–51. https://doi.org/10.1177/0959683609345075.

Murra, John. 1978. *La Organización Económica del Estado Inca*. Mexico City: Fondo de Cultura Económica.

Parnell, Andrew C., and Richard Inger. 2021. "Stable Isotope Mixing Models in R with simmr." Stable Isotope Mixing Models in R with simmr (website), https://cran.r-project.org/web/packages/simmr/vignettes/simmr.html.

Parnell, Andrew C., Donald L. Phillips, Stuart Bearhop, Brice X. Semmens, Eric J. Ward, Jonathan W. Moore, Andrew L. Jackson, Jonathan Grey, David J. Kelly, and Richard Inger. 2013. "Bayesian Stable Isotope Mixing Models." *Environmetrics* 24 (6): 387–99. https://doi.org/10.1002/env.2221.

Stehberg, Ruben. 1995. Instalaciones Incaicas en el Centro y Centro Norte de Chile. Santiago, Chile: DIBAM.

Troncoso, Andrés. 2004. "Relaciones Socio-Culturales de Producción, Formas de Pensamiento y Ser en el Mundo: Un Acercamiento a los Períodos Intermedio Tardío y Tardío en la Cuenca del Río Choapa." *Werkén* 5:61–68.

Troncoso, Andrés. 2018. "Inca Landscapes of Domination: Rock Art and Community in Northcentral Chile." In *The Oxford Handbook of Inca Culture*, edited by Sonia Alconini and Alan Covey, 453–69. New York: Oxford University Press.

Troncoso, Andrés 2022. "Relational communities, Leaders, and Social Reproduction: Discussing the Engagement Between Tawantinsuyu and Local Communities in the Southern Part of Qullasuyu." In *Rethinking the Inka: Community, Landscape, and Empire in the Southern Andes*, edited by Frances Hayashida, Andrés Troncoso, and Diego Salazar, 185–202. Austin: University of Texas Press.

Troncoso, Andrés, Cristian Becker, Daniel Pavlovic, Paola González, Jorge Rodríguez, and Claudia Solervicens. 2009. "El Sitio LV099-B 'Fundo Agua

Amarilla' y la Ocupación del Período Incaico en la Costa de la Provincia del Choapa, IV Región." *Chungará Revista Chilena de Antropología* 41 (2): 241–59. http://dx.doi.org/10.4067/S0717-73562009000200006.

Troncoso, Andrés, Gabriel Cantarutti, and Paola González. 2016. "Desarrollo Histórico y Variabilidad Espacial de las Comunidades Alfareras del Norte Semiárido (ca 300 años a.C. a 1450 años d.C.)." In *Prehistoria en Chile: Desde sus Primeros Habitantes Hasta los Incas*, edited by Fernanda Falabella, Mauricio Uribe, Lorena Sanhueza, Carlos Aldunate, and Jorge Hidalgo, 319–64. Santiago, Chile: Editorial Universitaria y Sociedad Chilena de Arqueología.

Tuross, Noreen, Marilyn L. Fogel, and P. E. Hare. 1988. "Variability in the Preservation of the Isotopic Composition of Collagen from Fossil Bone." *Geochimica et Cosmochimica Acta* 52 (4): 929–35. https://doi.org/10.1016/0016-7037(88)90364-X.

Uribe, Mauricio, and Rodrigo Sánchez. 2016. "Los Inca en Chile: Aportes de la Arqueología Chilena a la Historia del Tawantinsuyu (ca. 1.400 a 1.536 años d.C)." In *Prehistoria en Chile: Desde sus Primeros Habitantes a los Incas*, edited by Fernanda Falabella, Mauricio Uribe, Carlos Aldunate, and Jorge Hidalgo, 529–72. Santiago, Chile: Editorial Universitaria y Sociedad Chilena de Arqueología.

Veit, Heinz. 1996. "Southern Westerlies During the Holocene Deduced from Geomorphological and Pedological Studies in the Norte Chico, Northern Chile (27–33°S)." *Palaeogeography, Palaeoclimatology, Palaeoecology* 123 (1–4): 107–19. https://doi.org/10.1016/0031-0182(95)00118-2.

14

Inka Kallawayas

Cuisine, Identity, and Status Negotiations in the Eastern Antisuyu Chuncho Margins

Sonia Alconini

The Titicaca Basin and its eastern regions were populated by earthly mountain beings that protected their human progeny. Despite the drastic transformations of the Colonial era, Mount Kaata is still a sacred divinity with overtly anthropomorphic features in the Kallawaya region. At the center of the mountain's body is Kaata Pata, the pumping heart (Bastien 1978). Considering that for local Kaateños, the heart is the place where reasoning, wisdom, and memories are recurrently created and evoked, the symbolic appropriation of the ancient site of Kaata Pata by the Inkas reveals the blunt way in which particular organs of earthly deities were especially targeted. Archaeological research on the mountain's heart allows us to explore the geopolitics of feasting and food sharing, and the construction of collective memories as the Inka empire established control of the Antisuyu tropics.

This chapter addresses three research questions utilizing different lines of evidence, including faunal analysis, archaeobotany, and changes in the form and stylistic decorations of the serving wares. (1) How did commensal celebrations promote community cohesion and social difference along the fringes of the Inka empire? (2) How were such festivities used by emerging elites as avenues to attain and maintain status and power? (3) How did such events serve to metaphorically reproduce and transform the sacred geography for emerging imperial interests?

THE INKA CONQUEST OF THE TITICACA BASIN AND ITS EASTERN VALLEYS

The Inka ruler Tupac Inka Yupanki conquered the Titicaca Basin, and the neighboring eastern valleys (map 14.1), by mobilizing a sizable army to support the Lupacas in their endemic conflict against the Collas. The

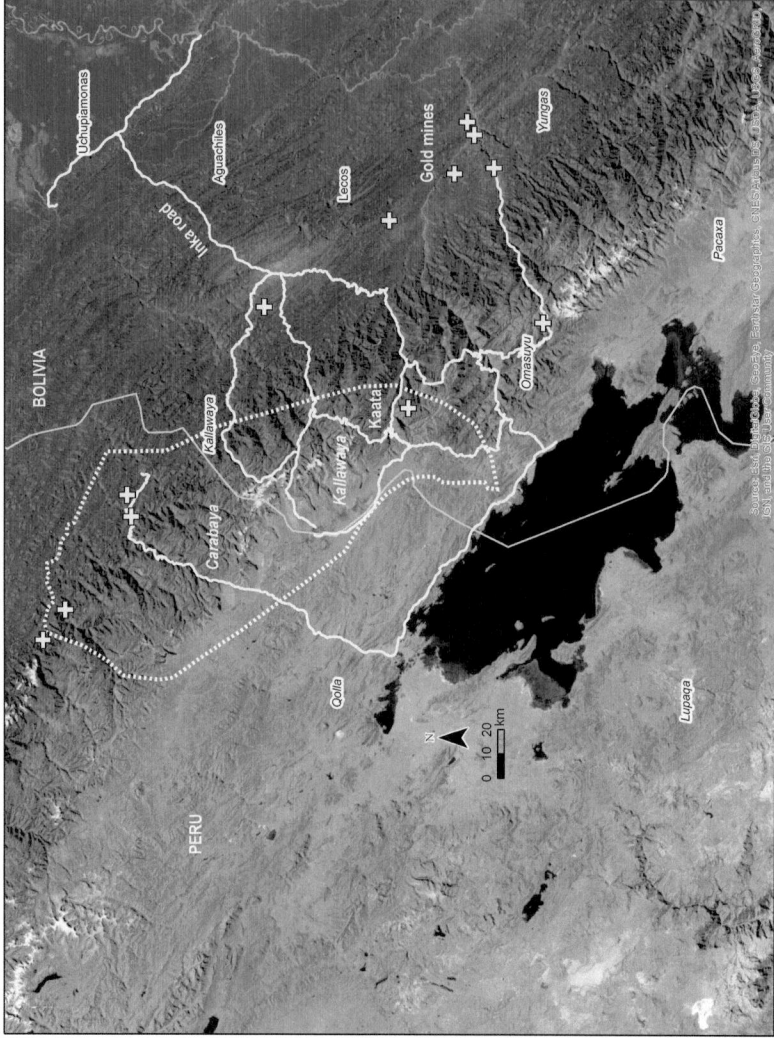

Map 14.1 Map of the Titicaca Basin and the province of Kallawaya. It also shows the Inka road and the gold mines in the region (based on Bouysse-Cassagne 2017; Saignes 1985; Tyuleneva 2015). Illustration by Sonia Alconini/Esri.

region was then reorganized into provinces, and the most valuable lands (northwest of Lake Titicaca and Copacabana), fell under the direct control of the ruler's royal *panaca* (Bouysse-Cassagne 1986; Rostworowski de Diez Canseco 1962; Stanish 2003). The rugged eastern valleys and Yunga tropical mountains were also the targets of strategic incorporation. They formed a natural corridor leading to southwestern Amazonia. To the east were the gold mines of Larecaja and Mapiri (Chavez and Alconini 2016; map 14.1). The corridor was inhabited by diverse peoples such as the Kallawayas, Lecos, and Takanas, many of whom were broadly known as Chunchos. They maintained varying forms of relations with the Inkas.

The Inka established the Kallawaya province following traditional principles of dual organization. Hatun Carabaya was founded to the northwest of the Titicaca Basin (Peru), whereas Lurin Kallawaya (or Carabaya la Chica) encompassed the southern portion of today's Bolivia (Alconini 2013, 2014; Saignes 1984, 1985; map 14.1). Many highland colonies that once dwelled in these valleys were expelled. Gaining control over their territory, the Kallawaya lords became valuable administrators and imperial representatives. Guaman Poma de Ayala ([1613] 2006) illustrates Kallawaya men carrying the royal couple's litter, an honor that was given only to trusted ethnicities. Known for their extensive knowledge of medicinal plants from the eastern tropics, the Kallawayas were renowned traveling shamans, traders, and herbal healers. Perhaps because of these skills, Kallawayas were highly valued by the Inkas as cultural brokers and traders with the outer tropical Chuncho populations, with whom they shared a similar language and cultural traditions (Meyers 2002; Saignes 1984, 1985).

REGIONAL INKA IMPERIAL APPROPRIATIONS: THE MOUNTAIN'S HEART

The Inka's radical socioeconomic transformations in the Kallawaya territory included an unprecedented expansion of the agrarian terrace system (*andenes*) and the construction of clusters of storage facilities, residences, and temporary shelters at different locales. In the upper Puna, the number and size of corrals peaked, suggesting specialized camelid pastoralism. Retention canals, dams, and interconnected stone wells (*tajanas*) were built to facilitate water retention in the *qocha* water reservoirs (Alconini 2011, 2020). Ethnohistoric narratives document that the Inkas mobilized many nonlocal workers (*mitmaqkunas*) to foment economic growth (Meyers 2002; Saignes 1985). Our pedestrian survey revealed a radical increase in the number of settlements compared with the preceding Late Intermediate Period (from 397 to 1,694 settlements).

To control this region, the Inkas established two main centers next to an ancient trading road that led to the eastern tropics. To the west and at the core of the Kallawaya domain was Kaata Pata in the Kaata Valley, and to the east was the Inka Tambo de Maukallajta in the Camata Valley. As the dominant center in the Kallawaya territory, Kaata Pata was strategically positioned in the prominent saddle of Mount Kaata. Placed in front of the Akhamani mountain, a paramount divinity in Kallawaya cosmology, Kaata Pata, controlled the trading route juxtaposed to the Inka imperial road.

As one of the anthropomorphized sacred earthly beings (*apus*) that dwelled in the landscape, Mount Kaata maintained kindred relations with other regional divinities who cared for and fed their human descendants (Bastien 1978; Arnold, Yapita, and Espejo 2016). Mount Kaata's discernible anthropomorphic features (map 14.2) included (1) the head (in the upper Puna), (2) the eyes (two shining lakes, *qochas*, that were portals to *uma pacha*, the world of the dead), (3) hair (growing bunchgrass), (4) the mouth (a hidden cavity known as Wayra Wishani, Door of the Wind), where community members feed the mountain with llama hearts to prevent the excessive rain that damages the fields, and (5) legs and arms (flowing river), where kindred sociopolitical organizations (*ayllus*) were established on each side (Bastien 1978, map 14.2). For example, the town of Niño Korin was conceived as part of the left leg, where multiple Tiwanaku burials in a funerary cave were exhumed. It contained textile bundles and ritual paraphernalia from the *rapé* hallucinogenic complex (Wassén 1972). Above Niño Korin and next to the road is the site of Kalla Kallan, a main Tiwanaku ceremonial and exchange center (Chavez and Alconini 2016).

The town of Kaata is divided into two halves: Kaata Pata (upper Kaata) and main Kaata (lower Kaata). Local residents considered the upper Inka center of Kaata Pata to be the mountain's heart and lower Kaata to be the bowels. For ethnographer Joseph Bastien (1978, 46), "the hamlets are joined together as are the vital organs surrounding the heart: Kaata Pata, the oldest and highest of these hamlets." The surrounding agrarian

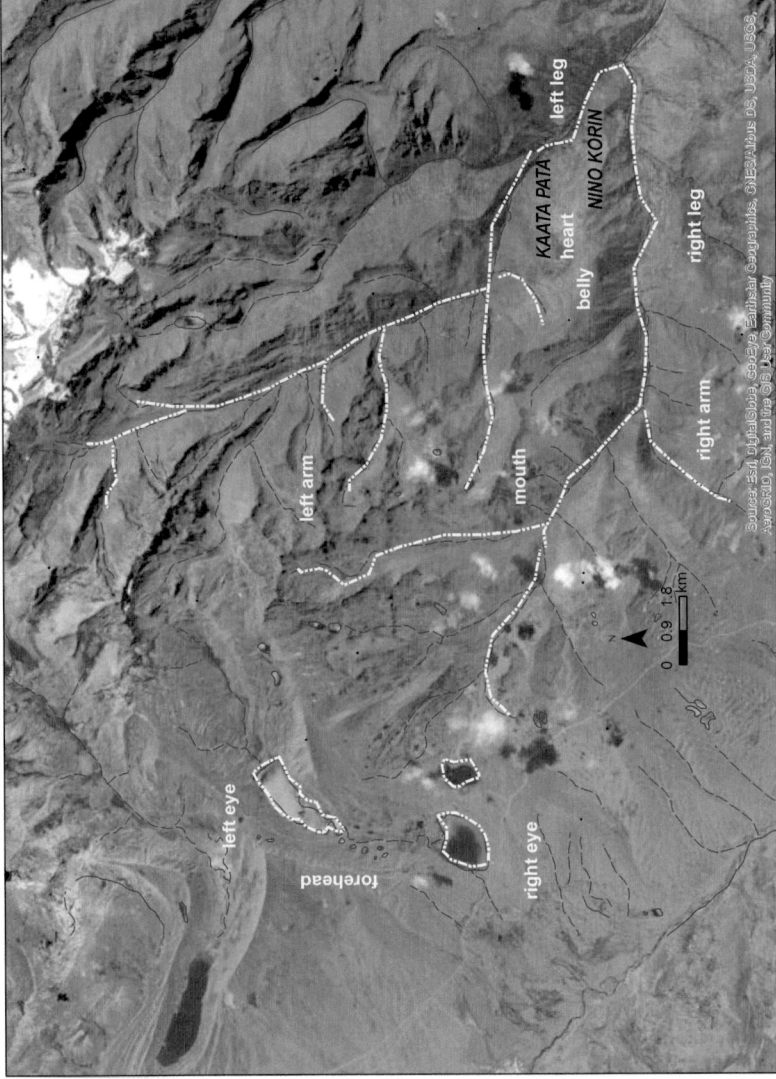

Map 14.2 Mount Kaata anthropomorphized *apu* divinity (based on Bastien 1978). Illustration by Sonia Alconini/Esri.

terraces are conceived as alternating layers of fat in the mountain's body and, hence, bodily sources of energy (Bastien 1978). Our excavations revealed that Kaata Paata was established over an early Formative and Tiwanaku site that lay next to a *qocha* water reservoir. In the rest of this chapter, we will argue that the Inkas purposefully established Kaata Pata over an ancient site to appropriate a sacred node in the Kallawaya geography.

THE INKA CENTER OF KAATA PATA

Kaata Pata (3 ha) sat on a small elevation and was distributed over a series of terraces in the Kaata Valley. On its lower northwestern portion was the said *qocha* water reservoir (map 14.3). This area is now the modern plaza, where the broken head of an anthropomorphic stone monolith stylistically associated with the Formative era was recovered.

The center of Kaata Pata was in the higher portion of the site and extended below in a series of platforms (map 14.3). Platforms in the upper portion were elite residential terraces or spaces for public use. Platforms in the lower flanks were utilized for agriculture or mortuary ends. Constructions were made of partially cut red sandstone blocks in the typical intermediate provincial Inka architectural style. A sacred outcrop used as a shrine (*ushnu*) lay at the center of a trapezoidal enclosure (Platform 6), surrounded by lower terraces that held groups of rectangular residential constructions. Among them was Platform 9, which was flanked by a rectangular hall (*kallanka*) that opened into the trapezoidal plaza enclosing the *ushnu* outcrop.

Platforms 6 and 9 were established over an earlier Tiwanaku settlement. Excavations in those platforms revealed three main periods of occupation based on architectural renovation episodes and associated radiocarbon dates: (a) Early Inka period (1400–1470 AD), which was roughly contemporaneous with the reigns of Wiracocha and Pachacuti; (b) Middle Inka period (1470–1520 AD), which encompassed the military incorporations during Tupac Inka Yupanki and Huayna Capac's ruling (map 14.3); and (c) Late Inka–Early Colonial period (1520–1600 AD), which comprised the reigns of Huayna Capac and the later downfall of the empire.

During the Early Inka period, Kaata Pata was a residential compound. Nearby to the south were the stone foundations of three aligned quadrangular rooms. Within and around were trash scatters, and small camelid dedicatory offerings were deposited below the stone foundations.

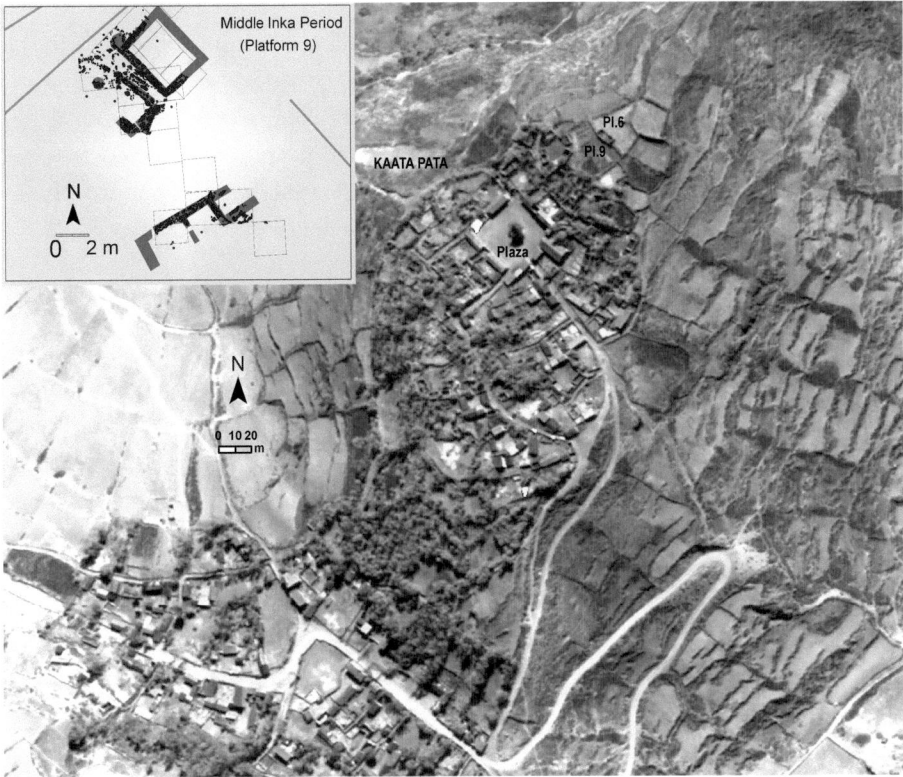

Map 14.3 The Inka site of Kaata Pata. The map shows the modern plaza, and to the north, Platforms 6 and 9. Illustration by Sonia Alconini.

In the following Middle Inka period, the range of activities expanded. An elite residential compound was constructed in the northern portion of Platform 9 (map 14.3). It had two preserved rooms and wall segments. The first stone structure was built over an earlier canal, while the second revealed food preparation activities. The residents enjoyed status-based adornments like copper *tupu* pins, *tumi* knives, tiny bells, and facial tweezers. To the south, the line of three quadrangular rooms continued in use, and small-scale metal smelting probably took place in some of them. With the proximity of the mines of Carabaya and Larecaja, local Kallawaya residents might have enjoyed privileged access to such valuable metal resources (map 14.1; Berthelot 1986; Bouysse-Cassagne 2017).

During this period, Kaata Pata became integral to the Inka imperial economy. As the state held control over the exchange networks that penetrated deep into the eastern tropics, the site residents gained prestige and wealth and sponsored lavish commensal celebrations on behalf of the state. Evidence of periodic feasting events of a scale well beyond the needs of the elite household is found in stratified midden pits outside the elite residences, patio areas, and the exterior of the specialized production rooms. These midden pits show alternating layers of refuse with soft organic soil mixed with medium to high densities of broken pottery, animal remains, and charcoal flakes.

During the Late Inka–Early Colonial period, Platform 9 was expanded, indicating its more prominent public role. A larger rectangular *kallanka* was also constructed to the northeast of the trapezoidal plaza enclosure. To the center of this plaza was the ritual *ushnu* outcrop. To accommodate the edification of the *kallanka*, the foundations of the earlier elite residence were leveled. Hence, the elite area was progressively transformed into a more public space as the site grew in regional importance.

Kaata Pata was progressively abandoned as Spanish conquistadors took hold over the Andes. As the occupation declined, the *kallanka* was repurposed. Its original entrance was deliberately closed to prevent Indigenous access to the sacred *ushnu*. Some of the local residents were possibly moved to the lower plaza, where a new Catholic chapel was erected.

FEASTING, EATING, AND SHARING IN KAATA PATA

Inhabited by elite residents, Kaata Pata was an important center for feasting, food sharing, and political incorporation. I will focus on broad temporal comparisons to explore the foods consumed, the sorts of meals prepared, and the changes that the site underwent. These comparisons are used to trace major transformations at the site. The analysis will consider animal foodways, types of plants consumed, and the serving equipment utilized.

ANIMAL FOODWAYS

A percentage estimate of the Number of Identified Specimens (NISP) from all the samples distributed across the different periods and taxa reveals an emphasis on domestic camelid specimens, including llamas and alpacas (n = 6,207, 61.2%). The next largest category was unidentified large-size mammals (n = 3,136, 30.92%) that were also most likely camelids. In smaller quantities were deer (*Cervidae* sp., n = 252, 2.48%), guinea pigs (*Cavia porcellus*, n = 99, 0.98%), and birds (n = 15, 0.15%). Felines (n = 8, 0.08%; perhaps small pumas or lesser felines) and domesticated and/or wild dogs (n = 33, 0.33%) were also found. The late, although limited introduction of domesticated pigs (*Suidae* sp.) and cattle (*Bovidae* sp.) in the archaeological inventory, unveils important economic transformations that took place at the onset of the Colonial era.

Camelids' dominance in the diet is foreseen, considering the rich Puna wetlands, where specialized pastoralists probably raised large herds of domesticated llamas and alpacas. Wild camelids (vicuña and guanaco) might have also been hunted, as they were prized for their fine wool fibers. To foment specialized pastoralism, extensive pasture lands and a system of *qocha* water reservoirs were expanded by the Inkas in the upper Puna.

As also observed in the Titicaca Basin and adjacent highlands, camelids' prominence in the regional political economy persisted through time (see Baitzel et al. and Miller et al., this volume). Following standard metrics, the Minimum Number of Elements (MNE) was estimated for each archaeological context, level, and floor. In contrast, the Minimum Number of Individuals (MNI) was calculated by dividing the MNE by the portion of the element within a typical camelid skeleton. This was done considering the side, size, and symmetry of the bone elements present in each archaeological context (Capriles 2017; Benavente et al. 1993; Pacheco Torres, Enciso, and Porras 1986).

Aggregation of MNI values from each context, floor, and activity area were the basis for the relative camelid estimates per period, which led to three important observations. (a) Camelid MNI counts increased from the Early Inka period (MNI = 99) into the Middle Inka period (MNI = 214) and then declined in the Late Inka–Early Colonial period (MNI = 99; fig. 14.1). (b) Thus, the consumption of camelids during the Middle Inka period was more intense as recurring feasting events grew in scale. Afterward, there was a progressive abandonment of the site. (c) The combined number of specimens from all periods reveals that a minimum of 434 camelid individuals were consumed in the excavated areas of Kaata Pata. This underestimates the actual number of camelids utilized but

Kata Pata: Distribution of camelid packs ratio
(Pack/MNI)

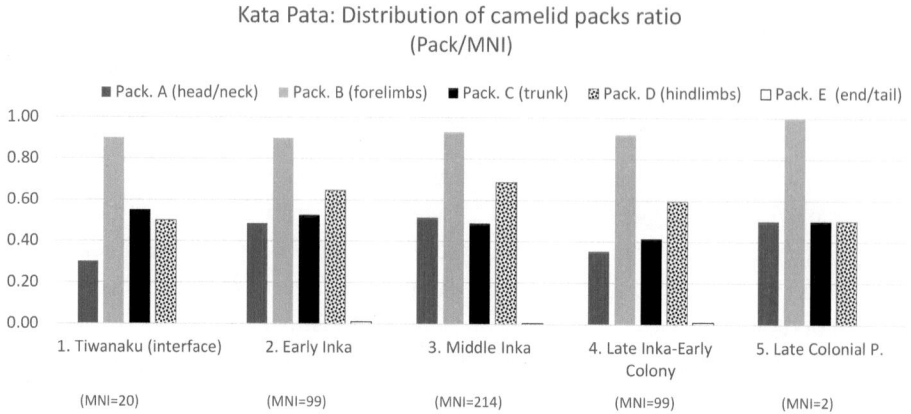

Figure 14.1 Camelid pack ratios (pack/MNI) show meat pack preferences over time. Illustration by Sonia Alconini.

allows for broader intersite comparisons. For example, this estimate is more than double that of the earlier Tiwanaku center of Kalla Kallan, where we excavated a similar area. This reveals an intensification in the exploitation of camelids in the Inka era.

We also calculated meat utility packages following Aldenderfer (1998) to further understand the nature of camelid consumption in the Inka center of Kaata Pata (table 14.1). The trunk (Pack C), which comprises valuable parts such as the ribs and the scapula, had the highest meat value. Second in value were packages D (hindlimbs) and B (forelimbs), with a roughly similar usefulness value, whereas package E (end/tail) had a limited meat contribution. The smallest meat contribution came from Package A (head/neck; Aldenderfer 1998, 107). However, the latter had wider economic functions (e.g., teeth used as cutting tools).

Broad temporal comparisons were possible using an aggregated meat package/MNI ratio. It allowed for standardized comparisons across periods because the values were adjusted to a scale of one. Therefore, whereas MNI camelid counts tracked actual quantity changes per period, the package/MNI ratios recorded the proportional preferences for each meat package.

While the MNI results showed the largest values in the Middle Inka period, the package/MNI ratios revealed a considerable diversity of meat packages across periods (fig. 14.1). Package B (forelimbs), which was ranked third in the nonstandardized data, was dominant in all periods,

Table 14.1 Camelid meat packages

Meat package	Body part	Utility index	Rank
Package A	Head/neck	20.5	5
Package B	Forelimbs	100.1–116.1	3
Package C	Trunk	209.2	1
Package D	Hindlimbs	108.9–142.0	2
Package E	End/tail	44.8	4

Note: Estimates follow Aldenderfer (1998).

followed by second-ranked Package D (hindlimbs). The best cuts in package C (trunk) were some of the lowest. They may have been moved as dry *charki* ribs to finance the Inka imperial expansion into the farther tropics or to feed the state army and imperial representatives. Alternatively, these packs could have been exchanged for desirable tropical goods.

The diversity of meat packages and the partially articulated tarsals and metatarsals from the middens indicate that the animals were slaughtered nearby. Depending on the religious calendar, camelids of various sizes were possibly killed at nearby Kaata Pata for consumption in the festivities or as part of ritual sacrifices (e.g., *wilanchas*). It is also feasible that a portion of the adult camelids in the llama caravans remained at the Inka center to be consumed there while the rest continued in their travels to the lower tropics.

PLANT FOODWAYS

Along with lavish quantities of meat prepared for the periodic banquets, the diversity of plants is noteworthy. Maria Bruno and Mabel Ramos collaborated with the flotation and analysis of the charred macrobotanical remains. Species identification was used to estimate ubiquity scores based on the presence or absence of taxa (fig. 14.2A). This allowed us to trace temporal shifts in the kinds of crops and plants consumed across the site (e.g., if a taxon appeared in seven of ten samples, the ubiquity score was 70%; Bruno 2014). All samples from different features and contexts were included in the ubiquity analysis (phase 1). In a select number of samples, we also counted the quantities of each taxon (phase 2; Bruno 2014). An average density per liter (density/L) was estimated for each compared period to assess the number of seeds per taxon and the amount of wood/parenchyma fragments in the flotation samples. Here, only crops and wild plants probably consumed are discussed (fig. 14.2*B*).

Ubiquity scores revealed a consistent presence of maize (*Zea mays*) and tubers such as potatoes (*Solanum* spp.) and oca (*Oxalis tuberosa*) across the different periods (fig. 14.2*A*). Quinoa's (*Chenopodium quinoa*) ubiquity increased over time until the Late Inka–Early Colony Period. Quinoa is suited to the higher altiplano (see Miller et al., this volume), and thus it was either imported or grown locally on a limited scale. Seeds from tuberous Puna species, *Solanum* sp. (potato) and *Oxalis* sp. (oca), were rare and only present in the later Middle and Late Inka–Early Colonial periods. The increased ubiquity of quinoa and the appearance of crops like potato and oca suggest an escalation in trade with populations from the upper Puna. A vertical economy may have allowed Kaata Pata's residents direct access to the upper Puna, although they may have adapted such cultigens in high elevation terraces.

The average density scores supported some of these interpretations, although new trends became apparent. For example, there was a relative increase in maize during the Middle Inka (4.7 density/L) and Late Inka–Early Colonial (4.9 density/L) periods. In contrast, parenchyma and quinoa average densities were low, perhaps because their local production was not encouraged (fig. 14.2*B*). Altogether, the steady increase of maize responds to the fact that the scale of state-sanctioned feasting expanded in the later periods. This trend is consistent with other Inka provincial regions, such as in Hatun Xauxa (Mantaro Valley), where an increase in the density and ubiquity of maize was linked with a decline of quinoa and potatoes (Hastorf 1990, 1993). In the Kallawaya region, the specialized production of maize took place in the expansive system of terraces along the temperate mountain flanks. The importance of this region is highlighted by the fact that the density of maize in the Inka center of Kaata Pata is even higher than in the Mantaro Valley (0.78 maize density/L; see Wright, Hastof, and Lennstrom 2003, 386).

Other domesticated and wild resources probably flowed from the eastern tropics. Charred remains of Cucurbitaceae, hallucinogenic *wilka* plants (*Anadenanthera colubrina* sp.), and coca seeds (*Erythroxylum coca* sp.) were identified. Coca and chili pepper (Solanaceae family) were extensively farmed in the lower Camata Valley, about 30 km southeast (Kim 2020).

A

Kaata Pata: Crops (ubiquity)

■ Chenopodium (Quinoa)   ▨ Oxalidaceae (Oxalis sp.)   ■ Parenchyma (Tubers)
■ Poaceae (Zea mays)   □ Solanaceae (Solanum sp.)

B

Kaata Pata: Crops (Mean density/liter)

■ Chenopodium (Quinoa)   ■ Parenchyma (Tubers)   ■ Poaceae (Zea mays)

(n=12 contexts sampled)

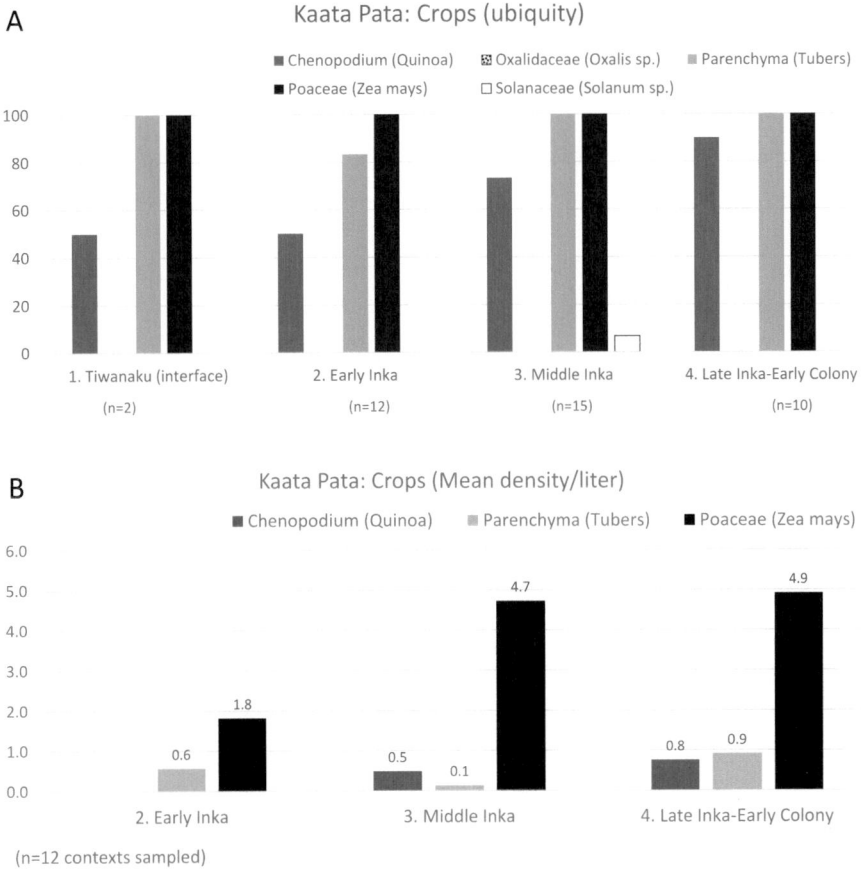

Figure 14.2 Crop distribution in Kaata Pata. *A*, crop ubiquity estimates. *B*, average densities (seeds/liter) per period based on selected contexts (phase 2). Illustration by Sonia Alconini.

The Kallawayas probably obtained them in their travels to Camata and the lower eastern Yunga tropical mountains. It is also possible that nearby Chuncho residents brought some of these preciosities to the Inka centers. Likely, the Kaata Pata residents enjoyed privileged access to such valuables.

SERVING EQUIPMENT

Serving equipment was studied to understand the scale of food consumption and feasting at Kaata Pata. Three broad functional categories were identified: (a) cooking and food preparation vessels (ollas, pedestal ollas, and basins of various sizes), (b) storage containers (large jars and sizable arybaloids), and (c) serving vessels (e.g., bowls, plates, *tazones*, pitchers, small jars, *keru* cups, and small *aryballos*; fig. 14.3*A*). The proportion of serving vessels increased steadily over time and peaked during the Middle Inka period. These vessels were probably used to drink corn chicha and serve foods such as stews and dishes made with maize, potato, quinoa, and camelid meat, as well as roasted meat and vegetables prepared in sunken earth ovens (*pachamanqa*; fig. 14.3*A*). This highlights that Kaata Pata was an important Inka center dedicated to feasting celebrations and food sharing, particularly in the Middle Inka period.

Storage receptacles had limited distribution (fig. 14.3*A*) and show an inverse relationship with serving vessels. As the latter increased over time, the frequency of storage vessels concurrently declined. The center probably became the focus of commensal celebrations to politically integrate different population segments in the region. Therefore, storage tasks might have been progressively delegated to ancillary facilities. Considering the dominance of maize in the charred botanical remains, it is very likely that *chicha* corn beer was the dominant beverage consumed in these events, whether in public or private settings. This fermented substance might have been brewed and stored elsewhere or in yet to be excavated platforms at the site. Similarly, the limited presence of cooking equipment reveals that the center did not have a large residential population or large kitchen areas. More likely, and considering the high density of charcoal in the outdoor stratified midden pits, *pachamanqa* earth ovens might have been utilized in recurrent communal food preparation events. Festive and collective, such meal preparations might have eased social interaction through drinking and food sharing.

The culinary equipment consists of a variety of local and imported (provincial or otherwise) ceramic styles. Local utilitarian ceramic forms were most frequent along the sequence, but the proportion of local to imported ceramic styles varied. Two of the most common decorated styles were the Inka Urcosuyo Polychrome, characterized by the presence of white and creamy kaolin in the paste and slip, and the Inka Chucuito Polychrome, with naturalistic motifs and painted with bright orange colors. These two styles were found along with other local Inka

A

B

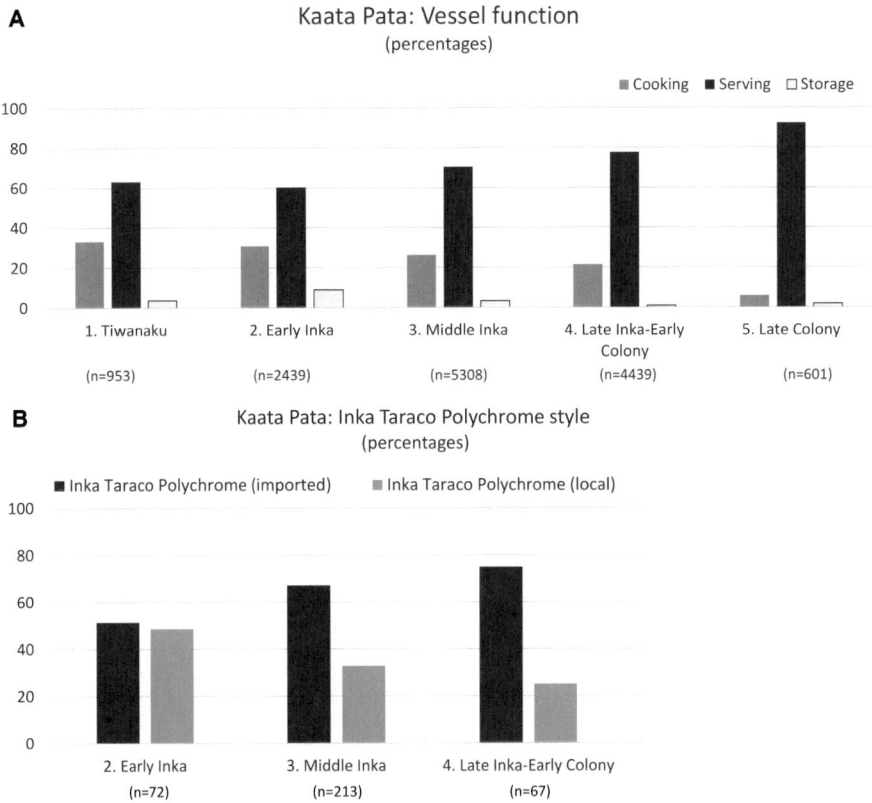

Figure 14.3 Ceramic assemblages at Kaata Pata. *A*, ceramic vessels grouped by function. *B*, Distribution of the Inka Taraco Polychrome styles, whether imported or manufactured locally. Illustration by Sonia Alconini.

variants. Motifs included chili peppers, ferns, corn stalks, fish, vizcachas, and a variety of reticular and geometric motifs painted in black or dark red (fig. 14.4). These styles originated in the northern portion of the Titicaca Basin, and were valued Inka provincial styles of ample distribution in Cuzco and other provinces. Motifs Variant A (*khipus* and ferns) and B (panels of diamonds) are both hallmarks of the Inka imperial style and were locally reproduced. A limited number of bowls and jars in the Inka Pacajes style, peculiar for its stylized black llama motifs, were also found. They might have entered the region through trade along the imperial roads.

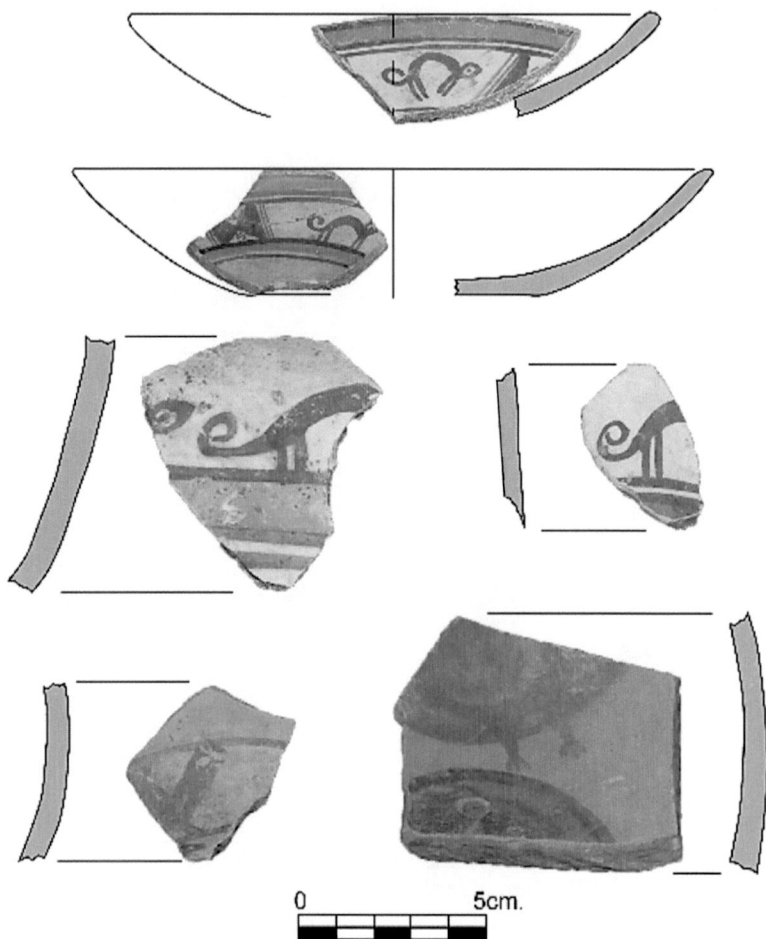

Figure 14.4 Example of Inka Taraco Polychrome serving bowls, plates, and jars depicting animal motifs. Illustration by Sonia Alconini.

A portion of the imported styles was probably manufactured in the state ceramic workshop of Milliraya in the Titicaca Basin (Alconini 2013, 2014). During the Lake Inka–Early Colonial era, Kaata Pata witnessed a relative increase in Inka Taraco Polychrome imported ceramics, perhaps at the expense of local reproductions (fig. 14.3*B*). I suggest that Yunga-Kallawaya elite segments were progressively incorporated into the Inka state economy through the Titicaca Basin.

FEEDING THE MOUNTAINS AND BEING FED

This study shows that state commensalism was a critical component in the range of activities conducted at the Inka provincial center of Kaata Pata. Located in the eastern frontier region that opened into the lands of the Chunchos, this facility served to integrate populations of distinct ethnic origins along different altitudinal ecologies. Changes in the assemblage quantities and proportions, reveal that the Middle Inka period witnessed important socioeconomic transformations. At this time, Kaata Pata had access to the largest camelid meat packs, maize average density, and serving vessels compared to the rest of the periods. The Middle Inka period roughly corresponds to the territorial expansion of rulers Tupac Inka Yupanki and Huayna Capac into the Antisuyu region to the south of the Madre de Dios River, which included the regions of Apolobamba, Larecaja, and Moxos.

Three questions guided this chapter. The first relates to the ways in which commensal celebrations simultaneously promoted community cohesion and social difference on the fringes of the Inka empire. A comparison of the quantities and diversity in the faunal, macrobotanical, and ceramic assemblages revealed that Kaata Pata was the focus of lavish banquets regularly sponsored by the elite. This is also documented in the alternating layers of trash deposited in deep midden pits of the site's public areas, perhaps the remains of *pachamanqas*. Judging by the density of camelid remains, in addition to other animal species, abundant meat cuts were prepared and served to the guests, while chicha corn beer was distributed and toasted on behalf of the state and the Inka ruler. Although in lower quantities, quinoa and a variety of tubers were also part of the meals in addition to plants from temperate environments such as Cucurbitaceae and possible capsicum species that might have arrived from trading networks. Likely, coca leaves and wilka stimulant plants were also consumed at these events.

All these foods were served in local and Inka provincial style plates and dishes, including traditional aryballos, *kerus*, and pitchers. Whether imported from the Titicaca Basin or manufactured locally, some of these vessels included Inka Taraco and Inka Urcosuyo polychrome styles, along with local Inka variants. Through common principles of reciprocity and redistribution, the elite residents at this Inka center became important imperial representatives who utilized commensal celebrations and feasting as strategies to cement alliances. These feasts built new social relations and legitimized imperial power through recursive rituals. Altogether, the variety of resources that flowed from different directions and altitudinal ecologies to this Inka frontier center unveils its political and economic importance.

The second question interrogated how emerging elites utilized such festivities as venues to attain and maintain status and power. As a frontier facility, Kaata Pata played a pivotal role in creating a new social order forged afar on behalf of the Inka state. As such, feasting celebrations and the recurrent rituals at the center fostered social cohesion; paradoxically, they also publicized emerging social inequalities. These rituals also made visible the privileged alliances that select Yunga-Kallawaya elite segments had established with the Inkas. The access to high-status metal adornments (rings, tweezers, tupu copper pins, and tiny bells attached to clothing) signals the rise of elite factions that broadcasted their new sociopolitical allegiances with the imperial core.

Strategically placed along an ancient trading node established in the Formative era, Kaata Pata became vital in the thriving exchange corridors that linked the Titicaca Basin with the eastern tropical Yunga mountains and farther Amazonian lowlands. We do not know whether these occupants were originally from the imperial core, were local Yunga-Kallawaya lords that strategically adopted imperial institutions and practices, or were Inka-Kallawaya elite established through privileged marriage relations. It is possible that what started as a selective migration of imperial emissaries from the Titicaca Basin and beyond resulted in the emergence of privileged Inka-Kallawaya elites that increasingly spoke Machajuyu (a mix of Quechua and Arawak Puquina). This elite segment was compartively more conservative than its counterparts in other provinces. Conservative Inka elite segments were economically and politically dependent on imperial patronage to maintain their status and power in comparison with more independent elite factions (for a larger discussion on conservative elites, see Alconini 2020).

The third question assessed was whether such commensal events served to reproduce and transform the sacred geography as an avenue to reinforce emerging imperial interests. The investigation revealed that the

Inka center of Kaata Pata was located in the midaltitude of Mount Kaata. Bastien's (1978) detailed ethnography documented that Mount Kaata was conceived as an animated earthly divinity with anthropomorphized attributes. Therefore, it is no surprise that the mountain's heart was deliberately positioned in the Inka center of Kaata Pata, an ancient seat of power occupied since the Formative and Tiwanaku eras.

Ethnohistoric and ethnographic research has abundantly documented how Andean populations envisioned their landscape as animated, with prominent geographic features such as mountains and rivers having particular importance as sacred *wak'a* divinities (Bastien 1978; Arnold, Yapita, and Espejo 2016; Bray 2015). The Collasuyu mountains were the subject of special veneration, considered to be legendary warriors turned into stone and actively engaged in combat with other godly mountains. These majestic *apus* were a special category of *wak'as*; they had personalities, aspirations and rivalries, and a network of kin and allies that also included humans.

This research contributes to understanding the epistemics of mountain veneration by focusing on a special organ: the heart (*sonqo*). In Quechua, the *sonqo* was conceived as a pivotal organ in human and nonhuman beings. As defined in the seventeenth century Quechua dictionary by González Holguín (1608, 218) *sonqo* (soncco) was "the heart and stomach entrails. It was the conscience, wisdom, reason, and memory. It was also conceived as the will and understanding, and the wood's core." In Mount Kaata, current Quechua residents envision the heart as a vital organ. As it pumps blood, it provides the human and earthly bodies with thoughts, intentions, and emotions. By comparison, the fat (*wira*) is generated in the bowels, endowing the body with energy (Bastien 1978, 46). Geopolitically, the heart of the mountain was located in the Inka center of Kaata Pata, whereas the bowels were in lower Kaata. The surrounding agrarian terraces formed alternating layers of fat, providing the settlement with the required source of vital energy.

The strategic positioning of the Inka center of Kaata Pata at the mountain's heart materialized the bodily geopolitics of Inka power in the region. Hence, the heart was fundamental in the creation and understanding of a new social reality that the Inkas sought to promote and legitimize by becoming their representatives. The pumping mountain heart brought life, consciousness, memory, and reasoning to the animated body of the *apu* earthly being and the human children and communities dwelling within. In this context, the acts of both feeding and communally eating with the mountain *apu* at its geopolitical heart must have been emotionally charged, cathartic, and life-changing events (see also Bray, this volume). Food and chicha corn beer were served, and camelids were sacrificed, as communities from various ecologies traveled and converged at the Inka center of Kaata Pata. These events had critical importance in the bodily geopolitics of state incorporation but also in the construction of shared memories as new group identities were forged along the Inka frontier. Through such recursive celebrations, life was ensured to those communities dwelling on the sacred mountain, including the promise of successful advances into the eastern lands of the Chunchos on behalf of the Inka empire.

ACKNOWLEDGMENTS

This research was possible thanks to the support of the National Science Foundation (BCS-0635342) and the Wenner Gren Foundation for Anthropological Research (grant N. 7363). I thank all my colleagues and friends in Bolivia and the United States for their constant encouragement and inspiration. I want to thank Maria Bruno, Rebecca Friedel, Ricardo Vasquez, Mabel Ramos, Juan Carlos Chavez, Jenny Martinez, and Vanessa Jimenez for the research presented in this chapter. My deepest gratitude goes to all Kaateños in Charazani.

REFERENCES

Alconini, Sonia. 2011. "Imperial Marginality and Frontier: Kallawayas and Chunchos in the Eastern Inka Borders. Final Project Report (2006–2010)." Report submitted to the National Science Foundation, award No. 0635342, San Antonio, Tex.

Alconini, Sonia. 2013. "El Territorio Kallawaya y el Taller Alfarero de Milliraya y la Región Kallawaya: Evaluación de la Producción, Distribución e Intercambio Interregional de la Cerámica Inka Provincial." *Chungará Revista Chilena de Antropología* 45 (2): 277–92. http://dx.doi.org/10.4067/S0717-7356201300 0200005.

Alconini, Sonia. 2014. "Producción y Distribución del Estilo Cerámico Inka Taraco Polícromo: Milliraya y Charazani en Perspectiva." In *Ocupación Inka y*

Dinámicas Regionales en los Andes (siglos XV–XVIII), edited by Claudia Rivera Casanovas, 177–96. La Paz, Bolivia: IFEA, Plural Editores.

Alconini, Sonia. 2020. "Inka Province of the Kallawaya and Yampara: Imperial Power, Regional Political Developments, and Elite Competition." In *Archaeologies of Empire: Local Participants and Imperial Trajectories*, School of Advanced Research, Advanced Seminar Series, edited by Anna L. Boozer, Bleda S. Düring, and Bradley Parker, 89–114. Santa Fe: University of New Mexico Press.

Aldenderfer, Mark S. 1998. *Montane Foragers: Asana and the South-Central Andean Archaic*. Iowa: University of Iowa Press.

Arnold, Denise Y., Juan de Dios Yapita, and Elvira Espejo. 2016. "Wak'as, Objetos Poderosos y la Personificación de lo Material en los Andes Meridionales: Pugnas de Exégesis Sobre la Economía Religiosa Según las Experiencias del Género." in *Wak'as, Diablos y Muertos: Alteridades Significantes en el Mundo Andino*, edited by Lucila Bugallo and Mario Vilca, 30–109. Jujuy, Argentina: Universidad Nacional de Jujuy.

Bastien, Joseph W. 1978. *Mountain of the Condor: Metaphor and Ritual in an Andean Ayllu*. Illinois: Waveland Press.

Benavente M. A., L. Adaro, P. Gelece, and C. Cunazza. 1993. *Contribución a la Determinación de Especies Animales en Arqueología: Familia Camelidae y Taruca del Norte*. Santiago: Universidad de Chile.

Berthelot, Jean. 1986. "The Extraction of Precious Metals at the Time of the Inka." In *Anthropological History of Andean Polities*, edited by John V. Murra, Nathan Wachtel, and Jacques Revel, 69–88. Cambridge: Cambridge University Press.

Bouysse-Cassagne, Thérèse. 1986. *La Identidad Aymara: Aproximación Histórica (siglo XV, siglo XVI)*. La Paz, Bolivia: Hisbol.

Bouysse-Cassagne, Thérèse. 2017. "Las Minas de Oro de los Incas, el Sol y las Culturas del Collasuyu." *Bulletin de l'Institut Français d'Études Andines* 46:9–36.

Bray, Tamara, ed. 2015. *The Archaeology of Wak'as: Explorations of the Sacred in the Pre-Columbian Andes*. Boulder: University Press of Colorado.

Bruno, Maria. 2014. "Beyond Raised Fields: Exploring Farming Practices and Processes of Agricultural Change in the Ancient Lake Titicaca Basin of the Andes." *American Anthropologist* 116 (1):1–16.

Capriles, José M. 2017. *Arqueología del Pastoralismo Temprano de Camélidos en el Altiplano Central de Bolivia*. La Paz, Bolivia: IFEA, Plural Editores.

Chavez, Juan Carlos, and Sonia Alconini. 2016. "Los Yunga-Kallawaya y Tiwanaku: Repensando los Procesos de Interacción Regional en los Andes Orientales Septentrionales." In *Entre la Vertiente Tropical y los Valles: Sociedades Regionales e Interacción Prehispánicas en los Andes Centro-Sur*, edited by Sonia Alconini, 67–86. La Paz, Bolivia: Plural Editores.

González Holguín, Diego. 1608. *Vocabulario de la Lengua General de Todo el Peru Llamada Lengua Qquichua o del Inca*. Lima: Francisco del Canto.

Guaman Poma de Ayala, Felipe. (1613) 2006. *El Primer Nueva Corónica y Buen Gobierno*. Mexico City: Editorial Siglo Veintiuno.

Hastorf, Christine. A. 1990. "The Effect of the Inka on Sausa Agricultural Production and Crop Consumption." *American Antiquity* 55 (2): 262–90.

Hastorf, Christine. A. 1993. *Agriculture and the Onset of Political Inequality Before the Inka*. Cambridge: Cambridge University Press.

Kim, Lynn. 2020. "Local Responses to Inka Imperialism." PhD diss., University of Texas at San Antonio.

Meyers, Rodica. 2002. *Cuando el Sol Caminaba por la Tierra: Orígenes de la Intermediación Kallawaya*. La Paz, Bolivia: Plural Editores.

Pacheco Torres, V. R., A. Altamirano Enciso, and E. Guerra Porras. 1986. *The Osteology of South American Camelids*. Translated by E. Sandefur. Los Angeles: Institute of Archaeology, University of California.

Rostworowski de Diez Canseco, Maria. 1962. "Nuevos Datos Sobre Tenencia de Tierras Reales en el Incario." *Revista del Museo Nacional, Lima, Perú* 31:130–59.

Saignes, Thierry. 1984. "Quienes son los Callahuayas: Notas Sobre un Enigma Histórico." In *Espacio y Tiempo en el Mundo Callahuaya*, edited by Teresa Gisbert, 111–29. La Paz, Bolivia: Instituto de Estudios Bolivianos, Facultad de Humanidades, Universidad Mayor de San Andrés.

Saignes, Thierry. 1985. *Los Andes Orientales: Historia de un Olvido*. Cochabamba: IFEA/CERES.

Stanish, Charles. 2003. *Ancient Titicaca: The Evolution of Complex Society in Southern Peru and Northern Bolivia*. Berkeley: University of California Press.

Tyuleneva, Vera. 2015. *Buscando Ayavirezamo: Nuevos Datos Sobre la Historia de Apolobamba*. La Paz, Bolivia: FOBOMADE.

Wassén, Henry S. 1972. "A Medicine-Man's Implements and Plants in a Tiahuanacoid Tomb in Highland Bolivia." *Etnologiska Studier* 32:1–109.

Wright, Melanie F., Christine Hastof, and Heidi Lennstrom. 2003. "Pre-Hispanic Agriculture and Plant Use at Tiwanaku: Social and Political Implications." In *Tiwanaku and Its Hinterland: Archaeology and Paleoecology of an Andean Civilization*. Vol. 2, *Urban and Rural Archaeology*, edited by Alan L. Kolata, 384–403. Washington, D.C.: Smithsonian Institute Press.

15

The Vital Matter of Food

Tamara L. Bray

Work and ritual associated with both the production and consumption of food constitute a key integrative mechanism of societies present and past. With respect to consumption, what, how, and with whom we eat is widely recognized as one of the fundamental ways we define ourselves (and are defined by others) as social beings and members of specific groups. Countless recent studies make clear that food preferences and prejudices are closely tied to questions of cultural, community, and individual identities. Most such studies implicitly recognize that food has both symbolic and material dimensions. Until recently, however, emphasis has been placed mainly on the former concern, that is, on the symbolic and communicative aspects of food and eating practices, rather than on the latter.

From the earliest days of anthropology, investigation into the ways in which food is symbolically used to draw lines between insiders and outsiders, assert membership, negotiate status, compel allegiance, and make political claims has been highly productive and has provided many insights into the entanglement of food, identity, and politics. But food is neither inert nor nonsubstantive. It does not merely symbolize or represent in a constant, stable, or abstract way—rather it moves, changes, penetrates, and transforms (Fajans 1988, 165). Thus, while it is important to analyze the various ways that food signifies, it is equally important that we attend to its materiality, mutability, and agentive nature. This is the point of departure for the present chapter.

In line with recent feminist, posthumanist, and neomaterialist thinking (e.g., Alaimo 2010; Alaimo and Hekman 2008; Bennett 2007, 2010; Haraway 1990, 2016), I take the *matter* of food as a key point of entry for thinking about what food does and what it means. To work against modernity's acceptance of material passivity, it is important to attend to the capacities of foods—as active and critical elements within broader relational networks—to generate not only biological effects but social and political ones as well and to consider how such substances can activate, suppress, or neutralize the circumstances of which they are a part.

The notion of transcorporeality, hinted at in various Andean texts and contexts (e.g., Allen 1988; Swenson 2018; Weismantel 1995) foregrounds the significance of materiality and allows for rethinking the connection between food and bodies as well as the concept and locus of agency. While much of the Western world's everyday orientation toward the human body constructs it as a stable, self-contained, and autonomous unit, it is important to recognize that this is not a universal disposition. Various anthropological studies have highlighted the communitarian nature of traditional societies and the ways in which the corporate or familial body is expressed and materialized through practices of consumption (e.g., Busby 1997; Marriott 1976; Walens 1981; Weismantel 1988). The shift in orientation from the relational "dividual" of traditional society to the stand-alone individual of the Western world is generally associated with the spread of capitalism and the condition of modernity (Strathern 1988).

Falk (1994) discusses the distinction between dividual and individual in terms of "open" (relational) bodies versus "closed" bodies. His concern is with what different ontologies of the body entail with respect to consumption practices. How the body is understood bears critically on where the boundaries between inside and outside are drawn—a key consideration for Falk in thinking about ingestion, incorporation, and the consuming body. In developing his argument, he contrasts "primitive society" with the modern version, suggesting that the former "is in a fundamental sense an 'eating community'"—one characterized by "a certain kind of openness . . . focused primarily on the eating mouth" (Falk 1994, 20). In such contexts, he states, the sharing of food involves simultaneously "eating into one's body/self and being eaten into the community," noting further that "sharing implies a two-way open body" (Falk 1994, 20). The idea of the "eating community" and the open body resonate to some degree with the notion of transcorporeality.

The concept of transcorporeality emphasizes the materiality of bodies (as opposed to their discursive construction) and movement within, across, and between these. The term was introduced into the ecofeminist and new materialist literature slightly more than a decade ago by Stacy

Alaimo (2010), who presented it as a way out of the essentialist dilemmas and dichotomies of bounded bodies, human exceptionalism, and the culture-nature divide. The idea of transcorporeality highlights the interconnections and interchanges among and between different bodies, both human and otherwise, directing us toward the permeability of bodily boundaries and underscoring the various ways in which humans are inextricably meshed with the material world.

Alaimo (2010, 22) has described the human body as transcorporeal and porous—a site where "biology and politics merge as people, places and substances amalgamate." From this perspective, the matter that enters our bodies is viewed not as inert, awaiting the actions of our interior enzymes or antibodies but rather as agentive in its own right, with the capacity to modify, affect, enhance, or diminish the bodies through which it passes and with which it interacts. The permeability—and vulnerability—of the human body was made painfully evident in the very recent past by an invisible virus with deadly agency and global reach. Beyond pathogens and the ways in which they are transmitted across bodies, food is one of the more readily recognizable of transcorporeal substances, highlighting the irreducible enmeshment of nature-culture and offering another approach for thinking relationally.

In the Andean context, a variety of sources both contemporary and historic indicate that Native peoples of this region see the world and all that it is made up of as deeply interconnected and mutually interdependent (Allen 1988, 1997, 2015; Arnold 2018; Bolin 1998; Cereceda 1986; Gose 1994; Stensrud 2016). The ethnographic data point to the idea of an Indigenous Andean ontology that is profoundly relational, wherein the nature of something is understood to be a function of the social-relational matrix within which it is embedded and that it helps constitute. Such a relational approach, which corresponds in some ways to both assemblage and actor-network theory (e.g., DeLanda 2016; Latour 2005; Law and Hassard 1999), has implications for the way bodies are understood—as separate yet dependent and conjoinable. As Allen (1997) observes, the Andean world is one "premised on *consubstantiality*, [in which] all beings are intrinsically interconnected through their sharing of a matrix of animated substance" (81, emphasis added). Associated with this way of understanding the relational nature of bodies is the idea of transcorporeality, which various Andean accounts suggest was mediated through food and drink.

Spanish conquistador and chronicler Pedro Pizzaro, for instance, in reporting on remembrances of the Inka emperor Huayna Capac, wrote that "[it was said that] he was wont to drink much more than three Indians together, but that they never saw him drunk, and that, when his captains and chief Indians asked him how, though drinking so much, he never got intoxicated, they say that he replied that he drank for the poor of whom he supported many" (Pizzaro [1571] 1921, 198–99). The Inka ruler, by imbibing large quantities of drink, could be understood, from a transcorporeal perspective, as uniting his body with that of his subjects through the substance of *chicha*, nourishing their bodies through his own (see also Bray 2018b). Similar observations regarding the role of chiefly personages in sustaining their subjects through excessive consumption have been reported for numerous traditional societies ranging from the Pacific Northwest to West Africa (e.g., Walens 1981; Warnier 2007).

The ability to link and sustain different, and different kinds of, bodies across both space and time via food is attested, as well, in various contemporary Andean contexts. Allen (1988, 151–75), for instance, reports on the importance of *mihuq*, or ritual eaters, who were critical to mediating relations between the living and the dead on special occasions such as All Soul's Day (see also Gifford and Hoggarth 1976, 79, cited by Allen 1988). Ritual activities associated with the fertility of livestock, during which owners would force-feed their animals while simultaneously imbibing to excess themselves, further illustrates this point (Allen 1988, 165–8; Carter 1977, 205). Allen herself was subject to various episodes of "forced-feeding" wherein it was explained to her by her hosts that she was, in fact, consuming food for her physically distant husband (Allen 1988, 165), which, from a transcorporeal perspective, could be viewed as an important way of conjoining bodies across spatial divides.

These accounts suggest that within the relational ontological framework of Andean people, bodies—be they human, animal, mineral, or other—were understood as holding the potential for transcorporeal enmeshment via the vital matter of food. These reports also suggest an augmented understanding of causality that does not map precisely onto traditional Western understandings—one that allows for the spatial noncontiguity of cause and effect. Additionally, as is found among many Amerindian societies, temporalities for Andean peoples are not strictly linear (Bray 2018a; Swenson and Roddick 2018).

Studies that emphasize food's materiality, relationality, and transcorporeality can generate new insights into Indigenous ontologies and the past lifeways we seek to better understand—in the Andean world and potentially elsewhere as well. If cultural meanings, identities, and structures are understood to be relationally constituted in the intra-actions between humans and things, then there is much to be learned by focusing on the relationship among specific foods, peoples, and contexts; among different types of foods; and between foodstuffs and other artifacts. What types of networks or assemblages come into focus by following the connections associated with foodstuffs, cuisines, and culinary affects, and what do these reveal in terms of social ecologies, political economies, and social strategies? A number of studies that take food chains and foodscapes as their unit of analysis have already begun to illuminate the value of such approaches (e.g., Kurlansky 1997; Jackson 2013; Mintz 1996; Psarikidou and Szerszynski 2012).

Here I develop an Andean example of "following the food" by focusing on a special viand known as *sanco* whose use by the Inka on specific ritual occasions was recorded by several chroniclers. Sanco is defined in early Quechua dictionaries as "masa de maiz cocido, o bollo," that is, as "cooked corn dough, or a bun," and also as "food or something thick and dry lacking broth" (González Holguín [1608] 1952, 77; Santo Tomás 1560, 116), and in Bertonio's ([1612] 1879) Aymara dictionary as "a thick porridge [*mazzamorro*] made of quinoa flour" (308). Contextual references to sanco describe it as a coarsely ground maize paste (Molina [ca. 1575] 2010, 54–66), as "cakes" or "balls" of cornmeal (Arriaga [1621] 1968, 46; Garcilaso de la Vega [1609] 1960, bk. 7, chap. 6), and as "consecrated bread" (Garcilaso de la Vega [1609] 1960, bk. 6, chap. 20). These descriptions suggest that this ritual foodstuff existed in at least two different states, specifically, raw and cooked.

In an image of a sacrifice being offered to the *wak'a*[1] Pariacaca-Pachacamac by the Chinchaysuyo (a conglomerate term for various ethnic groups making up the northern sector of the Inka Empire), Guaman Poma de Ayala ([1615] 1936, 266–67) depicts the female participant as holding a plate of small, round foodstuffs referred to as *uaccri zanco* in

---

1. The term *wak'a* generally refers to "a sacred thing," be it a place, idol, or image (Garcilaso de la Vega [1609] 1960, bk. 2, chap. 3–5).

the accompanying text, which indicates the solid, if not baked, nature of the offering in this particular context (fig. 15.1). It is important to note that baked bread was not a regular element of the everyday Andean diet (Garcilaso de la Vega [1609] 1960, bk. 6, chap. 20). As Garcilaso de la Vega, the son of an Andean noblewoman and a Spanish conquistador, comments in his discussion of sanco, Andean peoples (his maternal relatives) did not utilize ovens; he also specified that sanco was "cooked into balls, dry, in ollas" (Garcilaso de la Vega [1609] 1960, bk. 7, chap. 6).

In Cusco, sanco was prepared in large quantities with corn from the royal gardens of the Inkas by the *mamacuna* (chosen women) for a critical state ceremony known as *Citua* that occurred in the months of August and September and was associated with the *coya*, or queen (Cobo [1653] 1990, 145–47; Garcilaso de la Vega [1609] 1960, bk. 4, chap. 3; Polo de Ondegardo [1571] 1916, 23). Citua was one of the most important ceremonial events on the Inka calendar—lasting a week, if not longer—involving fasting, various purification rituals, camelid sacrifice, and feasting. Sanco, mixed with the blood of the sacrificed animals (i.e., *yaguarsanco*) played a critical role in this ritual event as a cleansing agent, sacrificial offering, and sacrament. Garcilaso de la Vega makes special reference to the fact that in Cusco, two separate batches of sanco were prepared. One variety contained the blood of young (living) boys drawn "from between the eyebrows above the nose"; the other did not (Garcilaso de la Vega [1609] 1960, bk. 7, chap. 6). The two batches were cooked separately and served different purposes: the first (prepared with the blood of young boys) was for external cleansing of the body by wiping or smearing (on the skin), the second was for consumption after breaking the fast observed during the previous day.

The Spanish clergyman Cristóbal de Molina ([ca. 1575] 2010, 54–56), who provides the most detailed description of Citua, reports that everyone—from the Sapa Inka to regular nobles to provincial elites to houses, wak'as, and mummies—wiped (or had wiped) sanco all over their bodies to conjure good fortune and banish illness. He describes this process, which occurred after ritual bathing with water, as warming (*calentando*) the body, a term that may be understood as enlivening or strengthening (the body) based on earlier Spanish usages (*Diccionario de la Lengua Castellana* 1726–39). Subsequently, all, including the wak'as, the mummified dead, priests, nobility, and provincials, would partake of the yaguarsanco either through the inhalation of the burned food or

Figure 15.1 Guaman Poma's depiction of residents of Chinchaysuyu making an offering of a child and foodstuffs to the wak'a Pariacaca-Pachacamac; note the round food items on the plate held by the woman that the author labels as "uaccri zanco" (Guaman Poma de Ayala [1615] 1936, 266–67). Image courtesy of the Royal Library of Denmark.

through ingestion (contrary to Garcilaso's account given just above), in this way in-corporating the sacramental substance.

The relationships embedded and embodied in sanco represent various human and nonhuman beings and interests assembled and materialized in a foodstuff. The making of this consecrated aliment, which involved a crucial cereal grain specially grown in royal soils mixed with the blood of young boys and/or male camelids prepared by special female hands, conjoined an array of important components with distinct properties into a single substance. The incorporation of this sanctified matter, via ingestion, inhalation, or physical application had the effect of cleansing, protecting, and warming the bodies with which it came in contact—enacting a kind of transcorporeal apotropaism through the medium of food. The assembly of elements represented in this vital viand were considered essential to the well-being of the entirety of Inka society, which we can clearly understand comprised not only human persons but buildings, possessions, livestock, springs, wak'as, and the dead, all recipients of sanco during Citua, as well.

Other foodstuffs construed as special within the context of Tawantinsuyu similarly seemed to have involved more than just the elemental substance of the viand itself. The foods of which the Inka partook, for instance, were distinguished from those that commoners ate by such qualities as color, rarity, primacy in terms of harvest, time involved in preparation, and abundance. This can be seen in a passage from Guaman Poma, wherein he describes the typical repast of the Sapa Inka: "he ate select maize called *capya utco sara* [tender white corn], and early potatoes [*papas mauay* or *chaucha*], and the meat of white camelids; and tiny fish called *chiche*, white cuy, and much fruit and ducks, and very smooth chicha called *yamor aca* that takes a month to mature. And he ate other things [as well], which the Indians were not to touch upon pain of death" (Guaman Poma de Ayala [1615] 1936, 332).[2] Other foods could apparently be transformed from the ordinary to the sublime via the persons who prepared and presented them—as seen above with sanco. A particular royal food called *tupa cocau*, for instance, which consisted of a

---

2. "Comía escogido mays, capya utco sara y papas mauay, chaucha, y carnero llamado cuyro blanco, y comía chiche, conejo blanco y mucha fruta y patos y chicha muy suaui que madoraua un mes que le llaman yamor aca. Y comía otras cosas que no tocaua los yndios, so pena de la muerte."

small bag of maize that was given by the Sapa Inka to those he ordered to travel on state business, was said to be so potent that one grain per day could sustain an individual (González Holguín [1608] 1952, 227). Extraordinary foodstuffs were thus seemingly distinguished by both their materiality and the larger networks of which they were a part.

Following on from the way in which the vital viand of sanco was deployed in Cusco, I would like to foreground one particular point: the idea that food, through its materiality and mutability, acted in the Andean context to create linkages across ontological divides, that is, between different categories of beings potentially existing in different temporal or spatial realms. The types of foods, the manner of preparation, the mode of presentation, and the form of consumption all seem to have figured importantly in the creation and maintenance of connections across such divides. This is a proposition that I made in an earlier paper (Bray 2012) that I wish to expand here.

For some time, I have been interested in the possibility of exploring alternative ontologies via the material evidence associated with foodstuffs, cuisine, and culinary practices. I have previously made the argument that commensality offers a window into what, and what kinds of, other-than-human entities may have formed part of the social worlds of pre-Columbian peoples (Bray 2012). The starting point for this proposition is the understanding that commensality, whether ritual or quotidian, has, as either a goal or a consequence, the construction of specific relations of sociality. What may distinguish these two principal forms of commensality—that is, the extraordinary versus the everyday—are the types of persons engaged in the acts of shared consumption as well as modes of ingestion and temporal-spatial distances involved.

If everyday commensality is understood to produce and re-produce social relations among close kin (e.g., Anigbo 1987; Weismantel 1988), then ritual commensality may be seen as a way of creating social relations with extrafamilial and/or spaciotemporally distant others—a process that (not coincidentally) establishes non-kin others as social beings. Based on this proposition, I further suggest that evidence of ritual commensality can offer insights into ontological systems potentially distinct from our own by indicating with whom (or what), where, and how foodstuffs were or could be shared. My approach to commensality, then, takes it as a method for ascertaining the kinds of persons with whom it was possible to establish social relations via shared consumption.

In the earlier paper, I illustrated this approach with reference to archaeological data and the identification of pre-Columbian wak'as (Bray
2012; for additional discussion of pre-Columbian wak'as, see also Alconini, this volume). My argument was that evidence of ritual commensality in the archaeological record could be expected to provide insight
into who was or could be included in the social universe of a given
community. Several archaeological studies in recent decades have documented the presence of rock outcrops and monoliths that were accorded
special treatment by site inhabitants (e.g., Bazán del Campo 2007; Makowski et al. 2005; McEwan, Gibaja, and Chatfield 2005; Topic, Topic,
and Cava 2002). The material remains found in association with these
features lend themselves to an interpretation of ritual commensality.

A prime example can be seen at the site of Pueblo Viejo in the lower
Lurin Valley on the south-central coast of Peru (Makowski et al. 2005).
Investigators working at this site identified an unusual, modified rock
outcrop containing several carved niches that was surrounded by a low
enclosure wall and located near an elite residential compound (Makowski et al. 2005, 307–13). Significant quantities of broken cooking vessels,
large-sized serving jars, and individually-sized plates and bowls were
recovered inside the enclosure wall. Excavators also recorded several
concentrations of disarticulated llama bones and ash; numerous worked
and broken pieces of spondylus shell; a few small metal items; and a
small stone effigy in the shape of a corn cob in this area. The assemblage
readily lends itself to an interpretation of ritual commensal activity. The
conduct of these activities adjacent to the modified outcrop (which we
may understand as an important wak'a, based on the evidence) suggests
a clear intent to include this entity in the commensal affair, in this way
affirming its personhood and social relationship with the local community (Bray 2012, 202–3).

The ethnohistoric record offers further insights along these lines and
provides ample cause for positing the existence of an Andean ontology
distinct from that of Europeans. In particular, the rich pictorial record
created by the Indigenous author Felipe Guaman Poma de Ayala during
the early seventeenth century provides a number of graphic illustrations
pertaining to the way in which food mediated social relations across
what—from a Western ontological perspective—would be viewed as
unbridgeable divides. In figure 15.2, for instance, Guaman Poma depicts

Figure 15.2 The fifth Sapa Inka, Capac Yupanqui Ynga, who is said to have invented the act of sharing a drink with his father, the Sun (Guaman Poma de Ayala [1615] 1936, 100–101). Image courtesy of the Royal Library of Denmark.

the fifth Inka king, Capac Yupanqui Ynga, "drinking with his father, the sun" (Guaman Poma de Ayala [1615] 1936, 100–101). This and other such images drew on and reflect a shared understanding among the subjects of Tawantinsuyu (and their descendants) that Inka men of royal birth claimed genealogical descent from the sun. The commensal act of drinking with and to the lord of the heavens was the material expression of a key social relationship linking the Inka ruler to his nonhuman progenitor.

Pizarro ([1571] 1921, 253–55) offers another description of a ritual event involving the sharing of food and drink with, in this case, the earthly manifestation of the Sun that took place on the central plaza of Cusco in what seems to have been a fairly regular affair. The religious caretakers of the Sun's image would bring it out to be seated on a richly adorned bench in the middle of the plaza together with a pair of highly decorated weapons that belonged to the deity. The Sun would then be presented with food and drink, which would be burned in a special fire built in front of it— incineration being the mechanism by which divine entities consumed their sustenance. Importantly, when the Sun's "dinner" was about to be lit, one of the guardians would yell loudly and, upon hearing his cry, all of the Cusqueños in the plaza—as well as those beyond but still within earshot— "would sit down, and, without speaking or coughing or moving, remain silent until the food was consumed" (Pizarro [1571] 1921, 254). Sharing the meal with the wak'a in this way—that is, by attending closely to its dining—can be considered a form of commensality, asymmetrical though it was. The episode described, again, seems to have been aimed at establishing social bonds across ontological divides, in this case creating connections between the human residents of Cusco and their divine patrons.

In addition to linking human persons to supernatural nonhuman persons, the sharing of food and drink also bridged the divide between the categories of living and dead, bringing these different modes of existence together within a single social world. In referring to the burial practices of peoples from the Collasuyu sector of the Inka Empire, for instance, Guaman Poma de Ayala ([1615]1936, 293) states that "they [the Collasuyus] give the deceased food, chicha, water, gold, silver, dinnerware, garments, and other things . . . [and] thus they are buried with their food and drink . . . [, and] the living always take care to send the dead food and drink." The commensal nature of these practices is depicted in figure 15.3. Eating with (and for) the dead remains an important activity

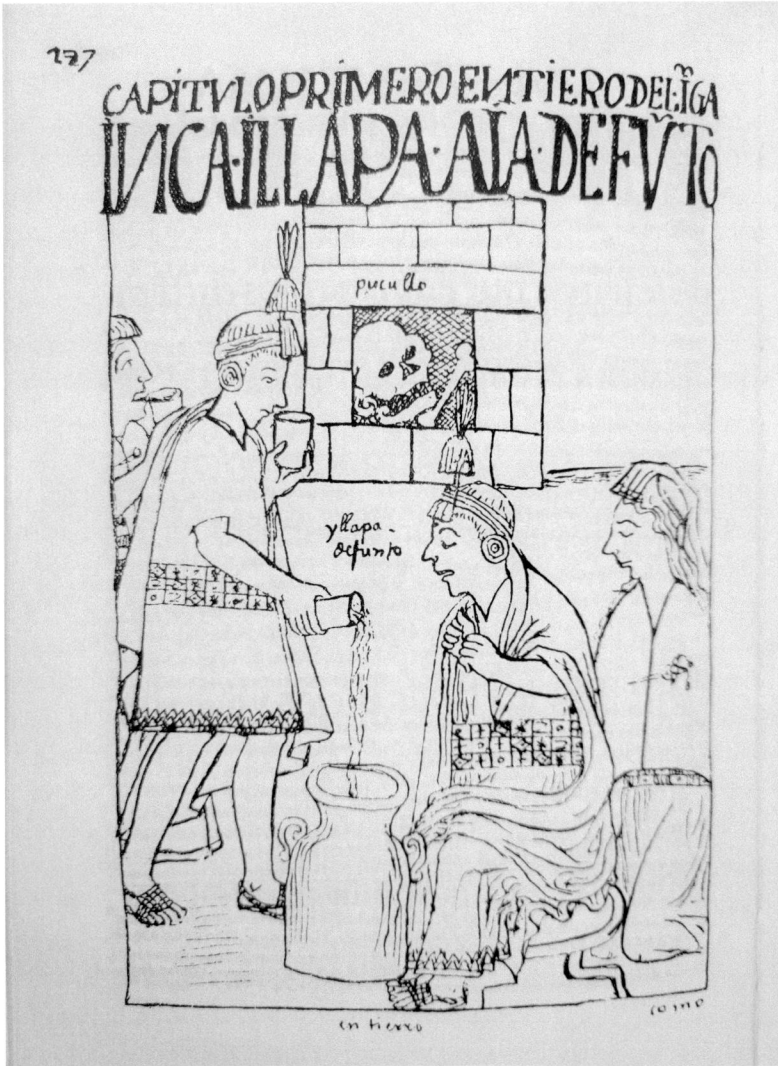

Figure 15.3 Inka nobles engaged in ritual commensal activities with a deceased member of their lineage (Guaman Poma de Ayala [1615] 1936, 287 [289]). Image courtesy of Royal Library of Denmark

among traditional Andean peoples today, as noted earlier (Allen 1988; also, Hartmann 1973).

One final intriguing example to bring forward is that in which Guaman Poma de Ayala ([1615] 1936, 369) illustrates an imagined meeting between the conquistador Pedro de Candia and the Inka king Huayna Capac. In the text the author writes that the Inka had been informed that "men with long beards who had the appearance of corpses" had landed in his kingdom, and he thereupon orders that one be brought to his court. In the accompanying drawing (fig. 15.4), the encounter between the two is depicted as a commensal event mediated by an array of foodstuffs in which the Inka is shown presenting a plate to the foreigner and simultaneously asking, "Is this the gold you eat?" with the Spaniard replying, "This is the gold we eat."

In this encounter, the Inka negotiates with what, to his eyes, was probably a nonhuman person via a commensal act. The main foodstuff being presented, in addition to all the other items indicated by the variety of serving vessels arranged between them, seems to be a plate of gold—not the normal fare of human persons, to be sure. In this provocative image, we are presented with a clear example of how social relations were constructed through ritual commensality and the way in which ontological status could be negotiated through food. The personhood of the Spaniard was both literally and figuratively constructed within a relational framework comprising a heterogeneous assemblage of human and nonhuman actors, among which foodstuffs and serving vessels featured prominently.

A century of anthropological research clearly indicates that cooking and eating are important arenas for the production and re-production of social life. I suggest that focusing on the culinary realm holds much promise for generating new insights into the social worlds made and inhabited by peoples of the pre-Columbian past. Following the food archaeologically can take us into materially mediated social domains that are well beyond dietary preferences and environmental reconstructions. The focus on food as vital matter may also offer insights into the ontological frameworks of different cultures and open new vistas for thinking relationally, transcorporeally, and nonpassively about sustenance and what it entails.

Figure 15.4 An imaginary meeting between the Inka Huayna Capac and a Spanish agent in which the Inka presumably attempts to negotiate a social relation with what probably seemed a nonhuman person through commensality (Guaman Poma de Ayala [1615] 1936, 369 [371]). Image courtesy of Royal Library of Denmark.

REFERENCES

Alaimo, Stacy. 2010. *Bodily Natures*. Bloomington: Indiana University Press.

Alaimo, Stacy, and Susan Hekman. 2008. *Material Feminisms*. Bloomington: Indiana University Press.

Allen, Catherine. 1988. *The Hold Life Has*. Washington, D.C.: Smithsonian Institution Press.

Allen, Catherine. 1997. "When Pebbles Move Mountains: Iconicity and Symbolism in Quechua Ritual." In *Creating Context in Andean Cultures*, edited by Rosaleen Howard-Malverde, 73–84. Oxford: Oxford University Press.

Allen, Catherine. 2015. "The Whole World Is Watching: New Perspectives on Andean Animism." In *The Archaeology of Wak'as: Explorations of the Sacred in the Pre-Columbian Andes*, edited by Tamara Bray, 23–46. Boulder: University Press of Colorado.

Anigbo, Osmund. 1987. *Commensality and Human Relationship Among the Igbo*. Nsukka: University of Nigeria Press.

Arnold, Denise. 2018. "Making Textiles into Persons: Gestural Sequences and Relationality in Communities of Weaving Practice of the South Central Andes." *Journal of Material Culture* 23 (2): 239–60. https://doi.org/10.1177/135 9183517750007.

Arriaga, Pablo Joseph de. (1621) 1968. *La Extirpación de la Idolatría en el Perú: Colección de Libros y Documentos Referentes a la Historia del Perú*. Vol. 1. Lima: Sanmarti.

Bazán del Campo, Francisco. 2007. "Las Ceremonias Especializadas de Veneración a los Huancas." *SIAN Revista Arqueológica* 18:3–17.

Bennett, Jane. 2007. "Edible Matter." *New Left Review* 45:133–45.

Bennett, Jane. 2010. *Vibrant Matter: A Political Ecology of Things*. Durham, N.C.: Duke University Press.

Bertonio, Ludovico. (1612) 1879. *Vocabulario de la Lengua Aymara*. Leipzig: B. G. Tuebner.

Bolin, Inge. 1998. *Rituals of Respect: The Secret of Survival in the High Peruvian Andes*. Austin: University of Texas Press.

Bray, Tamara. 2012. "Ritual Commensality Between Human and Non-Human Persons: Investigating Native Ontologies in the Late Pre-Columbian Andean World." *eTopoi: Journal of Ancient Studies* 2:197–212.

Bray, Tamara. 2018a. "Archaeology, Temporal Complexity, and the Politics of Time." In *Constructions of Time and History in the Pre-Columbian Andes*, edited by Edward Swenson and Andrew Roddick, 263–78. Boulder: University Press of Colorado.

Bray, Tamara. 2018b. "Partnering with Pots: The Work of Materials in the Imperial Inca Project." *Cambridge Archaeological Journal* 28 (2): 243–57. https://doi.org/10.1017/S0959774317000828.

Busby, Cecilia. 1997. "Permeable and Partible Persons: A Comparative Analysis of Gender and the Body in South India and Melanesia." *Journal of the Royal Anthropological Institute* 3 (2): 261–78. https://doi.org/10.2307/3035019.

Carter, Richard. 1977. "Trial Marriage in the Andes?" In *Kinship and Marriage in the Andes*, edited by Ralph Bolton and Enrique Mayer, 177–216. Washington, D.C.: American Anthropological Association.

Cereceda, Veronica. 1986. "The Semiology of Andean Textiles: The Talegas of Isluga." In *Anthropological History of Andean Polities*, edited by John Murra, Nathan Wachtel, and Jacques Revel, 149–73. Cambridge: Cambridge University Press.

Cobo, Bernabe. (1653) 1990. *Inca Religion and Customs*. Translated by Roland Hamilton. Austin: University of Texas Press.

DeLanda, Manuel. 2016. *Assemblage Theory*. Edinburgh: Edinburgh University Press.

Diccionario de la Lengua Castellana. 1726–39. 6 vols. Madrid: Imprenta de la Real Academia Española. https://webfrl.rae.es/DA.html.

Fajans, Jane. 1988. "The Transformative Value of Food: A Review Essay." *Food and Foodways* 3 (1/2): 143–66. https://doi.org/10.1080/07409710.1988.9961941.

Falk, Pasi. 1994. *The Consuming Body*. London: Sage.

Garcilaso de la Vega, El Inca. (1609) 1960. *Primera Parte de los Comentarios Reales de los Incas*. Vols. 133–35. Madrid: Biblioteca de Autores Españoles.

Gifford, Douglas, and Pauline Hoggarth. 1976. *Carnival and Coca Leaf: Some Traditions of the Peruvian Quechua Ayllu*. New York: St. Martin's Press.

González Holguín, Diego. (1608) 1952. *Vocabulario de la Lengua General de Todo el Perú Llamada Lengua Qquichua o del Inca*. 2nd ed. Prologue by Raúl Porras Barrenechea. Lima: Universidad Nacional Mayor de San Marcos.

Gose, Peter. 1994. *Deathly Waters and Hungry Mountains: Agrarian Ritual and Class Formation in an Andean Town*. Toronto: University of Toronto Press.

Guaman Poma de Ayala, Felipe. (1615) 1936. *El Primer Nueva Corónica y Buen Gobierno*. Paris.

Haraway, Donna. 1990. *Simians, Cyborgs and Women: The Reinvention of Nature*. London: Routledge.

Haraway, Donna. 2016. *Staying with the Trouble: Making Kin in the Chthulucene (Experimental Futures)*. Durham, N.C.: Duke University Press.

Hartmann, Roswith. 1973. "Conmemoración de Muertos en la Sierra Ecuatoriana." *Indiana* 1:179–97. https://doi.org/10.18441/ind.v1i0.179-197.

Jackson, Peter. 2013. *Food Words: Essays in Culinary Culture*. London: Bloomsbury.

Kurlansky, Mark. 1997. *Cod: A Biography of the Fish That Changed the World*. New York: Penguin Books.

Latour, Bruno. 2005. *Reassembling the Social: An Introduction to Actor-Network-Theory*. New York: Oxford University Press.

Law, John, and John Hassard. 1999. *Actor Network Theory and After*. Oxford: Wiley-Blackwell.

Makowski, Krzysztof, María Fe Córdova, Patricia Habetler, and Manuel Lizárraga. 2005. "La Plaza y la Fiesta: Reflexiones Acerca de la Función de los Patios en la Arquitectura Pública Prehispánica de los Períodos Tardíos." *Boletín de Arqueología, PUCP* 9:297–333.

Marriott, McKim. 1976. "Hindu Transactions: Diversity without Dualism." In *Transaction and Meaning: Direction in the Anthropology of Exchange and Symbolic Behaviour*, edited by Bruce Kapferer, 109–42. Philadelphia: Institute for the Study of Human Issues.

McEwan, Gordon, Arminda Gibaja, and Melissa Chatfield. 2005. "Arquitectura Monumental en el Cuzco del Periodo Intermedio Tardío: Evidencias de Continuidades en la Reciprocidad Ritual y el Manejo Administrativa entre los Horizontes Medio y Tardío." *Boletín de Arqueología, PUCP* 9:257–80.

Mintz, Sydney. 1996. *Tasting Food, Tasting Freedom: Excursions into Eating, Culture, and the Past*. Boston: Beacon Press.

Molina, Cristóbal de. (ca. 1575) 2010. *Relación de las Fábulas y Ritos de los Incas*. Edited by Paloma Jiménez del Campo. Madrid: Iberoamericana-Vervuert.

Pizarro, Pedro. (1571) 1921. *Relation of the Discovery and Conquest of the Kingdoms of Peru*. Translated by Philip A. Means. New York: Cortes Society.

Polo de Ondegardo, Juan. (1571) 1916. *Informaciones Acerca de la Religión y Gobierno de los Incas*. Edited by Horacio H. Urteaga. Lima: Imprenta y Librería Sanmartí.

Psarikidou, Katerina, and Bronislaw Szerszynski. 2012. "Growing the Social: Alternative Agro-food Networks and Social Sustainability in the Urban Ethical Foodscape." *Sustainability: Science, Practice, and Policy* 1 (8): 30–9. https://doi.org/10.1080/15487733.2012.11908082.

Santo Tomás, Domingo de. 1560. *Grammatica o Arte de la Lengua de los Indios de los Reynos del Peru*. Valladolid: Fernandez de Cordova.

Stensrud, Astrid. 2016. "Climate Change, Water Practices and Relational Worlds in the Andes." *Ethnos* 81 (1): 75–98. https://doi.org/10.1080/00141844.2014.929597.

Strathern, Marilyn. 1988. *The Gender of the Gift*. Berkeley: University of California Press.

Swenson, Edward. 2018. "Sacrificial Landscapes and the Anatomy of Moche Biopolitics (AD 200–800)." In *Powerful Places in the Ancient Andes*, edited by Justin Jennings and Edward Swenson, 247–86. Albuquerque: University of New Mexico Press.

Swenson, Edward, and Andrew Roddick. 2018. "Introduction: Rethinking Temporality and Historicity from the Perspective of Andean Archaeology." In *Constructions of Time and History in the Pre-Columbian Andes*, edited by Edward Swenson and Andrew Roddick, 3–43. Boulder: University Press of Colorado.

Topic, John, Theresa Topic, and Alfredo Melly Cava. 2002. "The Archaeology, Ethnohistory, and Ethnography of a Major Provincial Huaca." In *Andean*

Archaeology I: Variations in Sociopolitical Organization, edited by William Isbell and Helaine Silverman, 303–36. New York: Kluwer Academic; Plenum.

Walens, Stanley. 1981. *Feasting with Cannibals: An Essay on Kwaikutl Cosmology.* Princeton, N.J.: Princeton University Press.

Warnier, Jean-Pierre. 2007. *The Pot-King: The Body and Technologies of Power.* New York: Brill.

Weismantel, Mary. 1988. *Food, Gender, and Poverty in the Ecuadorian Andes.* Philadelphia: University of Pennsylvania Press.

Weismantel, Mary. 1995. "Making Kin: Kinship Theory and Zumbagua Adoptions." *American Ethnologist* 22 (4): 685–709.

PART V

FUTURE DIRECTIONS AND CONCLUSIONS

16

Foods, Diets, and Cuisines in the Andes

Some Concluding Thoughts

Susan D. deFrance

In order to create diets that fed and satiated both the living and diverse others, peoples and cultures of the ancient Andes engaged with plants, animals, the environment, and material culture in multiple and varied ways to transform raw products into foodstuffs that they further transformed into edible meals for consumption. During the sharing of meals and along each step of the food transformation process, social behaviors followed prescribed cultural norms, particularly as related to gender, age, identity, and status. At the same time, people conformed to expected behaviors. Meal preparation, and consumption, whether on a household scale or that of a community feast, consisted of performative actions reflecting a myriad of human desires and emotions. People created alliances, engaged in one-upmanship, jockeyed for recognition and praise, gossiped, and found future mates as well as countless other types of social interactions. Fortunately for archaeologists, many of the human-food interactions that took place in the past leave behind physical residues, spatial evidence, and biological and geochemical signatures in human and animal bodies. For behaviors that did not leave direct archaeological evidence, the rich ethnographies and ethnohistorical and historical accounts from the Andean region can be used cautiously to infer aspects of past food behavior.

The authors in this volume show both methodological skill in their analyses as well as creativity in constructing research questions and interpretations related to past foods, diets, and cuisines. To varying degrees the contributors employ new analytical methods, the integration and comparison of different food data, and interdisciplinary research to provide novel insights into ancient Andean foodways and important contributions to the recent literature addressing foods and diets in the Andean region (e.g., Cutright 2021; various authors in Staller 2021).

Here, I make suggestions for future research on foods, diets, and cuisines in the Andes and assess the analytical and interpretive challenges that researchers face. I also consider how some of the terminology commonly used in archaeological food and cuisine research may be shaping our interpretations unintentionally and negatively. There are many excellent volumes, essays, and case studies regarding different aspects of Andean cuisines; therefore, my essay is not a review of the literature that has gone before but rather an assessment of the challenges that archaeologists face when studying foods and cuisines and an exploration of possible new ways to think about diets and human behavior.

WHAT IS CUISINE?

Although various anthropological definitions of cuisine and meal structure are frequently cited (e.g., Douglas 1972; Goody 1996; Mintz and Du Bois 2002), the four-component definition of cuisine by Farb and Armelagos (1980, 190) is simple and elegant. Cuisine consists of (1) the limited number of foods that people select from what is environmentally available; (2) the manner of preparation; (3) traditional principles of flavoring, and; (4) all the rules related to food, including the number of meals consumed per day, whether meals are eaten with others or alone, whether some food is reserved for ceremonial use, and what and when foods are taboo. As Farb and Armelagos (1980, 190) note, these four elements include not only the artistic presentation of food "but everything concerned with eating." This definition is important because it reminds archaeologists that our analyses can only inform a limited portion of cuisine and that some aspects of cuisine are less visible or even invisible in our data (see Miller et al., this volume).

We also face issues of equifinality when considering cuisine—distinct processes can result in similar or identical outcomes. The issue of equifinality is most applicable to interpretations regarding methods of preparation and the physical properties of the resulting food refuse. For example, both open-pit cooking of meat and burning animal refuse might result in bone with similar degrees of burning. Likewise, pounding maize to add ground maize to soups or stews would result in the same evidence as chicha production (Matthew Biwer, personal communication, June 2021). The material culture for food preparation or consumption could also have served many nonfood uses. Multiple aspects of food rules and the absence of certain foods have the potential for equifinality as well. Explaining the absence of common foods in an assemblage (i.e., negative evidence) is particularly challenging. Larger samples and spatial comparisons across multiple contexts can help determine whether the absence of a foodstuff is the result of sampling or cultural practice.

Another issue related to identifying cuisine is that subtle differences in food preparation between different cultural groups may or may not reflect identity formation and intentionality. Identity formation implies an active acknowledgment by a group of people that this way of cooking is "what we do" to distinguish ourselves from others. Alternatively, the use of something local and naturally abundant may be out of necessity rather than an intentional selection of specific food items to express identity. Thus, when we speak of cuisine we need to acknowledge these various caveats.

ARCHAEOLOGICAL DATA IN STUDIES OF ANDEAN FOODS, DIETS, AND CUISINES

It is increasingly common for Andeanists to combine different archaeological food data sets to provide holistic interpretations (e.g., Duke 2019; Nash and deFrance 2019; Quave, Kennedy, and Covey 2019). Comparing different data, as several authors did in this volume, poses several challenges (see VanDerwarker 2010), including (as noted by Biwer, Alaica, and Quiñonez Cuzcano, this volume) that ubiquity identifies the presence of plant and animal foods but does not account for quantity, sample size variability, or the quality of the food material. The variability related to sample sizes for specific analyses can also make comparisons difficult. For example, the analyzed material may come from a small portion of a site, but because the volume of the total excavated site area versus the volume of the analyzed material is often not reported, generalizations may not be accurate. Similarly, certain analyses require different volumes of material for reliable analysis. For example, a volumetric sample of 25 L from a dense midden of refuse might be appropriate for zooarchaeological analysis, but a sample of 5 L from the same context might be suitable for archaeobotanical sampling. And excavation contexts can differ greatly in the volume of food refuse (e.g., a household floor versus a temple context).

There is also the issue of interpreting results from distinct analyses that contradict one another, particularly isotopic data on human diets and the food remains themselves. The studies by Miller et al. and Knudson et al. (this volume) present isotopic data indicating that people either did or did not eat particular foods. In the case of the Moquegua Valley samples (Knudson et al.), isotopes indicate that Tiwanaku inhabitants consumed freshwater fishes; however, freshwater fish remains are not found in Moquegua Tiwanaku sites. In contrast, the isotopic analysis by Miller et al. of Formative Period populations living in direct proximity to Lake Titicaca shows that children did not consume freshwater fishes even though fish remains are abundant in zooarchaeological materials. Ongoing improvements in mixing models (see Cheung and Szpak 2022) and more baseline studies will continue to refine these discrepancies.

Analyses that include multiple categories of food information require explanations of the methods used and clear data presentation (and data curation). But most importantly, the quantified data requires eloquent interpretations. Because many aspects of foods and cuisines are sensory, how we write about food and food-related behavior has great potential to provide both scientific information as well as humanistic and evocative understandings of how Andean peoples lived in the past. The studies in the volume advance that goal.

ONGOING CHALLENGES TO THE STUDY OF FOODS, DIETS, AND CUISINES

In addition to issues related to the integration of food and dietary data sets, there are other ongoing challenges for Andean food studies. Here, I address four topics of concern. First, the bony tissues of animals that end up in the archaeological record and the processed plant remains are biased assemblages of the total animal and plant matter that people consumed. There is very little consideration by analysts, myself included, of the organ tissues from animals. And since camelids are large mammals with large organ systems, we are probably discounting a large portion of the carcass in our analyses. A similar bias may apply to heavily processed or full consumed plant materials. I know of no analytical methods that will account for these unrecoverable food sources. However, greater consideration of the operational chain of processing could potentially fill in some of these gaps.

A second issue concerns past human behavior and the language we use to describe that behavior. Many of our food studies are analyses of food matter that people left behind. We commonly use terms such as discarded, disposal, refuse, and trash to describe food matter that people left behind. Although in some instances researchers acknowledge intentional placement of foodstuffs (e.g., Nash and deFrance 2019), in many cases, the semantics of discard terminology may be obscuring how past Andean peoples perceived consumed food matter or the products of food processing. If we acknowledge that Andean peoples functioned in a world where all matter was animate and food matter required the same moral code of reverence that was applied to the material world (Bray, this volume), wouldn't people view the remains of meals not as "waste" but as still vital matter? I don't think that all food that remained after Andean consumption events would be considered ceremonial trash (sensu Walker 1995), although some of it may have been. Yet the processed portions of plants and animals that provided food may have continued to live after consumption. Therefore, our food "discard" terminology could be more sensitive to that awareness.

A third topic relates to our lack of knowledge concerning household inhabitants and who ate what. Several of the authors in this volume provide empirical evidence of social and status differences in the food practices among past Andean populations. For elite populations, there is little to no consideration that households or elite compounds would have been occupied by individuals of different ranks and statuses. Andean households were not homogenous. The archaeological identification of people of different statuses within households, if possible, might allow us to understand the diversity of past food practices. For example, should the conquered and colonized pre-Columbian populations of the Andes be considered subalterns? Were these populations excluded from political and economic decision making, and if so, how were their food practices affected?

A fourth topic concerns the changing status of Andean peoples and their foodways following Spanish colonization (e.g., Belmar et al. this volume; deFrance 2021; Kennedy, Chiou, and VanValkenburgh 2019;

Weaver, Muñoz, and Durand 2019). Expanded research on Colonial changes to diets and cuisines promises to highlight the continuity of some food practices along with the significant changes that occurred.

FUTURE STUDIES AND CONCLUSIONS

As shown in these chapters, the foods, diets, and cuisines of Andean peoples were integral to their social, economic, political, and spiritual worlds. Food provided much more than nutritional substances. Future research on foods and diets will continue to provide novel insights into past Andean lives. I offer two suggestions, one methodological and one topical, for new avenues of future food and dietary studies.

Andean food research has great potential to use new methods that move analyses beyond studies of past food ingredients to study recipes and combinations of foods in greater detail. The studies by Weber and Young (this volume) and Belmar et al. (this volume) are very successful at identifying microbotanical materials in both ground stone and ceramics. One methodology to build on microbotanical and other food residue analysis is through metabolomics, or the identification and quantification of organic metabolite compounds. A recent study by Duffy (2021) extracted metabolites from a variety of ground stone artifacts, both curated and recently excavated, from Maya sites in Mesoamerica. Duffy extracted small quantities of ground stone fiber and used LC-MS (liquid chromatography–mass spectrometry) to generate metabolomic profiles of different foods and ingested substances (e.g., chili peppers, chocolate, tobacco). Similarly, Henkin is using two minimally invasive techniques, droplet probe LC-MS and direct analysis in real-time mass spectrometry (DART-MS), to identify plant residues on Andean ceramics, including direct identification of chicha made from molle (Henkin 2020; Williams et al. 2019). These minimally invasive methods have a phenomenal potential for future application in the Andean region where ground stone artifacts and ceramics are so common.

A future topical contribution could be greater comparative analyses of Andean foodways and diets across time and geography. As shown in this volume, food and dietary analyses commonly begin at the site level since this is the initial archaeological unit of study. The accumulation of site-level information can then be used for comparisons among multiple sites within time-specific periods or geographic regions (e.g., Alfonso-Durruty, Misarti, and Troncoso; Belmar et al; Berryman and Blom; Knudson et al.; Miller et al.; Santana-Sagredo et al.; Wilson and McCool, this volume). The examination of individual food items that people traded or exchanged over long distances can potentially show social connections that are not obvious in the archaeological record. For example, the long-distance trade of the Chilean Jack Mackerel to both colonial outposts of the Wari Empire as well as to local, politically independent inland sites in far southern Peru shows that coastal trade in marine fish was not an economic specialization that required political integration or oversight (deFrance 2021). Broad comparative studies might also examine whether environmental change or political and economic disruptions affected specific foods or diets.

The innovative studies in this volume show that the archaeological study of Andean diets, foods, and cuisines has made significant contributions to the social role of foods and diets in past lives, the creation of identity through foods, and the impact of foods on systems of production. Future research on Andean diets and cuisines will continue to highlight the centrality of food in Andean lives.

REFERENCES

Cheung, Christina, and Paul Szpak. 2022. "Interpreting Past Human Diets Using Stable Isotope Mixing Models: Best Practices for Data Acquisition." *Journal of Archaeological Method and Theory* 29:138–61. https://doi.org/10.1007/s10816-021-09514-w.

Cutright, Robyn E. 2021. *The Story of Food in the Human Past: How What We Ate Made Us Who We Are.* Tuscaloosa: University Alabama Press.

deFrance, Susan. 2021. "Fishing Specialization and the Inland Trade of the Chilean Jack Mackerel or Jurel, *Trachurus murphyi*, in Far Southern Peru." *Archaeological and Anthropological Sciences* 13:84–97. https://doi.org/10.1007/s12520-021-01326-z.

Douglas, Mary. 1972. "Deciphering a Meal." *Daedalus* 101 (1): 61–81. https://www.jstor.org/stable/20024058.

Duffy, Lisa. 2021. "Using Residue Analysis to Explore Ancient Maya Recipes and Food-Processing Technology." PhD diss., University of Florida.

Duke, Guy S. 2019. "'Doing' Llama Face Stew: A Late Moche Culinary Assemblage as a Domestic Dedicatory Deposit." *Cambridge Archaeological Journal* 29 (3): 517–35. https://doi.org/10.1017/S0959774319000179.

Farb, Peter, and George Armelagos. 1980. *Consuming Passions: The Anthropology of Eating*. Boston: Houghton Mifflin.

Goody, Jack. 1996. *Cooking, Cuisine and Class: A Study in Comparative Sociology*. Ill. ed. New York: Cambridge University Press.

Henkin, Joshua M. 2020. "Molecular Signatures of Plant Residues from Ceramics of Kala Uyuni Using Droplet Probe LC-MS." Poster presentation presented at the 48th Annual Midwest Conference on Andean and Amazonian Archaeology and Ethnohistory. Michigan State University, East Lansing, Mich., February 29–March 1, 2020.

Kennedy, Sarah A., Katherine L. Chiou, and Parker VanValkenburgh. 2019. "Inside the Reducción: Crafting Colonial Foodways at Carrizales and Mocupe Viejo, Zaña Valley, Peru (1570–1700)." *International Journal of Historical Archaeology* 23 (4): 980–1010. https://doi.org/10.1007/s10761-018-0481-2.

Mintz, Sidney W., and Christine M. DuBois. 2002. "The Anthropology of Food and Eating." *Annual Review of Anthropology* 31:99–119. https://doi.org/10.1146/annurev.anthro.32.032702.131011.

Nash, Donna J., and Susan D. deFrance. 2019. "Plotting Abandonment: Excavating a Ritual Deposit at the Wari Site of Cerro Baúl." *Journal of Anthropological Archaeology* 53 (2): 112–32. https://doi.org/10.1016/j.jaa.2018.12.002.

Quave, Kylie E., Sarah A. Kennedy, and R. Alan Covey. 2019. "Rural Cuzco Before and After Inka Imperial Conquest: Foodways, Status, and Identity (Maras, Peru)." *International Journal of Historical Archaeology* 23:868–92. https://doi.org/10.1007/S10761-018-0483-0.

Staller, John E., ed. 2021. *Andean Foodways: Pre-Columbian, Colonial, and Contemporary Food and Culture*. The Latin American Studies Book Series. New York: Springer. https://www.springer.com/gp/book/9783030516284.

VanDerwarker, Amber M. 2010. "Simple Measures for Integrating Plant and Animal Remains." In *Integrating Zooarchaeology and Paleoethnobotany: A Consideration of Issues, Methods, and Cases*, edited by Amber M. VanDerwarker and Tanya M. Peres, 65–74. New York: Springer. https://doi.org/10.1007/978-1-4419-0935-0.

Walker, William H. 1995. "Ceremonial Trash?" In *Expanding Archaeology*, edited by James M. Skibo, William H. Walker, and Axel E. Nielsen, 67–79. Salt Lake City: University of Utah Press.

Weaver, Brendan J. M., Lizette A. Muñoz, and Karen Durand. 2019. "Supplies, Status, and Slavery: Contested Aesthetics of Provisioning at the Jesuit Haciendas of Nasca." *International Journal of Historical Archaeology* 23 (4): 1011–38. https://doi.org/10.1007/s10761-018-0485-y.

Williams, Patrick R., Donna J. Nash, Joshua M. Henkin, and Ruth A. Armitage. 2019. "Archaeometric Approaches to Defining Sustainable Governance: Wari Brewing Traditions and the Building of Political Relationships in Ancient Peru." *Sustainability* 11 (8): art. no. 2333. https://doi.org/10.3390/su11082333.

CONTRIBUTORS

Aleksa K. Alaica is an Assistant Professor at the Department of Anthropology, University of British Columbia. She analyzes human-animal relationships and animal management during the first millennium CE in the Andes through zooarchaeological, isotopic, and iconographic methods.

Sonia Alconini is the David A. Harrison III Professor of Archaeology at the Department of Anthropology, University of Virginia. She specializes in the nature of frontier interaction, Inka imperialism, and local agency.

Marta Alfonso-Durruty is an Associate Professor of Anthropology at Kansas State University. Her research focuses on the bioarchaeological analysis of the peopling, adaptation, and diversity of human populations of Patagonia (Chile) as well as the diet of groups in the arid and semi-arid regions of Chile.

Sarah I. Baitzel is an Assistant Professor of Anthropology at Washington University in St. Louis. She specializes in mortuary archaeology and codirects archaeological research in Sama and Cuzco, Peru, on Andean pastoralism, mobility, and social identity in the context of state collapse.

Véronique Bélisle is an Associate Professor of Anthropology at Millsaps College. Her research focuses on the impact of Wari state expansion in the Cusco region of southern Peru. She has directed large-scale excavations at Ak'awillay and is currently working on a new project in the Wari colony in Cusco.

Carolina Belmar is an Assistant Professor at the Department of Anthropology, University of Chile. She specializes in paleoethnobotanical studies and researches different problems related to the complex relationship between humans and plants from the Late Pleistocene to Historic times in different areas of Chile.

Carrie Anne Berryman earned her PhD from the Department of Anthropology of Vanderbilt University. She is a specialist in bioarchaeology, dental anthropology, and forensic anthropology, and she has extensively studied the relationship between food and state formation. She has carried out fieldwork in Mesoamerican and the Andes.

Matthew E. Biwer is a Visiting Assistant Professor of Anthropology and Archaeology at Dickinson College. His research focuses on Andean archaeology and paleoethnobotany to investigate foodways and sociopolitics. He has conducted field and laboratory research in the south-central Andes of Peru focusing primarily on the Middle Horizon Wari Empire.

Deborah E. Blom is an Associate Professor of Anthropology in the Department of Anthropology at the University of Vermont, where she focuses on bioarchaeology and archaeology of the Andes, including mortuary ritual, health, diet, and human body modification as a means of expressing identity.

Tamara L. Bray is a Professor of Anthropology at Wayne State University in Detroit, Michigan. She specializes in the study of Inka imperialism and the archaeology of food. Her field research in Ecuador, Bolivia, Peru, and Argentina has addressed long-distance trade, imperial frontiers, sacred sites, and state pottery.

Matthew T. Brown is a doctoral student in the Department of Anthropology at the University of Michigan. His research focuses on transformations in social organization and the economy during the Formative Period in Cusco. He has supervised excavations in Cusco and the Puuc region of Yucatán as well as systematic surveys in Kosovo and Oaxaca, Mexico.

Maria C. Bruno is an Associate Professor of Anthropology and Archaeology at Dickinson College. She studies human-environmental relationships and the development of agriculture in South America. Her methodological specializations include ethnobotany and archaeobotany. Her primary region of study is the Lake Titicaca Basin of the Andes.

José M. Capriles is an Assistant Professor at Pennsylvania State University. He specializes in environmental archaeology, human ecology, and zooarchaeology. His research focuses on the peopling of South America and the socio-ecological factors involved in domestication and the disintegration of the Tiwanaku and Inka states.

Katherine L. Chiou is an Assistant Professor in the Department of Anthropology at the University of Alabama, where she directs the Ancient People and Plants Laboratory. She is an archaeologist and paleoethnobotanist interested in foodways, Andean archaeology, household archaeology, chili pepper domestication, GIS and data visualization, and ethics in archaeological practice.

Susan D. deFrance is a Professor of Anthropology in the Department of Anthropology, University of Florida. She is a specialist in zooarchaeology who conducts research on coastal adaptations, animal use in Andean empires, and Spanish and French Colonial archaeology. The geographic regions of study are the Central Andes, the Caribbean, and the U.S. Gulf Coast.

Marcos de la Rosa-Martinez is an advanced graduate student in the School of Human Evolution and Social Change at Arizona State University, where he focuses on the archaeology and paleodiet of North and South America.

Lucia M. Diaz is a doctoral student in the Department of Anthropology at Washington University in St. Louis. Her research utilizes stable isotopic analysis to investigate highland and lowland Andean pastoralism mobility and subsistence during the Late Horizon.

Richard P. Evershed is Chair of Biogeochemistry in the School of Chemistry, University of Bristol, and a Fellow of the Royal Society. He develops and applies chromatographic and mass spectrometric techniques that provide data for the reconstruction of prehistoric environments, diet, agriculture, and technologies.

Maureen E. Folk holds an MA from the Department of Anthropology at Binghamton University, New York. Her research specializes in paleoethnobotany and the cuisine of migrant communities in the ancient Andes.

Alexandra Greenwald is an Assistant Professor of Anthropology in the Department of Anthropology and the Curator of Ethnography at the Natural History Museum of Utah, University of Utah. She specializes in archaeological chemistry, North and South American prehistoric archaeology and ethnography, human behavioral ecology, biological anthropology, and bioarchaeology.

Chris Harrod is a Professor of Aquatic and Isotope Ecology at the Universidad de Antofagasta, Chile, where he is the director of the Instituto de Ciencias Naturales Alexander von Humboldt and the Universidad de Antofagasta Stable Isotope Facility. His research is largely directed at the ecology, function, and evolution of aquatic ecosystems and taxa using stable isotope analysis.

Christine A. Hastorf is a Professor of Anthropology, Director of the Archaeological Research Facility, Director of the McCown Archaeobotany Laboratory, and the Curator of South American Archaeology at the Phoebe A. Hearst Museum of Anthropology at the University of California, Berkeley. She specializes in paleoethnobotany focusing on plant production and use, particularly as foods, in the Andes of South America.

Iain Kendall is a postdoctoral researcher in the Organic Geochemistry Unit, School of Chemistry, University of Bristol. He specializes in compound-specific stable isotope techniques to investigate dietary sources and subsistence strategies of ancient human communities.

Kelly J. Knudson is a Professor of Anthropology in the School of Human Evolution and Social Change at Arizona State University, where she also directs the Center for Bioarchaeological Research and the Archaeological Chemistry Laboratory. Her research focuses on Andean paleodiet and paleomobility.

BrieAnna S. Langlie is an Assistant Professor of Anthropology at Binghamton University, New York, where she directs the Laboratory of

Ancient Food and Farming (LAFF). She specializes in paleoethnobotany and prehispanic Andean farming systems and explores human resilience and adaptation to social and climate change.

Cecilia Lemp is an adjunct professor at the Universidad Austral de Chile (Puerto Montt). She is in charge of the conservation and documentation of archaeological collections and teaches courses in archaeological conservation and collection management for archaeology students. She is a doctoral student at the National University of Córdoba, Argentina.

Petrus le Roux is a Chief Research Officer in the Department of Geological Sciences, University of Cape Town, where he is the Director of the MC-ICP-MS Facility. His interdisciplinary research focuses on the development of new analytical methods and novel application of existing methods to nontraditional geological fields.

Anahí Maturana-Fernández is a master's student in the Department of Anthropology at Trent University. Her research focuses on the analysis of stable isotopes in Northern Chile bioarchaeology, which goal is to understand patterns and changes in food consumption among archeological populations.

Weston C. McCool is a postdoctoral fellow in the Department of Anthropology, University of Utah. He focuses on human-environmental interactions through the lens of behavioral ecology and the use of geospatial modeling. His regional foci are the Nasca highlands of Peru and the Colorado Plateau.

Melanie J. Miller is a postdoctoral fellow in the Department of Anatomy at the University of Otago, New Zealand. Her research focuses on human diet, activity, and health and their relationships to social identities and inequalities. Melanie specializes in stable isotope analysis and has projects in South America and China.

Nicole Misarti is the Director of the Water and Environmental Research Center and an Associate Professor of Research at the University of Alaska, Fairbanks. She is also affiliated with the University of Alaska

Museum and the College of Fisheries and Ocean Sciences. She specializes in the historic ecology and paleoecology of nearshore marine ecosystems.

Flavia Morello is an Associate Professor at the Instituto de la Patagonia, Universidad de Magallanes, Chile. She specializes in the study of hunter-gatherer societies of Patagonia and the Fuegian archipelago (42°–56° South latitude). Her research focuses on lithic technology analyses and the dynamic interactions between culture, society, and the environment.

Patricia Quiñonez Cuzcano is a licensed archaeologist who specializes in malacological analysis and heritage management. She has worked at several Wari and Formative Period sites across Peru.

Omar Reyes, PhD, is a researcher and archaeologist at the Centro de Estudios del Hombre Austral, Universidad de Magallanes (Punta Arenas, Chile) and the Centro de Investigación en Ecosistemas de la Patagonia (Coyhaique, Chile). His research assesses the chronology and characteristics of marine hunter-gatherer settlements in the western Patagonian channels.

Arturo F. Rivera Infante is a licensed Peruvian archaeologist and a graduate of the Pontificia Universidad Católica del Perú. He specializes in ceramic and lithic analysis and has directed archaeological research projects throughout the central Andean region.

Manuel San Román is a researcher at the Centro de Estudios del Hombre Austral, Instituto de la Patagonia, Universidad de Magallanes, Chile.

Francisca Santana-Sagredo is an Assistant Professor of Archaeology at the Pontificia Universidad Católica de Chile. Her research focuses on human bioarchaeology, agropastoralism, paleodiet, ancient mobility patterns, and stable isotope analysis in the Atacama Desert.

Beth K. Scaffidi is an Assistant Professor of Anthropology and Heritage Studies in the School of Social Science, Humanities, and Arts at the University of California, Merced, where she directs the Skeletal and Environmental Isotope Laboratory (SEIL). Her research focuses on biocultural responses to social and environmental stress.

Augusto Tessone is a researcher at the National Council for Scientific and Technical Research (CONICET). Dr. Tessone specializes in the application of stable isotopes in archeology. He is currently researching different problems and materials, such as zooarcheology, ceramics, and human paleodiets in diverse socioeconomic contexts.

Andrés Troncoso is an Associate Professor in the Department of Anthropology, Universidad de Chile. His research has centered on the understanding of the Late Intermediate and Late period in central and north-central Chile, emphasizing the political and social dynamics of Inka and local communities using Landscape Archaeology as a framework.

Tiffiny A. Tung is a Professor and Chair of the Department of Anthropology at Vanderbilt University, where she is also the Director of the Bioarchaeology & Stable Isotope Research Lab. She is an anthropological bioarchaeologist, and her research is centered on exploring the health effects of sociocultural and political structures, particularly among early states in the Andes.

Mauricio Uribe is an Associate Professor of Archaeology in the Department of Anthropology at the University of Chile and a Counselor of the National Monuments Council of Chile. His research focuses on Andean cultures and archaeology using settlement and ceramic perspectives, particularly about social complexity processes in pre-state and state societies.

Natasha P. Vang is the laboratory manager for the Bioarchaeology and Stable Isotope Research Lab at Vanderbilt University. Her research interests focus on implementing and improving methods in archaeological chemistry to address questions about ancient diets and migration.

Sadie L. Weber is a postdoctoral scholar in the Laboratório de Arqueologia dos Trópicos in the Museu de Arqueologia e Etnologia at the Universidade de São Paulo. Her specialties are zooarchaeology and microbotany. Her research focuses on foodways, exchange, pastoralism, and the human-environment relation in the Central Andes and the Amazon.

Kurt M. Wilson is a PhD candidate at the Department of Anthropology, University of Utah. His research focuses on human-environment interactions, particularly studying how local ecologies influence human behavioral decisions regarding subsistence and influence diets, inequality, territoriality, and cooperation in western North America and the Central Andes.

Michelle E. Young is a postdoctoral fellow at the National Museum of the American Indian of the Smithsonian Institution. Her methodological foci are ceramic analysis and archaeometric techniques. Her research focuses on interregional interaction, long-distance exchange, ritual practices, and the emergence of new social identities during the Andean Formative.

INDEX

abalone, 183
achachillas, 80
achira, 74–76, 186
aclla, 7
agropastoralism, 6, 12, 83, 91, 111, 119,
    123, 172, 220–22, 228, 232, 234–36,
    259–60, 268–70, 305, 311
aguaymanto, 253
ají. *See* chili peppers
Ak'awillay, 11, 159–74, 252; style, 169
Álamos de San Juan, 46, 49, 51, 53,
    55–57
algae. *See* seaweed
algarroba (fruit). See *Prosopis* sp.
algarrobina (beverage), 81. See also
    Prosopis sp.
algarrobo (tree). See *Prosopis* sp.
aloja (beverage), 81. See also *Prosopis* sp.
alpaca, 5–6, 11, 93, 164, 181, 191, 228, 311.
    See also camelids
altiplano, 10, 12, 89, 91, 115, 117, 122–23,
    125, 221, 224–26, 232, 234, 259–60,
    265, 269, 314
amaranth, 76, 186, 203, 207, 252; wild,
    253
Amaranthaceae, 76, 78–79, 186. *See also*
    amaranth; Chenopodium or cheno-
    pod; quinoa
Amaranthus sp. *See* amaranth
Amazon and Amazonia, 4, 305
Amazonian: groups, 201, 203, 213;
    lowlands, 320; manioc, 80
amino acids, 97, 99, 101–2, 118
Amomyrtus luma, 54, 56–57, 60
amphibians, 227–28
Anadenanthera colubrina sp. *See* wilka

añapa, (beverage), 81. See also *Prosopis*
    sp.
Anas sp. *See* ducks
anchovy, 253
andenes. *See* terraces
animu, 8
Anser sp. *See* geese
Antisuyu, 303, 319
apatite (method), 117
apatite–collagen, 117, 118
apu, 13–14, 303, 306–7, 321–22. *See also*
    sacred geography
Arachis hypogea. See peanuts
Arawak Pukina, 320
Archaic, 262
Arequipa, 11, 12, 179, 202, 204, 216
arrope, 81
aryballos, 281, 297, 316, 319
Atacama Desert, 12, 259–60, 262, 268,
    270, 271, 284
Atalla, 9–10, 68–69, 71–72, 74, 76, 78–84
Atriplex sp. *See* grasses
ayahuasca, 213. *See also* hallucinogen
Ayawiri, 249
ayllu, 81, 306
Aymara, 329
ayni, 7
Azapa, 222

bean, common, 53–54, 149, 56–57, 184,
    186, 187, 191–92, 194, 203, 207, 222,
    235, 253–54, 282. *See also* legumes;
    Phaseolus
beer. *See* chicha
Berberis, 55, 57
Beringa, 205, 207

AMERIND STUDIES IN ANTHROPOLOGY
Series Editor **Eric Kaldahl**